D1098094

A BOOK OF ENGLAND

A BOOK OF ENGLAND

edited by

IVOR BROWN

With 110 photographs from

THE ✤✤✤ TIMES

Collins

LONDON AND GLASGOW

GENERAL EDITOR: J. B. FOREMAN

First published, 1958
Latest reprint 1961

ACKNOWLEDGMENTS

The publishers gratefully acknowledge the co-operation of the following authors, owners of copyright, publishers and literary agents who have given permission for poems and prose passages to appear in these pages.

EDWARD ARNOLD (PUBLISHERS) LTD. for the extract from *Abinger Harvest* by E. M. Forster.

MRS. GEORGE BAMBRIDGE, the publishers, MACMILLAN & CO. LTD., and the United States publishers, DOUBLEDAY & CO. INC., for *Puck's Song* from *Puck of Pook's Hill* by Rudyard Kipling. Copyright 1905, 1906 by Rudyard Kipling.

MR. EDMUND BLUNDEN for the lines (*Thence too when high wind through the black clouds' pouring*) from his *English Poems*.

SIR ARTHUR BRYANT for the extract from *The Years of Endurance*.

THE LATE MR. GERALD BULLETT for the poem *Saturday Cricket* from *News From the Village*.

JONATHAN CAPE LTD. for the extract from *London Perambulator* by James Bone; the stanzas from *The Stockdoves*, from *The Collected Poems* of Andrew Young; and the extracts from *Travels in England* by Thomas Platter, translated and edited by Clare Williams.

MR. NEVILLE CARDUS for the extract from *Second Innings*.

MISS D. E. COLLINS and DODD, MEAD & COMPANY for the poem *The Secret People* from *The Collected Poems of G. K. Chesterton*.

MR. NORMAN COLLINS for the two extracts from *London Belongs to Me*.

CHATTO AND WINDUS LTD. and HARCOURT, BRACE AND COMPANY INC. for the extract from *Queen Victoria* by Lytton Strachey. Copyright, 1921, by Harcourt, Brace and Company, Inc.; renewed 1949, by James Strachey.

CHATTO AND WINDUS LTD. and HARPER AND BROTHERS for the extract from *Do What You Will* by Aldous Huxley. Copyright, 1928, 1929, 1956, 1957, by Aldous Huxley.

MR. BERNARD DARWIN for the extracts from *Every Idle Dream* and *Out of the Rough*.

FABER AND FABER LTD., for the lines from *Poems of a Decade* by A. L. Rowse.

WILLIAM HEINEMANN LTD., and DODD, MEAD AND COMPANY for the extract from *More* by Sir Max Beerbohm.

HER MAJESTY'S STATIONERY OFFICE for the two extracts from Sir Winston Churchill's speeches to the House of Commons.

CONTENTS

History

London

Places

Gardens, Flowers and Trees

Going to the Play

Colleges and Schools

Seas and Sailors

Sport

Character and Comedy

First and Last Things

CONTENTS

ILLUSTRATIONS

The photographs are listed here, for convenient reference, in alphabetical order of counties, preceded by London. Their arrangement in the book follows an imaginary tour, starting with London and the Home Counties, through the south-eastern counties, then westward to Land's End. From Bath the route goes north to the Lake District, and crosses from Carlisle into Northumberland, Durham and Yorkshire. The journey through the Midlands brings the tourist to Bedford, where he turns north to visit East Anglia before returning to London.

INTRODUCTION

This volume follows *A Book of Scotland* and *A Book of Wales*, and precedes *A Book of Ireland*; naturally it would not have been attempted had not the earlier books been highly regarded and widely enjoyed. Accordingly I have, as editor, followed in general the pattern set by my predecessors: there are only a few alterations in method and arrangement. London, with its size, status, and exciting history, has been parted from the portion described as Places. This implies, of course, no slighting of the latter since I have always been a happily interested traveller in the cities, towns, villages, and shires of England. The division was made only to prevent the topographical division of the book from swelling to an uncomfortable size, which would have occurred if it included both capital and counties. "People, Great and Small" have been absorbed into the categories of History and of Character and Comedy.

Despite a larger allowance of pages my problem has been, I can fairly claim, even more exacting than that of my colleagues. The territories and population of England, as well as its chronicles and literature, are vastly greater than those of Scotland and Wales. The diversity of country and of racial types has created a more complex tapestry of scene, industry, and personality. With such a mass of material the problems of covering the essentials and of rejecting, of necessity, what others will think essential, have been inevitably severe. There was so much that one longed to put in and so much that one had to leave out.

Anthologies are of many and different kinds. They can be general in scope, at least as applied to literature; such are the famous Golden Treasuries and Oxford

Books of English Verse and Prose. They can also be
particular, that is to say limited to a single period or
style of writing or to a single aspect of man's many
activities and amusements, such as watching birds,
seeing plays, or catching fish. The more restricted is
the subject, the easier is the anthologist's task. *A Book
of England* is obviously in the general class and so presents
an editor with the maximum amount of difficulty.
This explanation is necessary since there is bound to be
regret, and even astonishment, that certain popular
and familiar items are not to be found. These absentees
are not the victims of neglect; many things considered
were reluctantly passed over, for reasons of space.
There was also an economic consideration. The quantity
of recent or contemporary writing had to be rationed
for reasons of copyright if, in these times of soaring
costs of book-production, the volume was to be issued at
a price in any way comparable with that of its fore-
runners.

Particular anthologies, with a limited theme, are
compiled for a special public, the keen students of
literature during one epoch, for example, or the devotees
of a single sport or pastime. The maker of a general
anthology has to remember that he is seeking to serve
readers who are not experts or specialists. I have had
in mind, while making my choice, the foreign visitor
to England, curious about our customs and affairs, as
well as the younger British readers who are entering
on the discovery of the English heritage in history,
in letters, and in the richly diverse fabric of the English
way of life. I have therefore made my selection with an
eye to their needs and have included occasional explana-
tory notes that may seem obvious to those more fully
equipped with knowledge of the authors cited and the
subjects discussed.

Another problem had to be faced. How far should
one include the piece of writing expected to be there

because it is, on its conspicuous merits, established as an anthology favourite and consequently so familiar with many as to be almost a cliché? Here I decided that a compromise would best suit the general need. Many justified favourites will be found, but some of the best, and best loved, examples of English poetry and prose have been dropped in place of something less often encountered. For example, I have not used Kipling's *Sussex*, although that county is not forgotten; nor have I taken in full Gray's *Elegy Written in a Country Church-yard*. Thomas Hardy's superb description of Egdon Heath in the opening chapter of *The Return of the Native* has been so often reprinted that I have preferred to use a softer and really more typical Wessex landscape, that of the lush vales of the dairies which occurs in *Tess of the D'Urbervilles*. Swarthy Egdon is not what it was; the pastures and the dairy farms, despite electrical milking, are much less altered. I can only hope that, in making this kind of less usual choice, I have done proportionate justice to both the familiar and the unfamiliar writing, drawing sufficiently both on the acknowledged masters and on writers, ancient and modern, whose qualities, though admirable, are less well known. I have also striven to achieve a fair balance between praise and censure of the national deeds and habits: the satirist has his place beside the eulogist.

Having made these explanations and excuses, I shall not presume to generalise about England; the book, not the editor, must do that. Myself a Scot, I have known England for most of my life as a tolerant and kindly hostess and I trust that my national detachment has been more help than hindrance in the pleasures of appreciation. My gratitude goes to those who have invited me to undertake this task and assisted me in its execution. A sudden death sadly removed from my counsels Mr. G. F. Maine, who had edited so shrewdly the second edition of *A Book of Scotland*. He was a man

of wide reading and of unusual and challenging opinions
and it was a great blow that he could only set me on my
way and not see me through it. To his successor, Mr.
J. B. Foreman, and other colleagues in the house of
Collins my debt is great.

Mr. Maine ended his introduction with these lines:

"There are those who regard an anthology as of the
devil, but there are others who, in an age when the
tempo of life takes increasing toll of our physical and
nervous resources, find them stimulating, even rejuvena-
ting. I hope that Scots at home and beyond the seas will
relish this miscellany and that those of other national-
ities who sojourn with us for business or pleasure will
find here much that will help them better to understand
our nation's life and history."

With the substitution of "English" for "Scots", those
are my sentiments and my ambition. I hope, also, that
with understanding will come entertainment. That
English laughter is a precious part of English life has
not been forgotten.

IVOR BROWN

PROLOGUE

England Observed

I find the Englishman to be him of all men who stands firmest in his shoes.

R. W. EMERSON

The Englishman is like a stout ship which will weather the roughest storm uninjured, but rolls its masts overboard in the succeeding calm.

WASHINGTON IRVING

The people of England are never so happy as when you tell them they are ruined.

ARTHUR MURPHY
(18th century Irish Dramatist)

Englishmen never will be slaves: they are free to do whatever the Government and public opinion tell them to do.

BERNARD SHAW

England is the land of sects. An Englishman, like a free man, goes to heaven by the way which pleases him.

VOLTAIRE

History

LANDSCAPE CHRONICLE

See you the ferny ride that steals
Into the oak-woods far?
O that was whence they hewed the keels
That rolled to Trafalgar.

And mark you where the ivy clings
To Bayham's mouldering walls?
O there we cast the stout railings
That stand around St. Paul's.

See you the dimpled track that runs
All hollow through the wheat?
O that was where they hauled the guns
That smote King Philip's fleet.

(Out of the Weald, the secret Weald,
Men sent in ancient years
The horse-shoes red at Flodden Field,
The arrows at Poitiers!)

See you our little mill that clacks,
So busy by the brook?
She has ground her corn and paid her tax
Ever since Domesday Book.

See you our stilly woods of oak,
And the dread ditch beside?
O that was where the Saxons broke
On the day that Harold died.

See you the windy levels spread
About the gates of Rye?
O that was where the Northmen fled,
When Alfred's ships came by.

See you our pastures wide and lone,
Where the red oxen browse?
O there was a City thronged and known,
Ere London boasted a house.

And see you, after rain, the trace
Of mound and ditch and wall?
O that was a Legion's camping-place,
When Cæsar sailed from Gaul.

And see you marks that show and fade,
Like shadows on the Downs?
O they are the lines the Flint Men made,
To guard their wondrous towns.

Trackway and Camp and City lost,
Salt Marsh where now is corn—
Old Wars, old Peace, old Arts that cease,
And so was England born!

She is not any common Earth,
Water or wood or air,
But Merlin's Isle of Gramarye,
Where you and I will fare!

RUDYARD KIPLING (1865-1936)
Puck's Song
Enlarged from *Puck of Pook's Hill*

MAGNA CARTA

An island in the Thames between Staines and Windsor had been chosen as the place of conference: the King encamped on one bank, while the barons covered the marshy flat, still known by the name of Runnymede, on the other. Their delegates met in the island between them, but the negotiations were a mere cloak to cover John's purpose of unconditional submission. The Great Charter was discussed, agreed to, and signed in a single day.[1]

One copy of it still remains in the British Museum, injured by age and fire, but with the royal seal still hanging from the brown, shrivelled parchment. It is impossible to gaze without reverence on the earliest monument of English freedom which we can see with our own eyes and touch with our own hands, the great Charter to which from age to age patriots have looked back as the basis of English liberty. But in itself the Charter was no novelty, nor did it claim to establish any new constitutional principles. The Charter of Henry the First formed the basis of the whole, and the additions to it are for the most part formal recognitions of the judicial and administrative changes introduced by Henry the Second. But the vague expressions of the older charters were now exchanged for precise and elaborate provisions. The bounds of unwritten custom which the older grants did little more than recognise had proved too weak to hold the Angevins; and the baronage now threw them aside for the restraints of written law.

It is in this way that the Great Charter marks the transition from the age of traditional rights, preserved in the nation's memory and officially declared by the

[1] 1215: *June 16*

Primate, to the age of written legislation, of parliaments and statutes, which was soon to come. The Church had shown its power of self-defence in the struggle over the interdict, and the clause which recognised its rights alone retained the older and general form. But all vagueness ceases when the Charter passes on to deal with the rights of Englishmen at large, their right to justice, to security of person and property, to good government. "No freeman," ran the memorable article that lies at the base of our whole judicial system, " shall be seized or imprisoned, or dispossessed, or outlawed, or in any way brought to ruin: we will not go against any man nor send against him, save by legal judgment of his peers or by the law of the land." "To no man will we sell," runs another, "or deny, or delay, right or justice."

J. R. GREEN (1837-1883)
A Short History of the English People

THE SECRET PEOPLE

That Magna Carta did, in fact, liberate none but the barons has been strenuously argued. The English Socialists have contended that "economic power precedes political power " and that therefore the formulæ of democratic freedom are made meaningless by the poverty of the many. That was an underlying theme of G. K. Chesterton's social theory. Though no Socialist, he was no lover of politicians, however "progressive" their creed. In this remarkable summary of English history, a summary written before the First World War, he made his personal interpretation of our island story: it is noteworthy that he did not mention Magna Carta.

Smile at us, pay us, pass us; but do not quite forget.
For we are the people of England, that never has spoken
    yet.
There is many a fat farmer that drinks less cheerfully,
There is many a free French peasant who is richer and
    sadder than we.

There are no folk in the whole world so helpless or so wise.
There is hunger in our bellies, there is laughter in our
    eyes;
You laugh at us and love us, both mugs and eyes are wet;
Only you do not know us. For we have not spoken yet.

The fine French kings came over in a flutter of flags and
    dames.
We liked their smiles and battles, but we never could say
    their names.
The blood ran red to Bosworth and the high French lords
    went down;
There was naught but a naked people under a naked
    crown.
And the eyes of the King's Servants turned terribly every
    way,
And the gold of the King's Servants rose higher every
    day.
They burnt the homes of the shaven men, that had been
    quaint and kind,
Till there was no bed in a monk's house, nor food that
    man could find.
The inns of God where no man paid, that were the wall
    of the weak,
The King's Servants ate them all. And still we did not
    speak.

And the face of the King's Servants grew greater than
    the King:
He tricked them, and they trapped him, and stood round
    him in a ring.
The new grave lords closed round him, that had eaten
    the abbey's fruits,
And the men of the new religion, with their bibles in
    their boots,

We saw their shoulders moving, to menace or discuss,
And some were pure and some were vile; but none took
    heed of us.
We saw the King as they killed him, and his face was
    proud and pale,
And a few men talked of freedom, while England talked
    of ale.

A war that we understood not came over the world and
    woke
Americans, Frenchmen, Irish; but we knew not the
    things they spoke.
They talked about rights and nature and peace and the
    people's reign:
And the squires, our masters, bade us fight; and never
    scorned us again.
Weak if we be for ever, could none condemn us then;
Men called us serfs and drudges, men knew that we were
    men.
In foam and flame at Trafalgar, on Albuera plains,
We did and died like lions, to keep ourselves in chains,
We lay in living ruins; firing and fearing not
The strange fierce face of the Frenchmen who knew for
    what they fought,
And the man who seemed to be more than man we
    strained against and broke;
And we broke our own rights with him. And still we
    never spoke.

They have given us into the hand of the new unhappy
    lords,
Lords without anger and honour, who dare not carry
    their swords.
They fight by shuffling papers; they have bright dead
    alien eyes;
They look at our labour and laughter as a tired man
    looks at flies.

LONDON: YEOMAN OF THE GUARD

The Chief Yeoman Warder of the Tower of London, beside a display of armour of Henry VIII's reign. The Yeomen of the Guard, or "Beefeaters", were raised by Henry VII as a personal bodyguard. The corps is now formed of military pensioners of distinguished service, their duties being purely ceremonial.

LONDON: THE PALACE OF WESTMINSTER
A view of the Houses of Parliament, from the opposite bank of the Thames, with the 320 ft. tower of Big Ben to the right. The Commons Chamber, bombed and burned out in 1941, was restored by 1950.

LONDON: KENSINGTON GARDENS
The famous Round Pond, much loved by children, at the close of a winter's day. Not far off stands the statue of Peter Pan.

And the load of their loveless pity is worse than the
    ancient wrongs,
Their doors are shut in the evening; and they know no
    songs.

We hear men speaking for us of new laws strong and
    sweet,
Yet is there no man speaketh as we speak in the street.
It may be we shall rise the last as Frenchmen rose the first.
Our wrath come after Russia's wrath and our wrath be
    the worst.
It may be we are meant to mark with our riot and our
    rest
God's scorn for all men governing. It may be beer is
    best.
But we are the people of England; and we have not
    spoken yet.
Smile at us, pay us, pass us. But do not quite forget.

                       G. K. CHESTERTON (1874-1936)
                                 Poems

OTHER EDEN

This royal throne of kings, this scept'red isle,
This earth of majesty, this seat of Mars,
This other Eden, demi-Paradise;
This fortress built by Nature for herself
Against infection and the hand of war;
This happy breed of men, this little world;
This precious stone set in the silver sea,
Which serves it in the office of a wall,
Or as a moat defensive to a house,
Against the envy of less happier lands;
This blessed plot, this earth, this realm, this England,
This nurse, this teeming womb of royal kings,

Fear'd by their breed, and famous by their birth,
Renowned for their deeds as far from home,—
For Christian service and true chivalry,—
As is the sepulchre, in stubborn Jewry,
Of the world's ransom, blessed Mary's Son;—
This land of such dear souls, this dear dear land,
Dear for her reputation through the world,
Is now leased out—I die pronouncing it—
Like to a tenement or pelting farm;
England, bound in with the triumphant sea,
Whose rocky shore beats back the envious siege
Of watery Neptune, is now bound in with shame,
With inky blots, and rotten parchment bonds:
That England, that was wont to conquer others,
Hath made a shameful conquest of itself.

WILLIAM SHAKESPEARE (1564-1616)
Richard II

ANOTHER VIEW

DUKE OF BOURBON

Normans, but bastard Normans, Norman bastards!
Mort de ma vie! if they march along
Unfought withal, but I will sell my dukedom,
To buy a slobbery and a dirty farm
In that nook-shotten isle of Albion.

THE CONSTABLE OF FRANCE

Dieu de batailles! where have they this mettle?
Is not their climate foggy, raw, and dull;
On whom, as in despite, the sun looks pale,
Killing their fruit with frowns? Can sodden water,
A drench for sur-rein'd jades, their barley-broth,
Decoct their cold blood to such valiant heat?

And shall our quick blood, spirited with wine,
Seem frosty? O, for honour of our land,
Let us not hang, like roping icicles
Upon our houses' thatch, whiles a more frosty people
Sweat drops of gallant youth on our rich fields.

*   *   *   *

THE CONSTABLE OF FRANCE

If the English had any apprehension, they would run
away.

DUKE OF ORLEANS

That they lack; for if their heads had any intellectual
armour, they could never wear such heavy head-pieces.

RAMBURES

That island of England breeds very valiant creatures;
their mastiffs are of unmatchable courage.

DUKE OF ORLEANS

Foolish curs, that run winking into the mouth of a
Russian bear, and have their heads crusht like rotten
apples! You may as well say, that's a valiant flea that
dare eat his breakfast on the lip of a lion.

THE CONSTABLE OF FRANCE

Just, just; and the men do sympathize with the mastiffs
in robustious and rough coming-on, leaving their wits
with their wives: and then give them great meals of
beef, and iron and steel, they will eat like wolves, and
fight like devils.

DUKE OF ORLEANS

Ay, but these English are shrewdly out of beef.

THE CONSTABLE OF FRANCE

Then shall we find to-morrow they have only stomachs
to eat, and none to fight. Now is it time to arm; come,
shall we about it?

DUKE OF ORLEANS

It is now two o'clock: but, let me see,—by ten
We shall have each a hundred Englishmen.

WILLIAM SHAKESPEARE (1564-1616)
Henry V

SPOTLESS HARRY

Shakespeare's Henry V has been censured for his betrayal of Sir John
Falstaff, his old companion in mischief. But Sir John had been given
his warning that, when Prince Hal was King Henry, the partnership
in pleasure would be over. Thereafter Henry V, whatever his actual
faults, was, in his nation's eyes, the Hammer of the French, the victor
of Agincourt, and the ideal of monarchy. So, at any rate, did Holinshed, the Elizabethan historian, regard him.

This Henrie was a king, of life without spot; a prince
whome all men loued, and of none disdained; a capteine
against whome fortune neuer frowned, nor mischance
once spurned; whose people him so seuere a iusticer
both loued and obeied, (and so humane withall,) that
he left no offense vnpunished, nor freendship vnrewarded;
a terrour to rebels, and suppressour of sedition; his
vertues notable, his qualities most praise-worthie.

In strength and nimblenesse of bodie from his youth
few to him comparable; for in wrestling, leaping, and
running, no man well able to compare. In casting of
great iron barres and heauie stones he excelled commonlie
all men; neuer shrinking at cold, nor slothfull for heat;
and, when he most laboured, his head commonlie
vncouered; no more wearie of harnesse than a light
cloake; verie valiantlie abiding at needs both hunger

and thirst; so manful of mind as neuer seene to quinch
at a wound, or to smart at the paine; to turne his nose
from euil sauour, or to close his eies from smoke or
dust; no man more moderate in eating and drinking,
with diet not delicate, but rather more meet for men of
warre, than for princes or tender stomachs. Euerie
honest person was permitted to come to him, sitting at
meale; where either secretlie or openlie to declare his
mind. High and weightie causes, as well betweene men
of warre and other, he would gladlie heare; and either
determined them himselfe, or else for end committed
them to others. He slept verie little, but that verie
soundlie, in so much that when his soldiers soong at
nights, or minstrels plaied, he then slept fastest; of
courage inuincible, of purpose vnmutable; so wise-
hardie alwaies, as feare was banist from him; at euerie
alarum he first in armor, and formost in ordering.
In time of warre such was his prouidence, bountie and
hap, as he had true intelligence, not onelie what his
enimies did, but what they said and intended: of his
deuises and purposes, few, before the thing was at the
point to be done, should be made priuie.

He had such knowledge in ordering and guiding an
armie, with such a gift to incourage his people, that the
Frenchmen had constant opinion he could neuer be
vanquished in battell. Such wit, such prudence, and such
policie withall, that he neuer enterprised any thing,
before he had fullie debated and forecast all the maine
chances that might happen; which done, with all
diligence and courage, he set his purpose forward.
What policie he had in finding present remedies for sudden mischeeues, and what engines in sauing himselfe
and his people in sharpe distresses, were it not that by
his acts they did plainlie appeare, hard were it by words
to make them credible. Wantonnesse of life and thirst
in auarice had he quite quenched in him; vertues in deed
in such an estate of souereigntie, youth, and power,

as verie rare, so right commendable in the highest
degree. So staied of mind and countenance beside,
that neuer iolie or triumphant for victorie, nor sad or
damped for losse or misfortune. For bountifulnesse and
liberalitie, no man more free, gentle, and franke, in
bestowing rewards to all persons, according to their
deserts: for his saieng was, that he neuer desired monie
to keepe, but to giue and spend.

RAPHAEL HOLINSHED (Died c. 1580)
Chronicles

THE SCOUNDREL KING

It has recently been keenly argued that Richard Duke of Gloucester,
later King Richard III, has been much maligned and that his conqueror
and successor, Henry VII, saw to it that the historians not only stressed
his misdeeds but added to them viciously. However that may be,
Shakespeare accepted the traditional view of a remorseless villain
and made him the prologue to his own play, introducing himself
with candid confession of his plots and iniquities.

DUKE OF GLOUCESTER

Now is the winter of our discontent
Made glorious summer by this sun of York;
And all the clouds that lour'd upon our house
In the deep bosom of the ocean buried.
Now are our brows bound with victorious wreaths;
Our bruised arms hung up for monuments;
Our stern alarums changed to merry meetings,
Our dreadful marches to delightful measures.
Grim-visaged war hath smooth'd his wrinkled front;
And now—instead of mounting barbed steeds
To fright the souls of fearful adversaries—
He capers nimbly in a lady's chamber
To the lascivious pleasing of a lute.
But I, that am not shaped for sportive tricks,
Nor made to court an amorous looking-glass;

I, that am rudely stampt, and want love's majesty
To strut before a wanton ambling nymph;
I, that am curtail'd of this fair proportion,
Cheated of feature by dissembling nature,
Deform'd, unfinish't, sent before my time
Into this breathing world, scarce half made up,
And that so lamely and unfashionable
That dogs bark at me as I halt by them;—
Why, I, in this weak piping time of peace,
Have no delight to pass away the time,
Unless to spy my shadow in the sun,
And descant on my own deformity:
And therefore, since I cannot prove a lover,
To entertain these fair well-spoken days,
I am determined to prove a villain,
And hate the idle pleasures of these days.
Plots have I laid, inductions dangerous,
By drunken prophecies, libels, and dreams,
To set my brother Clarence and the king
In deadly hate the one against the other:
And, if King Edward be as true and just
As I am subtle, false, and treacherous,
This day should Clarence closely be mew'd up,
About a prophecy which says that G
Of Edward's heirs the murderer shall be.
Dive, thoughts, down to my soul:—here Clarence comes.

WILLIAM SHAKESPEARE (1564-1616)
Richard III

ROYAL CHRISTENING

Queen Elizabeth the First and the benefits of her reign were saluted
by Shakespeare in the Christening Scene which comes towards the
close of his historical play, *Henry VIII*, to which John Fletcher may
have been a contributor. Shakespeare's own hand seems to me present
in the speech allotted to Archbishop Cranmer, a speech which tactfully

includes James I in its hopeful benedictions and prophecies. Shake-speare's Company, presenting the play at the Globe Theatre, were the King's Men, and their patron could hardly be omitted when England's blessings were being listed.

CRANMER
Let me speak, sir,
For heaven now bids me; and the words I utter
Let none think flattery, for they'll find 'em truth.
This royal infant—heaven still move about her!—
Though in her cradle, yet now promises
Upon this land a thousand thousand blessings,
Which time shall bring to ripeness: she shall be—
But few now living can behold that goodness—
A pattern to all princes living with her,
And all that shall succeed: Saba was never
More covetous of wisdom and fair virtue
Than this pure soul shall be: all princely graces,
That mould up such a mighty piece as this is,
With all the virtues that attend the good,
Shall still be doubled on her: truth shall nurse her,
Holy and heavenly thoughts still counsel her:
She shall be loved and fear'd: her own shall bless her;
Her foes shake like a field of beaten corn,
And hang their heads with sorrow: good grows with
    her:
In her days every man shall eat in safety,
Under his own vine, what he plants; and sing
The merry songs of peace to all his neighbours:
God shall be truly known; and those about her
From her shall read the perfect ways of honour,
And by those claim their greatness, not by blood.
Nor shall this peace sleep with her: but as when
The bird of wonder dies, the maiden phoenix,
Her ashes new create another heir,
As great in admiration as herself,
So shall she leave her blessedness to one,

When heaven shall call her from this cloud of darkness,
Who from the sacred ashes of her honour
Shall star-like rise, as great in fame as she was,
And so stand fixt: peace, plenty, love, truth, terror,
That were the servants to this chosen infant,
Shall then be his, and like a vine grow to him:
Wherever the bright sun of heaven shall shine,
His honour and the greatness of his name
Shall be, and make new nations: he shall flourish,
And, like a mountain cedar, reach his branches
To all the plains about him:—our children's children
Shall see this, and bless heaven.

KING HENRY
      Thou speakest wonders.

CRANMER
She shall be, to the happiness of England,
An aged princess; many days shall see her,
And yet no day without a deed to crown it.
Would that I had known no more! but she must die,—
She must, the saints must have her,—yet a virgin,
A most unspotted lily shall she pass
To the ground, and all the world shall mourn her.

WILLIAM SHAKESPEARE (1564-1616)
Henry VIII

SWEET BESS

The Queen succeeded to the throne in November, 1558. Naturally
many welcomes were made in prose and verse: a charming absence
of formality and sycophancy is to be found in this "Song Between
the Queen's Majesty and England".

ENGLAND: Come over the bourn, Bessy,
               Come over the bourn, Bessy,
            Sweet Bessy, come over to me;
               And I will thee take,
               And my dear Lady make,
            Before all other that ever I see.

QUEEN: Methinks I hear a voice,
               At whom I do rejoice,
            And answer thee now I shall:—
               Tell me, I say,
               What art thou that bids me come away,
            And so earnestly does me call?

ENGLAND: I am thy lover fair,
               Hath chose thee to mine heir,
            And my name is merry England.
               Therefore come away,
               And make no delay!
            Sweet Bessy, give me thy hand.

QUEEN: Here is my hand,
               My dear lover England,
            I am thine both with mind and heart,
               For ever to endure,
               Thou mayest be sure,
            Until death us two do part.

ENGLAND: Lady, this long space,
              Have I loved thy grace,
      More than I durst well say:
              Hoping at the last,
              When all storms were past,
      For to see this joyful day. . . .

QUEEN: I trust all faithful hearts
              Will play true subjects' parts,
      Knowing me their true Queen and heir by
          right,
              And that much the rather
              For love of my father,
      That worthy prince King Henry th'eight.

ENGLAND: Therefore let us pray
              To God both night and day,
      Continually and never to cease,
              That he will preserve your grace
              To reign over us long space
      In tranquillity, wealth and peace.

BOTH: All honour, laud and praise,
              Be to Lord God always,
      Who hath all princes' hearts in His hands,
              That by His peace and might
              He may them guide aright
      For the wealth of all Christen lands.

FINIS

God save the Queen!

WILLIAM BIRCH (1559)
Song Between the Queen's Majesty and England

WISE QUEEN BESS

It is your shame, (I speake to you all, you yong Ientlemen
of England) that one mayd should go beyond you all,
in excellencie of learnyng, and knowledge of diuers
tonges. Pointe forth six of the best giuen Ientlemen of
this Court, and all they together shew not so much
good will, spend not so much tyme, bestow not so many
houres, dayly, orderly, and constantly, for the increase
of learning and knowledge, as doth the Queenes Maiestie
her selfe. Yea I beleue, that beside her perfit readines,
in *Latin*, *Italian*, *French*, and *Spanish*, she readeth here
now at Windsore more *Greeke* euery day, than some
Prebendarie of this Chirch doth read *Latin* in a whole
weeke. And that which is most praise worthie of all,
within the walles of her priuie chamber, she hath
obteyned that excellencie of learnyng, to vnderstand,
speake, and write, both wittely with head, and faire
with hand, as scarse one or two rare wittes in both the
Vniuersities haue in many yeares reached vnto.
Amongest all the benefites that God hath blessed me
with all, next the knowledge of Christes true Religion,
I counte this the greatest, that it pleased God to call me,
to be one poore minister in settyng forward these
excellent giftes of learnyng in this most excellent
Prince. Whose onely example, if the rest of our nobilitie
would folow, then might England be, for learnyng
and wisedome in nobilitie, a spectacle to all the world
beside. But see the mishap of men: The best examples
haue neuer such forse to moue to any goodnes, as the
bad, vaine, light and fond haue to all ilnes.

ROGER ASCHAM[1] (1515-1570)
The Schoolmaster

[1]Tutor to Queen Elizabeth the First

"GLORIANA" FADES

When I came to Court I found the Queen ill disposed, and she kept her inner lodging; yet she, hearing of my arrival, sent for me. I found her in one of her with-drawing chambers, sitting low upon her cushions. She called me to her; I kissed her hand, and told her it was my chiefest happiness to see her in safety and in health, which I wished might long continue. She took me by the hand and wrung it hard, and said, "No, Robin, I am not well," and then discoursed with me of her indisposition, and that her heart had been sad and heavy for ten or twelve days, and in her discourse she fetched not so few as forty or fifty great sighs. I was grieved at the first to see her in this plight; for in all my lifetime before I never knew her fetch a sigh, but when the Queen of Scots was beheaded. Then upon my knowledge she shed many tears and sighs, manifesting her innocence that she never gave consent to the death of that Queen.

I used the best words I could to persuade her from this melancholy humour; but I found by her it was too deep rooted in her heart, and hardly to be removed.

. . . On Wednesday, the twenty-third of March, she grew speechless. That afternoon, by signs, she called for her Council, and by putting her hand to her head, when the King of Scots was named to succeed her, they all knew he was the man she desired should reign after her.

About six at night she made signs for the Archbishop and her Chaplains to come to her, at which time I went in with them, and sat upon my knees full of tears to see that heavy sight. Her Majesty lay upon her back with one hand in the bed, and the other without. The Bishop

kneeled down by her, and examined her first of her
faith, and she so punctually answered all his several
questions, by lifting up her eyes and holding up her
hand, as it was a comfort to all the beholders. Then the
good man told her plainly what she was, and what she
was to come to; and though she had been long a great
Queen here upon earth, yet shortly she was to yield an
account of her stewardship to the King of kings. After
this he began to pray, and all that were by did answer
him. After he had continued long in prayer, till the
old man's knees were weary, he blessed her, and meant
to rise and leave her. The Queen made a sign with her
hand. My sister Scroope, knowing her meaning, told
the Bishop the Queen desired he would pray still. He
did so for a long half-hour after, and then thought to
leave her. The second time she made sign to have him
continue in prayer. He did so for half an hour more,
with earnest cries to God for her soul's health, which
he uttered with that fervency of spirit as the Queen to
all our sight much rejoiced thereat, and gave testimony
to us all of her Christian and comfortable end. By this
time it grew late and every one departed, all but her
women that attended her.

SIR ROBERT CAREY (c. 1560-1639)
Memoirs

THE PURITANS

We would speak first of the Puritans, the most remarkable body of men, perhaps, which the world has ever
produced. The odious and ridiculous parts of their
character lie on the surface. He that runs may read
them; nor have there been wanting attentive and
malicious observers to point them out. For many years
after the Restoration, they were the theme of un-

measured invective and derision. They were exposed to the utmost licentiousness of the press and of the stage, at the time when the press and the stage were most licentious. They were not men of letters; they were, as a body, unpopular; they could not defend themselves; and the public would not take them under its protection. They were therefore abandoned, without reserve, to the tender mercies of the satirists and drama-tists. The ostentatious simplicity of their dress, their sour aspect, their nasal twang, their stiff posture, their long graces, their Hebrew names, the Scriptural phrases which they introduced on every occasion, their contempt of human learning, their detestation of polite amuse-ments, were indeed fair game for the laughers. But it is not from the laughers alone that the philosophy of history is to be learnt. And he who approaches this subject should carefully guard against the influence of that potent ridicule which has already misled so many excellent writers.

Those who roused the people to resistance, who directed their measures through a long series of eventful years, who formed, out of the most unpromising materials, the finest army that Europe had ever seen, who trampled down King, Church, and Aristocracy, who, in the short intervals of domestic sedition and rebellion, made the name of England terrible to every nation on the face of the earth, were no vulgar fanatics. Most of their absurdities were mere external badges, like the signs of freemasonry, or the dresses of friars. We regret that these badges were not more attractive. We regret that a body, whose courage and talents mankind has owed inestimable obligations, had not the lofty elegance which distinguished some of the adherents of Charles the First, or the easy good-breeding for which the court of Charles the Second was celebrated. But, if we must make our choice, we shall, like Bassanio in the play, turn from the specious caskets which contain only the Death's head and the Fool's head, and fix on the plain leaden chest which conceals the treasure.

. . . Thus the Puritan was made up of two different men, the one all self-abasement, penitence, gratitude, passion; the other proud, calm, inflexible, sagacious. He prostrated himself in the dust before his Maker: but he set his foot on the neck of his king. In his devotional retirement, he prayed with convulsions, and groans, and tears. He was half-maddened by glorious or terrible illusions. He heard the lyres of angels or the tempting whispers of fiends. He caught a gleam of the Beatific Vision, or woke screaming from dreams of everlasting fire. Like Vane, he thought himself intrusted with the sceptre of the millennial year. Like Fleetwood, he cried in the bitterness of his soul that God had hid his face from him. But when he took his seat in the council, or girt on his sword for war, these tempestuous workings of the soul had left no perceptible trace behind them. People who saw nothing of the godly but their uncouth visages, and heard nothing from them but their groans and whining hymns, might laugh at them. But those had little reason to laugh who encountered them in the hall of debate or in the field of battle. These fanatics brought to civil and military affairs a coolness of judgment and an immutability of purpose which some writers have thought inconsistent with their religious zeal, but which were in fact the necessary effects of it. The intensity of their feelings on one subject made them tranquil on every other. One overpowering sentiment had subjected to itself pity and hatred, ambition and fear. Death had lost its terrors and pleasure its charms. They had their smiles and their tears, their raptures and their sorrows, but not for the things of this world. Enthusiasm had made them stoics, had cleared their minds from every vulgar passion and prejudice, and raised them above the influence of danger and of corruption. It sometimes might lead them to pursue unwise ends, but never to choose unwise means. They went through the world, like Sir Artegal's iron man Talus with his flail, crushing and trampling down oppressors, mingling with human beings, but having neither part nor lot in human infirmities, insensible to fatigue, to pleasure, and to pain, not to be pierced by any weapon, not to be withstood by any barrier.

Such we believe to have been the character of the Puritans. We perceive the absurdity of their manners. We dislike the sullen gloom of their domestic habits. We acknowledge that the tone of their minds was often injured by straining after things too high for mortal reach: and we know that, in spite of their hatred of Popery, they too often fell into the worst vices of that bad system, intolerance and extravagant austerity, that they had their anchorites and their crusaders, their Dunstans and their De Montforts, their Dominics and their Escobars. Yet, when all circumstances are taken into consideration, we do not hesitate to pronounce them a brave, a wise, an honest, and an useful body.

LORD MACAULAY (1800-1859)
Essays: Milton

LEARNED CAVALIER

The opponents of the Puritans are so often thought of as light gallants, men as shallow as sparkish, that it is interesting to meet in Dr. William Harvey a very different type, the Scholar Cavalier. He was lecturing on the Circulation of the Blood while Shakespeare was dying (in 1616) and was therefore well on in years when he joined King Charles's army, presumably as a doctor.

He was always very contemplative, and the first that I heare of that was curious in anatomie in England. He had made dissections of frogges, toades, and a number of other animals, and had curious observations on them, which papers, together with his goods, in his lodgings at Whitehall, were plundered at the beginning of the Rebellion, he being for the king, and with him at Oxon; but he often sayd, that of all the losses he sustained, no greife was so crucifying to him as the losse of these papers, which for love or money he could never retrive or obtaine. When Charles I by reason of the tumults left London, he attended him, and was at the fight of Edge-hill with him; and during the fight, the Prince and duke of Yorke were committed to his care: he told me that he withdrew with them under a hedge, and tooke out of his pocket a booke and read; but he had not read very long before a bullet of a great gun grazed on the ground neare him, which made him remove his station.

. . . His brother Eliab bought, about 1654, Cockaine-house, now (1680) the Excise-Office, a noble house, where the Doctor was wont to contemplate on the leads of the house, and had his severall stations, in regard of the sun, or wind.

He did delight to be in the darke, and told me he could then best contemplate. He had a house heretofore at Combe, in Surrey, a good aire and prospect, where he had caves made in the earth, in which in summer time he delighted to meditate.

. . . He was wont to say that man was but a great mischievous baboon.

He would say, that we Europeans knew not how to order or governe our woemen, and that the Turkes were the only people used them wisely.

He was far from bigotry.

He had been physitian to the Lord Chancellor Bacon, whom he esteemed much for his witt and style, but would not allow him to be a great philosopher. "He writes philosophy like a Lord Chancellor," said he to me, speaking in derision; "I have cured him."

. . . He was not tall; but of the lowest stature, round faced, olivaster complexion; little eie, round, very black, full of spirit; his haire was black as a raven, but quite white 20 yeares before he dyed.

. . . I have heard him say, that after his booke of the Circulation of the Blood came-out, that he fell mightily in his practize, and that 'twas beleeved by the vulgar that he was crack-brained; and all the physitians were against his opinion, and envyed him; many wrote against him, as Dr. Primige, Paracisanus, etc. With much adoe at last, in about 20 or 30 yeares time, it was received in all the Universities in the world; and, as Mr. Hobbes sayes in his book "De Corpore," *he is the only man, perhaps, that ever lived to see his owne doctrine established in his life time.*

He understood Greek and Latin pretty well, but was no critique, and he wrote very bad Latin. His majestie king Charles I gave him the Wardenship of Merton Colledge in Oxford, as a reward for his service, but the times suffered him not to recieve or injoy any benefitt by it.

. . . He was much and often troubled with the gowte, and his way of cure was thus: he would then sitt with his legges bare, if it were frost, on the leads of Cockaine house, putt them into a payle of water, till he was almost dead with cold, and betake himselfe to his stove, and so 'twas gonne.

He was hott-headed, and his thoughts working would many times keepe him from sleepinge; he told me that then his way was to rise out of his bed and walke about his chamber in his shirt till he was pretty coole, i.e. till he began to have a horror, and then returne to bed, and sleepe very comfortably.

I remember he was wont to drinke coffee; which he and his brother Eliab did, before Coffee-houses were in fashion in London.

All his profession would allowe him to be an excellent anatomist, but I never heard of any that admired his therapeutique way. I knew severall practisers in London that would not have given 3d. for one of his bills;[1] and that a man could hardly tell by one of his bills what he did aime at. He did not care for chymistrey, and was wont to speake against them with an under-value.

JOHN AUBREY (1626-1695)
Brief Lives

[1] Medical Prescriptions

THE CROWN RESTORED

April 23, 1661. About four I rose and got to the Abbey, where I followed Sir J. Denham, the surveyor, with some company he was leading in. And with much ado, by the favour of Mr. Cooper, his man, did get up into a great scaffold across the north end of the Abbey, where with a great deal of patience I sat from past four till eleven before the King came in. And a great pleasure it was to see the Abbey raised in the middle, all covered with red, and a throne (that is, a chair) and footstool on the top of it; and all the officers of all kinds, so much as the very fiddlers, in red vests. At last comes in the Dean and Prebendaries of Westminster, with the Bishops (many of them in cloth of gold copes), and after them the nobility, all in their Parliament robes, which was a most magnificent sight. Then the Duke, and the King with a sceptre (carried by my Lord Sandwich) and sword and wand before him, and the crown too. The King in his robes, bareheaded, which was very fine. And after all had placed themselves, there was a sermon and the service; and then in the choir at the high altar, the King passed through all the ceremonies of the Coronation, which to my great grief I and most in the Abbey could not see.

The crown being put upon his head, a great shout begun, and he come forth to the throne, and there passed through more ceremonies: as taking the oath, and having things read to him by the Bishop; and his lords (who put on their caps as soon as the King put on his crown) and bishops come, and kneeled before him. And three times the King-at-Arms went to the three open places on the scaffold, and proclaimed, that if any one could show any reason why Charles Stuart should not be King of England, that now he should come and speak. And a General Pardon also was read by the Lord Chancellor, and medals flung up and down by my Lord Cornwallis, of silver, but I could not come by any. But so great a noise that I could make but little of the music; and indeed, it was lost to everybody.

I went out a little while before the King had done all his ceremonies, and went round the Abbey to Westminster Hall, all the way within rails, and 10,000 people with the ground covered with blue cloth; and scaffolds all the way. Into the Hall I got, where it was very fine with hangings and scaffolds one upon another full of brave ladies; and my wife in one little one, on the right hand. Here I stayed walking up and down, and at last upon one of the side stalls I stood and saw the King come in with all the persons (but the soldiers) that were yesterday in the cavalcade; and a most pleasant sight it was to see them in their several robes. And the King came in with his crown on, and his sceptre in his hand, under a canopy borne up by six silver staves, carried by barons of the Cinque Ports, and little bells at every end. And after a long time, he got up to the farther end, and all set themselves down at their several tables, and that was also a brave sight: and the King's first course carried up by the Knights of the Bath.

And many fine ceremonies there was of the heralds leading up people before him, and bowing; and my Lord of Albemarle's going to the kitchen and eating a bit of the first dish that was to go to the King's table. But, above all, was these three lords, Northumberland, and Suffolk, and the Duke of Ormond, coming before the courses on horseback, and staying so all dinner-time, and at last bringing up the King's Champion, all in armour on horseback, with his spear and target carried before him. And a herald proclaims "That if any dare deny Charles Stuart to be lawful King of England, here was a Champion that would fight with him"; and with these words, the Champion flings down his gauntlet and all this he do three times in his going up towards the King's table. To which, when he is come, the King drinks to him, and then sends him the cup which is of gold, and he drinks it off, and then rides back again with the cup in his hand.

I took a great deal of pleasure to go up and down, and look upon the ladies, and to hear the music of all sorts, but above all, the twenty-four violins. About six at night they had dined, and I went up to my wife. And strange it is to think, that these two days have held up fair till now that all is done, and the King gone out of the Hall; and then it fell a-raining and thundering and lightning as I have not seen it do for some years; which people did take great notice of; God's blessing of the work of these two days, which is a foolery to take too much notice of such things.

At Mr. Bowyer's; a great deal of company, some I knew, others I did not. Here we stayed upon the leads and below till it was late, expecting to see the fireworks, but they were not performed to-night, only the City had a light like a glory round about it, with bonfires. At last I went to King Street, and there sent Crockford to my father's and my house, to tell them I could not come home to-night, because of the dirt, and a coach could not be had. And so I took my wife and Mrs. Frankleyn (who I proffered the civility of lying with my wife at Mrs. Hunt's to-night) to Axe-yard, in which, at the further end, there were three great bonfires, and a great many gallants, men and women; and they laid hold of us, and would have us drink the King's health upon our knees, kneeling upon a faggot, which we all did, they drinking to us one after another, which we thought a strange frolic; but these gallants continued there a great while, and I wondered to see how the ladies did tipple.

At last, I sent my wife and her bedfellow to bed, and Mr. Hunt and I went in with Mr. Thornbury (who did give the company all their wine, he being yeoman of the wine-cellar to the King); and there, with his wife and two of his sisters, and some gallant sparks that were there, we drank the King's health, and nothing else, till one of the gentlemen fell down stark drunk, and there lay, and I went to my lord's pretty well. But no sooner abed with Mr. Shepley, but my head began to turn, and I to vomit, and if ever I was foxed, it was now, which I cannot say yet, because I fell asleep, and slept till morning. Thus did the day end with joy every-where; and blessed be God, I have not heard of any mischance to anybody through it all, but only to Serjeant Glynne, whose horse fell upon him yesterday, and is like to kill him, which people do please themselves to see how just God is to punish the rogue at such a time as this; he being now one of the King's Serjeants, and rode in the cavalcade with Maynard, to whom people wish the same fortune. There was also, this night in

King Street, a woman had her eye put out by a boy's flinging a firebrand into the coach. Now, after all this, I can say, that, besides the pleasure of the sight of these glorious things, I may now shut my eyes against any other objects, nor for the future trouble myself to see things of state and show, as being sure never to see the like again in this world.

24th. Waked in the morning, with my head in a sad taking through the last night's drink, which I am very sorry for: so rose, and went out with Mr. Creed to drink our morning draught, which he did give me in chocolate to settle my stomach. At night, set myself to write down these three days' diary, and, while I am about it, I hear the noise of the chambers, and other things of the fireworks, which are now playing upon the Thames before the King; and I wish myself with them, being sorry not to see them.

SAMUEL PEPYS (1633-1703)
Diary

LONDON BURNING

John Dryden celebrated (and lamented) the great (and sad) events of 1665 which he described in a long poem called *Annus Mirabilis, The Year of Wonders*. He recorded both England's naval victories, its great civic loss, the destruction of the old City of London by the Great Fire, and the noble rebuilding. The poet was moved to a profusion of rhetorical verse of which the following selected stanzas give a fair example.

Swell'd with our late Successes on the Foe,
Which *France* and *Holland* wanted power to cross,
We urge an unseen Fate to lay us low,
And feed their envious Eyes with *English* loss.

Each Element his dread Command obeys,
Who makes or ruines with a Smile or Frown;
Who as by one he did our Nation raise,
So now, he with another pulls us down.

Yet *London*, Empress of the Northern Clime,
By an high Fate thou greatly didst expire:
Great as the Worlds, which, at the death of time,
Must fall, and rise a nobler frame by fire.

         ✸   ✸   ✸

In this deep quiet, from what source unknown,
Those seeds of Fire their fatal Birth disclose;
And first, few scatt'ring Sparks about were blown,
Big with the flames that to our Ruin rose.

Then, in some close-pent Room it crept along,
And, smouldring as it went, in silence fed;
Till th' infant Monster, with devouring strong,
Walk'd boldly upright with exalted head.

Now like some rich or mighty Murderer,
Too great for Prison, which he breaks with Gold,
Who fresher for new Mischiefs does appear
And dares the World to tax him with the old:

So scapes th' insulting Fire his narrow Jail
And makes small out-lets into open air:
There the fierce Winds his tender Force assail,
And beat him down-ward to his first repair.

The Winds, like crafty Courtezans, withheld
His Flames from burning, but to blow them more;
And every fresh attempt he is repell'd
With faint Denials, weaker than before.

And now, no longer letted of his Prey,
He leaps up at it with inrag'd desire:
O'relooks the Neighbours with a wide survey,
And nods at every House his threatening Fire.

* * *

The next to Danger, hot persu'd by Fate,
Half-cloth'd, half-naked, hastily retire:
And frighted Mothers strike their Breasts, too late,
For helpless Infants left amidst the Fire.

Their Cries soon waken all the Dwellers near;
Now murmuring Noises rise in every Street;
The more remote run stumbling with their fear,
And, in the dark, Men justle as they meet.

* * *

A Key of Fire ran all along the Shore,
And lighten'd all the River with a blaze:
The waken'd Tides began again to roar,
And wond'ring Fish in shining waters gaze.

Old Father Thames rais'd up his reverend head,
But fear'd the fate of *Simoeis* would return:
Deep in his *Ooze* he sought his sedgy Bed,
And shrunk his Waters back into his Urn.

The Fire, mean time walks in a broader gross;
To either hand his Wings he opens wide:
He wades the Streets, and streight he reaches cross,
And plays his longing Flames on th' other side.

At first they warm, then scorch, and then they take;
Now with long Necks from side to side they feed:
At length, grown strong, their Mother-fire forsake,
And a new Colony of Flames succeed.

* * *

Night came, but without darkness or repose,
A dismal Picture of the gen'ral Doom;
Where Souls distracted when the Trumpet blows,
And half unready with their Bodies come.

Those who have Homes, when Home they do repair,
To a last Lodging call their wand'ring Friends;
Their short uneasie Sleeps are broke with Care,
To look how near their own Destruction tends.

* * *

Some stir up Coals, and watch the Vestal fire,
Others in vain from sight of Ruin run:
And, while through burning Lab'rinths they retire,
With loathing Eyes repeat what they would shun.

The most in Fields like herded Beasts lie down,
To Dews obnoxious on the grassie Floor;
And while their Babes in Sleep their Sorrows drown,
Sad Parents watch the remnants of their Store.

While by the Motion of the Flames they guess
What Streets are burning now, and what are near,
An infant waking to the Paps would press,
And meets, instead of Milk, a falling Tear.

* * *

At length th' Almighty cast a pitying Eye,
And Mercy softly touch'd his melting Breast:
He saw the Towns one half in Rubbish lie,
And eager flames drive on to storm the rest.

An hollow chrystal Pyramid he takes,
In firmamental Waters dipt above;
Of it a broad Extinguisher he makes
And hoods the Flames that to their quarry strove.

The vanquish'd Fires withdraw from every place,
Or, full with feeding, sink into a sleep:
Each household Genius shows again his face,
And, from the hearths, the little Lares creep.

Our King this more than natural change beholds;
With sober Joy his heart and eyes abound:
To the All-good his lifted hands he folds,
And thanks him low on his redeemed ground.

As when sharp Frosts had long constrain'd the earth
A kindly Thaw unlocks it with mild Rain,
And first the tender Blade peeps up to birth,
And streight the Green fields laugh with promis'd grain:

By such degrees the spreading Gladness grew
In every heart, which Fear had froze before:
The standing Streets with so much joy they view,
That with less grief the Perish'd they deplore.

＊　　　　＊　　　　＊

Me-thinks already, from this Chymick flame,
I see a city of more precious mold:
Rich as the town which gives the *Indies* name,
With Silver pav'd, and all divine with Gold.

Already labouring with a mighty fate,
She shakes the Rubbish from her mounting Brow,
And seems to have renew'd her Charters date,
Which Heav'n will to the death of time allow.

More great than human now, and more *August*,[1]
New deified she from her Fires does rise:
Her widening Streets on new Foundations trust,
And, opening, into larger parts she flies.

Before, she like some Shepherdess did shew,
Who sate to bathe her by a River's side;
Not answering to her fame, but rude and low,
Nor taught the beauteous Arts of Modern pride.

Now, like a Maiden Queen, she will behold,
From her high Turrets, hourly Suitors come:
The East with Incense, and the West with Gold,
Will stand, like Suppliants, to receive her Doom.

The silver *Thames*, her own domestick Floud,
Shall bear her Vessels, like a sweeping Train,
And often wind (as of his Mistress proud)
With longing eyes to meet her Face again.

The wealthy *Tagus*, and the wealthier *Rhine*,
The glory of their Towns no more shall boast,
And *Sein*, that would with Belgian Rivers join,
Shall find her Lustre stain'd, and Traffick lost.

The vent'rous Merchant who design'd more far,
And touches on our hospitable Shore,
Charm'd with the Splendour of this Northern Star,
Shall here unlade him, and depart no more.

[1]Augusta, *the old name of* London

Our pow'rful Navy shall no longer meet,
The wealth of *France* or *Holland* to invade:
The beauty of this Town without a Fleet,
From all the World shall vindicate her Trade.

JOHN DRYDEN (1631-1700)
Annus Mirabilis

MERRY MARY, 1688

I saw the *new Queene* and *King* proclaim'd the very next
day after her coming to *Whitehall*, Wednesday, 13 Feb.,
with greate acclamation and generall good reception.
Bonfires, bells, guns, &c. It was believ'd that both,
especially the Princesse, would have shew'd some
(seeming) reluctance at least, of assuming her father's
Crown, and made some apology, testifying by her
regret, that he should by his mismanagement necessitate
the Nation to so extraordinary a proceeding, w'ch would
have shew'd very handsomely to the world, and according to the character given of her piety: consonant also
to her husband's first declaration, that there was no
intention of deposing the King, but of succouring the
Nation: but nothing of all this appear'd; she came into
Whitehall laughing and jolly, as to a wedding, so as to
seem quite transported. She rose early the next morning,
and in her undresse, as it was reported, before her women
were up, went about from roome to roome to see the
convenience of *Whitehall*; lay in the same bed and
apartm't where the late Queene lay, and within a night
or two sate down to play at basset, as the Queene her
predecessor us'd to do. She smil'd upon and talk'd to
every body, so that no change seem'd to have taken place
at Court since her last going away, save that infinite
crouds of people throng'd to see her, and that she went
to our prayers. This carriage was censur'd by many.

She seems to be of a good nature, and that she takes nothing to heart; whilst the Prince her husband has a thoughtful countenance, is wonderfull serious and silent, and seems to treat all persons alike gravely, and to be very intent on affaires.

JOHN EVELYN (1620-1706)
Memoirs

JOHN CHURCHILL
DUKE OF MARLBOROUGH

Our chief, whom England and all Europe, saving only the Frenchmen, worshipped almost, had this of the godlike in him, that he was impassible before victory, before danger, before defeat. Before the greatest obstacle or the most trivial ceremony; before a hundred thousand men drawn in battalia, or a peasant slaughtered at the door of his burning hovel; before a carouse of drunken German lords, or a monarch's court, or a cottage table where his plans were laid, or an enemy's battery vomiting flame and death, and strewing corpses round about him,—he was always cold, calm, resolute, like fate.

*   *   *

His qualities were pretty well known in the army, where there were parties of all politics, and of plenty of shrewdness and wit; but there existed such a perfect confidence in him, as the first captain of the world, and such a faith and admiration of his prodigious genius and fortune, that the very men whom he notoriously cheated of their pay, the chiefs whom he used and injured—for he used all men, great and small, that came near him, as his instruments alike, and took something of theirs, either some quality or some property—the blood of a soldier, it might be, or a jewelled hat, or a hundred thousand crowns from a king, or a portion out of a starving sentinel's three-farthings; or, when he was young, a kiss from a woman, and the gold chain off her neck, taking all he could from woman or man, and having, as I have said, this of the godlike in him, that he could see a hero perish or a sparrow fall with the same amount of sympathy for either. Not that he had no tears: he could always order up this reserve at the proper moment to battle; he could draw upon tears or smiles alike, and whenever need was for using this cheap coin. He would cringe to a shoeblack, as he would flatter a minister or a monarch; be naughty, be humble, threaten, repent, weep, grasp your hand—or stab you whenever he saw occasion—but yet those of the army who knew him best, and had suffered most from him, admired him most of all; and as he rode along the lines to battle, or galloped up in the nick of time to a battalion reeling from before the enemy's charge or shot, the fainting men and officers got new courage as they saw the splendid calm of his face, and felt that his will made them irresistible.

After the great victory of Blenheim, the enthusiasm of the army for the Duke, even of his bitterest personal enemies in it, amounted to a sort of rage—nay, the very officers who cursed him in their hearts were among the most frantic to cheer him. Who could refuse his meed of admiration to such a victory and such a victor? Not he who writes. A man may profess to be ever so much a philosopher but he who fought on that day must feel a thrill of pride as he recalls it.

W. M. THACKERAY (1811-1863)
Henry Esmond

LONDON: TROOPING THE COLOUR

This ceremony, to mark the Sovereign's official birthday, takes place annually on Horse Guards Parade. In this picture, H.M. the Queen is taking the salute. Behind her are the Duke of Edinburgh and the Duke of Gloucester.

LONDON: THE TOWER AND TOWER BRIDGE

Construction of the Tower was begun by William I in 1078, probably on Roman foundations and at various times it has been a fortress, palace and prison. It stands in the south-east angle of the old city walls. Tower Bridge, in the background, was opened in 1894.

LONDON: BUCKINGHAM PALACE

Named after the 1st Duke of Buckingham, for whom it was built in 1703, Buckingham Palace was bought by George III in 1761. Reconstruction was begun by Nash, 1825, and Sir Aston Webb designed a new front in 1913. Before the palace is the Victoria Memorial.

LONDON: CHANGING THE GUARD

This has long been one of the most popular of public ceremonies in London, especially with the younger sight-seers, like A. A. Milne's Christopher Robin. In this picture, an Australian unit is taking over from the 2nd Battalion, Grenadier Guards, at Buckingham Palace.

OUT OF THE BLUE

Shakespeare's John of Gaunt began the chorus of tribute to the sea-safety of England, the island "set in the silver sea, which serves it in the office of a wall". That was the theme of James Thomson, when he sounded the powerful brass of naval patriotism.

When Britain first, at Heaven's command,
Arose from out the azure main,
This was the charter of the land,
And guardian angels sung this strain—
    "Rule, Britannia, rule the waves;
    Britons never will be slaves."

The nations, not so blest as thee,
Must in their turns to tyrants fall;
While thou shalt flourish great and free,
The dread and envy of them all.
    "Rule, Britannia, rule the waves;
    Britons never will be slaves."

Still more majestic shalt thou rise,
More dreadful from each foreign stroke;
As the loud blast that tears the skies
Serves but to root thy native oak.
    "Rule, Britannia, rule the waves;
    Britons never will be slaves."

            *   *   *

The Muses still with freedom found,
Shall to thy happy coast repair:

3

Blest isle! with matchless beauty crowned,
And manly hearts to guard the fair.
"Rule, Britannia, rule the waves;
Britons never will be slaves."

JAMES THOMSON (1700-1748)
Rule Britannia

The great actor (and versifier) David Garrick added the famous praise of the seamen as well as of the ships.

Come, cheer up, my lads! 'tis to glory we steer,
To add something more to this wonderful year;
To honour we call you, not press you like slaves,
For who are so free as the sons of the waves?
Heart of oak are our ships,
Heart of oak are our men:
We always are ready;
Steady, boys, steady;
We'll fight and we'll conquer again and again.

DAVID GARRICK (1717-1779)
Heart of Oak

But there have been Britons who disapproved of sailors. There was, for example, Jane Austen's Sir Walter Elliot, who disdained the sailor's profession. "Vanity," wrote Miss Austen, "was the beginning and end of Sir Walter's character." In his vanity, he spoke thus of a nautical career, despite the fact that the navy had just saved his country.

"Yes; it is in two points offensive to me; I have two strong grounds of objection to it. First, as being the means of bringing persons of obscure birth into undue distinction, and raising men to honours which their fathers and grandfathers never dreamt of; and, secondly, as it cuts up a man's youth and vigour most horribly; a sailor grows old sooner than any other man. I have

observed it all my life. A man is in greater danger in
the navy of being insulted by the rise of one whose
father his father might have disdained to speak to, and
of becoming prematurely an object of disgust himself,
than in any other line. One day last spring, in town,
I was in company with two men, striking instances of
what I am talking of: Lord St. Ives, whose father we
all know to have been a country curate, without bread
to eat: I was to give place to Lord St. Ives, and a certain
Admiral Baldwin, the most deplorable-looking personage
you can imagine; his face the colour of mahogany,
rough and rugged to the last degree; all lines and
wrinkles, nine grey hairs of a side, and nothing but a
dab of powder at top. "In the name of heaven, who is
that old fellow?" said I to a friend of mine who was
standing near (Sir Basil Morley). "Old fellow!" cried
Sir Basil. "It is Admiral Baldwin. What do you take
his age to be?" "Sixty," said I, "or perhaps sixty-two."
"Forty," replied Sir Basil, "forty, and no more."
Picture to yourselves my amazement: I shall not easily
forget Admiral Baldwin. I never saw quite so wretched
an example of what a sea-faring life can do; but to a
degree, I know it is the same with them all: they are
all knocked about, and exposed to every climate, and
every weather, till they are not fit to be seen. It is a pity
they are not knocked on the head at once, before they
reach Admiral Baldwin's age."

JANE AUSTEN (1775-1817)
Persuasion

THE GREAT UNNAMED

Let not ambition mock their useful toil,
Their homely joys, and destiny obscure;
Nor grandeur hear with a disdainful smile
The short and simple annals of the poor.

The boast of heraldry, the pomp of power,
And all that beauty, all that wealth e'er gave
Awaits alike th' inevitable hour:
The paths of glory lead but to the grave.

Nor you, ye proud, impute to these the fault
If memory o'er their tomb no trophies raise,
Where through the long-drawn aisle and fretted vault
The pealing anthem swells the note of praise.

Can storied urn or animated bust
Back to its mansion call the fleeting breath?
Can honour's voice provoke the silent dust,
Or flattery soothe the dull cold ear of death?

Perhaps in this neglected spot is laid
Some heart once pregnant with celestial fire;
Hands, that the rod of empire might have sway'd,
Or waked to ecstasy the living lyre:

But knowledge to their eyes her ample page
Rich with the spoils of time did ne'er unroll;
Chill penury repress'd their noble rage,
And froze the genial current of the soul.

Full many a gem of purest ray serene
The dark unfathom'd caves of ocean bear:
Full many a flower is born to blush unseen,
And waste its sweetness on the desert air.

Some village Hampden, that with dauntless breast
The little tyrant of his fields withstood,
Some mute inglorious Milton here may rest,
Some Cromwell, guiltless of his country's blood.

Th' applause of listening senates to command,
The threats of pain and ruin to despise,
To scatter plenty o'er a smiling land,
And read their history in a nation's eyes.

Their lot forbade: nor circumscribed alone
Their growing virtues, but their crimes confined;
Forbade to wade thro' slaughter to a throne,
And shut the gates of mercy on mankind;

The struggling pangs of conscious truth to hide,
To quench the blushes of ingenuous shame,
Or heap the shrine of luxury and pride
With incense kindled at the Muse's flame.

Far from the madding crowd's ignoble strife
Their sober wishes never learn'd to stray;
Along the cool sequester'd vale of life
They kept the noiseless tenour of their way.

THOMAS GRAY (1716-1771)
from *Elegy Written in a Country Churchyard*

"OLD NOBBS," 1789

But, when the Paris mob threatened the life of the
Queen and insulted the King, sober Britons began to
have their doubts. The King of England was no genius.
But his people were genuinely fond of him and looked
on a decent respect for the throne as a sign of good
citizenship. Old Nobbs, as they called him, had been
reigning for nearly thirty years, and, though he had
had his full and often deserved share of unpopularity
and troubles, his natural friendliness and good humour
and the personal integrity of his life had finally turned
him into a national institution. Since the end of the
American War and the revival of prosperity under the

brilliant young Minister whom he had so boldly placed
in office, George III's popularity had risen by leaps and
bounds. Not even the extravagance and indiscretions
of his eldest son were able to detract from it: indeed
by contrast they enhanced it. When in the autumn of
1788 the King's natural "rapid and rambling volubility"
degenerated under the strain of insomnia into insanity,
there was widespread grief and alarm.

He recovered suddenly at a time when hope had been
almost abandoned. While the States General was meeting at Versailles, England was giving itself up to a round
of thanksgiving services, illuminations and roasted
oxen. That summer the royal holiday pilgrimage to
Weymouth became a triumph, his Majesty driving
through flower-strewn villages and grassy forest rides
lined with cheering multitudes; the country folk
turning out with artless loyalty in their broadcloth,
loose white frocks and neckcloths, while chariots,
chaises, landaus, carts, waggons, gigs and phaetons,
drawn up in democratic disarray under the trees, shim-
mered with fluttering handkerchiefs. At Lyndhurst
the King on an evening walk was accompanied by
the entire village repeatedly singing the National
Anthem.

This loyalty of the rustic English to the Crown
afforded a curious contrast to the uneasy splendours of
the French monarchy. At the time of the storming of
the Bastille, Britain's sovereign was peacefully taking
the sea waters under the delighted eyes of a proprietary
multitude, a band concealed in a bathing machine
striking up "God save great George our King" as the
"Royal one entered the water."[1] Wherever he went the
same spontaneous acclamations attended him: "The
greatest conqueror," wrote Fanny Burney, "could never
pass through his dominions with fuller acclamations
of joy from his devoted subjects than George III experi-

[1] D'Arblay, II, 316

enced, simply from having won their love by the even tenor of an unspotted life." It was a loyalty founded on nature by a people who gave him their hearts, not because he was their sovereign but because, being what they wanted their sovereign to be, he deserved them.

For he was as natural as they. In his familiar Windsor uniform—the broadskirted blue frockcoat with its scarlet collar and cuffs—and round hat he looked what he was, an English country gentleman. He liked farming, the routine of his duties, but most of all the human beings about him. He talked incessantly, to every one, pouring out good-humoured comments and questions, such as how the apple got into the dumpling, and answering them mostly himself with a volley of hoarse "Tut! Tuts!" and "What! Whats!" which somehow removed all sense of ceremony and superiority.

Like his "cousin" of France, King George was a family man, but, unlike Louis, happy in being so since this was what the English, with their strong sense of the realities of life, wanted their sovereign to be. The Queen might be an over-frugal *hausfrau*, but Royal George was a faithful husband and a devoted father, and in his feckless eldest son an injured one, and his subjects loved him for it. They knew that he had a good heart. Nothing so won their affection as his manifest delight in children. When middle-class Dorothy Wordsworth accompanied her uncle and his family to one of the familiar summer evening parades on the terrace at Windsor, the old King stopped in front of little Christopher and Mary Wordsworth and allowed them to play with his stick. And when a day or two later Mary was wearing a new hat, the old man was quick to notice it. "Ah, Mary," says he, "that's a pretty hat! that's a pretty hat!"

Because of these things and because, despite black spots in the national existence, most Englishmen were tolerably satisfied with their lot, King George's subjects echoed Parson Woodforde's prayer:

"And may so good a King long live to reign over us—and pray God that his amiable and beloved Queen Charlotte may now enjoy again every happiness this world can afford with so good a man, and may it long, very long continue with them both here and eternal happiness hereafter."

They could not follow events across the Channel without their viewpoint being affected by such personal considerations: and when the French people rose in their majesty and established liberty by flinging drunken insults at their sovereign and butchering his retainers, they refused to approve such goings-on. Liberty was one thing; "anarchy and confusion" another. Even John Wilkes, that tried champion of the populace's right to do as it pleased, observed that the new France was not a democracy but a mobocracy.

ARTHUR BRYANT (Born 1899)
The Years of Endurance

THE GEORGIANS DEFENDED

An age can easily be misjudged owing to the predominance in art and letters of a few wits and grandees. The cynicism of the Georgians, their exhibitionism, and their pursuit of pleasure are remembered because of the famous books, plays, or pictures in which these characteristics so vividly survive. The unremembered Many may have had quite different ways of living and standards of morality. Eighteenth Century England has been regarded as heartless and callous as well as elegant and brilliant. So it is interesting to find that the nineteenth-century historian, J. R. Green, held another opinion and expressed it with his usual lucidity and force in his preface to an edition of Addison's Essays.

As the first of our lay-preachers, Addison marks the expansion of a thirst for moral and religious improve-

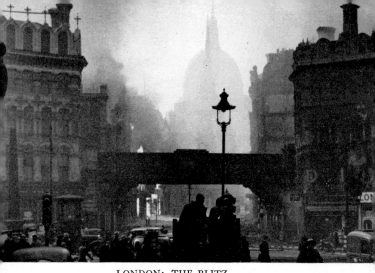

LONDON: THE BLITZ

A picture taken in 1940, at the height of the German raids on London, looking towards St. Paul's Cathedral from Ludgate Circus. An incendiary bomb has fallen on buildings in Ludgate Hill but to the Londoner it is just another incident on the way to work.

LONDON: ST. PAUL'S CATHEDRAL

Taken not far from the preceding fire-bomb scene, this post-war picture shows Wren's great masterpiece still standing, almost unscathed, but surrounded by the open "bomb sites" where buildings fell and many people died in 1940 and 1941.

LONDON: THE ROYAL BALLET

Formerly known as the Sadler's Wells Ballet Company, the Royal Ballet has become the most important in Western Europe. This picture, taken at the Royal Opera House, Covent Garden, shows Miss Nadia Nerina and members of the *corps de ballet* in a scene from *Coppelia*.

WINDSOR: SUMMER ON THE RIVER

Beyond the Thames stands Windsor Castle, with the Royal Standard flying from the Round Tower to show that the Sovereign is in residence. Between the towers lies St. George's Chapel, which is the chapel of the Knights of the Garter and burial place of British sovereigns.

ment beyond the circle of the clergy. He is thus the ancestor of Howard and Wilberforce, as he is the ancestor of Mr. Matthew Arnold. For a whole century the *Spectator* had greater weight on moral and religious opinions than all the charges of the bishops. And on the moral side, at least, it deserved to have such a weight. Addison was not only a moralist: he had what so few have had in the world's history, an enthusiasm for conduct. "The great aim of these my speculations," he says emphatically, "is to banish vice and ignorance out of the territories of Great Britain." It was this enthusiasm for morality which enabled him to discern, to sympathise with, to give shape to, the moral energy of his day. We hear sometimes that the last century is "repulsive": but what is it that repels us in it? Is it the age itself, or the picture of itself which the age so fearlessly presents? There is no historic ground for thinking the eighteenth century a coarser or a more brutal age than the centuries that had gone before; rather there is ground for thinking it a less coarse and a less brutal age. The features which repel us in it are no features of its own production. There were brutalized colliers at Ringwood before Wesley; there were brutal squires before Western; there were brutal mobs before the Gordon riots. Vile as our prisons were when Howard visited them, they were yet viler in the days of Elizabeth. Parliamentary corruption was a child of the Restoration; the immorality of the upper classes was as great under the Tudors as under the Georges. What makes the Georgian age seem repulsive is simply that it is the first age which felt these evils to be evils, which dragged them, in its effort to amend them, into the light of day. It is in fact the moral effort of the time which makes it seem so immoral. Till now social evil had passed unnoted, and uncensured, because, save by the directly religious world, it was unfelt. It was a sudden and general zeal for better things which made the eighteenth century note, describe, satirize the evil of society. Then, as now, the bulk of Englishmen were honest and right-minded. "Between the mud at the bottom and the scum of its surface," says Mons. Taine fairly enough, "rolled on the great current of the national life." Widely as it had parted from the theological and political doctrines of Puritanism, the moral conceptions of Puritanism lived on in the nation at large. The popular book of the upper and middle classes, the book that was in every lady's closet, was *The Whole Duty of Man*. But then, for the first time, this moral temper of the individual Englishman quickened into a passion for moral reform in the whole structure of English society. The moral preaching which bores the reader of to-day was the popular literature of the eighteenth century. Not only can the essayist make conduct the groundwork of his essays, but the novelist takes it as the groundwork of his novels, the play-wright as the basis of his plays. *The Beggar's Opera*, in which Gay quizzes political corruption, is played amidst thunders of applause. Everybody reads Pope's *Satires*. Whatever in fact men put their hands to takes somehow this shape of moral reform. "Give us some models of letters for servant maids to write to their homes," said the publishers to Richardson; and Richardson, honestly striving to produce a Complete Letter-writer, gave them *Pamela*.

J. R. GREEN (1837-1883)
Essays of Addison: Introduction

KENTISH COURAGE

This is not one of the most notable of Wordsworth's Sonnets, but it seemed to me worthy of inclusion for a historical reason. In the last war Kent had to endure not only a particularly large share of the general bombing which began in 1940, but also the long-range bombardment by big German guns on the French shore. Then came the stream of Flying Bombs which began in 1944. Most of these passed over Kent and many fell upon it. The aerial Battle of Britain was largely fought over Kent. So once more the people of Kent were in the "Vanguard of Liberty" and certainly the Kentish people had to face far more of death and danger than came to them in the Napoleonic Wars.

> Vanguard of Liberty, ye men of Kent,
> Ye children of a Soil that doth advance
> Her haughty brow against the coast of France,
> Now is the time to prove your hardiment!
> To France be words of invitation sent!
> They from their fields can see the countenance
> Of your fierce war, may ken the glittering lance,
> And hear you shouting forth your brave intent.
> Left single, in bold parley, ye, of yore,
> Did from the Norman win a gallant wreath;
> Confirmed the characters that were yours before;—
> No parleying now. In Britain is one breath;
> We all are with you now from shore to shore;—
> Ye men of Kent, 'tis victory or death!

WILLIAM WORDSWORTH (1770-1850)
Sonnets

THE DEATH OF NELSON

The cockpit was crowded with wounded and dying men over whose bodies he was with some difficulty conveyed, and laid upon a pallet in the midshipmen's berth. It was soon perceived upon examination that the wound was mortal. This, however, was concealed from all except Captain Hardy, the chaplain, and the medical attendants. He himself being certain from the sensation in his back and the gush of blood which he felt momently within his breast that no human care could avail him, insisted that the surgeon should leave him, and attend to those to whom he might be

useful. "For," said he, "you can do nothing for me."
All that could be done was to fan him with paper, and
frequently to give him lemonade, to alleviate his intense
thirst.

He was in great pain, and expressed much anxiety
for the event of the action, which now began to declare
itself. As often as a ship struck the crew of the *Victory*
hurrahed, and at every hurrah a visible expression of
joy gleamed in the eyes and marked the countenance
of the dying hero. But he became impatient to see
Captain Hardy, and as that officer, though often sent
for, could not leave the deck, Nelson feared that some
fatal cause prevented him, and repeatedly cried, "Will
no one bring Hardy to me? He must be killed! He is
surely dead!" An hour and ten minutes elapsed from
the time when Nelson received his wound before Hardy
could come to him. They shook hands in silence;
Hardy in vain struggling to suppress the feelings of that
most painful and yet sublimest moment. "Well,
Hardy," said Nelson, "how goes the day with us?"
"Very well," replied Hardy; "ten ships have struck,
but five of their van have tacked, and show an intention
of bearing down upon the *Victory*. I have called two or
three of our fresh ships round, and have no doubt of
giving them a drubbing." "I hope," said Nelson,
"none of our ships have struck?" Hardy answered,
"There was no fear of that." Then, and not till then,
Nelson spoke of himself. "I am a dead man, Hardy,"
said he; "I am going fast; it will be all over with me
soon. Come nearer to me. Let my dear Lady Hamilton
have my hair, and all other things belonging to me."
Hardy observed that he hoped Mr. Beatty could yet hold
out some prospect of life. "Oh, no!" he replied, "it is
impossible. My back is shot through. Beatty will tell
you so." Captain Hardy then once more shook hands
with him, and with a heart almost bursting hastened
upon deck.

By this time all feeling below the breast was gone, and Nelson, having made the surgeon ascertain this, said to him, "You know I am gone. I know it. I feel something rising in my breast"— putting his hand on his left side—"which tells me so." And, upon Beatty's inquiring whether his pain was very great, he replied, "So great that he wished he was dead. Yet," said he in a lower voice, "one would like to live a little longer too!" And after a few minutes in the same undertone he added, "What would become of poor Lady Hamilton if she knew my situation?" Next to his country she occupied his thoughts. Captain Hardy, some fifty minutes after he had left the cockpit, returned; and again taking the hand of his dying friend and commander, congratulated him on having gained a complete victory. How many of the enemy were taken he did not know, as it was impossible to perceive them distinctly; but fourteen or fifteen at least. "That's well," cried Nelson, "but I bargained for twenty." And then, in a stronger voice he said, "Anchor, Hardy, anchor."

Hardy upon this hinted that Admiral Collingwood take upon himself the direction of affairs. "Not while I live, Hardy!" said the dying Nelson, ineffectually endeavouring to raise himself from the bed; "do you anchor." His previous order for preparing to anchor had shown how clearly he foresaw the necessity of this. Presently, calling Hardy back, he said to him in a low voice, "Don't throw me overboard;" and he desired that he might be buried by his parents, unless it should please the King to order otherwise. Then reverting to private feelings, "Take care of my dear Lady Hamilton, Hardy; take care of poor Lady Hamilton. Kiss me, Hardy," said he. Hardy knelt down and kissed his cheek, and Nelson said, "Now I am satisfied. Thank God I have done my duty." Hardy stood over him in silence for a moment or two, then knelt again and kissed his forehead. "Who is that?" said Nelson; and

being informed, he replied, "God bless you, Hardy."
And Hardy then left him—for ever.

. . . There was reason to suppose, from the appearances
upon opening the body, that in the course of nature he
might have attained, like his father, to a good old age.
Yet he cannot be said to have fallen prematurely whose
work was done; nor ought he to be lamented who
died so full of honours and at the height of human
fame. The most triumphant death is that of the martyr;
the most awful, that of the martyred patriot; the most
splendid, that of the hero in the hour of victory; and
if the chariots and the horses of fire had been vouch-
safed for Nelson's translation, he could scarcely have
departed in a brighter blaze of glory.

ROBERT SOUTHEY (1774-1843)
The Life of Nelson

BRUSSELS, 1815

There never was, since the days of Darius, such a brilliant
train of camp-followers as hung round the Duke of
Wellington's army in the Low Countries in 1815, and
led it, dancing and feasting as it were, up to the very
brink of battle. A certain ball which a noble Duchess
gave at Brussels on the 15th June in the above-named
year is historical. All Brussels had been in a state of
excitement about it, and I have heard, from ladies who
were in that town at the period, that the talk and interest
of persons of their own sex regarding the ball was much
greater even than in respect of the enemy in their front.
The struggles, intrigues, and prayers to get tickets
were such as only English ladies will employ, in order
to gain admission to the society of the great of their
own nation. . . .

LAST PARTING

At last, George took Emmy's hand, and led her back into the bedroom, from whence he came out alone. The parting had taken place in that moment, and he was gone.

"Thank Heaven that is over," George thought, bounding down the stair, his sword under his arm, as he ran swiftly to the alarm ground, where the regiment was mustered, and whither trooped men and officers hurrying from their billets; his pulse was throbbing and his cheeks flushed: the great game of war was going to be played, and he one of the players. What a fierce excitement of doubt, hope, and pleasure! What tremendous hazards of loss or gain! What were all the games of chance he had ever played compared to this one? Into all contests requiring athletic skill and courage, the young man, from his boyhood upwards, had flung himself with all his might. The champion of his school and his regiment, the bravos of his companions had followed him everywhere; from the boys' cricket match to the garrison races, he had won a hundred of triumphs; and wherever he went, women and men had admired and envied him. What qualities are there for which a man gets so speedy a return of applause, as those of bodily superiority, activity, and valour? Time out of mind strength and courage have been the theme of bards and romances; and from the story of Troy down to to-day, poetry has always chosen a soldier for a hero. I wonder is it because men are cowards in heart that they admire bravery so much, and place military valour so far beyond every other quality for reward and worship?

So, at the sound of that stirring call to battle, George jumped away from the gentle arms in which he had been dallying; not without a feeling of shame (although his wife's hold on him had been but feeble), that he should have been detained there so long. The same feeling of eagerness and excitement was amongst all those friends of his of whom we have had occasional glimpses, from the stout senior Major, who led the regiment into action, to little Stubble, the Ensign, who was to bear its colours on that day.

The sun was just rising as the march began—it was a gallant sight—the band led the column, playing the regimental march—then came the Major in command, riding upon Pyramus, his stout charger—then marched the grenadiers, their Captain at their head; in the centre were the colours, borne by the senior and junior Ensigns—then George came marching at the head of his company. He looked up, and smiled at Amelia, and passed on; and even the sound of the music died away.

. . . All that day, from morning until past sunset, the cannon never ceased to roar. It was dark when the cannonading stopped all of a sudden.

All of us have read of what occurred during that interval. The tale is in every Englishman's mouth; and you and I, who were children when the great battle was won and lost, are never tired of hearing and recounting the history of that famous action. Its remembrance rankles still in the bosoms of millions of the countrymen of those brave men who lost the day. They pant for an opportunity of revenging that humiliation; and if a contest, ending in a victory on their part, should ensue, elating them in their turn, and leaving its cursed legacy of hatred and rage behind to us, there is no end to the so-called glory and shame, and to the alternations of successful and unsuccessful murder, in which two high-spirited nations might engage. Centuries hence, we Frenchmen and Englishmen might be boasting and killing each other still, carrying out bravely the Devil's code of honour.

All our friends took their share and fought like men in the great field. All day long, whilst the women were praying ten miles away, the lines of the dauntless English infantry were receiving and repelling the furious charges of the French horsemen. Guns which were heard at Brussels were ploughing up their ranks, and comrades falling, and the resolute survivors closing in. Towards evening, the attack of the French, repeated and resisted so bravely, slackened in its fury. They had other foes beside the British to engage, or were preparing for a final onset. It came at last: the columns of the Imperial Guard marched up the hill of Saint Jean, at length and at once to sweep the English from the height which they had maintained all day, and spite of all. Unscared by the thunder of the artillery, which hurled death from the English line, the dark rolling column pressed on and up the hill. It seemed almost to crest the eminence, when it began to wave and falter. Then it stopped, still facing the shot. Then at last the English troops rushed from the post from which no enemy had been able to dislodge them, and the Guard turned and fled.

No more firing was heard at Brussels—the pursuit rolled miles away. Darkness came down on the field and city, and Amelia was praying for George, who was lying on his face, dead, with a bullet through his heart.

W. M. THACKERAY (1811-1863)
Vanity Fair

WELLINGTON AND WATERLOO

The first thing I did, of course, was to put out my hand and congratulate him (the Duke) upon his victory.

He made a variety of observations in his short, natural, blunt way, but with the greatest gravity all the time, and without the least approach to anything like triumph or joy.—"It has been a damned serious business," he said. "Blücher and I have lost 30,000 men. It has been a damned nice thing—the nearest run thing you ever saw in your life. Blücher lost 14,000 on Friday night, and got so damnably licked I could not find him on Saturday morning; so I was obliged to fall back to keep up my communications with him."—Then, as he walked about, he praised greatly those Guards who kept the farm (meaning Hugomont) against the repeated attacks of the French; and then he praised all our troops, uttering repeated expressions of astonishment at our men's courage. He repeated so often its being *so nice a thing—so nearly run a thing*, that I asked him if the French had fought better than he had ever seen them do before.—"No," he said, "they have always fought the same since I first saw them at Vimeiro." Then he said:—"By God! I don't think it would have done if I had not been there."

When I left the Duke, I went instantly home and wrote to England by the same courier who carried his dispatch. I sent the very conversation I have just related to Bennet. I think however, I omitted the Duke's observation that he did not think the battle would have been won had he not been there, and I remember my reason for omitting this sentence. It did not seem fair to the Duke to state it without full explanation. There was nothing like vanity in the observation in the way he made it. I considered it only as meaning that the battle was so hardly and equally fought that nothing but confidence of our army in himself as their general could have brought them thro'. Now that seven years have elapsed since that battle, and tho' the Duke has become—very foolishly, in my opinion—a politician, and has done many wrong and foolish things since that time, yet I

think of his conversation and whole conduct on the
19th—the day after the battle—exactly the same as I did
then: namely—that nothing could do a conqueror
more honour than his gravity and seriousness at the
loss of lives he had sustained, his admission of his great
danger, and the justice he did his enemy.

THOMAS CREEVEY (1768-1838)
The Creevey Papers

FAREWELL TO WELLINGTON

Bury the Great Duke
  With an empire's lamentation,
Let us bury the Great Duke
  To the noise of the mourning of a mighty nation,
Mourning when their leaders fall,
Warriors carry the warrior's pall,
And sorrow darkens hamlet and hall.

*   *   *

All is over and done:
Render thanks to the Giver,
England, for thy son.
Let the bell be toll'd.
Render thanks to the Giver,
And render him to the mould.
Under the cross of gold
That shines over city and river,
There he shall rest for ever
Among the wise and the bold.

*   *   *

Who is he that cometh, like an honour'd guest,
With banner and with music, with soldier and with
     priest,
With a nation weeping, and breaking on my rest?
Mighty Seaman, this is he
Was great by land as thou by sea.
Thine island loves thee well, thou famous man,
The greatest sailor since our world began.
Now, to the roll of muffled drums,
To thee the greatest soldier comes;
For this is he
Was great by land as thou by sea;
His foes were thine; he kept us free;
O give him welcome, this is he
Worthy of our gorgeous rites,
And worthy to be laid by thee.

          *   *   *

Mighty Seaman, tender and true,
And pure as he from taint of craven guile,
O saviour of the silver-coasted isle,
O shaker of the Baltic, and the Nile,
If aught of things that here befall
Touch a spirit among things divine,
If love of country move thee there at all,
Be glad, because his bones are laid by thine!
And thro' the centuries let a people's voice
In full acclaim,
A people's voice,
The proof and echo of all human fame,
A people's voice, when they rejoice
At civil revel and pomp and game,
Attest their great commander's claim
With honour, honour, honour, honour to him,
Eternal honour to his name.

A people's voice! we are a people yet,
Tho' all men else their nobler dreams forget,
Confused by brainless mobs and lawless Powers;
Thank Him who isled us here, and roughly set
His Briton in blown seas and storming showers,
We have a voice, with which to pay the debt
Of boundless love and reverence and regret
To those great men who fought, and kept it ours.
And keep it ours, O God, from brute control;
O Statesmen, guard us, guard the eye, the soul
Of Europe, keep our noble England whole,
And save the one true seed of freedom sown
Betwixt a people and their ancient throne,
That sober freedom out of which there springs
Our loyal passion for our temperate kings;
For, saving that, ye help to save mankind
Till public wrong be crumbled into dust,
And drill the raw world for the march of mind,
Till crowds at length be sane and crowns be just.

      *   *   *

Yea, let all good things await
Him who cares not to be great,
But as he saves or serves the state.
Not once or twice in our rough island-story,
The path of duty was the way to glory:
He that walks it, only thirsting
For the right, and learns to deaden
Love of self, before his journey closes,
He shall find the stubborn thistle bursting
Into glossy purples, which outredden
All voluptuous garden-roses.
Not once or twice in our fair island-story,
The path of duty was the way to glory;
He that ever following her commands,
On with toil of heart and knees and hands,

Thro' the long gorge to the far light has won
His path upward, and prevail'd,
Shall find the toppling crags of Duty scaled
Are close upon the shining table-lands
To which our God Himself is moon and sun.
Such was he: his work is done.
But while the races of mankind endure,
Let his great example stand
Colossal, seen of every land,
And keep the soldier firm, the statesman pure:
Till in all lands and thro' all human story
The path of duty be the way to glory:
And let the land whose hearths he saved from shame
For many and many an age proclaim
At civic revel and pomp and game,
And when the long-illumined cities flame,
Their ever-loyal iron leader's fame,
With honour, honour, honour, honour to him,
Eternal honour to his name.

ALFRED, LORD TENNYSON (1809-1892)
Ode on the Death of the Duke of Wellington

MORAL INDIGNATION

We know no spectacle so ridiculous as the British public
in one of its periodical fits of morality. In general,
elopements, divorces, and family quarrels, pass with
little notice. We read the scandal, talk about it for a
day, and forget it. But once in six or seven years our
virtue becomes outrageous. We cannot suffer the laws
of religion and decency to be violated. We must make
a stand against vice. We must teach libertines that the
English people appreciate the importance of domestic
ties. Accordingly some unfortunate man, in no respect
more depraved than hundreds whose offences have

been treated with lenity, is singled out as an expiatory sacrifice. If he has children, they are to be taken from him. If he has a profession, he is to be driven from it. He is cut by the higher orders and hissed by the lower. He is, in truth, a sort of whipping-boy, by whose vicarious agonies all the other transgressors of the same class are, it is supposed, sufficiently chastised. We reflect very complacently on our own severity, and compare with great pride the high standard of morals established in England with the Parisian laxity. At length our anger is satiated. Our victim is ruined and heart-broken. And our virtue goes quietly to sleep for seven years more.

It is clear that those vices which destroy domestic happiness ought to be as much as possible repressed. It is equally clear that they cannot be repressed by penal legislation. It is therefore right and desirable that public opinion should be directed against them. But it should be directed against them uniformly, steadily, and temperately, not by sudden fits and starts. There should be one weight and one measure. Decimation is always an objectionable mode of punishment. It is the resource of judges too indolent and hasty to investigate facts and to discriminate nicely between shades of guilt. It is an irrational practice, even when adopted by military tribunals. When adopted by the tribunal of public opinion it is infinitely more irrational. It is good that a certain portion of disgrace should constantly attend on certain bad actions. But is is not good that the offenders should merely have to stand the risks of a lottery of infamy, that ninety-nine out of every hundred should escape, and that the hundredth, perhaps the most innocent of the hundred, should pay for all.

LORD MACAULAY (1800-1859)
Essays: Moore's Life of Byron

THE CHILDREN'S CRY

Among the worst horrors of the Industrial Revolution was the driving of almost infantile labour into the mines, mills, and factories. Elizabeth Browning's protest greatly helped the ending of this crime against children.

Do ye hear the children weeping, O my brothers,
    Ere the sorrow comes with years?
They are leaning their young heads against their
        mothers,
    And *that* cannot stop their tears.
The young lambs are bleating in the meadows,
    The young birds are chirping in the nest,
The young fawns are playing with the shadows,
    The young flowers are blowing toward the west—
But the young, young children, O my brothers,
    They are weeping bitterly!
They are weeping in the playtime of the others,
    In the country of the free.

*   *   *

"For oh," say the children, "we are weary
    And we cannot run or leap;
If we cared for any meadows, it were merely
    To drop down in them and sleep.
Our knees tremble sorely in the stooping,
    We fall upon our faces, trying to go;
And underneath our heavy eyelids drooping
    The reddest flower would look as pale as snow.
For, all day, we drag our burden tiring
    Through the coal-dark, underground;
Or, all day, we drive the wheels of iron
    In the factories, round and round.

ETON: THE FOURTH OF JUNE

The annual cricket match on Agar's Plough, played on June 4th, George III's birthday. Henry VI founded the College in 1440, and many of Britain's great soldiers and statesmen have been educated there, including the Duke of Wellington, who claimed that "The battle of Waterloo was won on the playing-fields of Eton."

HARROW: ROLL CALL ON SPEECH DAY

Harrow School was founded in 1571 and towards the end of the 18th century it became one of the chief schools of England. Famous pupils have included Byron, Sheridan, Peel, Palmerston, Baldwin, Galsworthy and Winston Churchill.

HERTFORDSHIRE: CASSIOBURY PARK, WATFORD

A popular beauty spot suggesting summer in winter, after a hard night's frost. Watford, 18 miles north-west of London, is a busy and thriving borough with important chocolate, brewing, milling and printing industries.

ST. ALBAN'S: THE ABBEY

The cathedral, or abbey church, was founded in Saxon times, the greater part being built during the reign of William the Conqueror. To the south-west of St. Alban's lie the remains of the ancient Romano-British town of Verulamium.

"For all day the wheels are droning, turning;
    Their wind comes in our faces,
Till our hearts turn, our heads with pulses burning,
    And the walls turn in their places:
Turns the sky in the high window, blank and reeling,
    Turns the long light that drops adown the wall,
Turn the black flies that crawl along the ceiling:
    All are turning, all the day, and we with all.
And all day, the iron wheels are droning,
    And sometimes we could pray,
'O ye wheels' (breaking out in a mad moaning)
    'Stop! be silent for to-day!'"

Ay! be silent! Let them hear each other breathing
    For a moment, mouth to mouth!
Let them touch each other's hands, in a fresh wreathing
    Of their tender human youth!
Let them feel that this cold metallic motion
    Is not all the life God fashions or reveals:
Let them prove their living souls against the notion
    That they live in you, or under you, O wheels!
Still, all day, the iron wheels go onward,
    Grinding life down from its mark;
And the children's souls, which God is calling sunward,
    Spin on blindly in the dark.

      *   *   *

They look up with their pale and sunken faces,
    And their look is dread to see,
For they mind you of their angels in high places,
    With eyes turned on Deity.
"How long," they say, "how long, O cruel nation,
    Will you stand, to move the world, on a child's
        heart,—
Stifle down with a mailed heel its palpitation,
    And tread onward to your throne amid the mart?

Our blood splashes upward, O gold-heaper,
    And your purple shows your path!
But the child's sob in the silence curses deeper
    Than the strong man in his wrath."

ELIZABETH BARRETT BROWNING (1806-1861)
The Cry of the Children

QUEEN VICTORIA

And so, after the toils and tempests of the day, a long
evening followed—mild, serene, and lighted with a
golden glory. For an unexampled atmosphere of success
and adoration invested the last period of Victoria's life.
Her triumph was the summary, the crown, of a greater
triumph—the culminating prosperity of a nation. The
solid splendour of the decade between Victoria's two
jubilees can hardly be paralleled in the annals of England.
The sage counsels of Lord Salisbury seemed to bring
with them not only wealth and power, but security;
and the country settled down with calm assurance, to
the enjoyment of an established grandeur. And—it was
only natural—Victoria settled down too. For she was a
part of the establishment—an essential part as it seemed
—a fixture—a magnificent, immovable sideboard in the
the huge saloon of state. . . .

She had given proof of one of the most admired
characteristics of the race—persistent vitality. She had
reigned for sixty years, and she was not out. And then,
she was a character. The outlines of her nature were
firmly drawn, and, even through the mists which
envelop royalty, clearly visible. In the popular imagination her familiar figure filled, with satisfying ease, a
distinct and memorable place. It was, besides, the kind
of figure which naturally called forth the admiring
sympathy of the great majority of the nation. Goodness
they prized above every other human quality; and

Victoria, who, at the age of twelve, had said that she
would be good, had kept her word. Duty, conscience,
morality—yes! in the light of those high beacons the
Queen had always lived. She had passed her days in
work and not in pleasure—in public responsibilities
and family cares. The standard of solid virtue which
had been set up so long ago amid the domestic happiness
of Osborne had never been lowered for an instant. For
more than half a century no divorced lady had
approached the precincts of the Court. Victoria, indeed,
in her enthusiasm for wifely fidelity, had laid down a
still stricter ordinance: she frowned severely upon any
widow who married again. Considering that she herself
was the offspring of a widow's second marriage, this
prohibition might be regarded as an eccentricity; but,
no doubt, it was an eccentricity on the right side. The
middle classes, firm in the triple brass of their respectability, rejoiced with a special joy over the most respectable of Queens. They almost claimed her, indeed, as
one of themselves; but this would have been an
exaggeration. For, though many of her characteristics
were most often found among the middle classes, in
other respects—in her manners, for instance, Victoria
was decidedly aristocratic. And, in one important
particular, she was neither aristocratic nor middle-class:
her attitude toward herself was simply regal.

Such qualities were obvious and important; but, in
the impact of a personality, it is something deeper,
something fundamental and common to all its qualities,
that really tells. In Victoria, it is easy to discern the
nature of this underlying element: it was a peculiar
sincerity. Her truthfulness, her single-mindedness, the
vividness of her emotions and her unrestrained expression
of them, were the varied forms which this central
characteristic assumed. It was her sincerity which
gave her at once her impressiveness, her charm, and
her absurdity. She moved through life with the imposing

certitude of one to whom concealment was impossible—
either towards her surroundings or towards herself.
There she was, all of her—the Queen of England,
complete and obvious; the world might take her or
leave her; she had nothing more to show, or to explain,
or to modify; and, with her peerless carriage, she
swept along her path. . . .

The personality and the position, too—the wonderful
combination of them—that, perhaps, was what was
finally fascinating in the case. The little old lady,
with her white hair and her plain mourning clothes,
in her wheeled chair or her donkey-carriage—one saw
her so; and then—close behind—with their immediate
suggestion of singularity, of mystery, and of power—
the Indian servants. That was the familiar vision, and
it was admirable; but, at chosen moments, it was right
that the widow of Windsor should step forth apparent
Queen. The last and the most glorious of such occasions
was the Jubilee of 1897. Then, as the splendid procession
passed along, escorting Victoria through the thronged
re-echoing streets of London on her progress of thanksgiving to St. Paul's Cathedral, the greatness of her
realm and the adoration of her subjects blazed out
together. The tears welled to her eyes, and, while the
multitude roared round her, "How kind they are to
me! How kind they are!" she repeated over and over
again. That night her message flew over the Empire:
"From my heart I thank my beloved people. May God
bless them!" The long journey was nearly done. But
the traveller, who had come so far, and through such
strange experiences, moved on with the old unfaltering
step. The girl, the wife, the aged woman, were the
same: vitality, conscientiousness, pride, and simplicity
were hers to the latest hour.

GILES LYTTON STRACHEY (1880-1932)
Queen Victoria

PRIME MINISTER

On 10th May, 1940, Hitler began his westward sweep across Holland and Belgium, which was to end with the surrender of France less than six weeks later. Mr. Churchill became Prime Minister, succeeding Mr. Neville Chamberlain, on the same day. He addressed the House of Commons on 13th May.

On Friday evening last I received His Majesty's commission to form a new administration. It was the evident wish and will of Parliament and the nation that this should be conceived on the broadest possible basis, and that it should include all parties, both those who supported the late Government and also the parties of the Opposition. I have completed the most important part of this task. A War Cabinet has been formed of five Members, representing, with the Opposition Liberals, the unity of the nation. The three party leaders have agreed to serve, either in the War Cabinet or in high executive office. The three fighting services have been filled. It was necessary that this should be done in one single day, on account of the extreme urgency and rigour of events. A number of other key positions were filled yesterday, and I am submitting a further list to His Majesty to-night. I hope to complete the appointment of the principal Ministers during to-morrow. The appointment of the other Ministers usually takes a little longer, but I trust that, when Parliament meets again, this part of my task will be completed, and that the administration will be complete in all respects.

I considered it in the public interest to suggest that the House should be summoned to meet to-day. Mr. Speaker agreed, and took the necessary steps, in accordance with the powers conferred upon him by the Resolution of the House. At the end of the proceedings to-day, the adjournment of the House will be proposed until Tuesday,

May 21, with, of course, provision for earlier meeting if need be. The business to be considered during that week will be notified to Members at the earliest opportunity. I now invite the House, by the Resolution which stands in my name, to record its approval of the steps taken and to declare its confidence in the new Government.

To form an administration of this scale and complexity is a serious undertaking in itself, but it must be remembered that we are in the preliminary stage of one of the greatest battles in history, that we are in action at many points in Norway and in Holland, that we have to be prepared in the Mediterranean, that the air battle is continuous, and that many preparations have to be made here at home. In this crisis I hope I may be pardoned if I do not address the House at any length to-day. I hope that any of my friends and colleagues, or former colleagues, who are affected by the political reconstruction, will make all allowance for any lack of ceremony with which it has been necessary to act. I would say to the House, as I said to those who have joined this Government: "I have nothing to offer but blood, toil, tears and sweat."

We have before us an ordeal of the most grievous kind. We have before us many, many long months of struggle and of suffering. You ask what is our policy? I will say: It is to wage war, by sea, land and air, with all our might and with all the strength God can give us: to wage war against a monstrous tyranny, never surpassed in the dark, lamentable catalogue of human crime. That is our policy. You ask, What is our aim? I can answer in one word: Victory—victory at all costs, victory in spite of all terror, victory, however long and hard the road may be; for without victory, there is no survival. Let that be realised; no survival for the British Empire; no survival for all that the British Empire has stood for, no survival for the urge and impulse of the ages, that mankind will move forward towards its goal. But I take up my task with buoyancy and hope. I feel sure that our cause will not be suffered to fail among men. At this time I feel entitled to claim the aid of all, and I say, "Come, then, let us go forward together with our united strength."

On 18th June, after the fall of France, Mr. Churchill delivered a speech in the House of Commons which was also broadcast to the nation.

For all of us, at this time, whatever our sphere, our station, our occupation or our duties, it will be a help to remember the famous lines:

> "He nothing common did or mean,
> Upon that memorable scene."

I have thought it right upon this occasion to give the House and the country some indication of the solid, practical grounds upon which we base our inflexible resolve to continue the war. There are a good many people who say, "Never mind. Win or lose, sink or swim, better die than submit to tyranny—and such a tyranny." And I do not dissociate myself from them. But I can assure them that our professional advisers of the three Services unitedly advise that we should carry on the war, and that there are good and reasonable hopes of final victory. We have fully informed and consulted all the self-governing Dominions, these great communities far beyond the oceans who have been built up on our laws and on our civilisation, and who are absolutely free to choose their course, but are absolutely devoted to the ancient Motherland, and who feel themselves inspired by the same emotions which lead me to stake our all upon duty and honour. We have fully consulted them, and I have received from their Prime Ministers, Mr. Mackenzie King of Canada, Mr. Menzies of Australia, Mr. Fraser of New Zealand and General Smuts of South Africa—that wonderful man, with his immense profound mind, and his eye watching from a distance the whole panorama of European affairs—I have received from all these eminent men, who all have Governments behind them elected on wide franchises, who are all there because they represent the will of their people, messages couched in the most moving terms in which they endorse our decision to fight on, and declare themselves ready to share our fortunes and to persevere to the end. That is what we are going to do.

. . . We do not yet know what will happen in France or whether the French resistance will be prolonged, both in France and in the French empire overseas. The French Government will be throwing away great opportunities and casting adrift their future if they do not continue the war in accordance with their treaty obligations, from which we have not felt able to release them. The House will have read the historic declaration in which, at the desire of many Frenchmen—and of our own hearts—we have proclaimed our willingness at the darkest hour in French history to conclude a union of common citizenship in this struggle. However matters may go in France or with the French Government, or other French Governments, we in this island and in the British Empire will never lose our sense of comradeship with the French people. If we are now called upon to endure what they have been suffering, we shall emulate their courage, and if final victory rewards our toils they shall share the gains, aye, and freedom shall be restored to all. We abate nothing of our just demands; not one jot or tittle do we recede. Czechs, Poles, Norwegians, Dutch, Belgians have joined their causes to our own. All these shall be restored.

What General Weygand called the Battle of France is over. I expect that the battle of Britain is about to begin.

KENT: THE PANTILES, TUNBRIDGE WELLS

A view of the Pantiles or Parade, a fashionable walk since the healing waters of the town were discovered in the 17th century. The street was paved with pantiles in the reign of Queen Anne.

KENT: THE FORGE AT COWDEN, EDENBRIDGE

Here and there the traditional crafts still live in country places. This village blacksmith is fashioning an iron lily bracket for the outside wall of his forge.

KENT: THE GARDEN OF ENGLAND

Typical of large areas of Kent in springtime, is this cherry orchard at Newington. The buildings with cone-shaped roofs are

Upon this battle depends the survival of Christian civilisation. Upon it depends our own British life, and the long continuity of our institutions and our Empire. The whole fury and might of the enemy must very soon be turned on us. Hitler knows that he will have to break us in this island or lose the war. If we can stand up to him, all Europe may be free and the life of the world may move forward into broad, sunlit uplands. But if we fail, then the whole world, including the United States, including all that we have known and cared for, will sink into the abyss of a new dark age made more sinister, and perhaps more protracted, by the lights of perverted science. Let us therefore brace ourselves to our duties, and so bear ourselves that, if the British Empire and its Commonwealth last for a thousand years, men will still say, "This was their finest hour."

SEPTEMBER, 1940

This, like the passage from *Vanity Fair* about Waterloo, is an extract from fiction, but our novelists have often told our history and added their own quality to that of the historians. Here are seen, in a story of London life, the common man's endurances during the bombing on a grand scale of that city, bombing shared by many other towns. Norman Collins is telling us of a night of din and flame. His Mr. Puddy, an adenoidal night-watchman, a very ordinary fellow, fond of his food and his own safety, is on guard in a tea-warehouse in South London.

He was standing by the front-door when the sirens began. They were faint at first, a mere flickering disturbance of the atmosphere. But Mr. Puddy heard them all right. He had ears in his stomach. And, immediately, a large cold patch began to spread right through him. And this was absurd because sirens as indistinct as that hadn't got anything to do with the tea-warehouse. Those sirens were warning the sleepers of Gravesend or Dagenham.

All the same, as Mr. Puddy sat there listening, his heart was thumping so hard and his breathing was so noisy that he had to hold his breath altogether, simply so that he could listen. Then, before he was ready for it, the next rank of players in this queer nocturnal orchestra had taken up their fiddles. London itself was howling and whining away at him. And, next moment, Mr. Puddy's own personal siren, the one just outside the back entrance, went off. It was so near that it wasn't simply a matter of hearing it. Mr. Puddy was engulfed and surrounded by it. His stomach went up and down with the wailings. Mr. Puddy was the siren.

When it stopped, Mr. Puddy went on vibrating for several seconds all by himself.

It was at this point that Mr. Puddy was supposed to go up to the sand-bagged telephone kiosk on the roof and tell the London Fire Brigade about any incendiaries which might come his way. Right up there, with nothing but chimneys and a stirrup-pump and long-handled shovel for scooping up the things when the Germans had dropped them.

And did he go?

Have a heart. There were 58 stairs to the roof from where Mr. Puddy was sitting. And even if he had *wanted* to perch himself right under the bombs, fifty-eight is an awful lot of stairs. What was more, supposing he had gone, how long would he have to stay there? For all he knew, he might still be up there at breakfast-time, a lofty anchorite looking down on the ruins of smoking Babylon. Taking it for granted that was, that he himself was still all right. And, in air-raids, it isn't safe to take anything for granted. That was why he picked up his big box-torch—he had a terror of being left suddenly in the dark—and went down to the underground cubby-hole where the ham was.

Not a moment too soon, either. This wasn't just a siren-raid. Already there was a kind of summer-thunder, a rumble in the air, as though the suburbs were being racked by earthquakes. Mr. Puddy didn't wait to hear the drone of planes. What he had heard was quite enough. It was tympanum and double-bass of this ten-thousand-acre orchestra.

" Let's hobe it's odly recodaissance," he told himself stoutly. "just wud or two plades cub over to sby on us."

But, if it were only one or two, the guns were making an extraordinary fuss over them. Either that, or the gunners had lost their nerve and were simply loosing off wildly. Even down there in the basement it was noisy. Which just showed what it would have been like if he'd gone up on the roof. Mr. Puddy took his steel helmet off the hook and put it on.

Then came the kind of sound that Mr. Puddy liked least of all. The guns were going *woof-woof* in all directions: there was a kind of hollowness about them. But this last noise was quite different. It was a sort of *crrr-rump*. And it came the wrong way. Instead of coming through the air like all the other disturbances, it rose suddenly out of the ground at Mr. Puddy's feet. It was as though the hard concrete floor had growled and then kicked him.

"That's wud," Mr. Puddy told himself. "This isn't recodaissance. This is the real thig."

As he said it, the glove of cold in his stomach expanded and re-iced itself. And, with the rapid changes of temperature inside him, Mr. Puddy began sweating. He passed his hand across his forehead. It was sticky. And no wonder. Because they were overhead all right. The cello passage had started. Even from there where he was, with a roof and five floors above him, Mr. Puddy could hear them. Clear and distinct above the general uproar, the *throb-throb-throb* came through the walls as though bees were swarming. Mr. Puddy tried not to think about that sound. To produce it, the night sky must have been practically solid with planes.

But the cellos weren't the worst. The bar with the flute and piccolo had now been reached. And it was an altogether new sound. Beginning as not much more than a shrill whistle, it mellowed and rounded and then changed suddenly into a vulgar *whoosh*. As soon as Mr. Puddy appreciated what it was, that he was really hearing a bomb *coming down*, he forsook all dignity and crawled underneath the table—the table with the ham still on it. Even before he had got under it properly, the thing gave a little jump into the air and a lot of dust and cobwebs were dislodged from the ceiling.

But that was all. Even the *whoosh* hadn't meant that it was Mr. Puddy's bomb, the one with his name written on it.

. . . On the following morning, another character, Mr. Josser, comes from Essex to his still smoking, smouldering home-town, London.

. . . In a way, it was strange after last night even to be going to London at all. There seemed at least reasonable doubt that the place would still be there. But for the first half of the journey there was nothing to show that last night hadn't been as peaceful as any other night-time in September. Day had dawned on a beautiful silky morning and the little suburban villas with their small oblongs of garden backing onto the railway looked snug and comfortable. There were children playing in them and here and there a baby taking its nap in a perambulator. No matter out of which side of the carriage Mr. Josser looked, there was still nothing to show for that massed midnight spectacle of star-shells and illumination.

Then, round a curve in the line, he abruptly found

himself in the war-zone. He was getting into London
by now. And, under the balloons, the little villas were
packed and crowded. They were the suburbs of a previous
generation. And overnight, they had suddenly been
opened out. Disembowelled. A bomb—quite a big
bomb, it seemed—had come down in the midst of them.
Two of the little villas had disappeared completely.
There was simply a large untidy crater filled with litter
where they had been standing only eight hours before.
So little of them was left, indeed, that it was difficult
to feel any sense of loss. It was the houses on either
side that brought to mind the damage and destruction.
There was something shocking and vaguely indecent
about the way they were exposed. The back of one
of them had been pared clean off. And a bedroom,
complete with bed, was open to the railway. Another
bed, upside down this time, rested in the garden. And
on the end of a length of lead piping a bath, soiled and
abraded by the rubbings of countless bathers, hung
straight down over the remains of a staircase. In another
little villa there was an iron grate, with a mantelpiece
and picture over it. But it was simply a grate set in the
open air. There was no room for the iron grate to
warm any longer.

The man next to Mr. Josser leaned over.

"Lucky it didn't hit the line," he remarked con-
solingly.

Mr. Josser nodded politely. He was too shocked to
do more. Shocked by the sheer flimsiness of the houses
that people had been living in. Before the blast had
caught them, they had looked ugly, sordid, overcrowded
—anything you like. But solid. Undeniably solid. So
many dense little lumps of architecture. But he could
see now that they were shams really. The bricks that
they were made of were nursery bricks and the ceilings
matchwood. Against the sky, the broken rafters showed
up like fish-bones. The whole thing was makeshift and

temporary-looking. It might have been in a native kraal that the bomb had fallen.

It was quite a long time afterwards when he saw the next reminder of last night. The line ran high here and he could see out across the landscape of roof-tops. Against the sky-line stood the openwork girders of what up till yesterday had been a factory. Now Mr. Josser could see right through it. At one corner the tall chimney stack was still standing, even though there was no smoke coming out of it. But over the whole building there hung an opaque dirty mist. And, as the firemen were still pumping in the water, the mist was constantly renewing itself.

It was not until Mr. Josser reached Liverpool Street that he actually *smelt* burning. But it was there all right. A rank frowsty odour hung over everything as though an incinerator door had been opened. But there was more than a smell of burning to distract him. The streets outside the station were full of scorched paper. Charred embers of what might once have been office ledgers. And large cobwebby smuts that were all that was left of filing-systems and double-entry book-keeping. Under foot there was the crunch and jingle of good plate-glass.

NORMAN COLLINS (Born 1907)
London Belongs to Me

London

SALUTE FROM SCOTLAND

London, thou art of townes *A per se,*
   Soveraign of cities, seemliest in sight,
Of high renoun, riches and royaltie;
   Of lordis, barons, and many a goodly knyght;
   Of most delectable lusty ladies bright:
Of famous prelatis, in habitis clericall;
   Of merchauntis full of substaunce and of myght:
London, thou art the flour of Cities all.

Gemme of all joy, jaspre of jocunditie,
   Most myghty carbuncle of vertue and valour;
Strong Troy in vigour and in strenuytie;
   Of royall cities rose and geraflour;
   Empress of townes, exalt in honour;
In beawtie beryng the crone imperiall;
   Swete paradise precelling in pleasure;
London, thou art the flour of Cities all.

Above all ryvers thy Ryver hath renowne,
   Whose beryall stremys, pleasant and preclare,
Under thy lusty wallys renneth down,
   Where many a swan doth swymme with wyngis fair;
   Where many a barge doth saile and row with are;
Where many a ship doth rest with top-royall.
   O, towne of townes! patrone and not compare,
London, thou art the flour of Cities all.

Strong be thy wallis that about the standis;
  Wise be the people that within the dwellis;
Fresh is thy ryver with his lusty strandis;
  Blith be thy chirches, wele sownyng be thy bellis;
  Rich be thy merchauntis in substaunce that excellis;
Fair be their wives, right lovesom, white and small;
  Clere be thy virgyns, lusty under kellis: [1]
London, thou art the flour of Cities all.

Thy famous Maire, by pryncely governaunce,
  With sword of justice thee ruleth prudently.
No Lord of Parys, Venyce, or Floraunce
  In dignitye or honour go'th to hym nigh.
  He is exempler, loode-ster, and guye; [2]
Principall patrone and rose orygynalle,
  Above all Maires as maister most worthy:
London, thou art the flour of Cities all.

WILLIAM DUNBAR (1465-1520)
London

[1] Kellis, hoods   [2] Guye, guide

A POET'S ESCAPE

The Reverend Robert Herrick was a natural Londoner by taste and
origin, born in Cheapside and brought up at Hampton Court. As a
young man he relished the roystering life of the poets and adored
Ben Jonson. But he had to earn a living, took holy orders, and was
given the parish of Dean Prior in "Dull Devonshire", as he called it.
The return to London in 1648, celebrated in the poem below, was not
for long.

From the dull confines of the drooping West,
To see the day spring from the pregnant East,
Ravisht in spirit, I come, nay more, I flie
To thee, blest place of my Nativitie!
Thus, thus with hallowed foot I touch the ground,
With thousand blessings by thy Fortune crown'd.
O fruitfull Genius! that bestowest here
An everlasting plenty, yeere by yeere.

O Place! O People! Manners! fram'd to please
All Nations, Customes, Kindreds, Languages!
I am a free-born Roman; suffer then,
That I amongst you live a Citizen.
London my home is; though by hard fate sent
Into a long and irksome banishment;
Yet since call'd back; henceforward let me be,
O native countrey, repossest by thee!
For, rather than Ile to the West return,
Ile beg of thee first here to have mine Urn.
Weak I am grown, and must in short time fall;
Give thou my sacred Reliques Buriall.

ROBERT HERRICK (1591-1674)
His Returne to London

WESTMINSTER ABBEY

When I am in a serious humour, I very often walk by
myself in Westminster Abbey; where the gloominess
of the place, and the use to which it is applied, with the
solemnity of the building, and the condition of the people
who lie in it, are apt to fill the mind with a kind of
melancholy, or rather thoughtfulness, that is not
disagreeable. I yesterday passed a whole afternoon in the
churchyard, the cloisters, and the church, amusing myself with the tombstones and inscriptions that I met
with in those several regions of the dead.

. . . Upon my going into the church, I entertained
myself with the digging of a grave; and saw in every
shovelful of it that was thrown up, the fragment of a
bone or skull intermixt with a kind of fresh mouldering
earth, that some time or other had a place in the composition of a human body. Upon this I began to consider with myself what innumerable multitudes of
people lay confused together under the pavement of that

ancient cathedral; how men and women, friends and enemies, priests and soldiers, monks and prebendaries, were crumbled amongst one another, and blended together in the same common mass; how beauty, strength, and youth, with old age, weakness, and deformity, lay undistinguished in the same promiscuous heap of matter.

After having thus surveyed this great magazine of mortality, as it were, in the lump I examined it more particularly by the accounts which I found on several of the monuments which are raised in every quarter of that ancient fabric. Some of them were covered with such extravagant epitaphs, that, if it were possible for the dead person to be acquainted with them, he would blush at the praises which his friends have bestowed upon him. There are others so excessively modest, that they deliver the character of the person departed in Greek or Hebrew, and by that means are not understood once in a twelve-month. In the poetical quarter, I found there were poets who had no monuments, and monuments which had no poets. I observed, indeed, that the present war had filled the church with many of these uninhabited monuments, which had been erected to the memory of persons whose bodies were perhaps buried in the plains of Blenheim, or in the bosom of the ocean.

I could not but be very much delighted with several modern epitaphs, which are written with great elegance of expression and justness of thought, and therefore do honour to the living as well as to the dead. As a foreigner is very apt to conceive an idea of the ignorance or politeness of a nation, from the turn of their public monuments and inscriptions, they should be submitted to the perusal of men of learning and genius, before they are put in execution.

. . . I have left the repository of our English kings for the contemplation of another day, when I shall find

my mind disposed for so serious an amusement. I
know that entertainments of this nature are apt to raise
dark and dismal thoughts in timorous minds and
gloomy imaginations; but for my own part, though I
am always serious, I do not know what it is to be melancholy; and can therefore take a view of nature in her
deep and solemn scenes, with the same pleasure as in her
most gay and delightful ones. By this means I can
improve myself with those objects which others consider with terror. When I look upon the tombs of the
great, every emotion of envy dies in me; when I read
the epitaphs of the beautiful, every inordinate desire
goes out; when I meet with the grief of parents upon
a tombstone, my heart melts with compassion; when
I see the tomb of the parents themselves, I consider the
vanity of grieving for those whom we must quickly
follow: when I see kings lying by those who deposed
them, when I consider rival wits placed side by side,
or the holy men that divided the world with their
contests and disputes, I reflect with sorrow and astonishment on the little competitions, factions, and debates
of mankind. When I read the several dates of the tombs,
of some that died yesterday, and some six hundred
years ago, I consider that great day when we shall all of
us be contemporaries, and make our appearance together.

JOSEPH ADDISON (1672-1719)
The Spectator

GRAVE THOUGHTS

Mortality, behold and fear!
What a change of flesh is here!
Think how many royal bones
Sleep within this heap of stones:
Here they lie had realms and lands,
Who now want strength to stir their hands:

Where from their pulpits seal'd with dust
They preach, "In greatness is no trust".
Here's an acre sown indeed
With the richest, royall'st seed
That the earth did e'er suck in
Since the first man died for sin:
Here the bones of birth have cried—
"Though gods they were, as men they died."
Here are sands, ignoble things,
Dropt from the ruin'd sides of kings;
Here's a world of pomp and state,
Buried in dust, once dead by fate.

FRANCIS BEAUMONT (1584-1616)
On the Tombs in Westminster Abbey

ONE MAN, TWO VIEWS

For who would leave, unbrib'd, *Hibernia*'s Land,
Or change the Rocks of *Scotland* for the *Strand*?
There none are swept by sudden Fate away,
But all whom Hunger spares, with Age decay;
Here Malice, Rapine, Accident, conspire,
And now a Rabble rages, now a Fire;
Their Ambush here relentless Ruffians lay,
And here the fell Attorney prowls for Prey;
Here falling Houses thunder on your Head,
And here a female Atheist talks you dead.

LONDON! the needy Villain's gen'ral Home,
The Common Shore of *Paris* and of *Rome*,
With eager Thirst, by Folly or by Fate,
Sucks in the Dregs of each corrupted State.
Forgive my Transports on a Theme like this,
I cannot bear a *French* Metropolis.

When a man is tired of London, he is tired of life; for there is in London all that life can afford.

I think the full tide of human existence is at Charing Cross.

DR. SAMUEL JOHNSON (1709-1784)
poem *London*; and remarks on
London, according to Boswell

INEXHAUSTIBLE

Talking of London, Johnson observed, "Sir, if you wish to have a just notion of the magnitude of this city, you must not be satisfied with seeing its great streets and squares, but must survey the innumerable little lanes and courts. It is not in the showy evolutions of buildings, but in the multiplicity of human habitations which are crowded together, that the wonderful immensity of London consists."—I have often amused myself with thinking how different a place London is to different people. They, whose narrow minds are contracted to the consideration of some one particular pursuit, view it only through that medium. A politician thinks of it merely as the seat of government in its different departments; a grazier, as a vast market for cattle; a mercantile man, as a place where a prodigious deal of business is done upon 'Change; a dramatick enthusiast, as the grand scene of theatrical entertainments; a man of pleasure, as an assemblage of taverns, and the great emporium for ladies of easy virtue. But the intellectual man is struck with it, as comprehending the whole of human life in all its variety, the contemplation of which is inexhaustible.

JAMES BOSWELL (1740-1795)
The Life of Dr. Johnson

GOOD FOR WIVES

MRS. SULLEN: *London*, dear *London*, is the place for managing and breaking a Husband.

DORINDA: And has not a Husband the same opportunities there for humbling a Wife?

MRS. SULLEN: No, no, Child, 'tis a standing Maxim in Conjugal Discipline, that when a Man wou'd enslave his Wife, he hurries her into the Country; and when a Lady wou'd be arbitrary with her Husband, she wheedles her Booby up to Town.— A man dare not play the Tyrant in *London*, because there are so many Examples to encourage the Subject to rebel. O *Dorinda*, *Dorinda*! a fine Woman may do any thing in *London*: O' my Conscience, she may raise an Army of Forty thousand Men.

GEORGE FARQUHAR (1678-1707)
The Beaux' Stratagem

VISION OF LONDON

The fields from Islington to Marybone,
To Primrose Hill and Saint John's Wood,
Were builded over with pillars of gold,
And there Jerusalem's pillars stood.
Her Little-ones ran on the fields,
The Lamb of God among them seen,

And fair Jerusalem his Bride,
Among the little meadows green.

Pancrass & Kentish-town repose
Among her golden pillars high,
    Among her golden arches which
Shine upon the starry sky.

The Jew's-harp-house & the Green Man,
The Ponds where Boys to bathe delight,
    The fields of Cows by Willan's farm,
Shine in Jerusalem's pleasant sight.

She walks upon our meadows green,
The Lamb of God walks by her side,
    And every English Child is seen
Children of Jesus & his Bride.

WILLIAM BLAKE (1757-1827)
Jerusalem

A LONDON "PARTICULAR"

LONDON. Michaelmas Term lately over, and the Lord
Chancellor sitting in Lincoln's Inn Hall. Implacable
November weather. As much mud in the streets, as if
the waters had but newly retired from the face of the
earth, and it would not be wonderful to meet a Megalo-
saurus, forty feet long or so, waddling like an elephantine
lizard up Holborn Hill. Smoke lowering down from
chimney-pots, making a soft black drizzle, with flakes
of soot in it as big as full grown snow-flakes—gone
into mourning one might imagine, for the death of the
sun. Dogs, undistinguishable in mire. Horses, scarcely

better; splashed to their very blinkers. Foot passengers, jostling one another's umbrellas, in a general infection of ill-temper, and losing their foot-hold at street-corners, where tens of thousands of other foot passengers have been slipping and sliding since the day broke (if this day ever broke), adding new deposits to the crust upon crust of mud, sticking at those points tenaciously to the pavement, and accumulating at compound interest.

Fog everywhere. Fog up the river, where it flows among green aits and meadows; fog down the river, where it rolls defiled among the tiers of shipping, and the waterside pollutions of a great (and dirty) city. Fog on the Essex marshes, fog on the Kentish heights. Fog creeping into the cabooses of collier-brigs; fog lying out on the yards, and hovering in the rigging of great ships; fog drooping on the gunwales of barges and small boats. Fog in the eyes and throats of ancient Greenwich pensioners, wheezing by the firesides of their wards; fog in the stem and bowl of the afternoon pipe of the wrathful skipper, down in his close cabin; fog cruelly pinching the toes and fingers of his shivering little 'prentice boy on deck. Chance people on the bridges peeping over the parapets into a nether sky of fog, with fog all round them, as if they were up in a balloon, and hanging in the misty clouds.

Gas looming through the fog in divers places in the streets, much as the sun may, from the spongy fields, be seen to loom by husbandman and ploughboy. Most of the shops lighted two hours before their time—as the gas seems to know, for it has a haggard and unwilling look.

The raw afternoon is rawest, and the dense fog is densest, and the muddy streets are muddiest, near that leaden-headed old obstruction, appropriate ornament for the threshold of a leaden-headed old corporation: Temple Bar. And hard by Temple Bar, in Lincoln's

Inn Hall, at the very heart of the fog, sits the Lord High Chancellor in his High Court of Chancery.

Never can there come fog too thick, never can there come mud and mire too deep, to assort with the groping and floundering condition which this High Court of Chancery, most pestilent of hoary sinners, holds, this day, in the sight of heaven and earth.

CHARLES DICKENS (1812-1870)
Bleak House

THE DEVOTEE

(From a letter written by Charles Lamb in London to William Wordsworth in the Lakes, January, 1801)

I have passed all my days in London, until I have formed as many and intense local attachments, as any of you mountaineers can have done with dead nature. The lighted shops of the Strand and Fleet Street, the innumerable trades, tradesmen and customers, coaches, waggons, playhouses, all the bustle and wickedness round about Covent Garden, the very women of the Town, the Watchmen, drunken scenes, rattles,—life awake, if you awake, at all hours of the night, the impossibility of being dull in Fleet Street, the crowds, the very dirt and mud, the Sun shining upon houses and pavements, the print shops, the old book stalls, parsons cheap'ning books, coffee houses, steams of soups from kitchens, the pantomimes, London itself a pantomime and a masquerade,—all these things work themselves into my mind and feed me, without a power of satiating me. The wonder of these sights impells me into night-walks about her crowded streets, and I often shed tears in the motley Strand from fulness of joy at so much life. All these emotions must be strange to you. So are your rural emotions to me. But consider, what must I have been doing all my life, not to have lent great portions of my heart with usury to such scenes?——

My attachments are all local, purely local. I have no passion (or have had none since I was in love, and then it was the spurious engendering of poetry and books) to groves and vallies. The rooms where I was born, the furniture which has been before my eyes all my life, a book case which has followed me about (like a faithful dog, only exceeding him in knowledge) wherever I have moved—old chairs, old tables, streets, squares, where I have sunned myself, my old school,—these are my mistresses. Have I not enough, without your mountains? I do not envy you. I should pity you, did I not know, that the Mind will make friends of anything. Your sun and moon and skys and hills and lakes affect me no more, or scarcely come to me in more venerable characters, than as a gilded room with tapestry and tapers, where I might live with handsome visible objects. I consider the clouds above me but as a roof, beautifully painted but unable to satisfy the mind, and at last, like the pictures of the apartment of a connoisseur, unable to afford him any longer a pleasure. So fading upon me, from disuse, have been the Beauties of Nature, as they have been confinedly called; so ever fresh and green and warm are all the inventions of men and assemblies of men in this great city.

CHARLES LAMB (1775-1834)
Letters

VAUXHALL

The pleasure gardens of a great city are often a world-famous asset as well as a happy resort for its citizens. Vauxhall, on the banks of the Thames, has long ceased to be a centre of lawns and gay lights, but to our ancestors it was the essential spot for a summer evening in the open. Here are three views of the old Vauxhall, the first recording the raptures of Oliver Goldsmith, the second containing the nocturnal adventures of Thackeray's Josiah Sedley and his amorous party, and the third describing the disillusion of Charles Dickens when he visited Vauxhall by daylight. He had, however, the relief of watching the then fashionable spectacle of an ascent in a balloon.

(1) THE LAWNS LIT UP

The People of *London* are as fond of walking, as our friends at *Pekin* of riding; one of the principal entertainments of the citizens here in summer, is to repair about nightfall to a garden not far from town, where they walk about, shew their best clothes and best faces, and listen to a concert provided for the occasion.

I accepted an invitation a few evenings ago from my old friend, the man in black, to be one of a party that was to sup there, and at the appointed hour waited upon him at his lodgings. There I found the company assembled and expecting my arrival. Our party consisted of my friend in superlative finery, his stockings rolled, a black velvet waistcoat, which was formerly new, and his grey wig combed down in imitation of hair. A pawn-broker's widow, of whom, by the bye, my friend was a professed admirer, dressed out in green damask, with three gold rings on every finger. Mr. *Tibbs*, the second-rate beau, I have formerly described, together with his lady, in flimsy silk, dirty gauze instead of linnen, and an hat as big as an umbrello. . . .

The illuminations began before we arrived, and I must confess, that upon entring the gardens, I found every sense overpaid with more than expected pleasure; the lights every where glimmering through the scarcely moving trees; the full-bodied concert bursting on the stillness of the night, the natural concert of the birds in the more retired part of the grove, vying with that which was formed by art; the company gayly dressed, looking satisfaction, and the tables spread with various delicacies, all conspired to fill my imagination with the visionary happiness of the *Arabian* lawgiver, and lifted me into an extasy of admiration. Head of *Confucius*, cried I to my friend, this is fine! this unites rural beauty with courtly magnificence; if we except the virgins of immortality that hang on every tree, and may be plucked at every desire, I don't see how this falls short of *Mahomet's Paradise*! As for virgins, cries my friend, it is true they are a fruit that don't much abound in our gardens here; but if ladies as plenty as apples in autumn, and as complying as any *houry* of them all, can content you, I fancy we have no need to go to heaven for Paradise.

OLIVER GOLDSMITH (1728-1774)
Citizen of the World

(2)   LOVE IS BLIND

"I say, Dobbin," says George, "just look to the shawls and things, there's a good fellow." And so while he paired off with Miss Sedley, and Jos squeezed through the gate into the Gardens with Rebecca at his side, honest Dobbin contented himself by giving an arm to the shawls, and by paying at the door for the whole party.

He walked very modestly behind them. He was not willing to spoil sport. About Rebecca and Jos he did not care a fig. But he thought Amelia worthy even of the brilliant George Osborne, and as he saw that good-looking couple threading the walks to the girl's delight

and wonder, he watched her artless happiness with a
sort of fatherly pleasure. Perhaps he felt that he would
have liked to have something on his own arm besides
a shawl (the people laughed at seeing the gawky young
officer carrying this female burthen); but William
Dobbin was very little addicted to selfish calculation at
all, and so long as his friend was enjoying himself,
how should he be discontented? And the truth is, that
of all the delights of the Gardens; of the hundred
thousand *extra* lamps, which were always lighted; the
fiddlers in cocked-hats, who played ravishing melodies
under the gilded cockle-shell in the midst of the Gardens;
the singers, both of comic and sentimental ballads, who
charmed the ears there; the country dances, formed by
bouncing cockneys and cockneyesses, and executed
amidst jumping, thumping, and laughter; the signal
which announced that Madame Saqui was about to
mount skyward on a slack rope ascending to the stars;
the hermit that always sat in the illuminated hermitage;
the dark walks, so favourable to the interviews of young
lovers; the pots of stout handed about by the people in
the shabby old liveries; and the twinking boxes, in
which the happy feasters made-believe to eat slices
of almost invisible ham;—of all these things, and of the
gentle Simpson, that kind smiling idiot, who, I daresay,
presided even then over the place—Captain William
Dobbin did not take the slightest notice.

W. M. THACKERAY (1811-1863)
Vanity Fair

(3) UP AND ABOUT

We paid our shilling at the gate, and then we saw for
the first time, that the entrance, if there had been any
magic about it at all, was now decidedly disenchanted,
being, in fact, nothing more nor less than a combina-

tion of very roughly-painted boards and sawdust. We
glanced at the orchestra and supper-room as we hurried
past—we just recognised them, and that was all. We
bent our steps to the fire-work ground; there, at least,
we should not be disappointed. We reached it, and
stood rooted to the spot with mortification and astonishment. *That* the Moorish tower—that wooden shed
with a door in the centre, and daubs of crimson and
yellow all round, like a gigantic watch-case! *That* the
place where night after night we had beheld the un-
daunted Mr. Blackmore make his terrific ascent, surrounded by flames of fire, and peals of artillery, and
where the white garments of Madame Somebody (we
forget even her name now), who nobly devoted her life
to the manufacture of fireworks, had so often been
seen fluttering in the wind, as she called up a red, blue
or parti-coloured light to illumine her temple! *That*
the—but at this moment the bell rang; the people
scampered away, pell-mell, to the spot from whence the
sound proceeded; and we, from the mere force of habit,
found ourself running among the first, as if for very
life.

. . . Some half-dozen men were restraining the impetuosity of one of the balloons, which was completely
filled, and had the car already attached; and as rumours
had gone abroad that a Lord was "going up", the
crowd were more than usually anxious and talkative.
There was one little man in faded black, with a dirty
face and a rusty black neckerchief with a red border,
tied in a narrow wisp round his neck, who entered into
conversation with everybody, and had something to say
upon every remark that was made within his hearing.
He was standing with his arms folded, staring up at the
balloon, and every now and then vented his feelings of
reverence for the aeronaut, by saying, as he looked
round to catch somebody's eye, "He's a rum 'un is

Green; think o' this here being up'ards of his two hundredth ascent; ecod, the man as is ekal to Green never had the toothache yet, nor won't have within this hundred year, and that's all about it. When you meets with real talent, and native, too, encourage it, that's what I say."

. . . "What's the ladies a-laughing at, sir?" inquired the little man, condescendingly.

"It's only my sister Mary," said one of the girls, "as says she hopes his lordship won't be frightened when he's in the car, and want to come out again."

"Make yourself easy about that there, my dear," replied the little man. "If he was so much as to move a inch without leave, Green would jist fetch him a crack over the head with the telescope, as would send him into the bottom of the basket in no time, and stun him till they come down again."

. . . Just at this moment all eyes were directed to the preparations which were being made for starting. The car was attached to the second balloon, the two were brought pretty close together, and a military band commenced playing with a zeal and fervour which would render the most timid man in existence but too happy to accept any means of quitting that particular spot of earth on which they were stationed. Then Mr. Green, sen., and his noble companion entered one car, and Mr. Green, jun., and *his* companion the other; and then the balloons went up, and the aerial travellers stood up, and the crowd outside roared with delight, and the two gentlemen who had never ascended before tried to wave their flags, as if they were not nervous, but held on very fast all the while; and the balloons were wafted gently away, our little friend solemnly protesting, long after they were reduced to mere specks in the air, that he could still distinguish the white hat of Mr. Green.

The gardens disgorged their multitudes, boys ran up
and down screaming "bal-loon"; and in all the crowded
thoroughfares people rushed out of their shops into the
middle of the road, and having stared up in the air at
two little black objects till they almost dislocated their
necks, walked slowly in again, perfectly satisfied.

CHARLES DICKENS (1812-1870)
Sketches by Boz

EARLY YEARS OF "THE YARD"

SCOTLAND YARD is a small—a very small—tract of
land, bounded on one side by the River Thames, on the
other by the gardens of Northumberland House: abut-
ting at one end on the bottom of Northumberland
Street, at the other on the back of Whitehall Place.
When this territory was first accidentally discovered
by a country gentleman who lost his way in the Strand,
some years ago, the original settlers were found to be a
tailor, a publican, two eating-house keepers, and a fruit-
pie maker; and it was also found to contain a race of
strong and bulky men, who repaired to the wharfs in
Scotland Yard regularly every morning about five or
six o'clock to fill heavy waggons with coal, with which
they proceeded to distant places up the country, and
supplied the inhabitants with fuel. When they had
emptied their waggons they again returned for a fresh
supply; and this trade was continued throughout the
year.

As the settlers derived their subsistence from ministering to the wants of these primitive traders, the articles
exposed for sale, and the places where they were sold,
bore strong outward marks of being expressly adapted
to their tastes and wishes. The tailor displayed in his
window a Lilliputian pair of leather gaiters, and a
diminutive round frock, while each doorpost was

appropriately garnished with a model of a coal-sack. The two eating-house keepers exhibited joints of a magnitude and puddings of a solidity, which coal-heavers alone could appreciate; and the fruit-pie maker displayed on his well-scrubbed window-board large pink stains, giving rich promise of the fruit within, which made their huge mouths water, as they lingered past.

But the choicest spot in all Scotland Yard was the old public-house in the corner. Here, in a dark wainscoted room of ancient appearance, cheered by the glow of a mighty fire, and decorated with an enormous clock, whereof the face was white, and the figures black, sat the lusty coal-heavers, quaffing large draughts of Barclay's best, and puffing forth volumes of smoke, which wreathed heavily above their heads, and involved the room in a thick dark cloud. From this apartment might their voices be heard on a winter's night, penetrating to the very bank of the river, as they shouted out some sturdy chorus, or roared forth the burden of a popular song; dwelling upon the last few words with a strength and length of emphasis which made the very roof tremble above them.

Here, too, would they tell old legends of what the Thames was in ancient times, when the Patent Shot Manufactory wasn't built, and Waterloo Bridge had never been thought of; and then they would shake their heads with portentous looks, to the deep edification of the rising generation of heavers, who crowded round them, and wondered where all this would end. . . .

One of the eating-house keepers began to court public opinion, and to look for customers among a new class of people. He covered his little dining-tables with white cloths, and got a painter's apprentice to inscribe something about hot joints from twelve to two in one of the little panes of his shop-window. Improvement began to march with rapid strides to the very threshold of Scotland Yard. A new market sprung up at Hungerford, and the Police Commissioners established their office in Whitehall Place. The traffic in Scotland Yard increased; fresh Members were added to the House of Commons, the Metropolitan Representatives found it a near cut, and many other foot passengers followed their example.

We marked the advance of civilisation, and beheld it with a sigh. The eating-house keeper, who manfully resisted the innovation of table-cloths, was losing ground every day, as his opponent gained it, and a deadly feud sprung up between them. The genteel one no longer took his evening's pint in Scotland Yard, but drank gin and water at a "parlour" in Parliament Street. The fruit-pie maker still continued to visit the old room, but he took to smoking cigars, and began to call himself a pastrycook, and to read the papers. The old heavers still assembled round the ancient fireplace, but their talk was mournful: and the loud song and the joyous shout were heard no more.

And what is Scotland Yard now?

CHARLES DICKENS (1812-1870)
Sketches by Boz

ON WESTMINSTER BRIDGE

Earth has not anything to show more fair:
   Dull would he be of soul who could pass by
A sight so touching in its majesty:
This City now doth like a garment wear
The beauty of the morning; silent, bare,
   Ships, towers, domes, theatres, and temples lie
   Open unto the fields, and to the sky,
All bright and glittering in the smokeless air.
Never did sun more beautifully steep
   In his first splendour valley, rock, or hill;

Ne'er saw I, never felt, a calm so deep!
   The river glideth at his own sweet will:
Dear God! the very houses seem asleep;
   And all that mighty heart is lying still!

WILLIAM WORDSWORTH (1770-1850)
Upon Westminster Bridge

END OF A GEORGIAN SUMMER

We are apt to think of a London Season in the eighteen-twenties as
something heavily gross, and we expect it to be described with the
irony and sarcasm which had been made fashionable by Byron.
W. M. Praed had a gentle humour and a vein of sentiment that made
him anticipate the Victorian touch in bright, neat, and facile versifica-
tion. He reminds one that there were nice people and genteel flirta-
tions amid the sensual luxury of George IV's London, a sensuality
vividly portrayed and attacked by Thackeray. Praed was a gallant
invalid who entered the House of Commons for a short time before
his very early death: he had enjoyed Eton, Cambridge, and the seaside life at his family home at Teignmouth in South Devon as much
as his London Seasons; he enjoyed also his light mockery of the
world that he enjoyed.

Good-night to the Season! 'tis over!
   Gay dwellings no longer are gay;
The courtier, the gambler, the lover,
   Are scatter'd like swallows away:
There's nobody left to invite one,
   Except my good uncle and spouse;
My mistress is bathing at Brighton,
   My patron is sailing at Cowes:
For want of a better employment,
   Till Ponto and Don can get out,
I'll cultivate rural enjoyment,
   And angle immensely for trout.

Good-night to the Season!—the dances,
   The fillings of hot little rooms,
The glancings of rapturous glances,
   The fancyings of fancy costumes;

The pleasures which Fashion makes duties,
  The praisings of fiddles and flutes,
The luxury of looking at beauties,
  The tedium of talking to mutes;
The female diplomatists, planners
  Of matches for Laura and Jane,
The ice of her ladyship's manners,
  The ice of his Lordship's champagne.

Good-night to the Season!—the flowers
  Of the grand horticultural fête,
When boudoirs were quitted for bowers,
  And the fashion was not to be late;
When all who had money and leisure
  Grew rural o'er ices and wines,
All pleasantly toiling for pleasure,
  All hungrily pining for pines,
And making of beautiful speeches,
  And marring of beautiful shows,
And feeding on delicate peaches,
  And treading on delicate toes.

Good-night to the Season!—another
  Will come with its trifles and toys,
And hurry away, like its brother,
  In sunshine, and odour, and noise.
Will it come with a rose or a briar?
  Will it come with a blessing or curse?
Will its bonnets be lower or higher?
  Will its morals be better or worse?
Will it find me grown thinner or fatter,
  Or fonder of wrong or of right,
Or married,—or buried?—no matter,
  Good-night to the Season, Good-night!

WINTHROP MACKWORTH PRAED (1802-1839)
New Monthly Magazine, 1828

HAPPY HAMPSTEAD

Among Britain's most notable refugees was Karl Marx, who was driven out of Germany and France and came to London in 1849. He worked as a journalist, especially for the *New York Tribune*, studied at the British Museum library and published the first volume of *Das Kapital* in 1867. When he had the money he was a hearty drinker and an incessant smoker. He greatly enjoyed taking his family on Hampstead Heath. His friend, Liebknecht, has left this account of their excursions in a book on Marx written in 1896.

When, from the beginning of the fifties, we lived in the North of London, in Kentish Town and Haverstock Hill, then our favourite walks were on the meadows and hills between and beyond Hampstead and Highgate. Here flowers were sought, plants analysed, which was a two-fold treat for the city children, in whom the cold, surging, bellowing stone sea of the metropolis created a veritable hunger for green nature. What a joy for us, when we discovered in our wanderings a little lake shaded by trees, and I could show to the children the first live " wild" forget-me-nots.

Our trips to Hampstead Heath! If I grew to be a thousand years old, I should not forget them. The "Heath" of Hampstead, beyond Primrose Hill, and like the latter known to the world outside of London through the Pickwick Papers of Dickens, is this day for the greater part a heath, that is, an undulating, uncultivated place covered with heather and clumps of trees, with miniature mountains and valleys, where everybody may move about and gambol at will without fear of being arrested and fined for trespassing by a guardian of holy private property. Forty years ago Hampstead Heath was much larger and much more natural and primeval than to-day. And a Sunday on Hampstead Heath was the highest pleasure to us. The children spoke of it the whole week, and we grown people, too, old and young, anticipated it with joy. The trip itself was a feast. The girls were good pedestrians, alert and tireless like cats. From Dean Street, where Marx lived—a short way from Church Street, where I had gone to anchor—it was at least one hour and a quarter, and as a rule the start was made as early as 11 o'clock a.m. Often, it must be admitted, we started later, for it is not customary in London to rise early, and some time was always consumed in getting everything in readiness, the children cared for and the basket properly packed.

That basket! It stands, or rather hangs before my mental vision as vivid, as real, as enticing, as appetizing, as if it were only yesterday that I had seen it last on Lenchen's arm.

It was our commissary department, and when a man has a healthy, strong stomach and very often not the necessary small change (large change did not come our way at all), then the question of provisions plays a very important role. And good Lenchen knew this and had for us often half-starved and, therefore, always hungry guests a sympathising heart. A mighty roast veal was the centre-piece hallowed by tradition for the Sunday on Hampstead Heath. After this tea with sugar, and occasionally some fruit. Bread and cheese was purchased on the heath, where one could, and still can, obtain dishes and hot water with milk, similarly to the coffee gardens of Berlin, and bread, butter, cheese, besides the local shrimps, water-cress and periwinkles, according to one's needs and purchasing power. Also beer. . . .

But after drinking and eating their fill, as Homer has it, the male and female comrades looked for the most comfortable place of repose or seat: and when this had been found, he or she—provided they did not prefer a little nap—produced the Sunday papers they had bought on the road, and now began the reading and discussing of politics—while the children, who rapidly found comrades, played hide and seek behind the heather bushes.

But this easy life had to be seasoned by a little diversion, and so we ran races, sometimes we also had wrestling matches, or putting the shot (stones) or some other sport. One Sunday we discovered a nearby chestnut tree with ripe nuts: "Let us see who can knock down the greatest number!" somebody cried, and with a great uproar we went to work. And only when the last chestnut had been captured amid wild shouts of triumph, the bombardment ceased. Marx could not move the right arm for eight days. And I was not better off.

The greatest treat was a general donkey riding. That was a mad laughing and whooping! And those ludicrous scenes! And how Marx amused himself and us. Us he amused twofold: by his more than primitive art of riding and by the fanatic zeal with which he affirmed his skill in this art.

Politics were tabooed on the march home as well as the misery of exile. Literature and art, however, were much discussed, and there Marx had an opportunity to show his gigantic memory. He recited long passages from the *Divina Commedia* that he knew almost entirely by heart; and scenes from Shakespeare at which his wife, also an excellent student of Shakespeare, frequently relieved him.

WILHELM LIEBKNECHT (1826-1900)
Karl Marx

HURDY-GURDY

The barrel-organ, or hurdy-gurdy, once as familiar in the London streets as the muffin-man with his wares on his head and his bell in his hand, has disappeared. But its manipulator lives on in C. S. Calverley's affectionate verses, harnessed with straps to his machine, accompanied by a sad-looking monkey in a red-flannel jacket, and seeking, with that animal's pathetic, soliciting glances, the coppers of those who either liked this maestro of the kerb or would pay him to plague the next street.

Grinder, who serenely grindest
    At my door the Hundredth Psalm,
'Till thou ultimately findest
    Pence in thy unwashen palm:

Grinder, jocund-hearted Grinder,
    Near whom Barbary's nimble son,
Poised with skill upon his hinder
    Paws, accepts the proffered bun:

Dearly do I love thy grinding;
    Joy to meet thee on thy road
Where thou prowlest through the blinding
    Dust with that stupendous load,

'Neath the baleful star of Sirius,
    When the postmen slowlier jog,
And the ox becomes delirious,
    And the muzzle decks the dog.

'Tell me by what art thou bindest
    On thy feet those ancient shoon:
Tell me, Grinder, if thou grindest
    Always, always out of tune.

KENT: FOX HUNTING

"'Unting is all that's worth living for . . . it's the sport of kings, the image of war without its guilt, and only five-and-twenty per cent of its danger."—*R. S. Surtees.* Opening meet of the Eridge Hunt at the Crest & Gun Inn, near Tunbridge Wells.

KENT: CHILHAM VILLAGE

A row of old half-timbered houses with fairy-tale roofs and leaded windows, the village tea-shop, the sweet-shop lady putting up the awning to keep the sun off her wares—just another pleasant summer's afternoon at Chilham, a few miles south-west of Canterbury.

KENT: CANTERBURY FROM THE AIR

The ecclesiastical capital of England, site of the shrine of Thomas Becket, to which Chaucer's famous pilgrims made their
way. The cathedral, seen in the centre, is one of the largest and most magnificent in England

Tell me if, as thou art buckling
   On thy straps with eager claws,
Thou forecastest, inly chuckling,
   All the rage that thou wilt cause.

Tell me if at all thou mindest
   When folks flee, as if on wings,
From thee as at ease thou grindest:
   Tell me fifty thousand things.

Grinder, gentle-hearted Grinder!
   Ruffians who lead evil lives,
Soothed by thy sweet strains, are kinder
   To their bullocks and their wives:

Children, when they see thy supple
   Form approach, are out like shots,
Half-a-bar sets several couple
   Waltzing in convenient spots;

Not with clumsy Jacks or Georges,
   Unprofaned by grasp of man
Maidens speed those simple orgies,
   Betsey Jane with Betsey Ann.

As they love thee in St. Giles's
   Thou art loved in Grosvenor Square:
None of those engaging smiles is
   Unreciprocated there.

      *   *   *

'Tis not that thy mien is stately,
   'Tis not that thy tones are soft;
'Tis not that I care so greatly
   For the same thing play'd so oft:

5

But I've heard mankind abuse thee;
    And perhaps it's rather strange,
But I thought that I would choose thee
    For encomium, as a change.

C. S. CALVERLEY (1831-1884)
Fly Leaves

FROM A SHIP, TOSSING

Ye flags of Piccadilly,
    Where I posted up and down,
And wished myself so often
    Well away from you and town,—

Are the people walking quietly,
    And steady on their feet,
Cabs and omnibuses plying
    Just as usual in the street?

Do the houses look as upright
    As of old they used to be,
And does nothing seem affected
    By the pitching of the sea?

Through the Green Park iron railings
    Do the quick pedestrians pass?
Are the little children playing
    Round the plane-tree in the grass?

This squally wild north-wester
    With which our vessel fights,
Does it merely serve with you to
    Carry up some paper kites?

Ye flags of Piccadilly,
   Which I hated so, I vow
I could wish with all my heart
   You were underneath me now!

A. H. CLOUGH (1819-1861)
Songs in Absence

ON THE WAY TO KEW

On the way to Kew
By the river old and gray,
Where in the Long Ago
We laughed and loitered so,
I met a ghost to-day,
A ghost that told of you—
A ghost of low replies
And sweet, inscrutable eyes
Coming up from Richmond
As you used to do.

By the river old and gray,
The enchanted Long Ago
Murmured and smiled anew.
On the way to Kew,
March had the laugh of May,
The bare boughs looked aglow,
And old immortal words
Sang in my breast like birds,
Coming up from Richmond
As I used with you.

With the life of Long Ago
Lived my thoughts of you.
By the river old and gray
Flowing his appointed way

As I watched I knew
What is so good to know—
Not in vain, not in vain,
Shall I look for you again
Coming up from Richmond
On the way to Kew.

W. E. HENLEY (1849-1903)
Poems

PORTLAND STONE   .

No poet has sung of Portland stone, although great ones have sung of sofas and mice and marine engines. Yet it is a great and magical stone, more beautiful, I think, even than the Roman travertine, with its marmoreal quality that responds so exquisitely to wear. Portland stone seemed ordained to form the face of London, its surface so finely mirroring the fitful lights that break through her river-mists, blanching in her towers and spires to a finer whiteness as the darker grow the coats of grime at the bases and sides. How those towers and spires come and go through the mists as you watch from Waterloo Bridge over the grey-blue Thames on a spring morning! Who can ever forget his first vision of it all as he beheld, round the bend of the river, the apparition of the mighty fleet of Wren, with their top-gallants and mainsails of stone?

The nautical simile leaps to the mind at the sight of Wren's white spires and towers, and it is appropriate, too, to the material in which Wren worked. Portland stone is a marine deposit of the Jurassic period before Britain first at Heaven's command arose from out the azure main. Its beds are full of fossils of marine creatures, cockles, sea-urchins, starfish, and oysters. You can see shell imprints on the freshly cut whitbed stone on the top of the new Bush Building, and you can see "horses' heads"—as certain shell fossils are called by masons—on the weather-beaten south parapet of St. Paul's. You can see and feel the shells projecting from the plinth of King Charles's statue at Charing Cross. It is a strange thought that the majesty of the capital of this sea-joined empire should come itself from beneath the sea, and that all the stone glories of London should be stamped so secretly with the seals of the creatures of the sea. How could our poets, how could Mr. Kipling, have missed such a theme? . . .

. . . Pretty it is, as Mr. Pepys would say, to study the doings of the rain-bearing south-west wind all over the town, how it puts its own high lights on London, touching the Portland stone with silver and spotting the plane tree-trunks with gold. In spring, especially when the light is fitful and the plane trees are shedding their bark, a sudden brightness will discover at times a secret London rhythm in these spotted buildings and trees, and even the flocks of pigeons suddenly wheeling round, like the spirit of Portland stone detaching itself from the buildings, play their part in the symphony. It is a vision one often has in the spring from the Temple windows.

But it is in autumn when Portland stone discloses its rarest beauties, when London is again the capital in a river-swamp and the mist oozes up out of the marshes of Westminster—the swamp-mist that destroys all frescoes in St. Stephen's unless they are under glass, and tarnishes the Templar's spoons three times a day—and the river and city fade away. Then the watcher at that unglazed window on Hungerford Bridge sees gently emerging the lovely façade of Somerset House with its triple screen, as its smooth, fine stone catches the coming light like a mirror, while Cleopatra's Needle and the granite Waterloo Bridge are still invisible; and as the light threads through the mist you are aware of gracious phantoms in the distance: St. Bride's and the City steeples and towers, and high over them the peristyle and lantern of St. Paul's.

JAMES BONE (Born 1872)
The London Perambulator

GOD IN LONDON

O world invisible, we view thee,
O world intangible, we touch thee,
O world unknowable, we know thee,
Inapprehensible, we clutch thee!

Does the fish soar to find the ocean,
The eagle plunge to find the air—
That we ask of the stars in motion
If they have rumour of thee there?

Not where the wheeling systems darken,
And our benumbed conceiving soars!—
The drift of pinions, would we hearken,
Beats at our own clay-shuttered doors.

The angels keep their ancient places:—
Turn but a stone, and start a wing!
'Tis ye, 'tis your estrangèd faces,
That miss the many-splendoured thing.

But (when so sad thou canst not sadder)
Cry;—and upon thy so sore loss
Shall shine the traffic of Jacob's ladder
Pitched betwixt Heaven and Charing Cross.

Yes, in the night, my Soul, my daughter,
Cry,—clinging Heaven by the hems;
And lo, Christ walking on the water
Not of Gennesareth, but Thames!

FRANCIS THOMPSON (1859-1907)
The Kingdom of God

ST. PAUL'S AFLOAT

Athwart the sky a lowly sigh
   From west to east the sweet wind carried;
The sun stood still on Primrose Hill;
   His light in all the city tarried:
The clouds on viewless columns bloomed
   Like smouldering lilies unconsumed.

"Oh sweetheart, see! how shadowy
   Of some occult magician's rearing,
Or swung in space of heaven's grace
   Dissolving, dimly reappearing,
Afloat upon ethereal tides
   St. Paul's above the city rides!"

A rumour broke through the thin smoke
   Enwreathing abbey, tower, and palace,
The parks, the squares, the thoroughfares,
   The million-peopled lanes and alleys,
An ever-muttering prisoned storm,
   The heart of London beating warm.

JOHN DAVIDSON (1857-1909)
Ballads and Songs

GRUB STREET

I see that alley hidden on the west side of Tottenham Court Road, where, after living in a back bedroom on the top floor, I had to exchange for the front cellar; there was a difference, if I remember rightly, of sixpence a week, and sixpence, in those days, was a very great consideration—why, it meant a couple of meals. (I once *found* sixpence in the street, and had an exultation which is vivid in me at this moment.) The front cellar was stone-floored; its furniture was a table, a chair, a wash-stand, and a bed; the window, which of course had never been cleaned since it was put in, received light through a flat grating in the alley above. Here I lived; here I *wrote*. Yes, "literary work" was done at that filthy deal table, on which, by the bye, lay my Homer, my Shakespeare, and the few other books I then possessed. At night, as I lay in bed, I used to hear the tramp, tramp of a *posse* of policemen who passed along the alley on their way to relieve guard; their heavy feet sometimes sounded on the grating above my window.

I recall a tragi-comical incident of life at the British Museum. Once, on going down into the lavatory to wash my hands, I became aware of a notice newly set up above the row of basins. It ran somehow thus: "Readers are requested to bear in mind that these basins are to be used only for casual ablutions." Oh, the significance of that inscription! Had I not myself, more than once, been glad to use this soap and water more largely than the sense of the authorities contemplated? And there were poor fellows working under the great dome whose need, in this respect, was greater than mine. I laughed heartily at the notice, but it meant so much.

Some of my abodes I have utterly forgotten; for one reason or another, I was always moving—an easy matter when all my possessions lay in one small trunk. Sometimes the people of the house were intolerable. In those days I was not fastidious, and I seldom had any but the slightest intercourse with those who dwelt under the same roof, yet it happened now and then that I was driven away by human proximity which passed my endurance. In other cases I had to flee from pestilential conditions. How I escaped mortal illness in some of those places (miserably fed as I always was, and always

KENT: THE CLIFFS AT DOVER

With associations stretching back to the very beginnings of British history, Dover is the only one of the Cinque Ports which remains a great port. During World War II Dover was constantly attacked from the air and was also a target for German guns at Cap Gris Nez.

SUSSEX: BEACHY HEAD

A prominent chalk headland over 500 ft. high, 3 miles south-west of Eastbourne, forming the eastern end of the South Downs.

SUSSEX: HAYMAKING AT GLYNDE

Mechanised farming in progress at the Home Farm, Glynde, not far from the famous Glyndebourne opera house, a small private theatre amid beautiful gardens, where many international artists of the first rank have given memorable performances.

SUSSEX: THE SOUTH DOWNS

Rolling downland country typical of the range of chalk hills which runs from Hampshire to the Sussex coast. The Southdown sheep pictured here, between Lewes and Newhaven, are now reared in many parts of the world, especially in the United States.

over-working myself) is a great mystery. The worst that befell me was a slight attack of diphtheria—traceable, I imagine, to the existence of a dust-bin *under the staircase*. When I spoke of the matter to my landlady, she was at first astonished, then wrathful, and my departure was expedited with many insults.

On the whole, however, I had nothing much to complain of except my poverty. You cannot expect great comfort in London for four-and-sixpence a week— the most I ever could pay for a "furnished room with attendance" in those days of pretty stern apprenticeship. And I was easily satisfied; I wanted only a little walled space in which I could seclude myself, free from external annoyance. Certain comforts of civilised life I ceased even to regret; a stair-carpet I regarded as rather extravagant, and a carpet on the floor of my room was luxury undreamt of. My sleep was sound; I have passed nights of dreamless repose on beds which it would now make my bones ache only to look at. A door that locked, a fire in winter, a pipe of tobacco— these were things essential; and, granted these, I have been often richly contented in the squalidest garret. One such lodging is often in my memory; it was at Islington, not far from the City Road; my window looked upon the Regent's Canal. As often as I think of it, I recall what was perhaps the worst London fog I ever knew; for three successive days, at least, my lamp had to be kept burning; when I looked through the window, I saw, at moments, a few blurred lights in the street beyond the Canal, but for the most part nothing but a yellowish darkness, which caused the glass to reflect the firelight and my own face. Did I feel miserable? Not a bit of it. The enveloping gloom seemed to make my chimney-corner only the more cosy. I had coals, oil, tobacco in sufficient quantity; I had a book to read; I had work which interested me; so I went forth only to get my meals at a City Road coffee-shop, and hastened

back to the fireside. Oh, my ambitions, my hopes!
How surprised and indignant I should have felt had I
known of any one who pitied me!

GEORGE GISSING (1857-1903)
The Private Papers of Henry Ryecroft

LONDON IN OCTOBER

Down through the ancient Strand
The spirit of October, mild and boon
And sauntering, takes his way
This golden end of afternoon,
As though the corn stood yellow in all the land
And the ripe apples dropped to the harvest-moon.
Lo! the round sun, half-down the western slope—
Seen as along an unglazed telescope—
Lingers and lolls, loth to be done with day:
Gifting the long, lean, lanky street
And its abounding confluences of being
With aspects generous and bland;
Making a thousand harnesses to shine
As with new ore from some enchanted mine,
And every horse's coat so full of sheen
He looks new-tailored, and every 'bus feels clean,
And never a hansom but is worth the feeing;
And every jeweller within the pale
Offers a real Arabian Night for sale;
And even the roar
Of the strong streams of toil, that pause and pour
Eastward and westward, sounds suffused—
Seems as it were bemused
And blurred, and like the speech
Of lazy seas on a lotus-haunted beach—
With this enchanted lustrousness,
This mellow magic, that (as a man's caress

Brings back to some faded face, beloved before,
A heavenly shadow of the grace it wore
Ere the poor eyes were minded to beseech)
Old things transfigures, and you hail and bless
Their looks of long-lapsed loveliness once more:
Till Clement's, angular and cold and staid,
Gleams forth in glamour's very stuffs arrayed;
And Bride's, her aëry, unsubstantial charm
Through flight on flight of springing, soaring stone
Grown flushed and warm
Laughs into life full-mooded and fresh-blown;
And the high majesty of Paul's
Uplifts a voice of living light, and calls—
Calls to his millions to behold and see
How goodly this his London Town can be!

W. E. HENLEY (1849-1903)
London Voluntary

Customs

CUSTOM, ITS POWER

The predominancy of custom is every where visible;
insomuch as a man would wonder to hear men profess,
protest, engage, give great words, and then do just as
they have done before; as if they were dead images and
engines moved only by the wheels of custom. We see
also the reign or tyranny of custom, what it is. The
Indians (I mean the sect of their wise men) lay themselves quietly upon a stack of wood, and so sacrifice
themselves by fire. Nay, the wives strive to be burned
with the corpses of their husbands. The lads of Sparta,
of ancient time, were wont to be scourged upon the
altar of Diana, without so much as queching. I remember, in the beginning of Queen Elizabeth's time of
England, an Irish rebel condemned put up a petition
to the deputy, that he might be hanged in a with and
not in an halter, because it had been so used with former
rebels. There be monks in Russia, for penance, that will
sit a whole night in a vessel of water, till they be engaged
with hard ice. Many examples may be put of the force
of custom, both upon mind and body.

Therefore, since custom is the principal magistrate
of man's life, let men by all means endeavour to obtain
good customs. Certainly, custom is most perfect when
it beginneth in young years: this we call education;
which is, in effect, but an early custom. So we see, in
languages the tongue is more pliant to all expressions
and sounds, the joints are more supple to all feats of
activity and motions, in youth than afterwards. For it is
true that late learners cannot so well take the ply;

except it be in some minds that have not suffered themselves to fix, but have kept themselves open and prepared
to receive continual amendment; which is exceeding
rare. But if the force of custom simply and separate be
great, the force of custom copulate and conjoined and
collegiate is far greater. For there example teacheth,
company comforteth, emulation quickeneth, glory
raiseth; so as in such places the force of custom is in his
exaltation. Certainly, the great multiplication of
virtues upon human nature resteth upon societies well
ordained and disciplined. For commonwealths and
good governments do nourish virtue grown, but do not
much mend the seeds. But the misery is, that the most
effectual means are now applied to the ends least to be
desired.

FRANCIS BACON, LORD VERULAM (1561-1626)
Essays

RAILING AT THE PRESENT

A Distaster of the Time is a *winter grashopper* all the yeare
long that looks back upon *harvest*, with a leane pair of
cheekes, never sets forward to meet it: his malice sucks
up the greatest part of his owne venome, and therewith
impoisoneth himselfe: and this sickness rises rather of
selfe-opinion, or over-great expectation; so in the conceit of
his own over-worthinesse, like a *coistrell*, he strives to
fill himselfe with wind, and flies against it. Any mans
advancement is the most capitall offence that can be to
his malice: yet this envy, like *Phalaris Bull*, makes that
a torment, first for himselfe, he prepared for others:
he is a *day-bed for the devill* to slumber on; his bloud is of
a yellowish colour; like those that have beene bitten
by vipers; and his gaule flowes as thick in him as oyle
in a poyson'd stomack. He infects all society, as thunder

sowres wine: war or peace, dearth or plenty, makes him equally discontented. And where he finds no cause to tax the state, he descends to raile against the rate of salt-butter. His wishes are *whirlewinds*; which breath'd forth, return into himselfe, and make him a most giddy and tottering vessell. When he is awake, and goes abroad, he doth but walk in his sleep, for his visitation is directed to none; his business is nothing. He is often dumb-mad, and goes fetter'd in his owne entrailes. Religion is commonly his pretence of discontent, though he can be of all religions; therefore truly of none. Thus by unnaturalizing himselfe, some would thinke him a very dangerous fellow to the state, but he is not greatly to be fear'd: for this dejection of his, is only like a rogue that goes on his knees and elbowes in the mire, to further his begging.

SIR THOMAS OVERBURY (1581-1613)
Characters

DECAY OF DANCING

The Court of England has much altered. Att a Solemne dancing, first you have the grave measures, then the Corantoes and the Galliards, and all this is kept upp with ceremony, att length they fell to Trenchmore, and so to the Cushion Dance, Lord and Groome, Lady and Kitchin Maid, no distinction: So in our Court. In Queen Eliz: time, Gravitie and state was kept upp. In King James time things were pretty well. But in K. Charles time there has binn nothing but Trenchmore and the Cushion dance, Omnium gatherum, tolly polly, hoyte come toyte.

JOHN SELDEN (1584-1664)
Table Talk

SHAKESPEARE-WORSHIP

Shakespeare, regarded as too romantic and even "barbaric" in the seventeenth century, came into full regard in the eighteenth. It is true that his plays were usually acted in "improved" versions, but Garrick, though he doctored Shakespeare's texts, revered his genius and established the first Shakespeare Festival at Stratford-upon-Avon in 1769. A special amphitheatre was constructed. There was abundance of feasting, dancing, horse-racing, and fire-works. Garrick wrote and delivered a Shakespeare Oration; he also wrote and recited several Odes. Others were moved to verse in praise of "Avonian Willy, Bard divine." There was much rain and the local landladies, so it was complained, were rapacious. But a good time was had by all, including many distinguished visitors from London, among whom was James Boswell. Nobody suggested acting one of Shakespeare's plays.

The happy period now arrived, when the first opening of the jubilee was announced by firing the cannon, ranged upon the banks of the Avon, about five o'clock on Wednesday morning, the 6th of September, 1769; and immediately afterwards, the principal ladies were serenaded under their windows, by a number of young men, fantastically dressed, belonging to the theatre, with the following song, accompanied by hautboys, flutes, clarionets, guitars, and other instruments:—

> Let beauty with the sun arise,
>   To Shakspeare tribute pay;
> With heav'nly smiles, and speaking eyes,
>   Give lustre to the day.

> Each smile she gives protects his name,
>   What face shall dare to frown?
> Not envy's self can blast the fame,
>   Which beauty deigns to crown.

Besides the foregoing, they also entertained the company with the Warwickshire ballad, written by Mr. Garrick. The whole town being roused by these performances, the Corporation assembled, about eight o'clock, in one of the principal streets. A public breakfast was held at the Town, or Shakspeare's hall, at nine, to which every purchaser of a guinea ticket for the various entertainments, (the masquerade only excepted, which, being of a peculiar nature, was rated separately at half a guinea) was admitted upon payment of a shilling and regaled with tea, coffee, and chocolate. Mr. Garrick, the steward, came to the breakfast-room soon after eight, to see that every thing was properly prepared for the reception of the company, as well as to be himself in readiness to receive them.

. . . From the town hall, the company proceeded in regular order, at half past ten, to the church; where the Oratorio of Judith, composed by Dr. Arne, and written by Mr. Bickerstaff, was well performed in a large temporary orchestra, erected under the organ. This piece opened at eleven; the principal vocal performers were Mrs. Baddeley, Mrs. Bartholemon, Miss Weller (a pupil of Dr. Arne's), Mr. Vernon, Mr. Champness, Master Brown, &c., first violin by Mr. Richards, and the whole conducted by Dr. Arne. The chorusses were very full; the band excellent, being composed of the whole of Drury Lane orchestra; and at the end of the first act, Mr. Bartholemon played a most enchanting solo, on the violin. When the Oratorio was finished, which had given great satisfaction to a very numerous, and polite audience, Mr. Garrick, at the head of the performers, walked in procession from the church, attended by a large cavalcade of the nobility, and gentry, in their coaches, chaises, &c., to the amphitheatre; Mr. Vernon, and the rest, singing the following chorus, to an accompanyment of proper instruments.

This is a day, a holiday! a holiday!
Drive spleen and rancour far away;
This is a day, a holiday! a holiday!
Drive care and sorrow far away.

Here Nature nurs'd her darling boy,
From whom all care and sorrow fly,
   Whose harp the Muses strung:
From heart to heart let joy rebound,
Now, now, we tread enchanted ground,
   Here Shakspeare walk'd and sung!

At three, a grand and sumptuous public ordinary for ladies and gentlemen (including all the rarities the season could afford) was given at the amphitheatre, and most numerously attended; Mr. Garrick presiding as steward. The company was occasionally diverted with a variety of new songs, catches, and glees, adapted to the purpose of the jubilee; during which time, the utmost harmony prevailed: and, after taking tea and coffee, the company retired to their respective apartments, to prepare for the assembly. The whole town was illuminated, and displayed a brilliant and lively appearance; drums were beating, and a tumult of perfect satisfaction every where predominated. The assembly at the amphitheatre was numerously attended by the nobility, ladies, and gentry; during which, immense quantities of beautiful fireworks were let off, under the management of Mr. Angelo. The minuets at the ball continued till twelve o'clock; at which time the country dances commenced: and about three all retired. The whole was conducted with the greatest decorum, and gave general satisfaction; and thus ended the first day's entertainment.

. . . On Thursday night the masquerade commenced, though not till twelve o'clock; the room was extremely

crowded, and nearly 1,000 persons were computed to
have been present. Several of the characters were well
dressed, and sustained their parts with great propriety;
among the most distinguished of which were Lady
Pembroke, Mrs. Bouverie, and Mrs. Crewe, habited as
witches, who excited general admiration: the astonishing contrast between the deformity of the feigned, and
the beauty of the real appearance, was every where
observed. Nor did a shepherdess and Dame Quickly, in
the Merry Wives of Windsor (personated by the two Miss
Ladbrokes) pass without the universal applause of the
company. Lord Grosvenor was magnificently dressed
in an eastern habit; but the greatest part of the nobility,
and most of the literary gentlemen, were in dominos.
Mrs. Yates personated a *petit-maître*: Mr. Yates, as a
waggoner, gave much satisfaction; as did a gentleman,
from Oxford, in Lord Ogleby. Mr. Boswell, the celebrated friend of Paoli, appeared in a corsican habit, with
pistol in his belt, and a musket at his back; in gold
letters, in the front of his cap, were the words *Paoli* and
Viva la Liberta. A person dressed as a devil was in-
expressibly displeasing: the three witches however
charmed the company into good humour, the shepherdess, with Mrs. Quickly, confirmed those agreeable
sensations; and about five every body retired.

On Friday (the 8th of September), as the weather
continued remarkably wet, and consequently prevented
the pageant, or representation of Shakspeare's principal
characters, part of the company (notwithstanding the
horse race) went out of town. The race for the jubilee
cup, value fifty guineas, commenced at twelve o'clock,
at Shottery race-ground, and afforded much diversion
to the lovers of the turf. " The course (says Mr. Garrick,
in his public advertisement) upon this beautiful meadow,
(allowed to be one of the finest in the kingdom) has been
altered, and made greatly more convenient, both for
horses and spectators. Indeed there was very little

occasion for art, where nature had been so lavish of her bounties: the stream of the surrounding Avon, the verdant lawns, and the rising hills and woods, form a scene too delicious for description."

The jubilee cup, whereon was engraved Shakspeare's arms, with other proper decorations, was won by a Mr. Pratt.

In the evening there was a full assembly at Shak-speare's hall, attended by many of the nobility, ladies, and gentry. Mrs. Garrick danced a minuet beyond description gracefully, and joined in the country dances, which ceased at four o'clock, and put an end to the jubilee.

R. B. WHELER
History and Antiquities of Stratford-upon-Avon, 1806

HORSE-WORSHIP

LADY UTTERWORD I assure you, all this house needs to make it a sensible, healthy, pleasant house, with good appetites and sound sleep in it, is horses.

MRS. HUSHABYE Horses! What rubbish!

LADY UTTERWORD Yes: horses. Why have we never been able to let this house? Because there are no proper stables. Go anywhere in England where there are natural, wholesome, contented, and really nice English people; and what do you always find? That the stables are the real centre of the household; and that if any visitor wants to play the piano the whole room has to be upset before it can be

opened, there are so many things
piled on it. I never lived until I
learned to ride; and I shall never
ride really well because I didn't
begin as a child. There are only two
classes in good society in England:
the equestrian classes and the neurotic
classes. It isn't mere convention:
everybody can see that the people
who hunt are the right people and
the people who don't are the wrong
ones.

BERNARD SHAW (1856-1950)
Heartbreak House

BIRD-WORSHIP

During the recent decades bird-watching has become popular with
amateurs and more exactly practised by professional naturalists and
photographers. Statistics of species and notes on their habits and
movements are carefully compiled: these supplement the old enjoyment of the English poets who were themselves shrewd observers,
as well as happy rhapsodists, among the fields, woods and hedge-rows.

The arching boughs unite between
The columns of the temple green;
And underneath the wingèd Quires
Echo about their tunèd fires.
The nightingale does here make choice
To sing the trials of her voice;
Low shrubs she sits in, and adorns
With music high the squatted thorns.
But highest oaks stoop down to hear
And listening elders prick the ear.
The thorn, lest it should hurt her, draws
Within the skin its shrunken claws.
But I have for my music found

A sadder, yet more pleasing sound;
The stock-doves, whose fair necks are graced
With nuptial rings, their ensigns chaste;
Yet always, for some cause unknown,
Sad pair, unto the elms they moan.
O why should such a couple mourn
That in so equal flames do burn!
Then, as I careless on the bed
Of gelid strawberries do tread,
And through the hazels thick espy
The hatching throstle's shining eye,
The heron from the ash's top
The eldest of its young lets drop,
As if it stork-like did pretend
That tribute to its lord to send.
But most the hewel's[1] wonders are,
Who here has the hot-felster's[2] care.
He walks still upright from the root,
Measuring the timber with his foot,
And all the way, to keep it clean,
Doth from the bark the wood-moths glean.
He, with his beak examines well
Which fit to stand, and which to fell.
The good he numbers up, and hacks,
As if he marked them with his axe.
But where he, tinkling with his beak,
Does find the hollow oak to speak,
That for his building he designs,
And through the tainted side he mines.
Who could have thought the tallest oak
Should fall by such a feeble stroke?
Nor would it, had the tree not fed
A traitor-worm within it bred.
And yet that worm triumphs not long,
But serves to feed the hewel's young.

[1] Hew-hole or Green Woodpecker
[2] Forester

Whiles the oak seems to fall content,
Viewing the treason's punishment.
Thus, I, easy philosopher,
Among the birds and trees confer,
And little now to make me wants
Or of the fowls, or of the plants.
Already I begin to call
In their most learned original;
And where I language want, my signs
The bird upon the bough divines.

ANDREW MARVELL (1621-1678)
Upon Appelton House

Elsewhere Marvell associated his own happiness with the avian gliding among greenery.

Meanwhile the mind from pleasure less
Withdraws into its happiness;
The mind, that ocean where each kind
Does straight its own resemblance find;
Yet it creates, transcending these,
Far other worlds, and other seas;
Annihilating all that's made
To a green thought in a green shade.
Here at the fountain's sliding foot
Or at some fruit-tree's mossy root,
Casting the body's vest aside
My soul into the boughs does glide;
There, like a bird, it sits and sings,
Then whets and claps its silver wings,
And, till prepared for longer flight,
Waves in its plumes the various light.

ANDREW MARVELL (1621-1678)
Thoughts in a Garden

Another close and devoted observer was John Clare, the ploughman-poet of the East Midlands.

THRUSH'S NEST

Within a thick and spreading hawthorn bush
   That overhung a molehill large and round,
I heard from morn to morn a merry thrush
   Sing hymns to sunrise, and I drank the sound
With joy; and, often an intruding guest,
   I watched her secret toils from day to day—
How true she warped the moss, to form a nest,
   And modelled it within with wood and clay;
And by and by, like heath-bells gilt with dew,
   There lay her shining eggs, as bright as flowers,
Ink-spotted over shells of greeny blue;
   And there I witnessed in the sunny hours
A brood of nature's minstrels chirp and fly,
   Glad as the sunshine and the laughing sky.

JOHN CLARE (1793-1864)
Poems

EMMONSAIL HEATH

I love to see the old heath's withered brake
Mingle its crimpled leaves with furze and ling,
While the old heron from the lonely lake
Starts slow and slaps his melancholy wing,
And oddling crow in idle motions swing
On the half rotten ashtree's topmost twig,
Beside whose trunk the gipsy makes his bed.
Up flies the bouncing woodcock from the brig
Where a black quagmire quakes beneath the tread,
The fieldfares chatter in the whistling thorn

And for the awe round fields and closen rove,
And coy bumbarrels[1] twenty in a drove
Flit down the hedgerows in the frozen plain
And hang on little twigs and start again.

JOHN CLARE (1793-1864)
Poems

[1] Long-tailed tits

THE STOCKDOVES

They rose up in a twinkling cloud
And wheeled about and bowed
To settle on the trees
Perching like small clay images.

Then with a noise of sudden rain
They clattered off again
And over Ballard Down
They circled like a flying town.

Though one could sooner blast a rock
Than scatter that dense flock
That through the winter weather
Some iron rule has held together.

Yet in another month from now
Love like a spark will blow
Those birds the country over
To drop in trees, lover by lover.

ANDREW YOUNG (Born 1885)
Collected Poems

SUSSEX: A GYPSY ENCAMPMENT NEAR CHAILEY
There are some thousands of gypsies in England and their horse-drawn
caravans are a common sight in many parts of the country, especially
in East Anglia and the South. Mostly the gypsies earn a living as tinkers
and makers of basketware, and many of the women tell fortunes.

SUSSEX: MORRIS DANCING
The Morris dance was originated by the Moors, and it may have been
brought to England by Eleanor of Castile, wife of Edward I. The
characters include Robin Hood and Maid Marian, usually with a hobby
horse. This picture was taken at Fulking, near Brighton.

SUSSEX: THE ROYAL PAVILION, BRIGHTON

The great popularity of Brighton as a pleasure resort, now only an hour from London by train, dates from the visits of George IV who, as Prince of Wales, built the Royal Pavilion in 1784-87. The Pavilion houses a museum, art galleries and assembly rooms.

SUSSEX: BRUNSWICK SQUARE, HOVE

A picture featuring the Regency architecture of which there are many fine examples in Brighton and neighbouring Hove, and recalling the popularity of the resort with men and women of fashion in the late 18th century. The promenade is nearly 4 miles long, with two piers.

RECEIVING REFUGEES

London, as well as England and Britain, has often been a good host to foreign refugees. But occasionally intolerance of alien workers breaks out among our own crafts and rarely has it had better rebuke than from Sir Thomas More in the Elizabethan play of that name. This is the more interesting to us because many scholars believe that the passage here quoted was not only written into this composite work by Shakespeare, but that the text of it in the surviving manuscript (British Museum, Harley 1368) is a specimen of Shakespeare's own hand-writing. Sir Thomas More is successfully denouncing the intolerant London mob which, on the "ill May Day" of 1517, has demanded the removing of the strangers who are competing in the London labour-market, and now threatens violence.

Grant them removed, and grant that this your noise
Hath chid down all the majesty of England;
Imagine that you see the wretched strangers,
Their babies at their backs, with their poor luggage
Plodding to th' ports and coasts for transportation,
And that you sit as kings in your desires,
Authority quite silenced by your brawl,
And you in ruff of your opinions clothed;
What had you got? I'll tell you. You had taught
How insolence and strong hand should prevail,
How order should be quelled. And by this pattern
Not one of you should live an aged man:
For other ruffians, as their fancies wrought,
With selfsame hand, self reasons, and self right,
Would shark on you; and men like ravenous fishes
Would feed on one another. . . .

                             What do you to your souls
In doing this, O desperate as you are?
Wash your foul minds with tears; and those same hands
That you like rebels lift against the peace,
Lift up for peace; and your unreverent knees,

Make them your feet. To kneel to be forgiven
Is safer wars than ever you can make
Whose discipline is riot. Why even your hurly
Cannot proceed but by obedience.
What rebel captain,
As mutinies are incident, by his name
Can still the rout? Who will obey a traitor?
Or how can well that proclamation sound
When there is no addition but a rebel
To qualify a rebel? You'll put down strangers,
Kill them, cut their throats, possess their houses,
And lead the majesty of law in lyam,[1]
To slip him like a hound. Say now the King—
As he is clement, if th' offender mourn—
Should so much come too short of your great trespass
As but to banish you, whither would you go?
What country, by the nature of your error,
Should give you harbour? Go you to France or Flanders,
To any German province, Spain or Portugal,
Nay anywhere that not adheres to England,
Why you must needs be strangers. Would you be pleased
To find a nation of such barbarous temper
That breaking out in hideous violence
Would not afford you an abode on earth,
Whet their detested knives against your throats,
Spurn you like dogs, and like as if that God
Owed not nor made not you, nor that the elements
Were not all appropriate to your comforts,
But chartered unto them? What would you think
To be thus used? This is the strangers' case.

Sir Thomas More: A Play by Several Hands
Written probably about 1595

[1] Leash

GOING TO SPAS

Going to take the waters at a Spa has long been a favourite English habit and that habit has been happily responsible for creating some of the most beautiful English towns. Bath, whose hot and curative springs were discovered and handsomely developed by the Romans, is a notable example.

Pepys enjoyed a visit in 1668 and Christopher Anstey, in his rhymed *Letters from Bath*, a century later, found the place delightful for sight-seeing and idling.

Up at four o'clock, being by appointment called up to the Cross Bath; where we were carried after one another, myself and wife and Betty Turner, Willet, and W. Hewer. And by and by, though we designed to have done before company come, much company come; very fine ladies; and the manner pretty enough, only methinks it cannot be clean to go so many bodies together in the same water. Good conversation among them that are acquainted here, and stay together. Strange to see how hot the water is; and in some places, though this is the most temperate bath, the springs so hot as the feet not able to endure. But strange to see, when women and men here, that live all the season in these waters, cannot but be parboiled and look like the creatures of the bath! Carried away wrapped in a sheet, and in a chair home: and there one after another thus carried (I staying above two hours in the water) home to bed, sweating for an hour. And by and by comes musick to play to me, extraordinary good as ever I heard at London almost any where: 5s.

SAMUEL PEPYS (1633-1703)
Diary

Of all the gay Places the World can afford,
By Gentle and Simple for Pastime ador'd,
Fine Balls, and fine Concerts, fine Buildings, and Springs,
Fine Walks, and fine Views, and a Thousand fine Things,
Not to mention the sweet Situation and Air,
What Place, my dear Mother, with *Bath* can compare?
Let *Bristol* for Commerce and Dirt be renown'd,
At *Sal'sbury* Pen-Knives and Scissors be ground;
The Towns of *Devizes*, of *Bradford*, and *Frome*,
May boast that they better can manage the Loom;
I believe that they may;—but the World to refine,
In Manners, in Dress, in Politeness to shine,
O *Bath*!—let the Art, let the Glory be thine.

*   *   *

You never can go, my dear Mother, where you
So much have to see and so little to do.

CHRISTOPHER ANSTEY
Letters from Bath, 1766

But Smollett gave a much less favourable description in 1771.

M. Bramble to Dr. Lewis

You must know, I find nothing but disappointment
at Bath; which is so altered, that I can scarce believe it is
the same place that I frequented about thirty years
ago. Methinks I hear you say, "Altered it is, without
all doubt: but then it is altered for the better; a truth
which, perhaps, you would own without hesitation, if
you yourself was not altered for the worse." The
reflection may, for aught I know, be just. The incon-
veniences which I overlooked in the high-day of health,
will naturally strike with exaggerated impression on
the irritable nerves of an invalid, surprised by premature
old age, and shattered with long-suffering—But, I

believe, you will not deny, that this place, which Nature and Providence seem to have intended as a resource from distemper and disquiet, is become the very centre of racket and dissipation. Instead of that peace, tranquillity, and ease, so necessary to those who labour under bad health, weak nerves, and irregular spirits; here we have nothing but noise, tumult, and hurry; with the fatigue and slavery of maintaining a ceremonial, more stiff, formal, and oppressive, than the etiquette of a German elector. A national hospital it may be, but one would imagine that none but lunatics are admitted; and truly, I will give you leave to call me so, if I stay much longer at Bath.

* * *

The Square, though irregular, is, on the whole, pretty well laid out, spacious, open, and airy; and, in my opinion, by far the most wholesome and agreeable situation in Bath, especially the upper side of it; but the avenues to it are mean, dirty, dangerous, and indirect. Its communication with the Baths is through the yard of an inn, where the poor trembling valetudinarian is carried in a chair, betwixt the heels of a double row of horses, wincing under the curry-combs of grooms and postilions, over and above the hazard of being obstructed, or overturned by the carriages which are continually making their exit or their entrance—I suppose after some chairmen shall have been maimed, and a few lives lost by those accidents, the corporation will think, in earnest, about providing a more safe and commodious passage.

The Circus is a pretty bauble, contrived for shew, and looks like Vespasian's amphitheatre turned outside in. If we consider it in point of magnificence, the great number of small doors belonging to the separate houses, the inconsiderable height of the different orders, the affected ornaments of the architrave, which are both childish and misplaced, and the areas projecting into the street, surrounded with iron rails, destroy a good part of its effect upon the eye; and, perhaps, we shall find it still more defective, if we view it in the light of convenience. The figure of each separate dwelling-house, being the segment of a circle, must spoil the symmetry of the rooms, by contracting them towards the street windows, and leaving a larger sweep in the space behind. If, instead of the areas and iron rails, which seem to be of very little use, there had been a corridor with arcades all round, as in Covent-garden, the appearance of the whole would have been more magnificent and striking; those arcades would have afforded an agreeable covered walk, and sheltered the poor chairmen and their carriages from the rain, which is here almost perpetual.

At present, the chairs stand soaking in the open street, from morning to night, till they become so many boxes of wet leather, for the benefit of the gouty and rheumatic; who are transported in them from place to place. Indeed this is a shocking inconvenience that extends over the whole city; and, I am persuaded, it produces infinite mischief to the delicate and infirm: even the close chairs, contrived for the sick, by standing in the open air, have their frize linings impregnated, like so many spunges, with the moisture of the atmosphere, and those cases of cold vapour must give a charming check to the perspiration of a patient, piping hot from the Bath, with all his pores wide open.

*   *   *

Every upstart of fortune, harnessed in the trappings of the mode, presents himself at Bath, as in the very focus of observation—Clerks and factors from the East Indies, loaded with the spoil of plundered provinces; planters, negro-drivers, and hucksters, from our American plantations, enriched they know not how; agents, commissaries, and contractors, who have fattened, in two successive wars, on the blood of the nation; usurers, brokers, and jobbers of every kind: men of low birth, and no breeding, have found themselves suddenly translated into a state of affluence, unknown to former ages; and no wonder that their brains should be intoxicated with pride, vanity, and presumption. Knowing no other criterion of greatness, but the ostentation of wealth, they discharge their affluence without taste or conduct, through every channel of the most absurd extravagance; and all of them hurry to Bath, because here, without any further qualification, they can mingle with the princes and nobles of the land. Even the wives and daughters of low tradesmen, who, like shovel-nosed sharks, prey upon the blubber of those uncouth whales of fortune, are infected with the same rage of displaying their importance; and the slightest indisposition serves them for a pretext to insist upon being conveyed to Bath, where they may hobble country-dances and cotillons among lordlings, squires, counsellors, and clergy.

These delicate creatures from Bedfordbury, Butcher-row, Crutched-friers, and Botolph-lane, cannot breathe in the gross air of the Lower Town, or conform to the vulgar rules of a common lodging-house; the husband, therefore, must provide an entire house, or elegant apartments in the new buildings. Such is the composition of what is called the fashionable company at Bath; where a very inconsiderable proportion of genteel people are lost in a mob of impudent plebeians, who have neither understanding nor judgment, not the least idea of propriety and decorum; and seem to enjoy nothing so much as an opportunity of insulting their betters.

TOBIAS SMOLLETT (1721-1771)
Humphry Clinker

There is a more kindly view expressed by Fag, "a gentleman's gentle-man", in the famous comedy, *The Rivals*, whose action is set in Bath.

COACHMAN: But pray, Mr. Fag, what kind of a place is
              this Bath?—I ha' heard a deal of it—
              here's a mort o' merry making—hey?

FAG: Pretty well, Thomas, pretty well—'tis a
              good lounge; in the morning we go to the
              pump-room (though neither my Master
              nor I drink the waters); after breakfast
              we saunter on the parades or play a game
              at billiards; at night we dance: but
              d--n the place, I'm tired of it; their regular
              hours stupify me—not a fiddle nor a card
              after eleven!—however, Mr. Faulkland's
              gentleman and I keep it up a little in
              private parties. . . .

                                   R. B. SHERIDAN (1751-1816)
                                                  The Rivals

OBSERVING SUNDAY

"And as for our good people's lawful Recreation, Our
pleasure likewise is, That, after the end of Divine Service,
Our good people be not disturbed, letted, or discouraged
from any lawful recreation, such as Dancing, either of
men or women, Archery for men, Leaping, Vaulting, or
any other such harmlesse Recreation, nor from having
of May Games, Whitsun Ales, and Morris-dances, and
the setting up of Maypoles, and other sports therewith
used so as the same be had in due and convenient time,
without impediment or neglect of Divine Service:
and that women shall have leave to carry rushes to the
Church for the decoring of it, according to their old
custome. But withall we doe here account still as

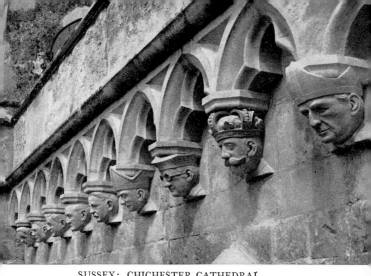

SUSSEX: CHICHESTER CATHEDRAL

This cathedral was consecrated in 1108, but the feature shown here is a modern and most unusual replacement. In 1932 the heads supporting the corbels were removed and effigies of contemporary persons holding leading positions in the State, and others closely connected with the Cathedral, were installed.

SURREY: BOX HILL

A famous landmark and beauty spot near Dorking, pictured here at the Whitsun holiday week-end. At the foot of the hill is the house once occupied by George Meredith. Since 1914 the hill has been the property of the National Trust.

BERKSHIRE: ROYAL ASCOT

The Queen drives up the course in an open landau during Ascot Week in Coronation Year. This famous race meeting, held annually in June, originated in 1711 and is still an event of importance in the social, as well as the racing, calendar.

OXFORDSHIRE: HENLEY ROYAL REGATTA

The amateur regatta each July at Henley-on-Thames is the principal rowing event in England and attracts the best oarsmen from all over the world. The first meeting was held in 1839.

prohibited all unlawful games to bee used upon Sundayes
onely, as Beare and Bull-baitings, Interludes, and at
all times, in the meaner sort of people, by Law prohibited, Bowling."

KING JAMES I OF ENGLAND AND VI OF SCOTLAND (1566-1625)
Royal Decree

It should be noted that the King, while relaxing the Sunday
disciplines, insisted that the new freedom of play be extended only to
those who had first been to Church. The Sabbatarians could hold
their own. In 1636 there was published "A Divine Tragedie lately
Acted giving fifty-six examples of God's Judgement on Sabbath-
breakers." Here is one example of the indignation and intervention of
a God strangely credited with loving kindness.

"At Chidlington upon the edge of Hertfordshire, not
farre from Hitchin, a company of fellowes upon a holy
day being to play a match, at foot ball, one of them was
tolling the bell, to assemble the rest, some being come
into the Church the randevoze of their meeting, sud-
dainly it thundering was seene a blacke ball come tumbling downe a hill neere by: which tooke its course
directly into the Church, there it flew into the bell free
and first slew him that tolled the bell, then it flustered
about the Church and hurted divers of them, and at
last bursting; left a filthy stinke like to that of brimstone
and so left a terror to all such spend thrifts of precious
time, and especially such as is dedicated to sacred uses,
who so is wise and will observe these things, even they
shall understand the loving kindness of the Lord."

*Quoted in composite volume on " The Englishman's Leisure in 17th
Century"*

———————

I am always very well pleased with a country Sunday,
and think, if keeping holy the seventh day were only a
human institution, it would be the best method that
could have been thought of for the polishing and
civilizing of mankind. It is certain the country people
would soon degenerate into a kind of savages and

6

barbarians, were there not such frequent returns of a stated time, in which the whole village meet together with their best faces, and in their cleanliest habits, to converse with one another upon indifferent subjects, hear their duties explained to them, and join together in adoration of the Supreme Being. *Sunday* clears away the rust of the whole week, not only as it refreshes in their minds the notions of religion, but as it puts both the sexes upon appearing in their most agreeable forms and exerting all such qualities as are apt to give them a figure in the eye of the village. A country-fellow distinguishes himself as much in the *Church-yard* as a citizen does upon the '*Change*, the whole parish-politicks being generally discussed in that place either after sermon or before the bell rings.

JOSEPH ADDISON (1672-1719)
The Spectator

DISLIKING SCOTS

Abusing Scotland has been a considerable English pastime and as much enjoyed as the English satirists' derision of England itself. First there was the enmity of warring neighbours in which
        "Treacherous Scotland, to no interest true,"
could be seen as a nest of marauding vermin.

But there's a saying, very old and true,—
    "If you will France win,
    Then with Scotland first begin":
For once the eagle England being in prey,
To her unguarded nest the weasel Scot
Comes sneaking, and so sucks her princely eggs;
Playing the mouse in absence of the cat,
To spoil and havoc more than she can eat.

WILLIAM SHAKESPEARE (1564-1616)
Henry V

Dr. Johnson's observations on the subject were so frequent and are so familiar as to be not worth repetition. After all, he found many and much to like when he went on his northern journey.

Sidney Smith also found Edinburgh society congenial and stimulating, but he had to keep up the raillery against "that knuckle-end of England—the land of Calvin, oat-cakes and sulphur". Even the gentle Elia had to make his grumble in the customary way.

I have been trying all my life to like Scotchmen, and am obliged to desist from the experiment in despair. They cannot like me—and in truth, I never knew one of that nation who attempted to do it. There is something more plain and ingenuous in their mode of proceeding. We know one another at first sight. There is an order of imperfect intellects (under which mine must be content to rank) which in its constitution is essentially anti-Caledonian. . . .

Persons of this nation are particularly fond of affirming a truth—which nobody doubts. They do not so properly affirm, as annunciate it. They do indeed appear to have such a love of truth—as if, like virtue, it were valuable for itself—that all truth becomes equally valuable, whether the proposition that contains it be new or old, disputed, or such as is impossible to become a subject of disputation. I was present not long since at a party of North Britons where a son of Burns was expected; and happened to drop a silly expression (in my south British way), that I wished it were the father instead of the son—when four of them started up at once to inform me, that "that was impossible, because he was dead." An impracticable wish, it seems, was more than they could conceive. Swift has hit off this part of their character, namely their love of truth, in his biting way, but with an illiberality that necessarily confines the passage to the margin. The tediousness of the Scotch is certainly proverbial. I wonder if they ever tire of one another!—In my early life I had a passionate fondness for the poetry of Burns. I have sometimes foolishly hoped to ingratiate myself with his countrymen by expressing it. But I have always found that a true Scot resents your admiration of his compatriot, even more than he would your contempt of him. The latter he imputes to your "imperfect acquaintance with many of the words which he uses;" and the same objection makes it a presumption in you to suppose that you can admire him. I have a great mind to give up Burns. There is certainly a bragging spirit of generosity, a swaggering assertion of independence, and *all that*, in his writings. Thomson they seem to have forgotten. Smollett they have neither forgotten nor forgiven, for his delineation of Rory and his companion, upon their first introduction to our metropolis.

CHARLES LAMB (1775-1834)
Essays of Elia:
Imperfect Sympathies

CATCHING A COLD

I dined privately with a friend to-day in the neighbour-hood. Last Saturday night I came home, and the drab had just washed my room, and my bed-chamber was all wet, and I was forced to go to bed in my own defence, and no fire: I was sick on Sunday, and now have got a swinging cold. I scolded like a dog at Patrick, although he was out with me: I detest washing of rooms: can't they wash them in a morning, and make a fire, and leave open the windows? I slept not a wink last night for hawking and spitting: and now every body has colds. Here's a clutter: I'll go to bed and sleep if I can.

DEAN SWIFT (1667-1745)
Journal to Stella

A QUAINT RELIEF

He was much troubled with flegme, and being so one winter at the court at Ludlowe (where he was one of the councesellours), sitting by the fire, spitting and spawling, he tooke a fine tender sprig, and tied a ragge at the end, and conceited he might putt it downe his throate, and fetch-up the flegme, and he did so. Afterwards he made this instrument of whale-bone. I have oftentimes seen him use it. I could never make it goe downe my throat, but for those that can 'tis a most incomparable engine. If troubled with the wind it cures you *immediately*. It makes you vomit without any paine, and besides, the vomits of apothecaries have *aliquid veneni* in them. He wrote a little octavo booke, of this way of medicine, called *Organon Salutis*: London, printed for Daniel Pakeman, at the Rainebowe, in Fleet-street, 1659, *scil.* the second edition, dedicated to Henry, marquess of Dorchester. I had a young fellow (Marc Collins), that was my servant, that used it incomparably, more easily than the Judge; he made of them. In Wilts, among my things, are some of his making still. The Judge sayd he never sawe any one use it so dextrously in his life. It is no paine, when downe your throate; he would touch the bottome of his stomach with it.

JOHN AUBREY (1626-1697)
Walter Rumsey in Brief Lives

RHUBARB TO THE RESCUE

1792. Janry. 12, Thursday . . . Mrs. Custance very finely this morning (thank God). I was taken very strangely this morning with a kind of a fainting fit owing I apprehend to the extreme cold weather, but soon got better thank God. Sent Briton this Morning to Mr. Jeanes's to enquire after them on their Loss of a Daughter. Dinner to day Giblet Soup, boiled Pork and rost Rabbit. Appetite rather better but still very poorly. Most bitter cold Day, froze very sharp within ag'n. Our Maid Betty Dade taken very ill this Even' with Wind-Cholic, gave her some Aether. She is very subject to Hysteric Wind.

Janry. 13, Friday . . . Mrs. Custance still continues getting better. Tolerably well (thank God) this Morning. As severe a Frost last Night as I ever remember. Betty something better this morning. Dinner to day Giblet Soup and a rost Chicken. Gave Betty some Rhubarb and Ginger this Evening going to bed, she is better this Evening. I took a small Quantity of Rhubarb and Ginger also going to bed, better to day thank God. Water Gruel generally my Supper now.

Janry. 14, Saturday . . . Mrs. Custance still continues getting better. Betty also a good deal better this Morning. The most severe Frost last Night and this Morning as I ever felt. The Milk in the Dairy in the Pans was one Piece of Ice and the Water above Stairs in the Basons froze in a few Minutes after being put there this Morn'. I don't know that I ever perceived the cold so piercing as this Morning, have kept a Charcoal-Fire in my Cellar since we brewed. Dinner to day a boiled Chicken with Pork and Greens and a fat Goose rosted, and Damson Tarts &c. Billy Bidewell brought our News for us.

Janry. 15 . . . Got up this morning very ill with a bad cold and sore Throat, so hoarse that I was not able to do my duty at Church this Afternoon. Sent round to my Parishioners this Morn' that there would be no Service at Church to day. Very poorly all day but rather better in the After [noon]. My Appetite very bad indeed. Poor Mrs. Custance much worse to day, but I hope she is not so bad as she has been. Weather much altered since Yesterday, much milder, which might have great effect upon her. Dinner to day Veal Soup, Calfs Fry, and Neck Veal rosted.

Janry. 16, Monday . . . Mrs. Custance some little matter better this Morn'. Mr. Custance but very poorly indeed which I wonder not much at, being so miserable abt. Mrs. C. Pray God send them both better soon. My Cold something better to day but still I am far from well, very dull and sleepy in the Mornings between Breakfast and dinner. Dinner to day a Leg of Mutton rosted &c.

Janry. 17, Tuesday . . . Mrs. Custance something better this Morn' and Mr. Custance. Thank God I find myself better and Appetite better. I walked to Weston Church this Morning married John Cutting and Anne Baker by Banns. Recd. for marrying John Cutting and Anne Baker having recd. before 2s. 6d., only o. 2. 6. Dinner to day boiled Beef and Damson Tarts. I relished my Dinner very well and eat tolerably hearty.

REV. JAMES WOODFORDE (1740-1803)
Diary of a Country Parson

DRINKING TEA

Johnson's defence of tea against Mr. Jonas Hanway's violent attack upon that elegant and popular beverage, shews how very well a man of genius can write upon the slightest subject, when he writes, as the Italians say, *con amore.* I suppose no person ever enjoyed with more relish the infusion of that fragrant leaf than Johnson. The quantities which he drank of it at all hours were so great, that his nerves must have been uncommonly strong, not to have been extremely relaxed by such an intemperate use of it. He assured me, that he never felt the least inconvenience from it; which is a proof that the fault of his constitution was rather a too great tension of fibres, than the contrary. Mr. Hanway wrote an angry answer to Johnson's review of his Essay on Tea, and Johnson, after a full and deliberate pause, made a reply to it; the only instance, I believe, in the whole course of his life when he condescended to oppose anything that was written against him.

JAMES BOSWELL (1740-1795)
The Life of Dr. Johnson

BLAMELESS BEVERAGE

Now stir the fire, and close the shutters fast,
Let fall the curtains, wheel the sofa round,
And, while the bubbling and loud-hissing urn
Throws up a steamy column, and the cups,
That cheer but not inebriate, wait on each,
So let us welcome peaceful ev'ning in.

WILLIAM COWPER (1731-1800)
The Winter Evening

TEA TO THE BRIM

The monthly meetings of the Brick Lane Branch of the United Grand Junction Ebenezer Temperance Association, were held in a large room, pleasantly and airily situated at the top of a safe and commodious ladder. The president was the straight-walking Mr. Anthony Humm, a converted fireman, now a schoolmaster, and occasionally an itinerant preacher; and the secretary was Mr. Jonas Mudge, chandler's shop-keeper, an enthusiastic and disinterested vessel, who sold tea to the members.

WILTSHIRE: SALISBURY CATHEDRAL

A 13th century cathedral noted for its Gothic architecture and its 404 ft. spire, the highest in England. The city gives its name to the great plain lying to the north, largely used as a military training area but also a rich hunting ground for the archæologist.

WILTSHIRE: STONEHENGE

The famous prehistoric stone circle, or solar temple, 2 miles west of Amesbury on Salisbury Plain. The largest stones are

Previous to the commencement of business, the ladies sat upon forms and drank tea, till such time as they considered it expedient to leave off; and a large wooden money-box was conspicuously placed upon the green baize cloth of the business table, behind which the secretary stood, and acknowledged, with a gracious smile, every addition to the rich vein of copper which lay concealed within.

On this particular occasion the women drank tea to a most alarming extent; greatly to the horror of Mr. Weller senior, who, utterly regardless of all Sam's admonitory nudgings, stared about him in every direction with the most undisguised astonishment.

"Sammy," whispered Mr. Weller, "if some o' these here people don't want tappin' to-morrow mornin', I ain't your father, and that's wot it is. Why, this here old lady next me is a drowndin' herself in tea."

"Be quiet, can't you," murmured Sam.

"Sam," whispered Mr. Weller, a moment afterwards, in a tone of deep agitation, "mark my vords, my boy. If that 'ere secretary fellow keeps on for only five minutes more, he'll blow hisself up with toast and water."

"Well, let him, if he likes," replied Sam; "it ain't no bis'ness o' yourn."

"If this here lasts much longer, Sammy," said M. Weller, in the same low voice, "I shall feel it my duty, as a human bein', to rise and address the cheer. There's a young 'ooman on the next form but two, as has drunk nine breakfast cups and a half; and she's a swellin' wisibly before my wery eyes."

There is little doubt that Mr. Weller would have carried his benevolent intention into immediate execution, if a great noise, occasioned by putting up the cups and saucers, had not very fortunately announced that the tea-drinking was over.

CHARLES DICKENS (1812-1870)
Pickwick Papers

HAVING A GOOD BREAKFAST

The Rev. Dr. Folliott: A man of taste is seen at once in
the array of his breakfast-table. . . . Chocolate, coffee,
tea, cream, eggs, ham, tongue, cold fowl,—all these are
good, and bespeak good knowledge in him who sets
them forth: but the touchstone is fish: anchovy is the
first step, prawns and shrimps the second; and I laud
him who reaches to these: potted char and lampreys
are the third, and a fine stretch of progression; but
lobster is, indeed, matter for a May morning, and
demands a rare combination of knowledge and virtue
in him who sets it forth.

Mr. MacQuedy: Well, sir, and what say you to a fine
fresh trout, hot and dry, in a napkin? or a herring out
of the water into the frying-pan, on the shore of Loch
Fyne?

The Rev. Dr. Folliott: Sir, I say every nation has some
eximious virtue; and your country is pre-eminent in
the glory of fish for breakfast. We have much to learn
from you in that line at any rate.

Mr. MacQuedy: And in many others, sir, I believe.
Morals and metaphysics, politics and political economy,
the way to make the most of all the modifications of
smoke; steam, gas, and paper currency; you have all
these to learn from us; in short, all the arts and sciences.
We are the modern Athenians.

The Rev. Dr. Folliott: I, for one, sir, am content to learn
nothing from you but the art and science of fish for
breakfast.

THOMAS LOVE PEACOCK (1785-1866)
Crotchet Castle

HAVING A GOOD DINNER

LOLLIO: Yes, sir, for every part has his hour: we
         wake at six and look about us, that's eye-
         hour; at seven we should pray, that's knee-
         hour; at eight, walk, that's leg-hour; at
         nine gather flowers and pluck a rose, that's
         nose-hour; at ten we drink, that's mouth-
         hour; at eleven lay about us for victuals,
         that's hand-hour; at twelve go to dinner,
         that's belly-hour.

ALIBIUS: Profoundly, Lollio! it will be long
          Ere all thy scholars learn this lesson. . . .
                        THOMAS MIDDLETON (1570-1627)
                                        The Changeling

———————

1790, Sept. 24, Friday . . . Nancy was taken very ill this
Afternoon with a pain within her, blown up so as if
poisoned, attended with a vomiting. I supposed it
proceeded in great measure from what she eat at Dinner
and after. She eat for Dinner some boiled Beef rather
fat and salt, a good deal of nice rost duck, and a plenty
of boiled Damson Pudding. After Dinner by way of
Desert, she eat some green-gage Plumbs, some Figgs,
and Rasberries and Cream. I desired her to drink a good
half pint Glass of warm Rum and Water which she did
and soon was a little better—for Supper she had Water-
gruel with a Couple of small Table Spoonfuls of Rum in
it, and going to bed I gave her a good dose of Rhubarb
and Ginger. She was much better before she went
to bed—And I hope will be brave to Morrow.

Sept. 25, Saturday . . . Nancy thank God Much better this Morning—The Rhubarb made her rise earlier than usual. She dined on a rost Neck of Mutton and supped on Water-gruel and at night quite hearty and well.

*   *   *

1792, Oct. 19, Friday. I breakfasted, supped and slept again at home. Nancy breakfasted, supped and slept again at home. It being a very fine morning and the Arch-Deacons Visitation at Reepham to day, I drove Nancy this morning in my Curricle to Reepham, set her down at Mr. Priests where she dined with Mrs. Priest, Mrs. Jeanes, Miss Baldwin and 2. Miss Priests. We set out at 9. and got to Reepham by ½ past 10. Put up the Curricle and Horse at Mr. Priests. I walked to the Kings Arms and from thence to Church with the Clergy, where Prayers were read by Mr. Priest and a very good constitutional Sermon preached by Dr. Grape of Horsted against the Seditious writings that have been and now are daily published by the Dissenters, Atheists, and ill designing Men. After Divine Service we returned to the Inn and there dined and spent the Afternoon. The Clergy that dined together were the Revd. Mr. Astley who officiated as Arch-Deacon, Revd. Dr. Grape, Revd. Mr. Priest, Revd. Mr. Whitmell, Revd. Mr. Carr, Revd. Mr. Bulwer, Revd. Mr. Jeans, Revd. Mr. Sandiford, Revd. Mr. Addison, Revd. Mr. Stouton, Revd. Mr. Maynard, Revd. Mr. Woodforde. Mr. Morphew, Notary, and his Clerk Mr. Stouton dined also with us—Ordinary and ext. pd. o. 3. o. We had a very good Dinner, Cod's Head and Shoulders, Surloin of Beef rosted, boiled Leg of Mutton and Caper Sauce, Pigeon Pye, Plumb and plain Puddings boiled, Bullace and Apple Pies, a rost Goose and a Couple of rost Ducks. Desert, Grapes, Apples and Walnuts. Soon after Dinner a Subscription for the French Clergy lately drove out of their Country by the

present Anarchical Government in France, was proposed
and set on foot by Mr. Astley, who subscribed, 2 Guineas,
Dr. Grape 1 Guinea.

REV. JAMES WOODFORDE (1740-1803)
Diary of a Country Parson

LOADED TABLES

The enormous feeding in Parson Woodforde's circle astonishes the
people of our more rationed and ascetic decades. The Victorians
kept up the great spread and the snobbery of entertaining *en masse*
and *de luxe*, even outside the ranks of aristocracy and plutocracy.

Why, then, do we of the middle classes persist in giving
entertainments so costly, and beyond our means? This
will be read by many mortals who are aware that they
live on leg of mutton themselves—or worse than this,
have what are called meat teas, than which I cannot
conceive a more odious custom; that ordinarily they are
very sober in their way of life; that they like in reality
that leg of mutton better than the condiments of that
doubtful French artist who comes from the pastrycook's,
and presides over the mysterious stewpans in the kitchen:
why, then, on their company dinners, should they flare
up in the magnificent manner in which they universally
do?

Everybody has the same dinner in London, and the
same soup, saddle of mutton, boiled fowls and tongue,
entrées, champagne, and so forth. I own myself to being
no better nor worse than my neighbours in this respect,
and rush off to the confectioners' for sweets, etc.; hire
sham butlers and attendants; have a fellow going
round the table with still and dry champagne, as if I
knew his name, and it was my custom to drink those
wines every day of my life. I am as bad as my neighbours.
But why are we so bad, I ask?—why are we not more
reasonable?

If we receive very great men or ladies at our houses, I will lay a wager that they will select mutton and goose-berry tart for their dinner, forsaking the *entrées* which the men in white Berlin gloves are handing round in the Birmingham plated dishes. Asking lords and ladies who have great establishments of their own to French dinners and delicacies, is like inviting a grocer to a meal of figs, or a pastrycook to a banquet of raspberry tarts. They have had enough of them. And great folks, if they like you, take no count of your feasts and grand preparations, and can but eat mutton like men.

One cannot have sumptuary laws nowadays, or restrict the gastronomical more than any other trade: but I wish a check could be put upon our dinner extravagances by some means, and am confident that the pleasures of life would greatly be increased by moderation. A man might give two dinners for one, according to the present pattern. Half your money is swallowed up in a dessert which nobody wants in the least, and which I always grudge to see arriving at the end of plenty. Services of culinary kickshaws swallow up money, and give nobody pleasure, except the pastrycook, whom they enrich. Everybody entertains as if he had three or four thousand a year.

Some one with a voice potential should cry out against this overwhelming luxury. What is mere decency in a very wealthy man is absurdity, nay, wickedness, in a poor one. A frog by nature, I am an insane, silly creature to attempt to swell myself to the size of the ox, my neighbour. Oh that I could establish in the middle classes of London an Anti-*entrée* and Anti-Dessert movement! I would go down to posterity not ill-deserving of my country in such a case, and might be ranked among the social benefactors.

W. M. THACKERAY (1811-1863)
Sketches and Travels in London

GOING TO "THE LOCAL," 1599

There are a great many inns, taverns, and beer-gardens scattered about the city, where much amusement may be had with eating, drinking, fiddling and the rest, as for instance in our hostelry, which was visited by players almost daily. And what is particularly curious is that the women as well as the men, in fact more often than they, will frequent the taverns or ale-houses for enjoyment. They count it a great honour to be taken there and given wine with sugar to drink; and if one woman only is invited, then she will bring three or four other women along and they gaily toast each other; the husband afterward thanks him who has given his wife such pleasure, for they deem it a real kindness.

In the ale-houses tobacco or a species of wound-wort are also obtainable for one's money, and the powder is lit in a small pipe, the smoke sucked into the mouth, and the saliva is allowed to run freely, after which a good draught of Spanish wine follows. This they regard as a curious medicine for defluctions, and as a pleasure, and the habit is so common with them, that they always carry the instrument on them, and light up on all occasions, at the play, in the taverns or elsewhere, drinking as well as smoking together, as we sit over wine, and it makes them riotous and merry, and rather drowsy, just as if they were drunk, though the effect soon passes—and they use it so abundantly because of the pleasure it gives, that their preachers cry out on them for their self-destruction, and I am told the inside of one man's veins after death was found to be covered in soot just like a chimney. The herb is imported from the Indies in great quantities, and some types are much stronger than others, which difference one can immediately taste; they perform queer antics when they take

it. And they first learned of this medicine from the
Indians, as Mr. Cope, a citizen of London who has spent
much time in the Indies, informed me.

THOMAS PLATTER
Travels in England, 1599
Translated and Edited by Clare Williams

SMOKING A PIPE

BOBADILL: Body o' me! here's the remainder of seven
pound since yesterday was seven-night. 'Tis
your right Trinidado; did you never take
any, Master Stephen?

STEPHEN: No, truly, sir; but I'll learn to take it now,
since you commend it so.

BOBADILL: Sir, believe me, upon my relation, for what
I tell you, the world shall not reprove.
I have been in the Indies, where this herb
grows, where neither myself nor a dozen
gentlemen more of my knowledge have
received the taste of any other nutriment in
the world for the space of one and twenty
weeks but the fume of this simple only;
therefore it cannot be, but 'tis most divine.
Further, take it in the nature, in the true
kind; so, it makes an antidote, that had you
taken the most deadly poisonous plant in
all Italy, it should expel it and clarify you
with as much ease as I speak. And for your
green wound—your Balsamum and your
St. John's wort are all mere gulleries and
trash to it, especially your Trinidado;
your Nicotian is good too. I could say what

I know of the virtue of it, for the expulsion of rheums, raw humours, crudities, obstructions, with a thousand of this kind, but I profess myself no quacksalver. Only thus much: by Hercules I do hold it, and will affirm it before any Prince in Europe, to be the most sovereign and precious weed that ever the earth tendered to the use of man.

BEN JONSON (1573-1637)
Every Man in His Humour

CURSING THE SUMMER

Letter to George Montagu, June 15, 1768

I perceive the deluge fell upon you before it reached us. It began here on Monday last, and then rained near eight and forty hours without intermission. My poor hay has not a dry thread to its back. I have had a fire these three days. In short, every summer one lives in a state of mutiny and murmur, and I have found the reason: it is because we will affect to have a summer, and we have no title to any such thing. Our poets learnt their trade of the Romans, and so adopted the terms of their masters. They talk of shady groves, purling streams, and cooling breezes, and we get sore throats and agues with attempting to realise these visions. Master Damon writes a song, and invites miss Chloe to enjoy the cool of the evening, and the deuce a bit have we of any such thing as a cool evening. Zephyr is a north-east wind, that makes Damon button up to the chin, and pinches Chloe's nose till it is red and blue; and then they cry, *this is a bad summer!* as if we ever had any other. The best sun we have is made of Newcastle coal, and I am determined never to reckon upon any other. We ruin ourselves with inviting over foreign trees, and make our houses clamber up hills to look at prospects. How our ancestors would laugh at us, who knew there was no being comfortable, unless you had a high hill before your nose, and a thick warm wood at your back! Taste is too freezing a commodity for us, and, depend upon it, will go out of fashion again.

Letter to the Rev. Mr. Cole, May 28, 1774

Nothing will be more agreeable to me, dear sir, than a visit from you in July. I will try to persuade Mr. Granger to meet you; and if you had any such thing as summer in the fens, I would desire you to bring a bag with you. We are almost freezing here in the midst of beautiful verdure, with a profusion of blossoms and flowers; but I keep good fires, and seem to feel warm weather while I look through the window; for the way to ensure summer in England, is to have it framed and glazed in a comfortable room.

HORACE WALPOLE (1717-1797)
Letters

CARRYING AN UMBRELLA

The umbrella, as its derivation from the Latin word, *umbra*, a shade, shows, began life as a defence against a scorching sun. In England there has been less need for that kind of protection and the umbrella was soon used against rain instead of rays. It is worth noting that Gay regarded it as a purely feminine weapon.

> Good housewives all the winter's rage despise,
> Defended by the riding-hood's disguise;
> Or, underneath th'umbrella's oily shade,
> Safe through the wet on clinking pattens tread.
> Let Persian dames th'umbrella's ribs display,
> To guard their beauties from the sunny ray;

Or sweating slaves support the shady load,
    When eastern monarchs show their state abroad;
    Britain in winter only knows its aid,
    To guard from chilly showers the walking maid.
                                    JOHN GAY (1685-1732)
                                                Trivia

The "brolly" in bent and battered form later became an asset to
the knockabout comedian, and, in its neatly rolled aspect, the mark
of a correct man-about-town. R. L. Stevenson in an essay on *The
Philosophy of the Umbrella* written in co-operation with J. W. Ferrier,
called it "the stamp of Respectability and the acknowledged index
of solid position".

THE GAMP

Mrs. Sairey Gamp has not only delighted millions of readers of
Martin Chuzzlewit, she has given an abiding name to what Calverley,
in his parody of Browning, called the *Ombrifuge*.

It was so amusing, that Tom, with Ruth upon his arm,
stood looking down from the wharf, as nearly regardless as it was in the nature of flesh and blood to be, of an
elderly lady behind him, who had brought a large
umbrella with her, and didn't know what to do with
it. This tremendous instrument had a hooked handle;
and its vicinity was first made known to him by a
painful pressure on the windpipe, consequent upon its
having caught him round the throat. Soon after dis-
engaging himself with perfect good humour, he had a
sensation of the ferrule in his back; immediately afterwards, of the hook entangling his ankles; then of the
umbrella generally, wandering about his hat, and
flapping at it like a great bird; and, lastly, of a poke or
thrust below the ribs, which gave him such exceeding
anguish, that he could not refrain from turning round
to offer a mild remonstrance.

Upon his turning round, he found the owner of the
umbrella struggling on tip-toe, with a countenance

expressive of violent animosity, to look down upon the
steam-boats; from which he inferred that she had
attacked him, standing in the front row, by design, and
as her natural enemy.

"What a very ill-natured person you must be!" said
Tom.

The lady cried out fiercely, "Where's the pelisse!"
meaning the constabulary—and went on to say, shaking
the handle of the umbrella at Tom, that, but for them
fellers never being in the way when they was wanted,
she'd have given him in charge, she would.

"If they greased their whiskers less, and minded the
duties which they're paid so heavy for, a little more,"
she observed, "no one needn't be drove mad by scroud-
ing so!"

She had been grievously knocked about, no doubt,
for her bonnet was bent into the shape of a cocked hat.
Being a fat little woman, too, she was in a state of great
exhaustion and intense heat. Instead of pursuing the
altercation, therefore, Tom civilly inquired what boat
she wanted to go on board of?

"I suppose," returned the lady, "as nobody but yourself can want to look at a steam package, without wanting
to go a-boarding of it, can they! Booby!"

"Which one do you want to look at then?" said Tom.
"We'll make room for you if we can. Don't be so ill-
tempered."

"No blessed creetur as ever I was with in trying
times," returned the lady, somewhat softened, "and
they're a many in their numbers, ever brought it as a
charge again myself that I was anythin' but mild and
equal in my spirits. Never mind a-contradicting of
me, if you seems to feel it does you good, ma'am, I
often says, for well you know that Sairey may be trusted
not to give it back again. But I will not denige that I
am worrited and wexed this day, and with good reagion,
Lord forbid."

By this time, Mrs. Gamp (for it was no other than that experienced practitioner) had, with Tom's assistance, squeezed and worked herself into a small corner between Ruth and the rail; where, after breathing very hard for some little time, and performing a short series of dangerous evolutions with her umbrella, she managed to establish herself pretty comfortably.

"And which of all them smoking monsters is the Ankworks boat, I wonder. Goodness me!" cried Mrs. Gamp.

"What boat did you want?" asked Ruth.

"The Ankworks package," Mrs. Gamp replied. "I will not deceive you, my sweet. Why should I?"

"That is the Antwerp packet in the middle," said Ruth.

"And I wish it was in Jonadge's belly, I do," cried Mrs. Gamp; appearing to confound the prophet with the whale in this miraculous aspiration.

CHARLES DICKENS (1812-1870)
Martin Chuzzlewit

GETTING IN A JAM

Crowding into Cocktail or Sherry Parties, at which thirty or forty people stand chattering shrilly in a room where six or eight might sit and talk comfortably, has proved a strangely popular custom in our time. But finding gaiety in sardine-fashion is not a new habit of the English, even at the highest social levels. Bacon, in his essay on Masques and Triumphs, wrote of such massed attendance at a revel and cautiously observed, "Some sweet odours, suddenly coming forth, without any drops falling, are, in such a company as there is steam and heat, things of great pleasure and refreshment".

De-odorising of this kind might have improved Horace Walpole's temper at a close-packed festivity "perfectly in character" with the taste of his time. This was in June, 1779.

The town has wound up the season perfectly in character by a fête at the Pantheon by subscription. Le Texier managed it; but it turned out sadly. The company was first shut into the galleries to look down on the supper, then let to descend to it. Afterwards they were led into the subterraneous apartment, which was laid with mould, and planted with trees, and crammed with nosegays: but the fresh earth, and the dead leaves, and the effluvia of breaths, made such a stench and moisture, that they were suffocated; and when they remounted, the legs and wings of chickens and remnants of ham (for the supper was not removed) poisoned them more. A druid in an arbour distributed verses to the ladies; then the Baccelli and the dancers of the opera danced; and then danced the company; and then, it being morning, and the candles burnt out, the windows were opened; and then the stewed danced assembly were such shocking figures, that they fled like ghosts, as they looked.—I suppose there will be no more balls unless the French land, and then we shall show we do not mind it.

HORACE WALPOLE (1717-1797)
Letters

BEING KIND TO ANIMALS

Thursday, July 11. This gale continued till towards noon; when the east end of the island bore but little ahead of us. The captain swaggered and declared he would keep the sea; but the wind got the better of him, so that about three he gave up the victory, and making a sudden tack stood in for the shore, passed by Spithead and Portsmouth, and came to an anchor at a place called Ryde on the island.

A most tragical incident fell out this day at sea. While the ship was under sail, but making as will appear no great way, a kitten, one of four of the feline inhabitants of the cabin, fell from the window into the water; an alarm was immediately given to the captain, who was then upon deck, and received it with the utmost concern and many bitter oaths. He immediately gave orders to the steersman in favour of the poor thing, as he called it; the sails were instantly slackened, and all hands, as the phrase is, employed to recover the poor animal. I was, I own, extremely surprised at all this; less indeed at the captain's extreme tenderness than at his conceiving any possibility of success; for if puss had had nine thousand instead of nine lives, I concluded they had been all lost. The boatswain, however, had more sanguine hopes, for, having stripped himself of his jacket, breeches, and shirt, he leaped boldly into the water, and to my great astonishment in a few minutes returned to the ship, bearing the motionless animal in his mouth. Nor was this, I observed, a matter of such great difficulty as it appeared to my ignorance, and possibly may seem to that of my fresh-water reader. The kitten was now exposed to air and sun on the deck, where its life, of which it retained no symptoms, was despaired of by all.

The captain's humanity, if I may so call it, did not so totally destroy his philosophy as to make him yield himself up to affliction on this melancholy occasion. Having felt his loss like a man, he resolved to shew he could bear it like one; and, having declared he had rather have lost a cask of rum or brandy, betook himself to threshing at backgammon with the Portuguese friar, in which innocent amusement they had passed about two-thirds of their time.

But as I have, perhaps, a little too wantonly endeavoured to raise the tender passions of my readers in this narrative, I should think myself unpardonable if I concluded it without giving them the satisfaction of hearing that the kitten at last recovered, to the great joy of the good captain, but to the great disappointment of some of the sailors, who asserted that the drowning a cat was the very surest way of raising a favourable

wind; a supposition of which, though we have heard
several plausible accounts, we will not presume to
assign the true original reason.

Friday, *July* 12. This day our ladies went ashore at
Ryde, and drank their afternoon tea at an ale-house
there with great satisfaction; here they were regaled
with fresh cream, to which they had been strangers since
they left the Downs.

HENRY FIELDING (1707-1754)
A Voyage to Lisbon

AVOIDING LECTURES

The American people have a reputation for enjoying lectures and for
paying readily to enjoy that fancy. The English have been less
fascinated by the prospect of listening, on hard chairs, to the voice of
wisdom proceeding from a dais. The talkers have been abundant,
but the audience not so eager. The student class has always been as
ready to "cut" lectures as to be regular in attendance and its members
have agreed with the opinions expressed by Peacock's Dr. Opimian.

The Rev. Dr. Opimian: Fish, Miss Gryll—I could discourse to you on fish by the hour; but for the present
I will forbear: as Lord Curryfin is coming down to
Thornback Bay, to lecture the fishermen on fish and
fisheries, and to astonish them all with the science of
their art. You will, no doubt, be curious to hear him.
There will be some reserved seats.

Miss Gryll: I shall be very curious to hear him, indeed.
I have never heard a lecturing lord. The fancy of lords
and gentlemen to lecture everybody on everything,
everywhere, seems to me something very comical;
but perhaps it is something very serious, gracious in the
lecturer, and instructive to the audience. I shall be

WILTSHIRE: MARLBOROUGH FAIR

In medieval England fairs were primarily occasions for buying and selling goods and it was later that the emphasis shifted from business to pleasure, as at Nottingham's Goose Fair, and at Marlborough. The town has a 16th century grammar school and a famous public school.

DORSET: CORFE CASTLE

The ruins of this strongly-placed castle, dating from Norman times but with traces of an earlier Saxon settlement, stand about 5 miles south-east of Wareham. King John often stayed at Corfe Castle, and it was a stronghold of the barons in the time of Henry III.

DEVON: EXETER CATHEDRAL BY MOONLIGHT

Exeter, county town of Devonshire, is the agricultural and commercial centre for a wide district. The cathedral dates from 1280, being restored in the 1870's, and is famous for its unusual transeptal towers. In 1942 it suffered a direct hit during an air raid.

DEVON: PONIES ON DARTMOOR

Dartmoor is a high plateau of wild country, 200 square miles in extent, lying between Exeter, Totnes, Plymouth and Okehampton, broken here and there by granite peaks or "tors". The moorland, a national park, is the home of a breed of wild ponies.

glad to be cured of my unbecoming propensity to laugh whenever I hear of a lecturing lord.

The Rev. Dr. Opimian: I hope, Miss Gryll, you will not laugh at Lord Curryfin: for you may be assured nothing will be farther from his lordship's intention than to say anything in the slightest degree droll.

Mr. Gryll: Doctor Johnson was astonished at the mania for lectures, even in his day, when there were no lecturing lords. He thought little was to be learned from lectures, unless where, as in chemistry, the subject required illustration by experiment. Now, if your lord is going to exhibit experiments in the art of cooking fish, with specimens in sufficient number for all his audience to taste, I have no doubt his lecture will be well attended, and a repetition earnestly desired.

The Rev. Dr. Opimian: I am afraid the lecture will not have the aid of such pleasant adventitious attractions. It will be a pure scientific exposition, carefully classified, under the several divisions and subdivisions of Ichthyology, Entomology, Herpetology, and Conchology. But I agree with Doctor Johnson, that little is to be learned from lectures. For the most part those who do not already understand the subject will not understand the lecture, and those who do will learn nothing from it. The latter will hear many things they would like to contradict, which the *bienséance* of the lecture-room does not allow. I do not comprehend how people can find amusement in lectures.

THOMAS LOVE PEACOCK (1785-1866)
Gryll Grange

SEEMING COLD FISH

If the English nature is cold, how is it that it has produced a great literature and a literature that is particularly great in poetry? Judged by its prose English literature would not stand in the first rank. It is its poetry that raises it to the level of Greek, Persian, or French. And yet the English are supposed to be so unpoetical. How is this? The nation that produced the Elizabethan drama and the Lake Poets cannot be a cold, unpoetical nation. We can't get fire out of ice. Since literature always rests upon national character, there must be in the English nature hidden springs of fire to produce the fire we see. The warm sympathy, the romance, the imagination, that we look for in Englishmen whom we meet, and too often vainly look for, must exist in the nation as a whole, or we could not have this outburst of national song. An undeveloped heart—not a cold one.

The trouble is that the English nature is not at all easy to understand. It has a great air of simplicity, it advertises itself as simple, but the more we consider it, the greater the problems we shall encounter. People talk of the mysterious East, but the West is also mysterious. It has depths that do not reveal themselves at the first gaze. We know what the sea looks like from a distance: it is of one colour, and level, and obviously cannot contain such creatures as fish. But if we look into the sea over the edge of a boat, we see a dozen colours, and depth below depth, and fish swimming in them. That sea is the English character—apparently imperturbable and even. The depths and the colours are the English romanticism and the English sensitiveness—we do not expect to find such things, but they exist. And—to continue my metaphor—the fish are the

English emotions, which are always trying to get up to the surface, but don't quite know how. For the most part we see them moving far below, distorted and obscure. Now and then they succeed and we exclaim, "Why the Englishman has emotions! He actually can feel!" And occasionally we see that beautiful creature the flying fish, which rises out of the water altogether into the air and the sunlight. English literature is a flying fish. It is a sample of the life that goes on day after day beneath the surface; it is a proof that beauty and emotion exist in the salt, inhospitable sea.

E. M. FORSTER (Born 1879)
Abinger Harvest

Places

ENGLISH SPRING

When daisies pied and violets blue,
   And lady-smocks all silver-white,
And cuckoo-buds of yellow hue
   Do paint the meadows with delight,
The cuckoo then on every tree
Mocks married men, for thus sings he,
      Cuckoo,
Cuckoo, cuckoo: O word of fear,
Unpleasing to a married ear!

When shepherds pipe on oaten straws,
   And merry larks are ploughmen's clocks,
When turtles tread, and rooks, and daws,
   And maidens bleach their summer smocks,
The cuckoo then on every tree,
Mocks married men, for thus sings he,
      Cuckoo,
Cuckoo, cuckoo: O word of fear,
Unpleasing to a married ear!

WILLIAM SHAKESPEARE (1564-1616)
Love's Labour's Lost

ENGLISH WINTER

When icicles hang by the wall,
   And Dick the shepherd blows his nail,
And Tom bears logs into the hall,
   And milk comes frozen home in pail,

When blood is nipp'd and ways be foul,
Then nightly sings the staring owl,
    Tu-whit;
Tu-who, a merry note,
While greasy Joan doth keel the pot.

When all aloud the wind doth blow,
  And coughing drowns the parson's saw,
And birds sit brooding in the snow,
  And Marian's nose looks red and raw,
When roasted crabs hiss in the bowl,
Then nightly sings the staring owl,
    Tu-whit;
Tu-who, a merry note,
While greasy Joan doth keel the pot.

WILLIAM SHAKESPEARE (1564-1616)
Love's Labour's Lost

TIMBER AND IRON

The Weald of Sussex still has its fine remnants of forest, but there was great devastation caused in the Middle Ages when its timber was cut down to feed the iron-forges and so to serve the hammers and anvils of the metal-workers and the needs of the soldiers mentioned by Kipling. The northern coal-fields subsequently carried industry in their direction, but not before Sussex had been largely denuded. But the foresters' loss has sometimes been the farmers' gain. Michael Drayton wrote with passion of the commerce that had been so profligate in tree-destruction.

These Forrests as I say, the daughters of the *Weald*
(That in their heavie breasts, had long their greefs con-
    ceal'd)
Foreseeing, their decay each howre so fast came on,
Under the axes stroak, fetcht many a grievous grone,

When as the anviles weight, and hammers dreadfull
　　sound,
Even rent the hollow Woods, and shook the queachy
　　ground.
So that the trembling Nymphs, opprest through gastly
　　feare,
Ran madding to the Downes, with loose dishev'ld hayre.
The *Sylvans* that about the neighbouring woods did
　　dwell,
Both in the tufty Frith and in the mossy Fell,
Forsook their bloomy Bowres, and wandred farre abroad,
Expeld their quiet seats, and place of their abode,
When labouring carts they saw to hold their dayly trade,
Where they in summer wont to sport them in the shade.
Could we, say they, suppose, that any would us cherish,
Which suffer (every day) the holiest things to perish?
Or to our daily want to minister supply?
These yron times breed none, that minde posteritie.
Tis but in vaine to tell, what we before have been,
Or changes of the world, that we in time have seen;
When, not devising how to spend our wealth with
　　waste,
We to the savage swine, let fall our larding mast.
But now, alas, our selves we have not to sustaine,
Nor can our tops suffice to shield our Roots from raine.
Joves Oke, the warlike Ash, veyn'd Elme, the softer
　　Beech,
Short Hazell, Maple plaine, light Aspe, the bending
　　Wych,
Tough Holly, and smooth Birch, must altogether burne:
What should the Builder serve, supplies the Forgers'
　　turne;
When under publike good, base private gaine takes holde,
And we poore woefull Woods, to ruine lastly solde.

MICHAEL DRAYTON (1563-1631)
Polyolbion

SHEPHERD'S COUNTRY

The Cotswold country, mainly in Gloucestershire, has been a great contributor to England's beauty, both in the natural scene and in man's contrivance. The turf of its rounded hills made good pasture for its sheep, and so its flock-masters became rich and were able to build nobly in the seventeenth century, when the builder's art was luckily at its highest. Below the turf lay the stone, the stone that has mellowed so richly in the light of the years. Hence the Cotswold churches and manor-houses, almost honey-coloured on a sunny day, have been, and happily remain, the perfect out-growth of the wolds about them and of the river-valleys where the cloth-mills used the local water-power for the working of the local wool. The Tudor and Jacobean poet, Michael Drayton, in his long and often over-learned poem on the English countryside and its history, paid his tribute to the Cotswolds, rich in the white fleeces that were golden in the market. He loved the hills also as the source of the Thames, which rises at Seven Springs near Cheltenham.

And, now that every thing may in the proper place
Most aptly be contriv'd, the Sheepe our *Wold* doth breed
(The simplest though it seeme) shall our description
    need,
And Shepheard-like, the Muse thus of that kind doth
    speak;
No browne, nor sullyed black the face or legs doth streak,
Like those of *Moreland*, *Cank*, or of the *Cambrian* hills
That lightly laden are: but *Cotswold* wisely fills
Her with the whitest kind: whose browes so woolly be,
As men in her faire Sheepe no emptiness should see.
The Staple deepe and thick, through, to the very graine,
Most strongly keepeth out the violentest raine:
A body long and large, the buttocks equall broad;
As fit to under-goe the full and weightie load.
And of the fleecie face, the flanks doth nothing lack,
But every-where is stor'd; the belly, as the back.
The faire and goodly Flock, the Shepheards only pride,
As white as Winters snowe, when from the Rivers side

He drives his new-washt Sheepe; or on the Sheering day,
When as the lusty Ram, with those rich spoyles of May
His crooked hornes hath crown'd; the Bell-weather, so
        brave
As none in all the Flock they like themselves would have.

    But Muse, returne to tell, how there the Sheepheards
        King,
Whose flock hath chanc't that yeere the earliest Lambe
        to bring,
In his gay Bauldrick sits at his lowe grassie Bord,
With Flawns, Curds, Clowted-creame, and Country
        dainties stor'd:
And, whilst the Bag-pipe playes, each lustie jocund
        Swaine
Quaffes Sillibubs in Kans, to all upon the Plaine,
And to their Country-Girles, whose Nosegayes they doe
        weare,
Some Roundelayes doe sing: the rest, the burthen beare.

    But *Cotswold*, be this spoke to th'onely praise of thee,
That thou of all the rest, the chosen soyle should'st bee,
Faire *Isis* to bring-forth (the Mother of great *Tames*)
With those delicious Brooks, by whose immortall
        streames
Her greatnesse is begunne: so that our Rivers King,
When he his long Descent shall from his Bel-sires
        bring,
Must needs (Great Pastures Prince) derive his stem by
        thee,
From kingly *Cotswolds* selfe, sprung of the third degree:
As th'old worlds Heroës wont, that in the times of yore,
On *Neptune*, *Jove*, and *Mars*, themselves so highly bore.

MICHAEL DRAYTON (1563-1631)
Polyolbion

ISLE OF WIGHT: YACHTING AT COWES

Cowes is the headquarters of the Royal Yacht Squadron and its regatta is the chief event in the yachting world. This picture was taken during Cowes Week, just before the start of the handicap race for cruising yachts. Other resorts are Ryde, Sandown, Shanklin and Ventnor.

HAMPSHIRE: NEW FOREST PONIES

The New Forest was established as a royal hunting preserve by William the Conqueror and is still the largest stretch of woodland in England. Wild ponies, such as those pictured here on one of the forest lawns, wander freely in the countryside around Lyndhurst, Brockenhurst, Beaulieu and other New Forest villages.

HAMPSHIRE: THE "CAT AND FIDDLE"

A famous old thatch-roofed New Forest inn, near Christchurch. The village inn has always been an important feature of the English scene, a congenial meeting point for local folk, as well as a place of refreshment for the weary traveller.

HAMPSHIRE: BOURNEMOUTH BEACH

Bournemouth is one of the most popular resorts in the South of England, its assets including a splendid sandy beach and a mild winter climate. This view is from near one of the "chines", or deep ravines, leading down to the beach.

SHEPHERD'S LOVE

Come live with me, and be my love;
And we will all the pleasures prove
That hills and valleys, dales and fields,
Woods or steepy mountain yields.

And we will sit upon the rocks,
Seeing the shepherds feed their flocks
By shallow rivers, to whose falls
Melodious birds sing madrigals.

And I will make thee beds of roses,
And a thousand fragrant posies;
A cap of flowers, and a kirtle
Embroider'd all with leaves of myrtle;

A gown made of the finest wool
Which from our pretty lambs we pull;
Fair-lined slippers for the cold,
With buckles of the purest gold;

A belt of straw and ivy-buds,
With coral clasps and amber studs:
And if these pleasures may thee move,
Come live with me, and be my love.

The shepherd swains shall dance and sing
For thy delight each May morning:
If these delights thy mind may move,
Then live with me, and be my love.

CHRISTOPHER MARLOWE (1564-1593)
Poems

7

THAMES VALLEY

From *Richmond* to *London* the River Sides are full of Villages, and those Villages are so full of beautiful Buildings, charming Gardens, and rich Habitations of Gentlemen of Quality, that nothing in the World can equal it; no, not the Country for Twenty Miles round *Paris*, tho' that indeed is a kind of Prodigy.

That these Houses and Gardens are admirably beautiful in their Kind, and in their separate and distinct Beauties, such as their Situation, Decoration, Architecture, Furniture, and the like, must be granted, and many Descriptions have been accurately given of them; But I find none has spoken of what I call the distant Glory of all these Buildings. There is a Beauty in these Things at a Distance, taking them *en passant*, and in *Perspective*, which few People value, and fewer understand; and yet here they are more truly great, than in all their private Glories whatsoever. Here they reflect Beauty and Magnificence upon the whole Country, and give a kind of Character to the Island of *Great Britain* in general. The Banks of the *Sein* are not thus adorn'd from *Paris* to *Roan*, or from *Paris* to the *Loign* above the City: The *Danube* can shew nothing like it above and below *Vienna*, or the *Po* above and below *Turin*; the whole Country here shines with a Lustre not to be describ'd.

In a Word, nothing can be more beautiful; here is a plain and pleasant Country, a rich fertile Soil, cultivated and inclosed to the utmost Perfection of Husbandry; then bespangled with Villages; those Villages fill'd with these Houses, and the Houses surrounded with Gardens, Walks, Vistos, Avenues, representing all the Beauties of Building, and all the Pleasures of Planting. It is impossible to view these Countries from any rising

Ground, and not be ravish'd with the delightful Prospect; For Example, suppose you take your View from the little rising Hills about *Clapham*, if you look to the East, there you see the pleasant Villages of *Peckham* and *Camberwell*, with some of the finest Dwellings about *London*. Then turning South, we see *Loughborough* House near Kennington; the Duchess of *Bedford*'s at Stretham; other fine Seats about *Croydon*; a whole Town of fine Houses at *Cashalton*; Sir *Theodore Janssen*'s (and that lately built by the Duchess Dowager of *Marlborough*, at *Wimbledon*); other fine Houses at *Tooting*; besides a very great Number in *Clapham* itself; On the South West also you have Mr. *Harvey*'s at *Coomb*, formerly the Palace of a King; with all the Villages mentioned above, and the Country adjoining, fill'd with the Palaces of the *British* Nobility and Gentry already spoken of; looking North, behold, to crown all, a fair Prospect of the whole City of *London* itself; the most glorious Sight without Exception, that the whole World at present can shew, or perhaps ever could shew since the Sacking of *Rome*.

Add to all this, that these fine Houses, and innumerable more, which cannot be spoken of here, are but very few of them the Mansion-Houses of Families, the antient Residences of Ancestors, the Capital Messuages of the Estates; nor have the rich Possessors any Lands to a considerable Value about them; but they are mostly Houses of Retreat, like the *Bastides* of *Marseilles*, Gentlemens mere *Summer-Houses*, or Citizens *Country-Houses*; whither they retire from the Hurries of Business, to draw their Breath in a clear Air, and to divert themselves and Families in the hot Weather; so that, in short, all this Variety, this Beauty, this glorious Shew of Wealth and Plenty, is really a View of the luxuriant Age which we live in, and of the prodigious Riches of the Citizens, who in their Abundance make these gay Excursions, and live thus deliciously all the Summer, retiring within themselves in the Winter, the better to lay up for the next Summer's Expence.

DANIEL DEFOE (1660-1731)
A Tour Through the Whole Island of Great Britain

RACKS AND TORMENTS

DORINDA: You share in all the Pleasures that the Country affords.

MRS. SULLEN: Country Pleasures! Racks and Torments! dost think, Child, that my Limbs were made for leaping of Ditches and clambring over Stiles; or that my Parents, wisely foreseeing my future Happiness in Country-Pleasures, had early instructed me in rural Accomplishments of drinking fat Ale, playing at Whisk, and smoaking Tobacco with my Husband; or of spreading of Plaisters, brewing of Diet-drinks, and stilling Rosemary-Water, with the good old Gentlewoman my Mother-in-Law?

DORINDA: I'm sorry, Madam, that it is not more in our power to divert you; I cou'd wish, indeed, that our Entertainments were a little more polite, or your Taste a little less refin'd: But pray, Madam, how came the Poets and Philosophers, that labour'd so much in hunting after Pleasure, to place it at last in a Country Life?

MRS. SULLEN: Because they wanted Money, Child, to find out the Pleasures of the Town: Did you ever see a Poet or Philosopher

worth ten Thousand Pound? If you
can shew me such a Man, I'll lay you
Fifty Pound you'll find him somewhere
within the weekly Bills.[1]—Not that I
disapprove rural Pleasures, as the Poets
have painted them; in their Landschape
every *Phillis* has her *Coridon*, every
murmuring Stream, and every flowry
Mead gives fresh Alarms to Love.—
Besides, you'll find that their Couples
were never marry'd.

GEORGE FARQUHAR (1678-1707)
The Beaux' Stratagem

[1] Bills of mortality were official returns of deaths in an urban district
and came to signify the districts themselves

COUNTRY SUNDAY

18th Century

My friend Sir Roger, being a good churchman, has
beautified the inside of his church with several texts
of his own choosing; he has likewise given a handsome
pulpit-cloth, and railed in the communion table at his
own expense. He has often told me, that at his coming
to his estate he found his parishioners very irregular;
and that in order to make them kneel and join in the
responses, he gave every one of them a hassock and a
common-prayer book: at the same time employed an
itinerant singing master, who goes about the country
for that purpose, to instruct them rightly in the tunes
of the psalms; upon which they now very much value
themselves, and indeed outdo most of the country
churches that I have ever heard.

As Sir Roger is landlord to the whole congregation,
he keeps them in very good order, and will suffer nobody

to sleep in it besides himself; for if by chance he has
been surprised into a short nap at sermon, upon recover-
ing out of it he stands up and looks about him, and if he
sees anybody else nodding, either wakes them himself, or
sends his servants to them. Several other of the old
knight's particularities break out upon these occasions:
sometimes he will be lengthening out a verse in the
singing-psalms, half a minute after the rest of the
congregation have done with it; sometimes, when he is
pleased with the matter of his devotion, he pronounces
Amen three or four times to the same prayer; and sometimes stands up when everybody else is upon their
knees, to count the congregation, or see if any of his
tenants are missing.

. . . The chaplain has often told me, that upon a cate-
chism day, when Sir Roger has been pleased with a boy
that answers well, he has ordered a bible to be given
him next day for his encouragement; and sometimes
accompanies it with a flitch of bacon to his mother.
Sir Roger has likewise added five pounds a year to the
clerk's place; and that he may encourage the young
fellows to make themselves perfect in the church service,
has promised, upon the death of the present incumbent,
who is very old, to bestow it according to merit.

JOSEPH ADDISON (1672-1719)
The Spectator

SINGING THE PSALMS

The good old practice of psalm-singing is, indeed,
wonderfully improved in many country churches since
the days of Sternhold and Hopkins; and there is scarce a
parish clerk who has so little taste as not to pick his
staves out of the New Version. This has occasioned
great complaints in some places, where the clerk has

been forced to bawl by himself, because the rest of the congregation cannot find the psalm at the end of their prayer-books; while others are highly disgusted at the innovation, and stick as obstinately to the Old Version as to the Old Style. The tunes themselves have also been new set to jiggish measures; and the sober drawl, which used to accompany the two first staves of the hundredth psalm, with the *gloria patri*, is now split into as many quavers as an Italian air. For this purpose there is in every county an itinerant band of vocal musicians, who make it their business to go round to all the churches in their turns, and, after a prelude with the pitch-pipe, astonish the audience with hymns set to the new Winchester measure, and anthems of their own composing. As these new-fashioned psalmodists are necessarily made up of young men and maids, we may naturally suppose, that there is a perfect concord and symphony between them: and, indeed, I have known it happen that these sweet singers have more than once been brought into disgrace, by too close an unison between the thorough-bass and the treble.

WILLIAM COWPER (1731-1800)
Essay on Country Congregations

TUNBRIDGE WELLS

The Ladies that appear here, are indeed the Glory of the Place; the coming to the Wells to drink the Water seems to be little more than a mere Matter of Custom; some drink, more do not, and few drink physically. But Company and Diversion is, in short, the main Business of the Place; and those People who have nothing to do any-where else, seem to be the only People who have any thing to do at *Tunbridge*.

After the Appearance is over at the Wells (where the

Ladies are all in an Undress) and at the Chapel, the Company go home; and, as if it was another Species of People, or a Collection from another Place, you are surpriz'd to see the Walks covered with Ladies completely dress'd, and gay to Profusion; where rich Cloaths, Jewels, and Beauty, dazzle the Eyes from one End of the Range to the other.

Here you have all the Liberty of Conversation that can be desir'd, and any Person that looks like a Gentleman, has an agreeable Address, and behaves with Decency and Good Manners, may single out whom he pleases, that does not appear engag'd, and may talk, rally, and say any decent Thing to them; but all this makes no Acquaintance, nor is it so taken or understood. If a Gentleman desires to enter into any particular Acquaintance, he must do it by proper Application, not by the ordinary Meeting on the Walks; for the Ladies will ask no Gentleman there to go off the Walk, or invite any one to their Lodgings, except it be a sort of Ladies of whom I am not now speaking.

As for Gaming, Sharping, Intriguing, as also Fops, Beaus, and the like, *Tunbridge* is as full of these as most other publick Places. However a Man of Character and good Behaviour cannot be there any Time, but he single out such Company as may be suitable to him.

The Air here is excellent good, the Country healthful, and the Provisions of all sorts very reasonable: Particularly they are supply'd with excellent Fish, and that of almost all Sorts, from *Rye*, and other Towns on the Sea-Coast; and I saw a Turbut of near twenty Pounds weight sold there for three Shillings. In the Season of Mackarel, they have them here from *Hastings*, within three hours of their being taken out of the Sea; and the Difference which that makes in their Goodness, I need not mention.

They have likewise here Abundance of Wild-Fowl,

DEVON: WIDECOMBE IN THE MOOR

Although its fame rests mainly on the old song *Widecombe Fair*, this little moorland village is deservedly popular with tourists because of its own special charm and the beauty of its setting in one of the loveliest corners of Glorious Devon.

DEVON: BUCKLAND IN THE MOOR

Cottages with neatly thatched roofs in the village of Buckland, near Ashburton. Thatch consists of reeds or straw arranged in bundles on a wooden framework, and pegged and tied down. The art of thatching is handed down from father to son, but it is a dying craft.

DEVON: TORQUAY

A popular holiday resort and yachting centre in South Devon, beautifully situated on Tor Bay and enjoying an equable climate. It was here that William of Orange landed in 1688.

of the best Sorts; such as Pheasant, Partridge, Wood-cock, Snipe, Quails, also Duck, Mallard, Teal, etc., particularly they have from the *South-Downs* the Bird call'd a *Wheatear*, or which I think I may call the *English Ortolans*, the most delicious Taste for a Creature of one Mouthful, (for 'tis little more) that can be imagin'd; but these are very dear at *Tunbridge*; They are much cheaper at *Seaford*, *Lewes*, and that Side of the Country.

Tunbridge is a Place in which a Lady, for want of good Conduct, may as soon shipwreck her Character as in any Part of *England*; and where, when she has once injur'd her Reputation, 'tis as hard to restore it. But then a Lady very seldom suffers that way at *Tunbridge*, without some apparent Folly of her own; for, after all, they do not seem so apt to make Havock of one another's Reputation here, by Tattle and Slander, as I think they do in some other Places in the World; the Reason of which I take to be, because the Company who frequent *Tunbridge*, seem to be a Degree or two above the Society that use some other Places, and therefore are not so very apt, either to meddle with other People's Affairs, or to censure rudely and causelessly if they do.

DANIEL DEFOE (1660-1731)
A Tour Through the Whole Island of Great Britain

KENTISH   YEOMAN   OF   TO-DAY

He tills the soil to-day,
Surly and grave, his difficult wage to earn.
Cities of discontent, the sickened nerve,
Are still a fashion that he will not learn.
His way is still the obstinate old way,
Even though his horses stare above the hedge,
And whinny, while the tractor drives its wedge
Where they were wont to serve,
And iron robs them of their privilege.

Still is his heart not given
To such encroachments on a natural creed;
Not wholly given, though he bows to need
By urgency and competition driven,
And vanity, to follow with the tide.
Still with a secret triumph he will say,
"Tractor for sand, maybe, but horse for clay."
And in his calling takes a stubborn pride
That nature still defeats
The frowsty science of the cloistered men,
Their theory, their conceits;

The faith within him still derides the pen,
Experience his text-book. What have they,
The bookish townsmen in their dry retreats,
Known of December dawns, before the sun
Reddened the east, and fields were wet and grey?
When have they gone, another day begun,
By tracks into a quagmire trodden,
With sack about their shoulders and the damp
Soaking until their very souls were sodden,
To help a sick beast, by a flickering lamp,
With rough words and kind hands?
Or felt their boots so heavy and so swere
With trudging over cledgy lands,
Held fast by earth, being to earth so near?

Book-learning they have known.
They meet together, talk, and grow most wise,
But they have lost, in losing solitude,
Something,—an inward grace, the seeing eyes,
The power of being alone;
The power of being alone with earth and skies,
Of going about a task with quietude,
Aware at once of earth's surrounding mood
And of an insect crawling on a stone.

V. SACKVILLE-WEST (Born 1892)
The Land

BAFFLED BY BEAUTY

I can never read in summer out of doors. Though in shadow the bright light fills it, summer shadows are broadest daylight. The page is so white and hard, the letters so very black, the meaning and drift not quite intelligible, because neither eye nor mind will dwell upon it. Human thoughts and imaginings written down are pale and feeble in bright summer light. The eye wanders away and rests more lovingly on greensward and green lime leaves. The mind wanders yet deeper and farther into the dreamy mystery of the azure sky. Once now and then, determined to write down that mystery and delicious sense while actually in it, I have brought out table and ink and paper, and sat there in the midst of the summer day. Three words, and where is the thought? Gone. The paper is so obviously paper, the ink so evidently ink, the pen so stiff; all so inadequate. You want colour, flexibility, light, sweet low sound— all these to paint it and play it in music, at the same time you want something that will answer to and record in one touch the strong throb of life and the thought or feeling, or whatever it is that goes out into the earth and sky and space, endless as a beam of light. The very shade of the pen on the paper tells you how utterly hopeless it is to express these things. There is the shade and the brilliant gleaming whiteness; now tell me in plain written words the simple contrast of the two. Not in twenty pages, for the bright light shows the paper in its common fibre-ground, coarse aspect, in its reality, not a mind-tablet.

The delicacy and beauty of thought or feeling is so extreme that it cannot be inked in; it is like the green and blue of field and sky, of veronica flower and grass blade, which in their own existence throw light and

beauty on each other, but in artificial colours repel.
Take the table indoors again, and the book: the thoughts
and imaginings of others are vain, and of your own too
deep to be written. For the mind is filled with the
exceeding beauty of these things, and their great won-
drousness and marvel. Never yet have I been able to
write what I felt about the sunlight only. Colour and
form and light are as magic to me. It is a trance. It
requires a language of ideas to convey it.

RICHARD JEFFERIES (1848-1887)
Meadow Thoughts

ILL FARES THE LAND

Sweet Auburn, loveliest village of the plain,
Where health and plenty cheared the labouring swain,
Where smiling spring its earliest visit paid,
And parting summer's lingering blooms delayed,
Dear lovely bowers of innocence and ease,
Seats of my youth, when every sport could please,
How often have I loitered o'er thy green,
Where humble happiness endeared each scene;
How often have I paused on every charm,
The sheltered cot, the cultivated farm,
The never failing brook, the busy mill,
The decent church that topt the neighbouring hill,
The hawthorn bush, with seats beneath the shade,
For talking age and whispering lovers made;
How often have I blest the coming day,
When toil remitting lent its turn to play,
And all the village train from labour free,
Led up their sports beneath the spreading tree;
While many a pastime circled in the shade,
The young contending as the old surveyed;
And many a gambol frolicked o'er the ground,
And slights of art and feats of strength went round;

And still as each repeated pleasure tired,
Succeeding sports the mirthful band inspired;
The dancing pair that simply sought renown
By holding out to tire each other down;
The swain mistrustless of his smutted face,
While secret laughter tittered round the place;
The bashful virgin's side-long looks of love,
The matron's glance that would those looks reprove:
These were thy charms, sweet village; sports like these,
With sweet succession, taught even toil to please;
These round thy bowers their chearful influence shed,
These were thy charms—But all these charms are fled.

Sweet smiling village, loveliest of the lawn,
Thy sports are fled, and all thy charms withdrawn;
Amidst thy bowers the tyrant's hand is seen,
And desolation saddens all thy green:
One only master grasps the whole domain,
And half a tillage stints thy smiling plain;
No more thy glassy brook reflects the day,
But choaked with sedges, works its weedy way.
Along thy glades, a solitary guest,
The hollow sounding bittern guards its nest;
Amidst thy desert walks the lapwing flies,
And tires their echoes with unvaried cries.
Sunk are thy bowers, in shapeless ruin all,
And the long grass o'ertops the mouldering wall,
And trembling, shrinking from the spoiler's hand,
Far, far away thy children leave the land.

Ill fares the land, to hastening ills a prey,
Where wealth accumulates, and men decay:
Princes and lords may flourish, or may fade;
A breath can make them, as a breath has made;
But a bold peasantry, their country's pride,
When once destroyed, can never be supplied.

A time there was, ere England's griefs began,
When every rood of ground maintained its man:
For him light labour spread her wholesome store,
Just gave what life required, but gave no more:
His best companions, innocence and health;
And his best riches, ignorance of wealth.

But times are altered; trade's unfeeling train
Usurp the land and dispossess the swain;
Along the lawn, where scattered hamlets rose,
Unwieldy wealth, and cumbrous pomp repose;
And every want to opulence allied,
And every pang that folly pays to pride.
These gentle hours that plenty bade to bloom,
Those calm desires that asked but little room,
Those healthful sports that graced the peaceful scene,
Lived in each look, and brightened all the green;
These far departing seek a kinder shore,
And rural mirth and manners are no more.

Sweet Auburn! parent of the blissful hour,
Thy glades forlorn confess the tyrant's power.
Here as I take my solitary rounds,
Amidst thy tangling walks, and ruined grounds,
And, many a year elapsed, return to view
Where once the cottage stood, the hawthorn grew,
Remembrance wakes with all her busy train,
Swells at my breast, and turns the past to pain.

OLIVER GOLDSMITH (1728-1774)
The Deserted Village

SUFFOLK—OR WILTSHIRE?

March, 1830

To conclude an account of Suffolk and not to sing the praises of Bury St. Edmunds would offend every creature of Suffolk birth; even at Ipswich, when I was praising *that place*, the very people of that town asked me if I did not think Bury St. Edmund's the nicest town in the world. Meet them wherever you will, they have all the same boast; and indeed, as a town *in itself*, it is the neatest place that ever was seen. It is airy, it has several fine open places in it, and it has the remains of the famous abbey walls and the abbey gate entire; and it is so clean and so neat that nothing can equal it in that respect. It was a favourite spot in ancient times; greatly endowed with monasteries and hospitals. Besides the famous Benedictine Abbey, there was once a college and a friary; and as to the abbey itself, it was one of the greatest in the kingdom; and was so ancient as to have been founded only about forty years after the landing of Saint Austin in Kent. The land all round about it is good; and the soil is of that nature as not to produce much dirt at any time of the year; but the country about it is *flat*, and not of that beautiful variety that we find at Ipswich.

After all, what is the reflection now called for? It is that this fine county, for which nature has done all that she can do, soil, climate, sea-ports, people; everything that can be done, and an internal government, civil and ecclesiastical, the most complete in the world, wanting nothing but to *be let alone*, to make every soul in it as happy as people can be upon earth; the peace provided for by the county rates; property protected by the law of the land; the poor provided for by the poor-rates; religion provided for by the tithes and the church-rates;

easy and safe conveyance provided for by the highway-rates; extraordinary danger provided against by the militia-rates; a complete government in itself; *but having to pay a portion of sixty millions a year in taxes over and above all this: and that, too, on account of wars carried on, not for the defence of England;* not for the upholding of *English liberty and happiness,* but for the purpose of crushing liberty and happiness in other countries; and all this because, and only because, a septennial parliament has deprived the people of their rights.

That which we *admire* most is not always that which would be *our choice.* One might imagine that after all that I have said about this fine county, I should certainly prefer it as a place of residence. I should not, however: my choice has been always very much divided between the woods of Sussex and the downs of Wiltshire. I should not like to be compelled to decide: but if I were compelled, I do believe that I should fix on some vale in Wiltshire. Water meadows at the bottom, corn-land going up towards the hills, those hills being *down land,* and a farm-house, in a clump of trees, in some little cross vale between the hills, sheltered on every side but the south. In short, if Mr. Bennet would give me a farm, the house of which lies on the right-hand side of the road going from Salisbury to Warminster, in the parish of Norton Bovant, just before you enter that village; if he would but be so good as to do that, I would freely give up all the rest of the world to the possession of whoever may get hold of it. I have hinted this to him once or twice before, but I am sorry to say that he turns a deaf ear to my hinting.

WILLIAM COBBETT (1763-1835)
Rural Rides

LEWES AND BRIGHTON

When Cobbett, a born and convinced countryman, wrote of "a wen" he meant a large town or what modern planners call "a conurbation". He frequently spoke of London as the worst of "wens". The Kremlin, about which he was so sarcastic, was the Pavilion built to the exotic taste of the Prince Regent, who had become George IV when this was written. It is still there and much used for public gatherings.

Nowadays we think of Brighton as a town of cream and white, gleaming in the sunshine, especially when its stucco has been freshly painted. The reference to "blue and purple brick" reminds us of a pre-stucco Brighton.

Lewes is in a valley of the *South Downs*, this town is at eight miles distance, to the south-south-west or there-abouts. There is a great extent of rich meadows above and below Lewes. The town itself is a model of solidity and neatness. The buildings all substantial to the very outskirts; the pavements good and complete; the shops nice and clean; the people well-dressed; and, though last not least, the girls remarkably pretty, as, indeed, they are in most parts of Sussex; round faces, features small, little hands and wrists, plump arms, and bright eyes. The Sussex men, too, are remarkable for their good looks. A Mr. Baxter, a stationer at Lewes, showed me a *farmer's account book*, which is a very complete thing of the kind. The inns are good at Lewes, the people civil and not servile, and the charges really (considering the taxes) far below what one could reason-ably expect.—From Lewes to Brighton the road winds along between the hills of the South Downs, which, in this mild weather, are mostly beautifully green even at this season, with flocks of sheep feeding on them.— Brighton itself lies in a valley cut across at one end by the sea, and its extension, *or Wen*, has swelled up the sides of the hills and has run some distance up the valley.— The first thing you see in approaching Brighton from

Lewes, is a splendid *horse-barrack* on one side of the road, and a heap of low, shabby, nasty houses, irregularly built, on the other side. This is always the case where there is a barrack. How soon a reformed parliament would make both disappear!

Brighton is a very pleasant place. For a *wen* remarkably so. The *Kremlin*, the very name of which has so long been a subject of laughter all over the country, lies in the gorge of the valley, and amongst the old houses of the town. The grounds, which cannot, I think, exceed a couple or three acres, are surrounded by a wall neither lofty nor good-looking. Above this rise some trees, bad in sorts, stunted in growth, and dirty with smoke. As to the "palace" as the Brighton newspapers call it, the apartments appear to be all upon the ground floor; and, when you see the thing from a distance, you think you see a parcel of *cradle-spits*, of various dimensions, sticking up out of the mouths of so many enormous squat decanters. Take a square box, the sides of which are three feet and a half, and the height a foot and a half. Take a large Norfolk-turnip, cut off the green of the leaves, leave the stalks 9 inches long, tie these round with a string three inches from the top, and put the turnip on the middle of the top of the box. Then take four turnips of half the size, treat them in the same way, and put them on the corners of the box. Then take a considerable number of bulbs of the crown-imperial, the narcissus, the hyacinth, the tulip, the crocus, and others; let the leaves of each have sprouted to about an inch, more or less according to the size of the bulb; put all these, pretty promiscuously, but pretty thickly, on the top of the box. Then stand off and look at your architecture. There! That's "a *Kremlin*!" Only you must cut some church-looking windows in the sides of the box. As to what you ought to put *into* the box, that is a subject far above my cut.

Brighton is naturally a place of resort for *expectants*,

and a shifty ugly-looking swarm is, of course, assembled here. Some of the fellows, who had endeavoured to disturb our harmony at the dinner at Lewes, were parading, amongst this swarm, on the cliff. You may always know them by their lank jaws, the stiffeners round their necks, their hidden or *no* shirts, their stays, their false shoulders, hips and haunches, their half-whiskers, and by their skins, colour of veal kidney-suet, warmed a little, and then powdered with dirty dust.— These vermin excepted, the people at Brighton make a very fine figure. The trades-people are very nice in all their concerns. The houses are excellent, built chiefly with a blue or purple brick; and bow-windows appear to be the general taste. I can easily believe this to be a very healthy place: the open downs on the one side and the open sea on the other. No inlet, cove, or river; and, of course, no swamps.

WILLIAM COBBETT (1763-1835)
Rural Rides

EAST ANGLIAN AUTUMN

It was a fair and mild autumnal sky,
And earth's ripe treasures met th'admiring eye,
As a rich beauty, when her bloom is lost,
Appears with more magnificence and cost.
The wet and heavy grass, where feet had stray'd,
Not yet erect, the wanderer's way betray'd;
Showers of the night had swell'd the deep'ning rill;
The morning breeze had urged the quick'ning mill;
Assembled rooks had wing'd their seaward flight,
By the same passage to return at night;
While proudly o'er them hung the steady kite,
Then turn'd him back, and left the noisy throng,
Nor deign'd to know them as he sail'd along.
Long yellow leaves from oziers, strew'd around,
Choked the small stream, and hush'd the feeble sound;

While the dead foliage dropt from loftier trees,
Our squire beheld not with his wonted ease,
But to his own reflections made reply,
And said aloud, "Yes! doubtless we must die."

GEORGE CRABBE (1754-1832)
The Hall

HUNTINGDON

The level country of the South-East Midlands of England has been loved by those who know it well. But it has rarely received the enthusiastic praise bestowed on it by William Cobbett, a Surrey man from Farnham, whose surrounding territory is the heathery commons and uplands which modern estate-agents like to call the Surrey Highlands. It is pleasant to meet such " beauty-spot" tributes paid to places not usually found on the beauty-spot list.

The country changes but little till you get quite to Huntingdon. The land is generally quite open, or in large fields. Strong wheatland, that wants a good deal of draining. Very few turnips of any sort are raised; and, of course, few sheep and cattle kept. Few trees, and those scrubbed. Few woods, and those small. Few hills, and those hardly worthy of the name. All which, when we see them, make us cease to wonder, that this country is so famous for *fox-hunting*. Such it has doubtless been, in all times, and to this circumstance Huntingdon, that is to say, Huntingdun, or Huntingdown, unquestionably owes its name; because *down* does not mean *unploughed* land, but open and *unsheltered* land, and the Saxon word is *dun*.—When you come down near to the town itself, the scene suddenly, totally, and most agreeably, changes. The *River Ouse* separates God-manchester from Huntingdon, and there is, I think, no very great difference in the population of the two. Both together do not make up a population of more than about five thousand souls.

Huntingdon is a slightly built town, compared with Lewes, for instance. The houses are not in general so high, nor made of such solid and costly materials. The shops are not so large and their contents not so costly. There is not a show of so much business and so much opulence. But Huntingdon is a very clean and nice place, contains many elegant houses, and the environs are beautiful. Above and below the bridge, under which the Ouse passes, are the most beautiful, and by far the most beautiful meadows that I ever saw in my life. The meadows at Lewes, at Guildford, at Farnham, at Winchester, at Salisbury, at Exeter, at Gloucester, at Hereford, and even at Canterbury, are nothing, compared with those of Huntingdon in point of beauty. Here are no reeds, here is no sedge, no unevennesses of any sort. Here are *bowling-greens* of hundreds of acres in extent, with a river winding through them, full to the brink. *One* of these meadows is the *race-course*; and so pretty a spot, so level, so smooth, so green, and of such an extent I never saw, and never expected to see. From the bridge you look across the valleys, first to the west and then to the east; the valleys terminate at the foot of rising ground; well set with trees, from amongst which church spires raise their heads here and there. I think it would be very difficult to find a more delightful spot than this in the world. To my fancy (and every one to his taste) the prospect from this bridge far surpasses that from Richmond Hill.—All that I have yet seen of Huntingdon I like exceedingly. It is one of those pretty, clean, unstenched, unconfined places that tend to lengthen life and make it happy.

WILLIAM COBBETT (1763-1835)
Rural Rides

AT BARNARD CASTLE
IN DURHAM

But, westward, Stanmore's shapeless swell,
And Lunesdale wild, and Kelton-fell,
And rock-begirdled Gilmanscar,
And Arkingarth, lay dark afar;
While, as a livelier twilight falls,
Emerge proud Barnard's bannered walls.
High crown'd he sits, in dawning pale,
The sovereign of the lovely vale.
What prospects, from his watch-tower high,
Gleam gradual on the warder's eye!—
Far sweeping to the east, he sees
Down his deep woods the course of Tees,
And tracks his wanderings by the steam
Of summer vapours from the stream;
And ere he pace his destined hour
By Brackenbury's dungeon-tower,
These silver mists shall melt away,
And dew the woods with glittering spray.
Then in broad lustre shall be shown
That mighty trench of living stone,
And each huge trunk that, from the side,
Reclines him o'er the darksome tide,
Where Tees, full many a fathom low,
Wears with his rage no common foe;
For pebbly-bank, nor sand-bed here,
Nor clay-mound, checks his fierce career,
Condemn'd to mine a channell'd way,
O'er solid sheets of marble grey.

SIR WALTER SCOTT (1771-1832)
Rokeby

YORKSHIRE AND YORKSHIRE FOLK

From one end to the other of the kingdom Yorkshiremen are looked upon as being keener than other people; more eager in pursuit of their own interests; more sharp and more selfish. For my part, I was cured with regard to the *people* long before I saw Yorkshire. In the army, where we see men of all counties, I always found York-shiremen distinguished for their frank manners and generous disposition. In the United States, my kind and generous friends of Pennsylvania were the children and descendants of Yorkshire parents; and, in truth, I long ago made up my mind that this hardness and sharpness ascribed to Yorkshiremen arose from the sort of envy excited by that quickness, that activity, that buoyancy of spirits which bears them up through adverse circum-stances and their consequent success in all the situations of life. They, like the people of Lancashire, are just the very reverse of being *cunning* and *selfish*; be they farmers, or be they what they may, you get at the bottom of their hearts in a minute. Everything they think soon gets to the tongue, and out it comes, heads and tails, as fast as they can pour it.

. . I have seen the vale of Honiton, in Devonshire, that of Taunton and of Glastonbury, in Somersetshire: I have seen the vales of Gloucester and Worcester, and the banks of the Severn and the Avon: I have seen the vale of Berkshire, that of Aylesbury, in Buckingham-shire: I have seen the beautiful vales of Wiltshire; and the banks of the Medway, from Tunbridge to Maidstone, called the Garden of Eden: I was born at one end of Arthur Young's "finest ten miles in England": I have ridden my horse across the Thames at its two sources: and I have been along every inch of its banks, from its sources to Gravesend, when I have sailed out of it into the channel; and having seen and had ability to judge of the goodness of the land in all these places, I declare that I have never seen any to be compared with the land on the banks of the Humber, from the Holderness country included, and with the exception of the land from Wisbeach to Holbeach, and Holbeach to Boston. Really, the single parish of Holbeach, or a patch of the same size in the Holderness country, seems to be equal in value to the whole of the county of Surrey, if we leave out the little plot of hop-garden at Farnham.

Nor is the town of Hull itself to be overlooked. It is a little city of London: streets, shops, everything like it; clean as the best parts of London, and the people as bustling and attentive. The town of Hull is *surrounded* with commodious docks for shipping. These docks are separated, in three or four places, by draw-bridges, so that, as you walk round the town, you walk by the side of the docks and the ships. The town on the outside of the docks is pretty considerable, and the walks from it into the country beautiful. I went about a good deal and I nowhere saw marks of beggary or filth, even in the outskirts: none of those nasty, shabby, thief-looking sheds that you see in the approaches to London: none of those off-scourings of pernicious and insolent luxury. I hate commercial towns in general: there is generally something so loathsome in the look, and so stern and unfeeling in the manners of sea-faring people, that I have always, from my very youth, disliked sea-ports; but really, the sight of this nice town, the manners of its people, the civil and kind and cordial reception that I met with, and the clean streets, and especially the pretty gardens in every direction, as you walk into the country, has made Hull, though a sea-port, a place that I shall always look back to with delight.

Beverley, which was formerly a very considerable city, with three or four gates, one of which is yet stand-

DEVON: PLYMOUTH HOE

The scene of the famous game of bowls played by Drake during the approach of the Spanish Armada. From Plymouth, too, the Pilgrim Fathers sailed for America, in 1620. Devonport, beyond the lighthouse in this picture, is an important naval station and dockyard.

CORNWALL: POLPERRO

A charming little fishing port between Looe and Fowey, on the south coast of Cornwall. Like Mevagissey, Clovelly and other Cornish seaside villages, Polperro attracts many artists and holiday-makers.

CORNWALL: ST. MICHAEL'S MOUNT

A small island in Mount's Bay linked with Marazion by a natural causeway
passable only at low tide. The chapel of St. Michael is a beautiful 15th
century building, and many relics of the island's colourful history are
preserved in the castle.

CORNWALL: LAND'S END

The most westerly point of England, a headland of granite nine miles
south-west of Penzance. It extends underwater into a group of dangerous
rocks marked, one mile out, by the Longships lighthouse.

ing, had a great college, built in the year 700 by the
Archbishop of York. It had three famous hospitals and
two friaries. There is one church, a very fine one, and
the minster still left; of which a bookseller in the town
was so good as to give me copper-plate representations.
It is still a very pretty town; the market large; the land
all round the country good; and it is particularly famous
for horses; those for speed being shown off here on the
market-days at this time of the year. The farmers and
gentlemen assemble in a very wide street, on the outside
of the western gate of the town; and at a certain time
of the day, the grooms come from their different stables
to show off their beautiful horses; blood horses, coach
horses, hunters, and cart horses; sometimes, they tell
me, forty or fifty in number. The day that I was there
(being late in the season) there were only seven or eight,
or ten at the most. When I was asked at the inn to go
and see " *the horses*," I had no curiosity, thinking it was
such a parcel of horses as we see at a market in the
south; but I found it a sight worth going to see, for,
besides the beauty of the horses, there were the adroitness,
the agility, and the boldness of the grooms, each running
alongside of his horse, with the latter trotting at the
rate of ten or twelve miles an hour, and then swinging
him round, and showing him off to the best advantage.
In short, I was exceedingly gratified by the trip to
Beverley: the day was fair and mild; we went by one
road and came back by another, and I have very seldom
passed a pleasanter day in my life.

WILLIAM COBBETT (1763-1835)
Rural Rides

THE BRONTËS' YORKSHIRE

It would not have been difficult to compile a volume out of the papers left by my sisters, had I, in making the selection, dismissed from my consideration the scruples and the wishes of those whose written thoughts these papers held. But this was impossible: an influence, stronger than could be exercised by any motive of expediency, necessarily regulated the selection. I have, then, culled from the mass only a little poem here and there. The whole makes but a tiny nosegay, and the colour and perfume of the flowers are not such as fit them for festal uses.

It has been already said that my sisters wrote much in childhood and girlhood. Usually, it seems a sort of injustice to expose in print the crude thoughts of the unripe mind, the rude efforts of the unpractised hand; yet I venture to give three little poems of my sister Emily's, written in her sixteenth year, because they illustrate a point in her character.

At that period she was sent to school. Her previous life, with the exception of a single half-year, had been passed in the absolute retirement of a village parsonage, amongst the hills bordering Yorkshire and Lancashire. The scenery of these hills is not grand—it is not romantic; it is scarcely striking. Long low moors, dark with heath, shut-in little valleys, where a stream waters, here and there, a fringe of stunted copse. Mills and scattered cottages chase romance from these valleys; it is only higher up, deep in amongst the ridges of the moors, that Imagination can find rest for the sole of her foot: and even if she finds it there, she must be a solitude-loving raven—no gentle dove. If she demand beauty to inspire her, she must bring it inborn: these moors are too stern to yield any product so delicate. The eye of the gazer must *itself* brim with a "purple light," intense enough to perpetuate the brief flower-flush of August on the heather, or the rare sunset-smile of June; out of his heart must well the freshness, that in latter spring and early summer brightens the bracken, nurtures the moss, and cherishes the starry flowers that spangle for a few weeks the pasture of the moor-sheep. Unless that light and freshness are innate and self-sustained, the drear prospect of a Yorkshire moor will be found as barren of poetic as of agricultural interest: where the love of wild nature is strong, the locality will perhaps be clung to with the more passionate constancy, because from the hill-lover's self comes half its charm.

My sister Emily loved the moors. Flowers brighter than the rose bloomed in the blackest of the heath for her; out of a sullen hollow in a livid hill-side her mind could make an Eden. She found in the bleak solitude many and dear delights; and not the least and best beloved was—liberty.

Liberty was the breath of Emily's nostrils; without it, she perished. The change from her own home to a school, and from her own very noiseless, very secluded, but unrestricted and inartificial mode of life, to one of disciplined routine (though under the kindliest auspices), was what she failed in enduring. Her nature proved here too strong for her fortitude. Every morning when she woke, the vision of home and the moors rushed on her, and darkened and saddened the day that lay before her. Nobody knew what ailed her but me—I knew only too well. In this struggle her health was quickly broken: her white face, attenuated form, and failing strength, threatened rapid decline. I felt in my heart she would die, if she did not go home, and with this conviction obtained her recall. She had only been three months at school; and it was some years before the experiment of sending her from home was again ventured on. After the age of twenty, having meantime studied alone with diligence and perseverance, she went with me to an establishment on the Continent: the same suffering and conflict ensued, heightened by the strong recoil of her upright, heretic and English spirit from the gentle Jesuitry of the foreign and Romish system. Once more she seemed sinking, but this time she rallied through the mere force of resolution: with inward remorse and shame she looked back on her former failure, and resolved to conquer in this second ordeal. She did conquer; but the victory cost her dear. She was never happy till she carried her hard-won knowledge back to the remote English village, the old parsonage house, and desolate Yorkshire hills. A very few years more, and she looked her last on those hills, and breathed her last in that house, and under the aisle of that obscure village church found her last lowly resting-place. Merciful was the decree that spared her when she was a stranger in a strange land, and guarded her dying bed with kindred love and congenial constancy.

The following pieces were composed at twilight, in the school-room, when the leisure of the evening play-hour brought back in full tide the thoughts of home:—

CHARLOTTE BRONTË (1816-1855)
Introduction to the Poems of Emily Brontë

*The following poem was written by Emily while
away at school, aged* 16

A little while, a little while,
  The weary task is put away,
And I can sing and I can smile,
  Alike, while I have holiday.

Where wilt thou go, my harassed heart—
  What thought, what scene invites thee now?
What spot, or near or far apart,
  Has rest for thee, my weary brow?

There is a spot, 'mid barren hills,
  Where winter howls, and driving rain;
But, if the dreary tempest chills,
  There is a light that warms again.

The house is old, the trees are bare,
  Moonless above bends twilight's dome;
But what on earth is half so dear—
  So longed for—as the hearth of home?

The mute bird sitting on the stone,
  The dank moss dripping from the wall,
The thorn-tree gaunt, the walks o'ergrown,
  I love them—how I love them all!

Still, as I mused, the naked room,
  The alien firelight died away;
And from the midst of cheerless gloom,
  I passed to bright, unclouded day.

A little and a lone green lane
  That opened on a common wide;
A distant, dreamy, dim blue chain
  Of mountains circling every side.

A heaven so clear, an earth so calm,
  So sweet, so soft, so hushed an air;
And, deepening still the dream-like charm,
  Wild moor-sheep feeding everywhere.

That was the scene, I knew it well;
  I knew the turfy pathway's sweep,
That, winding o'er each billowy swell,
  Marked out the tracks of wandering sheep.

Could I have lingered but an hour,
    It well had paid a week of toil;
But Truth has banished Fancy's power;
    Restraint and heavy task recoil.

Even as I stood with raptured eye,
    Absorbed in bliss so deep and dear,
My hour of rest had fleeted by,
    And back came labour, bondage, care.

EMILY BRONTË (1818-1848)
Poems

AFTER LIFE'S FITFUL FEVER

My walk home was lengthened by a diversion in the
direction of the kirk. When beneath its walls, I perceived decay had made progress, even in seven months:
many a window showed black gaps deprived of glass;
and slates jutted off, here and there, beyond the right
line of the roof, to be gradually worked off in coming
autumn storms.

I sought, and soon discovered, the three headstones
on the slope next the moor: the middle one grey, and
half buried in heath: Edgar Linton's only harmonised
by the turf and moss creeping up its foot: Heathcliff's
still bare.

I lingered round them, under that benign sky;
watched the moths fluttering among the heath and
harebells, listened to the soft wind breathing through
the grass, and wondered how any one could ever imagine
unquiet slumbers for the sleepers in that quiet earth.

EMILY BRONTË (1818-1848)
Wuthering Heights
(three last paragraphs)

THE MOORLAND MAP

I do not include these casual verses for any merit of their own, but as
a tribute to the native candour which calls hard places by hard
names, and as a tribute, also, to the superb wilderness in which they
occur. That is the northern tip of the North Riding of Yorkshire,
where the country runs up from Swaledale to meet Westmorland and
Durham in Tees-dale beside the great waterfall of High Force and
under the loftiest summit of the Pennine Chain, Cross Fell.

Our maps are music and our northern titles,
  Like wind among the grass and heather, grieve.
Our maps are candid charts of desolation
  And wear the Pennine weather on their sleeve.

There's Howl Moor, Wetshaw, Winterings and Gutters,
  Mirk Fell and Dirty Pool and Hagworm Hill,
Fog Close, Cold Syke, Ravock, and Crooks Altar,
  And Loups and Wham and Whaw and Rotten Gill.

Our maps are music and they sing the miners'
  Old wrestle with the rocks for yield of lead:
There's Old Gang, Windegg, Eskeleth, and Crackpot,
  And Racca Vein, forsaken. They are dead.

Our maps are music and they sing the farmers'
  Long battle to wring fodder from the fell:
There's Stony Mea and Nettlepot and Sour Nook,
  There's Pasture End and Halfpenny, and Farewell.

                              IVOR BROWN (Born 1891)

PRESTON, 1802

GOOD LOOKS AND BAD HABITS

The reference to pot-walling as a basis of civic rights is interesting.
The verb "wall" once meant to boil and the pot-waller was a man
with a fireplace who could keep his own pot boiling: before the

Reform Act of 1832 a householder of a certain degree of wealth could claim to be an elector because of his status as a pot-waller. The word pot-walloper is a lengthening of pot-waller and Devonian pot-wallopers were spoken of as such in a dispute about common land mentioned in the English papers in 1956.

Before we reached Preston, the manufacturers of that town and its neighbourhood appeared in some cotton-works, which we passed in our way; and the frequent recurrence of villages, hamlets, and gentlemen's seats, proved the great population as well as riches of the county. The situation of Preston is at once pleasant and salubrious; on a lofty rising ground, swelling from the river Ribble, who, though but an insignificant stream here, adds greatly to the beauty of the scenery of the surrounding country. This is best seen from the terrace called the *Walks*, the resort of all the beauty and fashion of Preston, in the cool hours of the summer evening, and during the genial influence of the noon-day winter's sun. At the foot of this the river flows, beyond whose banks an unbounded vale is opened to the eye, more remarkable for extent than interest.

Preston is a large, handsome town, with a population of nearly 12,000 and cursed with the right of returning members to the senate. I use the term in its harshest sense, as applied to this place; since the feuds, disagreements, malignity, and unhappiness, which the privilege has occasioned amongst its inhabitants, to the total destruction of all social intercourse, and comfortable neighbourhood, fully justify the expression. For nearly one hundred and fifty years, the question was undetermined whether the elective franchise were vested in the *pot-wallers* (such of the inhabitants as boiled a pot) or the burgesses of the corporation; and during this long period of indecision, as frequently as the election returned, the town was converted into one general scene of confusion, agitation, and hostility; and although four determinations of the House of

SOMERSET: CHEDDAR GORGE

A spectacular pass through the Mendip Hills, famous for its stalactitic caves. Remains found in the caves and neighbourhood show that Cheddar was the site of prehistoric and Roman settlements. Cheddar cheese was first made in the town and district during the 17th century.

SOMERSET: ROYAL CRESCENT, BATH

In the 18th century Beau Nash made Bath a fashionable health resort and these magnificent houses, built 1767-1769 by John Wood the Younger, form one of the most celebrated pieces of English street architecture. The remains of the Roman settlement at Bath are the most complete in Britain.

GLOUCESTERSHIRE: CLIFTON SUSPENSION BRIDGE

Brunel's famous bridge, built in 1832-1864, 250 ft. above the River Avon near Bristol. It has a span of 702 ft. Clifton is a residential suburb of Bristol, the great city and seaport which for centuries has carried on an extensive trade with America and the West Indies.

GLOUCESTERSHIRE: THE PROMENADE, CHELTENHAM

The borough of Cheltenham, a spa and summer resort, lies at the foot of the Cotswold Hills. It is a town of pleasant tree-lined streets and attractive shops, with some fine Georgian buildings. Cheltenham Ladies' College is one of the largest public schools for girls.

Commons have resolved that the right vests in the inhabitants at large, and thus prevented any future contests on that head, yet the *effects* of former ones are still felt in latent heats, which burst into open flame, as often as the political match is applied to this *irritabile genus*, the constituents of Preston. Amongst other privileges attached to the town, it has the peculiar one of holding once in every twenty years a sort of jubilee; which is generally resorted to by all the fashion of the neighbouring country. It continues through the whole month of August; during which the town is filled with amusements; the Mayor gives repeated entertainments; and the Corporation parade occasionally through the streets, attended by the trading companies of the place, arrayed in the *insignia* of their professions. The whole town, in short, is dissolved in idleness and pleasure.

REV. RICHARD WARNER
*A Tour Through the Northern Counties of England
and the Borders of Scotland, 1802*

IN LANCASHIRE, 1698

Celia Fiennes came of a Wiltshire family whose members had fought on the Parliament's side in the Civil War. She went riding round England and traversed the country from Land's End to the Scottish Border. This she did to regain her health by taking air and exercise: being of a serious mind, she also found it well to remark and record what she saw. She thought that travelling and the keeping of travel-diaries should be more widely practised; especially should our legislators know their own land first. Her spelling and grammar are her own and an ungrammatical sentence in what follows does not imply a misprint.

If all persons, both Ladies, much more Gentlemen, would spend some of their tyme in Journeys to visit their native Land, and be curious to inform themselves and make observations of the pleasant prospects, good buildings, different produces and manufactures of each

8

place, with the variety of sports and recreations they are
adapt to, would be a souveraign remedy to cure or
preserve from these epidemick diseases of vapours,
should I add Laziness? It would also form such an Idea
of England, add much to its Glory and Esteem in our
minds and cure the evil itch of over-valueing foreign
parts; at least furnish them with an equivalent to
entertain strangers when amongst us, or inform them
when abroad of their native Country, which has been
often a reproach to the English, ignorance and being
strangers to themselves. Nay the Ladies might have
matter not unworthy their observation, soe subject for
conversation, within their own compass in each county
to which they relate; and thence studdy how to be
serviceable to their neighbours especially the poor
amonge whom they dwell, which would spare them the
uneasye thoughts how to pass away tedious dayes,
and tyme would not be a burthen when not at a card or
dice table, and the fashions and manners of foreign
parts less minded or desired.

But much more requisite is it for Gentlemen in
general service of their country at home or abroad, in
town or country, especially those that serve in parliament, to know and inform themselves the nature of
Land, the Genius of the Inhabitants, so as to promote and
improve Manufacture and Trade suitable to each and
encourage all projects tending thereto, putting in
practice all Laws made for each particular good, maintaining their priviledges, procuring more as requisite;
but to their shame it must be own'd many if not most
are ignorant of anything but the name of the place for
which they serve in parliament; how then can they
speake for or promote their Good or redress their
Grievances? . . . And I shall conclude with a hearty
wish and recommendation to all, but especially my own
Sex, the studdy of those things which tends to improve
the mind and makes our Lives pleasant and comfortable

as well as proffitable in all the Stages and Stations of our
Lives, and render Suffering and Age supportable and
Death less formidable and a future State more happy.

The equestrian authoress was rightly modest about her writing.
Those who knew her, she said, would not expect "exactness and politeness in this book". Exactness presumably refers to syntax rather than
to observation. Her pen ran freely: her sentences are apt to seem
disorderly and interminable: but her vision was fresh and keen and
her curiosity produced a most valuable and agreeable record which
she herself left in manuscript. Her journeys were made between
1685-1703. Roads were bad and signposts scarce. Her courage was
shown by the fact that she made an expedition quite alone. She had
to put up at the roughest inns, and even in a then frequented Spaw
(Spa) like Buxton she noted that "if you have not company enough of
your own to fill a room they will be ready to put others into the same
chamber and sometimes they are so crowded that three or four must
lie in a bed".
She was particularly interested in Spaws and curative waters and
knew them all from Epsom, Tunbridge and Hampstead to Harrogate,
Scarborough and Buxton. Her records were first published under the
title of *Through England on a Side-Saddle in the time of William and
Mary*, by the Hon. Mrs. Emily Griffith in 1885. Christopher Morris,
of King's College, Cambridge, edited and introduced a better text in
1947. (*Cresset Press.*)

Leverpool [Liverpool] which is in Lancashire is built
just on the river Mersy [Mersey], mostly new built
houses of brick and stone after the London fashion;
the first original was a few fishermens houses and now is
grown to a large fine town and but a parish and one
Church, tho' there be 24 streetes in it; there is indeed a
little Chappell and there are a great many Dessenters
in the town; its a very rich trading town the houses of
brick and stone built high and even, that a streete
quite through lookes very handsome, the streetes well
pitched; there are abundance of persons you see very
well dress'd and of good fashion; the streetes are faire
and long, its London in miniature as much as ever I
saw any thing; there is a very pretty Exchange stands
on 8 pillars besides the corners which are each treble

pillars all of stone and its railed in over which is a very handsome Town Hall; over all is a tower and cupillow thats so high that from thence one has the whole view of the town and the country round; in a clear day you may see the Isle of Man. . . .

. . . Wiggons [Wigan] is another pretty market town built of stone and brick; here it is that the fine Channell [Cannel] Coales are in perfection, burns as light as a candle—set the coales together with some fire and it shall give a snap and burn up light—of this coale they make saltcellars standishes and many boxes and things which are sent about for Curiositys and sold in London and are often offer'd in the exchanges in company with white or black marble, and most people deceived by them, which have not been in those countrys and know it, but such persons discover it and will call for a candle to trye them wheather marble or coale; its very finely pollish'd and lookes much like jett or ebany wood for which one might easily take it when in boxes etc.; I bought some of them for Curiosity sake.

2 mile off Wigon towards Warrington—which was some of my way back againe but for the Curiosity's sake I did—is the Burning Well which burns like brandy; its a little sorry hole in one of the grounds 100 yards from the road that comes from Warrington to Wiggon, just by a hedge or banck, its full of dirt and mud almost but the water continually bubbles up as if it were a pott boyling which is the spring or severall springs in that place, nevertheless I felt the water and it was a Cold Spring; the man which shewed it me with a dish tooke out a good quantety of the water and threw away and then, with a piece of rush he lighted by a candle that he brought in a lanthorne, he set the water in the well on fire, and it burn'd blewish just like spirits and continued a good while, but by reason of the great raines that fell the night before the spring was weaker and had

not thrown off the raine water, otherwise it used to
flame all over the well a good height now it burnt
weaker; however at last the wind blew out the mans
candle, and he severall tymes lighted the bitt of rush
or splinter of wood by the flame that burnt in the well;
this is a little unacountable, I apprehend its a sort of an
unctious matter in the earth and soe through its veines
the springs run which causes it so to burn, for I observ'd
when they dug into the banck and opened the sort of
clay or mudd it burnt fiercer and more. . . .

. . . From Eland [Elland] I went to the Blackstone
Edge 8 mile; when I had gone 3 of the miles I came to a
greate precipice or vast descent of a hill as full of stones
as if paved and exceedingly steep, I take it to be much
steeper than Blackstone Edge tho' not soe long; the end
of this steep was a little village all stony alsoe; these
parts have some resemblance to Darbyshire only here are
more woody places and inclosures: then I came to
Blackstone Edge noted all over England for a dismal
high precipice and steep in the ascent and descent on
either end; its a very moorish ground all about and
even just at the top, tho' so high that you travel on a
Causey, which is very troublesome as its a moist ground,
soe as is usual on these high hills they stagnate the aire
and hold mist and raines almost perpetually; as I
ascended the morning was pretty faire but a sort of mist
met me and small raine just as I attained the top which
made me feare a wet day and that the aire would have
been so thick to have quite lost me the sight of the
Country, but when I attained the top where is a great
heap raised up which parts Yorkshire, and there I
entred Lancashire, the mist began to lessen, and as I
descended on this side the fog more and more went off
and a little raine fell, tho' at a little distance in our
view the sun shone on the vale which indeed is of a large
extent here, and the advantage of soe high a hight which

is at least 2 mile up, discovers the grounds beneath as a fruitfull valley full of inclosures and cut hedges and trees. . . .

. . . Manchester looks exceedingly well at the entrance, very substantiall buildings, the houses are not very lofty but mostly of brick and stone, the old houses are timber work, there is a very large Church all stone and stands high soe that walking round the Church yard you see the whole town; there is good carving in wood in the Quire of the Church and severall little Chappells, wherein are some little Monuments; there is one that was the founder of the Colledge and Library where hangs his picture, for just by the Church is the Colledge (Chetham Hospital), which is a pretty neate building with a large space for the boys to play in and a good garden walled in; there are 60 Blew Coate boys in it, I saw their appartments and was in the cellar and dranck of their beer which was very good I alsoe saw the kitchen and saw their bread cutting for their supper and their piggins[1] for their beer; there is a Cloyster round a Court; in it is a large roome called a parlour and over it a large room for the Judges to eate in, and also for the roomes for heareing and dispatching their buissness; there is a large Library 2 long walls full of books on each side there is alsoe the globes at the end and maps, there is alsoe a long whispering trumpet and there I saw the skinn of the Rattle Snake 6 foote long, with many other Curiositys, their anatomy of a man wired together, a jaw of a shark; there was a very fine clock and weather glass; out of the Library there are leads on which one has the sight of the town which is large as alsoe the other town that lyes below it called Salfor [Salford], and is divided from this by the river Uvall [Irwell] over which is a stone bridge with many arches.

Salfor has only a little Chappell of Ease and is belonging

[1] Mugs

o the Parish of Manchester; there is another river
alled the Shark (Irk), which runs into the Uval (Irwell);
he Market place is large it takes up two streetes length
vhen the Market is kept for their Linnen Cloth Cotten
Tickings Incles,[2] which is the manufacture of the town;
tere is a very fine schoole for young Gentlewomen as
good as any in London and musick and danceing, and
things are very plenty here this is a thriveing place.

CELIA FIENNES (1662-1741)
The Journeys of Celia Fiennes

[2] Linen tape

TEIGNMOUTH
seen from the Ness

raed, as was noted in connection with his London poem, *Good
Night to the Season*, had family roots in South Devon. The town of
Teignmouth was favoured in his time and John Keats spent some
months there, for his health's sake, in 1819. Now much more exposed
o mass-visitation, it retains some of its Georgian charm.

He looked across the river stream;
    A little town was there,
O'er which the morning's earliest beam
    Was wandering fresh and fair;
No architect of classic school
Had pondered there with line and rule;
And, stranger still, no modern master
Wasted there his lath and plaster;
The buildings in strange order lay,
As if the streets had lost their way,
Fantastic, puzzling, narrow, muddy,
Excess of toil from lack of study,
Where Fashion's very newest fangles
Had no conception of right angles.
But still about that humble place
There was a look of rustic grace;

'Twas sweet to see the sports and labours
And morning greetings of good neighbours,
The seamen mending sails and oars,
The matrons knitting at the doors,
The invalids enjoying dips,
The children launching tiny ships,
The beldames clothed in rags and wrinkles,
Investigating periwinkles.

WINTHROP MACKWORTH PRAED (1802-1839)
Fragments of a Descriptive Poem

WITH THE WORDSWORTHS

It is frequently said nowadays that the English Spring, with its bitter winds extending until May, is a new discomfort. Did not the poets continually praise sweet, jocund Spring, that came with April? It is perhaps consoling to realise that May has been snowy before now.

Friday, 14th May.—A very cold morning—hail and snow showers all day. We went to Brothers wood, intending to get plants, and to go along the shore of the lake to the foot. We did go a part of the way, but there was no pleasure in stepping along that difficult sauntering road in this ungenial weather. We turned again, and walked backwards and forwards in Brothers wood. William tired himself with seeking an epithet for the cuckoo. I sate a while upon my last summer seat, the mossy stone. William's, unemployed, beside me, and the space between, where Coleridge has so often lain. The oak trees are just putting forth yellow knots of leaves. The ashes with their flowers passing away, and leaves coming out; marsh marigolds in full glory; the little star plant, a star without a flower. We took home a great load of gowans, and planted them about the orchard. After dinner, I worked bread, then came and mended stockings beside William; he fell asleep.

After tea I walked to Rydale for letters. It was a strange

night. The hills were covered over with a slight covering
of hail or snow, just so as to give them a hoary winter
look with the black rocks. The woods looked miserable,
the coppices green as grass, which looked quite unnatural,
and they seemed half shrivelled up, as if they shrank
from the air. O, thought I! what a beautiful thing
God has made winter to be, by stripping the trees, and
letting us see their shapes and forms. What a freedom
does it seem to give to the storms! There were several
new flowers out, but I had no pleasure in looking at
them. I walked as fast as I could back again with my
letter from S.H. . . . Met William at the top of White
Moss. . . . Near ten when we came in. William and
Molly had dug the ground and planted potatoes in my
absence. We wrote to Coleridge; sent off bread and
frocks to the C's. Went to bed at half past eleven.
William very nervous. After he was in bed, haunted
with altering *The Rainbow*.

DOROTHY WORDSWORTH (1771-1855)
Journal

THE DAFFODILS

I wandered lonely as a cloud
That floats on high o'er vales and hills,
When all at once I saw a crowd,
A host, of golden daffodils;
Beside the lake, beneath the trees,
Fluttering and dancing in the breeze.

Continuous as the stars that shine
And twinkle on the milky way,
They stretched in never-ending line
Along the margin of a bay;
Ten thousand saw I at a glance,
Tossing their heads in sprightly dance.

The waves beside them danced; but they
Out-did the sparkling waves in glee:
A poet could not but be gay,
In such a jocund company:
I gazed—and gazed—but little thought
What wealth the show to me had brought:

For oft, when on my couch I lie
In vacant or in pensive mood,
They flash upon that inward eye
Which is the bliss of solitude;
And then my heart with pleasure fills,
And dances with the daffodils.

WILLIAM WORDSWORTH (1770-1850)
The Daffodils

Here is Dorothy Wordsworth's prose description of the same scene; it does not fall behind her brother's poetry. William paid full tribute to his sister's vision. "She gave me ears, she gave me eyes."

When we were in the woods beyond Gowbarrow Park we saw a few daffodils close to the water-side. We fancied that the lake had floated the seeds ashore, and that the little colony had so sprung up. But as we went along there were more and yet more; and at last, under the boughs of the trees, we saw that there was a long belt of them along the shore, about the breadth of a country turnpike road. I never saw daffodils so beautiful. They grew among the mossy stones about and about them; some rested their heads upon these stones, as on a pillow, for weariness; and the rest tossed and reeled and danced, and seemed as if they verily laughed with the wind, that blew upon them over the lake; they looked so gay, ever glancing, ever changing. This wind blew directly over the lake to them. There was here and there a little knot, and a few stragglers higher up; but they were so few as not to disturb the simplicity, unity, and life of that one busy highway. We rested again and again.

DOROTHY WORDSWORTH (1771–1855)
Journal

PEACE BY ULLSWATER

　　　　　　　. . . Not a breath of air
Ruffles the bosom of this leafy glen.
From the brook's margin, wide around, the trees
Are steadfast as the rocks; the brook itself,
Old as the hills that feed it from afar,
Doth rather deepen than disturb the calm
Where all things else are still and motionless.
And yet, even now, a little breeze, perchance
Escaped from boisterous winds that rage without,
Has entered, by the sturdy oaks unfelt,
But in its gentle touch how sensitive
Is the light ash! that, pendent from the brow
Of yon dim cave, in seeming silence makes
A soft eye-music of slow-waving boughs,
Powerful almost as vocal harmony
To stay the wanderer's steps and soothe his thoughts.

WILLIAM WORDSWORTH (1770–1850)
Airey Force Valley

STORM OVER LANGDALE

While at our pastoral banquet thus we sate
Fronting the window of that little cell,
I could not, ever and anon, forbear
To glance an upward look on two huge Peaks,
That from some other vale peered into this.

"Those lusty twins," exclaimed our host, "if here
It were your lot to dwell, would soon become
Your prized companions. Many are the notes
Which, in his tuneful course, the wind draws forth
From rocks, woods, caverns, heaths, and dashing shores;
And well those lofty brethren bear their part
In the wild concert—chiefly when the storm
Rides high; then all the upper air they fill
With roaring sound, that ceases not to flow,
Like smoke, along the level of the blast,
In mighty current; theirs, too, is the song
Of stream and headlong flood that seldom fails;
And, in the grim and breathless hour of noon,
Methinks that I have heard them echo back
The thunder's greeting. Nor have nature's laws
Left them ungifted with a power to yield
Music of finer tone; a harmony,
So do I call it, though it be the hand
Of silence, though there be no voice;—the clouds,
The mist, the shadows, light of golden suns,
Motions of moonlight, all come thither—touch,
And have an answer—thither come, and shape
A language not unwelcome to sick hearts
And idle spirits:—there the sun himself,
At the calm close of summer's longest day,
Rests his substantial orb;—between those heights
And on the top of either pinnacle,
More keenly than elsewhere in night's blue vault,
Sparkle the stars, as of their station proud.

WILLIAM WORDSWORTH (1770-1850)
The Excursion

AUTUMN ON THE WOLDS

Calm is the morn without a sound,
   Calm as to suit a calmer grief,
   And only thro' the faded leaf
The chestnut pattering to the ground:

Calm amid deep peace on this high wold,
   And on these dews that drench the furze,
   And all the silvery gossamers
That twinkle into green and gold:

Calm and still light on yon great plain
   That sweeps with all its autumn bowers,
   And crowded farms and lessening towers,
To mingle with the bounding main:

Calm and deep peace in this wide air,
   These leaves that redden to the fall;
   And in my heart, if calm at all,
If any calm, a calm despair:
          ALFRED, LORD TENNYSON (1809-1892)
          In Memoriam

WINTER

The frost is here,
The fuel is dear,
And woods are sear,
And fires burn clear,
And frost is here
And has bitten the heel of the going year.

Bite, frost, bite!
You roll up away from the light
The blue wood-louse, and the plump dormouse,
And the bees are still'd, and the flies are kill'd,
And you bite far into the heart of the house,
But not into mine.

Bite, frost, bite!
The woods are all the searer,
The fuel is all the dearer,
The fires are all the clearer,
My spring is all the nearer,
You have bitten into the heart of the earth,
But not into mine.

ALFRED, LORD TENNYSON (1809-1892)
Maud

THE COUNTRY BOY

HERMIONE

                    Come, I'll question you
Of my lord's tricks and yours when you were boys:
You were pretty lordlings then?

POLIXENES

                    We were, fair queen,
Two lads that thought there was no more behind
But such a day to-morrow as to-day,
And to be boy eternal.

HERMIONE

Was not my lord the verier wag o' the two?

POLIXENES

We were as twinn'd lambs that did frisk i' the sun,
And bleat the one at the other: what we changed

Was innocence for innocence; we knew not
The doctrine of ill-doing, no, nor dream'd
That any did. Had we pursued that life,
And our weak spirits ne'er been higher rear'd
With stronger blood, we should have answer'd heaven
Boldly, "Not guilty" . . .

WILLIAM SHAKESPEARE (1564-1616)
The Winter's Tale

Thence too when high wind through the black clouds'
    pouring,
Bowing the strong trees' creaking joints, went roaring,
Adventure was to splash through the sightless lane
When church-bells filled a pause of wind and rain,
And once within the venerable walls
To hear the alms without like waterfalls,
While the cold arches murmured every prayer,
And Advent hymns bade the round world prepare,
Prepare! The next day with pale seas amazed
We scarce had marvelled as we gaped and gazed
If this had been the tempest harbinger
Of the world's end and final Arbiter:
The pollards in the yellow torrent drowning,
The weir's huge jaw a-gnashing, all heaven frowning.

But there at length, beside that thunderous weir,
Our lot was cast, and no less generous here
Came each long day; not even the hours we spent
Under old Grammar's eye unkindly went.
We found his learning dry, in faith, and hit
Disaster in our sleights for leavening it;
But the big desks cut with heroic names,
The gilded panel trumpeting past fames,
Shields, pictures, solemn books of stars and sages,
Kindled our pride in sense of mightier ages,

That school had seen, and cannot see again.
Fair, fair befall her, though no urchin pen
Crawl through the summer hours beneath her beams,
Nor playground roystering shout bestir her dreams;
Honoured among her aspens may she rise,
And her red walls long soothe the traveller's eyes.

Thence issued we among the scampering crew,
And crossed the green, and from the bridge down threw
Our dinner crumbs to waiting roach; or soft
Marauding climbed the cobwebbed apple-loft,
And the sweet smell of Blenheims lapped in straw
Made stolen pleasure seem a natural law;
Escape and plunder hurried us at last
To the weir-cottage where our lot was cast,
Poor as church mice, yet rich at every turn,
Who never guessed that man was made to mourn.
In this same country as the time fulfilled
When hops like ribands on the maypole frilled
Their colonnaded props mile after mile,
And tattered armies gathered to the spoil,
We too invaded the green arbours ere
The day had glistened on earth's dewy hair,
And through the heat we picked and picked apace,
To fill our half-bin and not lose the chace,
While our bin partner, fierce of eye and tongue,
Disliked our style and gave " when I was young."
And all about the clearing setts revealed
The curious colours of the folk afield,
The raven hair, the flamy silk, the blue
Washed purple with all weathers; crime's dark crew;
Babes at the breast; old sailors chewing quids;
And hyacinth eyes beneath soon-dropt eyelids.
The conquest sped, the bramblings, goldings small,
The heavy fuggles to the bins came all,
Garden past garden heard the measurer's horn
Blow truce—advance! until a chillier morn

Saw the last wain load up with pokes and go,
And an empty saddened field looked out below
On trees where smouldered the quick fever-tinge
Of Autumn, on the river's glaucous fringe,
And our own cottage, its far lattice twinkling
Across tired stubble sown with sheep-bells' tinkling
On airy wings the warning spirit sighed,
But we, we heard not, thinking of Christmastide.

A love I had, as childhood ever will,
And our first meeting I'll remember still;
When to the farmhouse first we went, the may
With white and red lit hedgerows all the way,
And there I saw her, in a red-may cloak
To church going by; so delicately she spoke,
So gracefully stept, so innocent-gay was her look,
I took a flower; she put it in her book.
And after, many eves, we walked for hours
Like loving flowers among the other flowers,
And blushed for pride when other girls and boys
Laughed at us sweethearts in the playhour's noise—
No more, this was a silly simple thing;
Those two can never now walk so in spring;
But to look back to child with child primrosing
Is all the sweetness of each spring's unclosing.

EDMUND BLUNDEN (Born 1896)
English Poems

BINSEY POPLARS
felled 1879

My aspens dear, whose airy cages quelled,
Quelled or quenched in leaves the leaping sun,
All felled, felled, are all felled;
   Of a fresh and following folded rank
      Not spared, not one
      That dandled a sandalled

Shadow that swam or sank
On meadow and river and wind-wandering
weed-winding bank.

O if we but knew what we do
    When we delve or hew—
Hack and rack the growing green!
    Since country is so tender
To touch, her being so slender,
That, like this sleek and seeing ball
But a prick will make no eye at all,
Where we, even where we mean
        To mend her we end her,
    When we hew or delve:
After-comers cannot guess the beauty been.
    Ten or twelve, only ten or twelve
        Strokes of havoc unselve
            The sweet especial scene,
        Rural scene, a rural scene,
        Sweet especial rural scene.

                    GERARD MANLEY HOPKINS (1844-1889)
                                            Poems

DORSET FOR DAIRIES

The journey over the intervening uplands and lowlands
of Egdon, when she (Tess) reached them, was a more
troublesome walk than she had anticipated, the distance
being actually but a few miles. In two hours, after
sundry wrong turnings, she found herself on a summit
commanding the long-sought-for vale, the Valley of the
Great Dairies, the valley in which milk and butter
grew to rankness, and were produced more profusely,
if less delicately, than at her home—the verdant plain so
well watered by the river Var or Froom.

It was intrinsically different from the Vale of Little

Dairies, Blackmoor Vale, which, save during her disastrous sojourn at Trantridge, she had exclusively known till now. The world was drawn in a larger pattern here. The enclosures numbered fifty acres instead of ten, the farmsteads were more extended, and groups of cattle formed tribes here about; there only families. These myriads of cows stretching under her eyes from the far east to the far west outnumbered any she had ever seen at one glance before. The green lea was speckled as thickly with them as a canvas by Van Alsloot or Sallaert with burghers. The ripe hue of the red and dun kine absorbed the evening sunlight, which the white-coated animals returned to the eye in rays almost dazzling, even at the distant elevation on which she stood.

' The bird's-eye perspective before her was not so luxuriantly beautiful, perhaps, as that other one which she knew so well; yet it was more cheering. It lacked the intensely blue atmosphere of the rival vale, and its heavy soils and scents; the new air was clear, bracing, ethereal. The river itself, which nourished the grass and cows of these renowned dairies, flowed not like the streams in Blackmoor. Those were slow, silent, often turbid; flowing over beds of mud into which the incautious wader might sink and vanish unawares. The Var waters were clear as the pure River of Life shown to the Evangelist, rapid as the shadow of a cloud, with pebbly shallows that prattled to the sky all day long. There the water-flower was the lily; the crow-foot here.

. . . Suddenly there arose from all parts of the lowland a prolonged and repeated call—
"Waow! waow! waow!"
From the furthest east to the furthest west the cries spread as if by contagion, accompanied in some cases by the barking of a dog. It was not the expression of the valley's consciousness that beautiful Tess had arrived,

but the ordinary anouncement of milking-time—
half-past four o'clock, when the dairymen set about
getting in the cows.

The red and white herd nearest at hand, which had
been phlegmatically waiting for the call, now trooped
towards the steading in the background, their great
bags of milk swinging under them as they walked.
Tess followed slowly in their rear, and entered the
barton by the open gate through which they had
entered before her. Long thatched sheds stretched
round the enclosure, their slopes encrusted with vivid
green moss, and their eaves supported by wooden posts
rubbed to a glossy smoothness by the flanks of infinite
cows and calves of bygone years, now passed to an
oblivion almost inconceivable in its profundity. Between
the posts were ranged the milchers, each exhibiting
herself at the present moment to a whimsical eye in the
rear as a circle on two stalks, down the centre of which a
switch moved pendulum-wise; while the sun, lowering
itself behind this patient row, threw their shadows
accurately inwards upon the wall. Thus it threw
shadows of these obscure and homely figures every
evening with as much care over each contour as if it
had been the profile of a Court beauty on a palace wall;
copied them as diligently as it had copied Olympian
shapes on marble *façades* long ago, or the outline of
Alexander, Cæsar, and the Pharoahs.

They were the less restful cows that were stalled.
Those that would stand still of their own will were
milked in the middle of the yard, where many of such
better behaved ones stood waiting now—all prime
milchers, such as were seldom seen out of this valley,
and not always within it; nourished by the succulent
feed which the water-meads supplied at this prime
season of the year. Those of them that were spotted
with white reflected the sunshine in dazzling brilliancy,
and the polished brass knobs on their horns glittered

with something of military display. Their large-
veined udders hung ponderous as sandbags, the teats
sticking out like the legs of a gipsy's crock; and as
each animal lingered for her turn to arrive the milk
oozed forth and fell in drops to the ground.

THOMAS HARDY (1840-1928)
Tess of the D'Urbervilles

IN PRAISE OF RAIN

Now be you thankful, who in England dwell,
That to the starving trees and thirsty grass
Even at summer's height come cloudy fleets
Moist from the wastes of the Atlantic swell,
To spill their rain, and pass,
While fields renew their sweets.
Not as the Arab watches in despair
The scrannel promise of his harvest parch
Even before the sun climbs high in March
And only dust-notes dim the scorching air.
He who must yoke to wooden water-wheel
The bullock or the camel, turning slow
But constant in the round and trodden groove,
Slumberous as hypnotics move,
To the lamentation of the whining cogs,
While in the runnels rapid waters flow,
Lapped by the timid tongue of pariah dogs,
And in the trenches spread, to quench and heal.
Or as the Persian from his hills of snow
Gathers the freshet to the jealous pool,
And floods his garden with a hundred streams
Under the plane-trees when the evening's cool,
But still for all his pains
Sees roses languish with returning noon,
And in the heat of June
The leaves already flutter from the planes.

Such arid months as only exiles know,
With longing for the smell of English rains,
Some drops to lay the dust, some shower to stir
The earthly redolence of soaking loam,
Some saddening of the sky before the shower,
Some dew to hold a footprint for an hour;
When through the stones the lizard and the snakd
Rustle their brittle length, and crickets chirr
Day after day, and broom-pods crackling break,
Scavenger kites hang waiting for the dead
Over the old and solitary ram,
And the mule picks his way up the dried river-bed,—
This know, and know then how the heart can ache
With pining for the woods and clouds of home.
If I could take my England, and could wring
One living moment from her simple year,
One moment only, whether of place or time,
—One winter coppice feathery with rime,
One shred of dawn in spring—
Then should my voice find echo in English ear;
Then might I say, "That which I love, I am."

V. SACKVILLE-WEST (Born 1892)
The Land

APRIL IN CORNWALL

The cracked bell rings to Lenten service over
The April fields, lifting the mists that hover

Across the dun distances from wood to wood.
Each quiet stroke renews the familiar mood

Of a dream that has been dreamed, and again I hear
The interior, murmuring complaint of prayer.

Now the dark woods of Duporth are pierced with late
Innumerable sweet voices, separate

And clear above the burden of the sea.
The long sea-swell rolls in its symmetry

Of surf, breaking the springwhite flowers of foam
Upon the iron rocks amid the fume

And thunder of spring upon the heaving sea.
The sheltered slope is strewn with sticks that the

April winds have sown: the trees are yet bare.
A night-moth voyages on the uncertain air,

Seeking the dizzy region of the cliffs.
Somewhere in the domed sky a gull laughs

Above the turning world, and with shrill mirth
That the sea should mumble the corners of the earth.

A. L. ROWSE (Born 1903)
Poems of a Decade

Gardens, Flowers and Trees

THE EXCELLENT ART
OF SIMPLING

To the courteous and well willing Readers.

Although my paines hav not been spent (courteous Reader) in the gracious discoverie of golden Mines, nor in the tracing after silver veines, whereby my native country might be inriched with such merchandise as it hath most in request and admiration; yet hath my labour (I trust) been otherwise profitably imploied, in descrying of such a harmelesse treasure of herbes, trees and plants, as the earth frankely without violence offereth unto our most necessary uses.

Harmelesse I call them, because they were such delights as man in the perfectest state of his innocence did erst injoy: and treasure I may well terme them seeing both Kings and Princes have esteemed them as Jewels; sith wise men have made their whole life as a pilgrimage to attaine to the knowledge of them: by the which they have gained the hearts of all, and opened the mouthes of many, in commendation of those rare vertues which are contained in these terrestriall creatures. I confesse blind *Pluto*[1] is now adaies more sought after than quicke sighted *Phoebus*:[2] and yet this dusty mettall, or excrement of the earth (which was first deepely buried least it should be an eie-sore to grieve the corrupt heart of man) by forcible entry made into the bowels of the earth, is rather snatched at of man to his owne destruction, than directly sent of God to the comfort

[1] The God of Wealth   [2] The God of Light

of this life. And yet behold in the compassing of this worldly drosse, what care, what cost, what adventures, what mysticall proofes, and chymicall trials are set abroach; when as notwithstanding the chiefest end is but uncertaine wealth.

Contrariwise, in the expert knowledge of herbes, what pleasure still renewed with variety? what small expence? what security? and yet what an apt and ordinary meanes to conduct man to that most desired benefit of health? which as I devoutly wish unto my native countrey, and to the carfull nursing mother of the same; so having bent my labours to the benefit of such as are studiously practised in the conservation thereof, I thought it a chief pointe of my dutie, thus out of my poore store to offer up these my far-fetched experiments, together with mine owne countries unknowne treasure, combined in this compendious Herball (not unprofitable though unpolished) unto your wise constructions and courteous considerations. The drift whereof is a ready introduction to that excellent art of Simpling,[1] which is neither so base nor contemptible as perhaps the English name may seeme to intimate: but such as it is, altogether hath beene a study for the wisest, an exercise for the noblest, a pastime for the best.

JOHN GERARD (1543-1612)
The Herball

[1] Gathering herbs, especially curative herbs

TABACO OR
THE HEN-BANE OF PERU

The bad effects of smoking upon health have been so much stressed lately that one notes with interest the Elizabethan view of tobacco's curative qualities. Gerard, however, recommends the extraction and drinking of tobacco-juice, not the smoking of the dried leaf.

The plant was introduced into Europe from America in 1570, and named Nicotiana after Nicot, a French Ambassador in Portugal who arranged for seeds to be brought over. Sir Walter Raleigh popularised smoking in England.

Nicolaus Monardis saith, that the leaves hereof are a remedie for the paine of head called the Megram or Migram, that hath bin of long continuance.

It is a present remedie for the fits of the mother, it mitigateth the paine of the gout, if it be rosted in hot embers, and applied to the grieved part.

It is likewise a remedy for the tooth-ache, if the tooth and gumbs be rubbed with a linnen cloth dipped in the juice, and afterward a round ball of the leaves laid unto the place.

The weight of foure ounces of the juice hereof drunke procureth afterward a long and sound sleepe, as wee have learned of a friend by observation, who affirmed, That a strong countreyman of a middle age having a dropsie, took it, and being wakened out of his sleepe called for meat and drinke, and after that became perfectly cured.

Moreover, the same man reported, That he had cured many countreymen of agues, with the distilled water of the leaves drunke a little while before the fit.

Likewise there is an oile to be taken out of the leaves that healeth merri-galls, kibed heeles, and such like.

It is good against poyson, and taketh away the malignitie thereof, if the juice be given to drink, or the wounds made by venomous beasts be washed therewith.

The dry leaves are used to be taken in a pipe set on fire and suckt into the stomacke, and thrust forth againe at the nosthrils, against the paines in the head, rheumes, aches in any part of the bodie, whereof soever the originall proceed, whether from France, Italy, Spaine, Indies, or from our familiar and best knowne diseases. Those leaves do palliate or ease for a time, but never perform any cure absolutely: for although they empty the body of humors, yet the cause of the griefe cannot be so taken away.

. . . Some use to drink it (as it is termed) for wantonnesse, or rather custome, and cannot forbeare it, no not in the midst of their dinner; which kinde of taking is unwholsome and very dangerous: although to take it seldom, and that physically, is to be tolerated, and may do some good: but I commend the syrrup above this fume or smoky medicine.

It is taken of some physically in a pipe for that purpose once in a day at the most, and that in the morning fasting, against paines in the head, stomack, and griefe in the brest and lungs: against catarrhs and rheums, and such as have gotten cold and hoarsenesse.

Some have reported, That it doth little prevaile against an hot disease, and that it profiteth an hot complexion nothing at all. But experience hath not shewed as yet that it is injurious unto either.

They that have seene the proofe hereof, have credibly reported, That when the Moores and Indians have fainted either for want of food or rest, this hath bin a present remedie unto them, to supply the one, and to help them to the other.

The priests and Inchanters of the hot countries do take the fume thereof until they be drunke, that after they have lien for dead three or foure houres, they may tell the people what wonders, visions, or illusions they have seen, and so give them a prophetical direction or foretelling (if we may trust the Divell) of the successe of their businesse.

The juyce or distilled water of the first kind is very good against catarrhs, the dizzinesse of the head, and rheums that fall downe the eies, against the pain called the Megram, if either you apply it unto the temples, or take one or two green leaves, or a dry leafe moistened in wine, and dried cunningly upon the embers, and laid thereto.

It cleeres the sight, and taketh away the webs and spots thereof, being annointed with the juyce bloud-warme.

The oile or juyce dropped into the eares is good against deafnesse; a cloth dipped in the same and layd upon the face, taketh away the lentils, rednesse, and spots thereof.

Many notable medicines are made hereof against the old and inveterat cough, against asthmaticall or pectorall griefes, all which if I should set downe at large, would require a peculiar volume.

It is also given unto such as are accustomed to swoune.

It is used in outward medicines, either the herbe boiled with oile, wax, rosin, and turpentine, as before is set downe in yellow Henbane, or the extraction thereof with salt, oile, balsam, the distilled water, and such like, against tumours, apostumes, old ulcers of hard curation, botches, scabbes, stinging with nettles, carbuncles, poisoned arrowes, and wounds made with gunnes or any other weapons.

It is excellent good in burnings and scaldings with fire, water, oile, lightning, or such like, boiled with hogges grease into the forme of an ointment, as I have often prooved, and found most true; adding a little of the juice of Thorne-Apple leaves, spreading it upon a cloth and so applying it.

JOHN GERARD (1543-1612)
The Herball

TRAVELLERS' JOY

The Travellers' Joy is found in the borders of fields among thorns and briers, almost in every hedge, as you go from Gravesend to Canterbury in Kent; in many places of Essex, and in most of these southerly parts about London, but not in the north of England that

I can hear of. . . . The flowers come forth in July;
the beauty thereof appeareth in November and December.
It is called commonly *Viorna quasi vias ornans*, of decking
and adorning ways and hedges, where people travel,
and thereupon I have named it The Travellers' Joy.

JOHN GERARD (1545-1612)
The Herball

WILLOW

Perhaps it is the melody in the name, as well as the visible suggestion
of weeping, that has made the willow so dear to English poets. The
willow wails frequently and finely in Shakespeare's plays: how
magical sounds Viola's willow-cabin at Olivia's gate! An oaken
cabin, perhaps more serviceable, would not have made the same
music. "Sing all a green willow," cried Emilia in the hour of doom.
Ophelia was drowned beneath a willow. And in this song by Sir
William Davenant, who liked to be thought Shakespeare's natural
son, the willow is once more a grave-side tree.

> Roses and pinks will be strewn where you go;
> Whilst I walk in shades of willow, willow.
>   When I am dead let him that did slay me
>   Be but so good as kindly to lay me
>   There where neglected lovers mourn,
>   Where lamps and hallowed tapers burn,
>   Where clerks and choirs sad dirges sing,
>   Where sweetly bells at burials ring.

>   My rose of youth is gone,
>   Withered as soon as blown.
>   Lovers, go ring my knell,
>   Beauty and love, farewell.
>   And lest virgins forsaken
>   Should perhaps be mistaken
> In seeking my grave, alas! let them know
> I lie near a shade of willow, willow.

SIR WILLIAM DAVENANT (1606-1668)
Song from " The Unfortunate Lovers"

POET'S CHOICE (1)

See where she sits upon the grassy green,
    (O seemly sight!)
Yclad in scarlet, like a maiden Queen,
    And ermines white:
Upon her head a crimson coronet
With damask roses and daffadillies set,
    Bay leaves between,
    And primroses green,
Embellish the sweet violet.

Bring hither the pink and purple columbine,
    With gillyflowers;
Bring coronations and sops-in-wine
    Worn of paramours;
Strew me the ground with daffadowndillies
And cowslips and kingcups and lovèd lilies;
    The pretty pawnce
    And the chevisaunce
Shall match with the fair flower de lys.

EDMUND SPENSER (1552-1599)
The Shepheardes Calender

POET'S CHOICE (2)

PERDITA
   . . . Here's flowers for you;
Hot lavender, mints, savory, marjoram;
The marigold, that goes to bed wi' the sun,
And with him rises weeping: these are flowers
Of middle summer, and, I think, they are given
To men of middle age. Y'are very welcome.

CAMILLO

I should leave grazing, were I of your flock,
And only live by gazing.

PERDITA

Out, alas!
You'ld be so lean, that blasts of January
Would blow you through and through.—No, my fair'st
      friend,
I would I had some flowers o' the spring that might
Become your time of day;—and yours, and yours,
That wear upon your virgin branches yet
Your maidenheads growing:—O Proserpina,
For the flowers now, that, frighted, thou lett'st fall
From Dis's wagon! Daffodils,
That come before the swallow dares, and take
The winds of March with beauty; violets dim,
But sweeter than the lids of Juno's eyes
Or Cytherea's breath; pale primroses,
That die unmarried, ere they can behold
Bright Phoebus in his strength,—a malady
Most incident to maids; bold oxlips and
The crown-imperial, lilies of all kinds,
The flower-de-luce being one.

WILLIAM SHAKESPEARE (1564-1616)
The Winter's Tale

No, I will rob Tellus of her weed,
To strew thy green with flowers; the yellows, blues,
The purple violets, and marigolds,
Shall, as a carpet, hang upon thy grave,
While summer days do last.

WILLIAM SHAKESPEARE (1564-1616)
Pericles

POET'S CHOICE (3)

Now the lusty spring is seen;
  Golden yellow, gaudy blue,
Daintily invite the view.
Everywhere on every green,
Roses blushing as they blow,
  And enticing men to pull,
Lilies whiter than the snow,
    Woodbines of sweet honey full:
      All love's emblems, and all cry,
      "Ladies, if not plucked, we die".

Yet the lusty spring hath stayed;
  Blushing red and purest white
  Daintily to love invite
Every woman, every maid.
Cherries kissing as they grow,
  And inviting men to taste,
Apples even ripe below,
    Winding gently to the waist:
      All love's emblems, and all cry,
      "Ladies, if not plucked, we die."

JOHN FLETCHER (1579-1625)
Song from the tragedy of " Valentinian "

POET'S CHOICE (4)

Ye valleys low, where the mild whispers use
Of shades and wanton winds and gushing brooks,
On whose fresh lap the swart star sparely looks,
Throw hither all your quaint enamell'd eyes,

GLOUCESTERSHIRE: ARLINGTON ROW

The Cotswold Hills, a limestone range between Bristol and Stratford-on-Avon shelter many lovely villages such as this, built from the mellow Cotswold limestone with its warm and friendly appearance. Arlington lies near Bibury, about 6 miles north-east of Cirencester.

HEREFORDSHIRE: THE THREE COUNTIES SHOW

Being hardy, as well as good beef-producers, Hereford cattle are now bred extensively in America, Australia and New Zealand. This parade of Hereford bulls is taking place at the agricultural show held each year in Hereford, Gloucester and Worcester, in rotation.

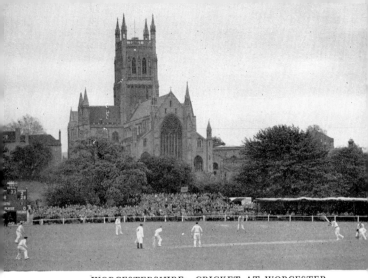

WORCESTERSHIRE: CRICKET AT WORCESTER
The cricket ground at Worcester is beautifully situated, close beside the fine cathedral which was founded in Norman times. The match in progress here is between Worcestershire and an Australian touring team

SHROPSHIRE: WENLOCK EDGE AND THE WREKIN
A prosperous farming area, viewed from Wenlock Edge and looking towards the Wrekin, an isolated hill, 1,335 ft. high. The county is often called Salop, the original name of the county town of Shrewsbury, an ancient market centre on routes leading into Wales.

That on the green turf suck the honied showers,
And purple all the ground with vernal showers.
Bring the rathe[1] primrose that forsaken dies,
The tufted crow-toe, and pale jessamine,
The white pink, and the pansy freaked with jet,
The glowing violet,
The musk-rose, and the well-attired woodbine,
The cowslips wan that hang the pensive head,
And every flower that sad embroidery wears:
Bid Amaranthus all his beauty shed,
And daffadillies fill their cups with tears,
To strew the laureate hearse where Lycid lies.

JOHN MILTON (1608-1674)
Lycidas

[1] Early. Our word "rather" originally meant "sooner" in time.

POET'S CHOICE (5)

I dream'd that, as I wander'd by the way,
    Bare Winter suddenly was changed to Spring;
And gentle odours led my steps astray,
    Mix'd with a sound of waters murmuring
Along a shelving bank of turf, which lay
    Under a copse, and hardly dared to fling
Its green arms round the bosom of the stream,
But kiss'd it and then fled, as thou mightest in dream.

There grew pied wind-flowers and violets;
    Daisies, those pearl'd Arcturi of the earth,
The constellated flower that never sets;
    Faint oxlips; tender bluebells, at whose birth
The sod scarce heaved; and that tall flower that wets—
    Like a child, half in tenderness and mirth—
Its mother's face with heaven-collected tears
When the low wind, its playmate's voice, it hears.

9

And in the warm hedge grew lush eglantine,
   Green cowbind and the moonlight-colour'd May,
And cherry-blossoms, and white cups whose wine
   Was the bright dew yet drain'd not by the day;
And wild roses, and ivy serpentine,
   With its dark buds and leaves wandering astray;
And flowers, azure, black, and streak'd with gold,
Fairer than any waken'd eyes behold.

And nearer to the river's trembling edge
   There grew broad flag-flowers, purple prank'd with
     white,
And starry river-buds among the sedge,
   And floating water-lilies, broad and bright,
Which lit the oak that overhung the hedge
   With moonlight beams of their own watery light;
And bulrushes, and reeds of such deep green
As soothed the dazzled eye with sober sheen.

PERCY BYSSHE SHELLEY (1792-1822)
The Question

POET'S CHOICE (6)

So, some tempestuous morn in early June,
   When the year's primal burst of bloom is o'er,
     Before the roses and the longest day—
   When garden-walks and all the grassy floor
     With blossoms red and white of fallen May
       And chestnut-flowers are strewn—
So have I heard the cuckoo's parting cry,
   From the wet field, through the vext garden-trees,
   Come with the volleying rain and tossing breeze:
The bloom is gone, and with the bloom go I!

Too quick despairer, wherefore wilt thou go?
  Soon will the high Midsummer pomps come on,
    Soon will the musk carnations break and swell,
  Soon shall we have gold-dusted snapdragon,
    Sweet-William with his homely cottage-smell,
      And stocks in fragrant blow;
  Roses that down the alleys shine afar,
    And open, jasmine-muffled lattices,
    And groups under the dreaming garden-trees,
  And the full moon, and the white evening-star.

MATTHEW ARNOLD (1822-1888)
Thyrsis

GARDEN AND STATE

Langley. The DUKE OF YORK'S *garden.*
Enter the QUEEN *and two* LADIES

QUEEN

What sport shall we devise here in this garden,
To drive away the heavy thought of care?

FIRST LADY

Madam, we'll play at bowls.

QUEEN

'Twill make me think the world is full of rubs,
And that my fortune runs against the bias.

FIRST LADY

Madam, we'll dance.

QUEEN

My legs can keep no measure in delight,
When my poor heart no measure keeps in grief;
Therefore, no dancing, girl; some other sport.

FIRST LADY

Madam, we'll tell tales.

QUEEN

Of sorrow or of joy?

FIRST LADY

Of either, madam.

QUEEN

Of neither, girl:
For if of joy, being altogether wanting,
It doth remember me the more of sorrow;
Or if of grief, being altogether had,
It adds more sorrow to my want of joy:
For what I have, I need not to repeat;
And what I want, it boots not to complain.

FIRST LADY

Madam, I'll sing.

QUEEN

'Tis well that thou hast cause;
But thou shoulds't please me better, wouldst thou weep.

FIRST LADY

I could weep, madam, would it do you good.

QUEEN

And I could weep, would weeping do me good,
And never borrow any tear of thee.
But stay, here come the gardeners.
Let's step into the shadow of these trees.
My wretchedness unto a row of pins,
They'll talk of state, for every one doth so
Against a change: woe is forerun with woe.

(QUEEN *and* LADIES *retire*)

Enter a GARDENER *and two* SERVANTS

GARDENER

Go, bind thou up yon dangling apricocks,
Which, like unruly children, make their sire
Stoop with oppression of their prodigal weight:
Give some supportance to the bending twigs.—
Go thou, and, like an executioner,
Cut off the heads of too-fast-growing sprays,
That look too lofty in our commonwealth:
All must be even in our government.—
You thus employ'd, I will go root away
The noisome weeds, that without profit suck
The soil's fertility from wholesome flowers.

FIRST SERVANT

Why should we, in the compass of a pale,
Keep law and form and due proportion,
Showing, as in a model, our firm estate,
When our sea-walled garden, the whole land,
Is full of weeds; her fairest flowers choked up,
Her fruit-trees all unpruned, her hedges ruin'd,
Her knots[1] disorder'd, and her wholesome herbs
Swarming with caterpillars?

GARDENER

           Hold thy peace;—
He that hath suffer'd this disorder'd spring
Hath now himself met with the fall of leaf.

WILLIAM SHAKESPEARE (1564-1616)
Richard II

[1] Flower-beds of intricate design

PRINCELY PLEASAUNCE

God Almighty first planted a garden. And indeed it is the purest of human pleasures. It is the greatest refreshment to the spirits of man; with which, buildings and palaces are but gross handyworks: and a man shall ever see that when ages grow to civility and elegancy, men come to build stately sooner than to garden finely; as if gardening were the greater perfection. I do hold it, in the royal ordering of gardens, there ought to be gardens for all the months in the year; in which, severally, things of beauty may be then in season. . . .

And because the breath of flowers is far sweeter in the air (where it comes and goes, like the warbling of music) than in the hand, therefore nothing is more fit for that delight, than to know what be the flowers and plants that do best perfume the air. Roses, damask and red, are fast flowers of their smells; so that you may walk by a whole row of them, and find nothing of their sweetness; yea, though it be in a morning's dew. Bays likewise yield no smell as they grow. Rosemary little; nor sweet marjoram. That which above all others yields the sweetest smell in the air, is the violet; specially the white double violet, which comes twice a year; about the middle of April, and about Bartholomewtide. Next to that is the musk-rose. Then the strawberry-leaves dying, which [yield] a most excellent cordial smell. Then the flower of the vines; it is a little dust, like the dust of a bent, which grows upon the cluster in the first coming forth. Then sweet-briar. Then wall-flowers, which are very delightful to be set under a parlour or lower chamber window. Then pinks and gillyflowers, specially the matted pink and clove gilly-flower. Then the flowers of the lime-tree. Then the honeysuckles, so they be somewhat afar off. Of bean flowers I speak not, because they are field flowers. But those which perfume the air most delightfully, not passed by as the rest, but being trodden upon and crushed, are three: that is, burnet, wild thyme, and water mints. Therefore you are to set whole alleys of them, to have the pleasure when you walk or tread.

For gardens (speaking of those which are indeed prince-like, as we have done of buildings), the contents ought not well to be under thirty acres of ground, and to be divided into three parts: a green in the entrance; a heath or desert in the going forth; and the main garden in the midst; besides alleys on both sides. And I like well that four acres of ground be assigned to the green; six to the heath; four and four to either side; and twelve to the main garden. The green hath two pleasures: the one, because nothing is more pleasant to the eye than green grass kept finely shorn; the other, because it will give you a fair alley in the midst, by which you may go in front upon a stately hedge, which is to enclose the garden. But because the alley will be long, and, in great heat of the year or day, you ought not to buy the shade in the garden by going in the sun thorough the green, therefore you are, of either side the green, to plant a covert alley, upon carpenter's work, about twelve foot in height, by which you may go in shade into the garden. As for the making of knots or figures with divers-coloured earths, that they may lie under the windows of the house on that side which the garden stands, they be but toys: you may see as good sights many times in tarts. . . .

For the ordering of the ground within the great hedge, I leave it to variety of device; advising, nevertheless, that whatsoever form you cast it into, first, it be not too busy or full of work. Wherein I, for my part, do not like images cut out in juniper or other garden stuff: they be for children. Little low hedges, round, like welts, with some pretty pyramides, I like well; and in some places, fair columns upon frames of carpenter's work. I would also have the alleys spacious and fair. You may have closer alleys upon the side grounds, but none in the main garden. I wish also, in the very middle, a fair mount, with three ascents, and alleys, enough for four to walk abreast; which I would have to be perfect circles, without any bulwarks or embossments; and the whole mount to be thirty foot high; and some fine banqueting-house, with some chimneys neatly cast, and without too much glass.

For fountains, they are a great beauty and refreshment; but pools mar all, and make the garden unwholesome and full of flies and frogs. Fountains I intend to be of two natures: the one, that sprinkleth or spouteth water; the other, a fair receipt of water, of some thirty or forty foot square, but without fish, or slime, or mud. For the first, the ornaments of images gilt, or of marble, which are in use, do well: but the main matter is, so to convey the water, as it never stay, either in the bowls or in the cistern; that the water be never by rest discoloured, green or red or the like, or gather any mossiness or putrefaction. Besides that, it is to be cleaned every day by the hand. Also some steps up to it, and some fine pavement about it, doth well. As for the other kind of fountain, which we may call a bathing pool, it may admit much curiosity and beauty, wherewith we will not trouble ourselves: as, that the bottom be finely paved, and with images; the sides likewise; and withal embellished with coloured glass, and such things of lustre; encompassed also with fine rails of low statuas. But the main point is the same which we mentioned in the former kind of fountain; which is, that the water be in perpetual motion, fed by a water higher than the pool, and delivered into it by fair spouts, and then discharged away under ground, by some equality of bores, that it stay little. And for fine devices, of arching water without spilling, and making it rise in

CHESHIRE: SAXON CROSSES AT SANDBACH

The Britons in Cheshire were subjugated in 830 and thereafter it became a Saxon stronghold. These crosses in the market town of Sandbach are of that period. Cheshire resisted the Norman invasion, and no Saxons retained estates there after the Conquest.

CHESHIRE: THE ROWS, CHESTER

Chester, once a Roman camp, became a busy port in medieval times, but the silting up of the River Dee caused its decline. The 14th century walls completely surround the city. The "Rows" are continuous galleries overlooking the streets, with shops approached by flights of steps.

LANCASHIRE: THE MANCHESTER SHIP CANAL

This important canal, over 35 miles long, connects Manchester with Eastham, on the estuary of the Mersey. Work on it was begun in 1887 and the canal opened for traffic in 1894, having cost about £20,000,000. It can accommodate vessels up to 12,500 tons.

several forms (of feathers, drinking glasses, canopies, and the like), they be pretty things to look on, but nothing to health and sweetness. . . .

For aviaries, I like them not, except they be of that largeness as they may be turfed, and have living plants and bushes set in them; that the birds may have more scope and natural nestling, and that no foulness appear in the floor of the aviary. So I have made a platform of a princely garden, partly by precept, partly by drawing, not a model, but some general lines of it; and in this I have spared for no cost. But it is nothing for great princes, that, for the most part, taking advice with workmen, with no less cost set their things together; and sometimes add statuas, and such things, for state and magnificence, but nothing to the true pleasure of a garden.

FRANCIS BACON, LORD VERULAM (1561-1626)
Essay on Gardens

EDEN

Southward through Eden went a river large,
Nor changed his course, but through the shaggy hill
Passed underneath engulfed, for God had thrown
That mountain as His garden mould high raised
Upon the rapid current, which through veins
Of porous earth with kindly thirst updrawn,
Rose a fresh fountain, and with many a rill
Watered the garden; thence united fell
Down the steep glade, and met the nether flood,
Which from his darksome passage now appears,
And now divided into four main streams,
Runs diverse, wand'ring many a famous realm
And country whereof here needs no account,
But rather to tell how, if art could tell,
How from that sapphire fount the crispèd brooks,
Rolling on orient pearl and sands of gold,

With mazy error under pendant shades
Ran nectar, visiting each plant, and fed
Flowers worthy of Paradise which not nice art
In beds and curious knots, but Nature boon
Poured forth profuse on hill and dale and plain,
Both where the morning sun first warmly smote
The open field, and where the unpierc'd shade
Embrowned the noontide bow'rs: Thus was this place
A happy rural seat of various view:
Groves whose rich trees wept odorous gums and balm,
Others whose fruit burnished with golden rind
Hung amiable, Hesperian fables true,
If true, here only, and of delicious taste:
Betwixt them lawns, or level downs, and flocks
Grazing the tender herb, were interposed,
Or palmy hillock, or the flowery lap
Of some irriguous valley spread her store,
Flowers of all hue, and without thorn the rose:
Another side, umbrageous grots and caves
Of cool recess, o'er which the mantling vine
Lays forth her purple grape, and gently creeps
Luxuriant; meanwhile murmuring waters fall
Down the slope hills, dispersed, or in a lake,
That to the fringèd bank with myrtle crowned
Her crystal mirror holds, unite their streams.

JOHN MILTON (1608-1674)
Paradise Lost

HEARTS OF OAK

England hath the best in the world, not for fineness,
but firmness. Indeed outlandish oaks have a smaller
grain; and therefore fitter for wainscot, and whilst
they make the best linings, our English oak is the
substantial outside. The best in England is in Dean
Forest in this country, and most serviceable for shipping;
so tough that, when it is dry, it is said to be as hard as

iron. I have read, that, in the reign of Queen Elizabeth, the Spaniard sent an ambassador over purposely to get this wood destroyed (by private practices and cunning contrivances); who, had he effected his embassy, deserved a good reward at his return.

THOMAS FULLER (1608-1661)
Worthies

PEPYS, PLEASED AND TROUBLED

May 27th, 1667 . . . My wife away down with Jane and W. Hewer to Woolwich, in order to a little ayre and to lie there to-night, and so to gather May dew to-morrow morning, which Mrs. Turner hath taught her is the only thing in the world to wash her face with; and I am contented with it. I by water to Fox-hall, and there walked in Spring-garden. A great deal of company, and the weather and garden pleasant: and it is very pleasant and cheap going thither, for a man may go to spend what he will, or nothing, all as one. But to hear the nightingale and other birds, and hear fiddles and there a harp, and here a Jew's trump, and here laughing, and there fine people walking, is mighty divertising.

July 27th, 1688 . . . To see my Lord Crewe, whom I find up; and did wait on him; but his face sore, but in hopes to do now very well again. Thence to Cooper's, where my wife's picture almost done, and mighty fine indeed. So over the water with my wife and Deb. and Mercer to Spring-garden, and there eat and walked; and observe how rude some of the young gallants of the town are become, to go into people's arbors where there are not men, and almost force the women; which troubled me, to see the confidence of the vice of the age: and so we away by water with much pleasure home.

SAMUEL PEPYS (1633-1703)
Diary

HIGGLEDY-PIGGLEDY

I am one, you must know, who am looked upon as a Humorist in Gardening. I have several Acres about my House, which I call my Garden, and which a skilful Gardener would not know what to call. It is a Confusion of Kitchen and Parterre, Orchard and Flower Garden, which lie so mixt and interwoven with one another, that if a Foreigner who had seen nothing of our Country should be conveyed into my Garden at his first landing, he would look upon it as a natural Wilderness, and one of the uncultivated Parts of our Country. My Flowers grow up in several Parts of the Garden in the greatest Luxuriancy and Profusion. I am so far from being fond of any particular one, by reason of its Rarity, that if I meet with any one in a Field which pleases me, I give it a Place in my Garden.

By this Means, when a Stranger walks with me, he is surprised to see several large Spots of Ground covered with ten thousand different Colours, and has often singled out Flowers that he might have met with under a common Hedge, in a Field, or in a Meadow, as some of the greatest Beauties of the Place. The only Method I observe in this Particular, is to range in the same Quarter the Products of the same Season, that they may make their Appearance together, and compose a Picture of the greatest Variety. There is the same Irregularity in my Plantations, which run into as great a Wildness as their Natures will permit. I take in none that do not naturally rejoyce in the Soil, and am pleased when I am walking in a Labyrinth of my own raising, not to know whether the next Tree I shall meet with is an Apple or an Oak, an Elm or a Pear-tree.

My Kitchen has likewise its particular Quarters assigned it; for besides the wholesome Luxury which that Place abounds with, I have always thought a Kitchen garden a more pleasant Sight than the finest Orangerie, or artificial Green-house. I love to see every thing in its perfection, and am more pleased to survey my Rows of Coleworts and Cabbages, with a thousand nameless Pot-herbs, springing up in their full Fragrancy and Verdure, than to see the tender Plants of Foreign Countries kept alive by artificial Heats, or withering in an Air and Soil that are not adapted to them.

JOSEPH ADDISON (1672-1719)
The Spectator

FLOWERS AND TREES

Flowers to the fair: to you these flowers I bring,
And strive to greet you with an earlier spring.
Flowers, sweet and gay and delicate like you,
Emblems of innocence and beauty too.
With flowers the Graces bind their yellow hair,
And flowery wreaths consenting lovers wear.
Flowers, the sole luxury which nature knew,
In Eden's pure and guiltless garden grew.
To loftier forms are rougher tasks assigned;
The sheltering oak resists the stormy wind,
The tougher yew repels invading foes,
And the tall pine for future navies grows;
But this soft family, to cares unknown,
Were born for pleasure and delight alone;
Gay without toil, and lovely without art,
They spring to cheer the sense, and glad the heart
Nor blush, my fair, to own you copy these,
Your best, your sweetest empire is—to please.

ANNA LAETITIA BARBAULD (1743-1825)
To a Lady, with some Painted Flowers

GARDEN SOUNDS

But now I sit with all the windows and the door wide
open, and am regaled with the scent of every flower
in a garden as full of flowers as I have known how to
make it. We keep no bees, but if I lived in a hive I should
hardly hear more of their music. All the bees in the
neighbourhood resort to a bed of mignonette, opposite
to the window, and pay me for the honey they get out
of it by a hum, which, though rather monotonous, is
as agreeable to my ear as the whistling of my linnets.
All the sounds that nature utters are delightful,—at
least in this country. I should not perhaps find the
roaring of lions in Africa, or of bears in Russia, very
pleasing; but I know no beast in England whose voice
I do not account musical, save and except always the
braying of an ass. The notes of all our birds and fowls
please me, without one exception. I should not indeed
think of keeping a goose in a cage, that I might hang
him up in the parlour for the sake of his melody, but
a goose upon a common, or in a farm-yard, is no bad
performer; and as to insects, if the black-beetle, and
beetles indeed of all hues, will keep out of my way, I
have no objection to any of the rest; on the contrary,
in whatever key they sing, from the gnat's fine treble to
the bass of the humble-bee, I admire them all.

WILLIAM COWPER (1751-1800)
Letters

TIMBER PENDENT

These hangers are woods on the sides of very steep hills.
The trees and underwood *hang*, in some sort, to the
ground, instead of *standing on* it. Hence these places

are called *Hangers*. From the summit of that which I had now to descend, I looked down upon the villages of Hawkley, Greatham, Selborne and some others.

From the south-east, round, southward, to the north-west, the main valley has cross-valleys running out of it, the hills on the sides of which are very steep, and, in many parts, covered with wood. The hills that form these cross-valleys run out into the main valley, like piers into the sea. Two of these promontories, of great height, are on the west side of the main valley, and were the first objects that struck my sight when I came to the edge of the hanger, which was on the south. The ends of these promontories are nearly perpendicular and their tops so high in the air, that you cannot look at the village below without something like a feeling of apprehension. The leaves are all off, the hop-poles are in stack, the fields have little verdure; but, while the spot is beautiful beyond description even now, I must leave to imagination to suppose what it is, when the trees and hangers and hedges are in leaf, the corn waving, the meadows bright, and the hops upon the poles.

WILLIAM COBBETT (1762-1835)
Rural Rides

RIPENESS TO THE CORE

Of a fine English writer it was said that, in his later years, "his mind was an autumn garden". The remark seems most apposite to all who age in mellowness, a little misty in memory, but ripe in benignity and wisdom. What Keats wrote of the autumn garden and its late flowers applies also to the qualities of man's September days and Indian Summers.

Season of mists and mellow fruitfulness,
    Close bosom-friend of the maturing sun;
Conspiring with him how to load and bless
    With fruit the vines that round the thatch-eaves run;

To bend with apples the moss'd cottage-trees,
 And fill all fruit with ripeness to the core;
  To swell the gourd, and plump the hazel shells
 With a sweet kernel; to set budding more,
And still more, later flowers for the bees,
Until they think warm days will never cease,
  For Summer has o'er-brimm'd their clammy cells.

Who hath not seen thee oft amid thy store?
 Sometimes whoever seeks abroad may find
Thee sitting careless on a granary floor,
 Thy hair soft-lifted by the winnowing wind;
Or on a half-reap'd furrow sound asleep,
 Drows'd with the fume of poppies, while thy hook
  Spares the next swathe and all its twinèd flowers;
 And sometimes like a gleaner thou dost keep
Steady thy laden head across a brook;
Or by a cyder-press, with patient look,
  Thou watchest the last oozings hours by hours.

Where are the songs of Spring? Ay, where are they?
 Think not of them, thou hast thy music too,—
While barrèd clouds bloom the soft-dying day
 And touch the stubble-plains with rosy hue;
Then in a wailful choir the small gnats mourn
 Among the river sallows, borne aloft
  Or sinking as the light wind lives or dies;
 And full-grown lambs loud bleat from hilly bourn;
Hedge-crickets sing; and now with treble soft
The red-breast whistles from a garden-croft;
  And gathering swallows twitter in the skies.

JOHN KEATS (1795-1821)
Ode to Autumn

A LESSON FOR THE LEARNED

Cobbett's love for a steady and self-sufficient countryman was equalled by his hatred of town-bred politicians, economists, and writers.

Chesham is a nice little town, lying in a deep and narrow valley, with a stream of water running through it. All along the country that I have come, the labourers' dwellings are good. They are made of what they call *brick-nog* (that is to say, a frame of wood, and a single brick thick, filling up the vacancies between the timber). They are generally covered with tile. Not *pretty* by any means, but they are good; and you see here, as in Kent, Sussex, Surrey, and Hampshire, and, indeed, in almost every part of England, that most interesting of all objects, that which is such an honour to England, and that which distinguishes it from all the rest of the world, namely, those *neatly kept and productive little gardens round the labourers' houses*, which are seldom un-ornamented with more or less of flowers. We have only to look at these to know what sort of people English labourers are: these gardens are the answer to the *Malthuses* and the *Scarletts*. Shut your mouths, you Scotch Economists; cease bawling, Mr. Brougham, and you Edinburgh Reviewers, till *you* can show us something, not *like*, but approaching towards a likeness of *this*!

WILLIAM COBBETT (1762-1835)
Rural Rides

WOODS IN AUTUMN

I saw old Autumn in the misty morn
   Stand shadowless like Silence, listening
To silence, for no lonely bird would sing
Into his hollow ear from woods forlorn
Nor lowly hedge nor solitary thorn;—
Shaking his languid locks all dewy bright
With tangled gossamer that fell by night,
   Pearling his coronet of golden corn.

Where are the songs of Summer?—With the sun,
Oping the dusky eyelids of the south,
Till shade and silence waken up as one,
And Morning sings with a warm odorous mouth.
Where are the merry birds?—Away, away,
On panting wings through the inclement skies,
      Lest owls should prey
      Undazzled at noonday,
And tear with horny beak their lustrous eyes.

Where are the blooms of Summer?—In the west,
Blushing their last to the last sunny hours,
When the mild Eve by sudden Night is prest
Like tearful Proserpine, snatch'd from her flow'rs
      To a most gloomy breast.
Where is the pride of Summer,—the green prime,—
The many, many leaves all twinkling?—Three
On the moss'd elm; three on the naked lime
Trembling,—and one upon the old oak-tree!
   Where is the Dryad's immortality?—
Gone into mournful cypress and dark yew,
Or wearing the long gloomy Winter through
   In the smooth holly's green eternity.

The squirrel gloats on his accomplish'd hoard,
The ants have brimm'd their garners with ripe grain,
   And honey bees have stored
The sweets of Summer in their luscious cells;
The swallows all have wing'd across the main;
But here the Autumn melancholy dwells,
   And sighs her tearful spells
Amongst the sunless shadows of the plain.
     Alone, alone,
     Upon a mossy stone,
She sits and reckons up the dead and gone
With the last leaves for a love-rosary,
Whilst all the wither'd world looks drearily,
Like a dim picture of the drownèd past
In the hush'd mind's mysterious far away,
Doubtful what ghostly thing will steal the last
Into that distance, gray upon the gray.

THOMAS HOOD (1798-1845)
Ode: Autumn

THREE TOWN GARDENS

If the regular City man, who leaves Lloyd's at five
o'clock, and drives home to Hackney, Clapton, Stamford
Hill, or elsewhere, can be said to have any daily recreation
beyond his dinner, it is his garden. He never does anything to it with his own hands; but he takes great
pride in it notwithstanding; and if you are desirous of
paying your addresses to the youngest daughter, be sure
to be in raptures with every flower and shrub it contains.
If your poverty of expression compel you to make any
distinction between the two, we would certainly recommend your bestowing more admiration on his garden
than his wine. He always takes a walk round it, before
he starts for town in the morning, and is particularly

anxious that the fish-pond should be kept specially neat.

. . . When he drives you down to dinner on a week-day, he is rather fatigued with the occupations of the morning, and tolerably cross into the bargain; but when the cloth is removed, and he has drunk three or four glasses of his favourite port, he orders the French windows of his dining-room (which of course look into the garden) to be opened, and throwing a silk handkerchief over his head, and leaning back in his armchair, descants at considerable length upon its beauty, and the cost of maintaining it. This is to impress you—who are a young friend of the family—with a due sense of the excellence of the garden, and the wealth of its owner; and when he has exhausted the subject, he goes to sleep.

There is another and a very different class of men, whose recreation is their garden. An individual of this class resides some short distance from town—say in the Hampstead Road, or the Kilburn Road, or any other road where the houses are small and neat, and have little slips of back garden. He and his wife—who is as clean and compact a little body as himself—have occupied the same house ever since he retired from business twenty years ago. They have no family. They once had a son, who died at about five years old. The child's portrait hangs over the mantelpiece in the best sitting-room, and a little cart he used to draw about is carefully preserved as a relic.

In fine weather the old gentleman is almost constantly in the garden; and when it is too wet to go into it, he will look out of the window at it, by the hour together. He has always something to do there, and you will see him digging, and sweeping, and cutting, and planting, with manifest delight. In spring-time, there is no end to the sowing of seeds, and sticking little bits of wood over them, with labels which look like epitaphs to their memory; and in the evening, when the sun has gone down, the perseverance with which he lugs a great watering-pot about is perfectly astonishing. The only other recreation he has is the newspaper, which he peruses every day, from beginning to end, generally reading the most interesting pieces of intelligence to his wife during breakfast. The old lady is very fond of flowers, as the hyacinth-glasses in the parlour-window, and geranium-pots in the little front court, testify. She takes great pride in the garden too: and when one of the four fruit-trees produces rather a larger gooseberry than usual, it is carefully preserved under a wineglass on the sideboard, for the edification of visitors, who are duly informed that Mr. So-and-So planted the tree, which produced it, with his own hands. On a summer's evening, when the large watering-pot has been filled and emptied some fourteen times, and the old couple have quite exhausted themselves by trotting about, you will see them sitting happily together in the little summer-house, enjoying the calm and peace of the twilight.

. . . Let us turn now to another portion of the London population, whose recreations present about as strong a contrast as can well be conceived—we mean the Sunday pleasurers; and let us beg our readers to imagine themselves stationed by our side in some well-known rural "Tea-gardens".

The heat is intense this afternoon, and the people, of whom there are additional parties arriving every moment, look as warm as the tables which have been recently painted, and have the appearance of being red-hot. What a dust and noise. Men and women—boys and girls—sweethearts and married people—babies in arms, and children in chaises—pipes and shrimps—cigars and periwinkles—tea and tobacco. Gentlemen in alarming waistcoats, and steel watch-guards, prom-

enading about, three abreast, with surprising dignity
(or as the gentleman in the next box facetiously observes,
"cutting it uncommon fat!")—ladies, with great, long,
white pocket-handkerchiefs like small table-cloths in
their hands, chasing one another on the grass in the
most playful and interesting manner, with the view of
attracting the attention of the aforesaid gentlemen—
husbands in perspective ordering bottles of ginger-beer
for the objects of their affections, with a lavish disregard
for expense; and the said objects washing down huge
quantities of "shrimps" and "winkles" with an equal
disregard of their own bodily health and subsequent
comfort—boys, with great silk hats just balanced on the
top of their heads, smoking cigars, and trying to look
as if they liked them—gentlemen in pink shirts and
blue waistcoats, occasionally upsetting either themselves, or somebody else, with their own canes.

. . . The party in the opposite box are a pretty fair
specimen of the generality of the visitors. These are the
father and mother, and old grandmother: a young man
and woman, and an individual addressed by the euphon-
ious title of "Uncle Bill", who is evidently the wit of the
party. They have some half-dozen children with them,
but it is scarcely necessary to notice the fact, for that is
a matter of course here. Every woman in "the gardens",
who has been married for any length of time, must have
had twins on two or three occasions; it is impossible
to account for the extent of juvenile population in any
other way.

Observe the inexpressible delight of the old grandmother, at Uncle Bill's splendid joke of "tea for four;
bread-and-butter for forty"; and the loud explosion of
mirth which follows his wafering a paper "pigtail"
on the waiter's collar. The young man is evidently
"keeping company" with Uncle Bill's niece: and Uncle
Bill's hints—such as "Don't forget me at the dinner,

you know," "I shall look out for the cake, Sally," "I'll
be godfather to your first—wager it's a boy," and so
forth, are equally embarrassing to the young people,
and delightful to the elder ones. As to the old grandmother, she is in perfect ecstasies, and does nothing but
laugh herself into fits of coughing, until they have
finished the "gin-and-water warm with" of which
Uncle Bill ordered "glasses round" after tea, "just to
keep the night air out, and do it up comfortable and
riglar arter sich an astonishing hot day!"

CHARLES DICKENS (1812-1872)
Sketches by Boz

UNDER THE TREES

This ingenious piece of light verse must surely be the longest ever
written with only a single rhyme. The allusions are to various
Victorian musicians, singers, artists and other personalities of whom
some are now forgotten.

"Under the trees!" Who but agrees
That there is magic in words such as these?
Promptly one sees shake in the breeze
Stately lime-avenues haunted of bees;
Where, looking far over buttercupp'd leas,
Lads and "fair shes" (that is Byron, and he's
An authority) lie very much at their ease;
Taking their teas, or their duck and green peas,
Or, if they prefer it, their plain bread and cheese,
Not objecting at all though it's rather a squeeze
And the glass is, I daresay, at 80 degrees.
Some get up glees, and are mad about Ries
And Sainton, and Temberlik's thrilling high Cs,
Or if painters, hold forth upon Hunt and Maclise,
And the tone and the breadth of that landscape of Lee's;
Or if learned, on nodes and the moon's apogees,
Or, if serious, on something of A.K.H.B.'s,
Or the latest attempt to convert the Chaldees;

Or in short about all things, from earthquakes to fleas.
Some sit in twos or (less frequently) threes,
With their innocent lambswool or book on their knees,
And talk, and enact, any nonsense you please,
As they gaze into eyes that are blue as the seas;
And you hear an occasional "Harry, don't tease"
From the sweetest of lips in the softest of keys,
And other remarks, which to me are Chinese.
And fast the time flees; till a ladylike sneeze,
Or a portly papa's more elaborate wheeze,
Makes Miss Tabitha seize on her brown muffatees,
And announce as a fact that it's going to freeze,
And that young people ought to attend to their Ps
And their Qs, and not court every form of disease.
Then Tommy eats up the three last ratafias,
And pretty Louise wraps her *robe de cerise*
Round a bosom as tender as Widow Machree's,
And (in spite of the pleas of her lorn *vis-à-vis*)
Goes to wrap up her uncle—a patient of Skey's,
Who is prone to catch chills, like all old Bengalese:—
But at bedtime I trust he'll remember to grease
The bridge of his nose, and preserve his rupees
From the premature clutch of his fond legatees;
Or at least have no fees to pay any M.D.'s
For the cold his niece caught, sitting under the Trees.

C. S. CALVERLEY (1831-1884)
Fly Leaves

LOVE IN THE GARDEN

Come into the garden, Maud,
    For the black bat, Night, has flown,
Come into the garden, Maud,
    I am here at the gate alone;
And the woodbine spices are wafted abroad,
    And the musk of the roses blown.

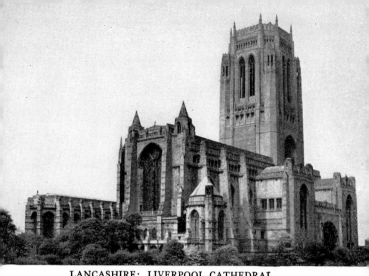

LANCASHIRE: LIVERPOOL CATHEDRAL
The building of Liverpool Cathedral was begun in 1904 and, although still unfinished, it is acknowledged to be one of the finest modern churches in the world. The main industry of the city is shipping, with cotton the chief import to feed the great cotton mills of Lancashire.

LANCASHIRE: PICCADILLY GARDENS, MANCHESTER
Manchester is the headquarters of the cotton industry in England, and a great distributing centre. In the world of music, it is famous for its Royal College of Music and as the home of the Hallé Orchestra. The city's leading newspaper, the *Manchester Guardian*, is known and respected throughout the world.

LANCASHIRE: BLACKPOOL ILLUMINATIONS

In 1800 Blackpool was little more than a village, but thereafter the rapid growth of industry in Lancashire brought the need for a playground for the workers. Now it is one of the most popular resorts in England, with a promenade 7 miles long

For a breeze of morning moves,
And the planet of Love is on high,
Beginning to faint in the light that she loves
   On a bed of daffodil sky,
To faint in the light of the sun she loves,
   To faint in his light, and to die.

All night have the roses heard
   The flute, violin, bassoon;
All night has the casement jessamine stirr'd
   To the dancers dancing in tune;
Till a silence fell with the waking bird,
   And a hush with the setting moon.

I said to the lily, " There is but one
   With whom she has heart to be gay.
When will the dancers leave her alone ?
   She is weary of dance and play."
Now half to the setting moon are gone,
   And half to the rising day;
Low on the sand and loud on the stone
   The last wheel echoes away.

I said to the rose, " The brief night goes
   In babble and revel and wine.
O young lord-lover, what sighs are those
   For one that will never be thine ?
But mine, but mine," so I sware to the rose,
   " For ever and ever, mine."

And the soul of the rose went into my blood,
   As the music clash'd in the hall;
And long by the garden lake I stood,
   For I heard your rivulet fall
From the lake to the meadow and on to the wood,
   Our wood, that is dearer than all;

From the meadow your walks have left so sweet
 That whenever a March-wind sighs
He sets the jewel-print of your feet
 In violets blue as your eyes,
To the woody hollows in which we meet
 And the valleys of Paradise.

The slender acacia would not shake
 One long milk-bloom on the tree;
The white lake-blossom fell into the lake,
 As the pimpernel dozed on the lea;
But the rose was awake all night for your sake,
 Knowing your promise to me;
The lilies and roses were all awake,
 They sigh'd for the dawn and thee.

Queen rose of the rosebud garden of girls,
 Come hither, the dances are done,
In gloss of satin and glimmer of pearls,
 Queen lily and rose in one;
Shine out, little head, sunning over with curls,
 To the flowers, and be their sun.

There has fallen a splendid tear
 From the passion-flower at the gate.
She is coming, my dove, my dear;
 She is coming, my life, my fate;
The red rose cries, " She is near, she is near ";
 And the white rose weeps, " She is late ";
The larkspur listens, "I hear, I hear ";
 And the lily whispers, "I wait."

She is coming, my own, my sweet;
 Were it ever so airy a tread,
My heart would hear her and beat,
 Were it earth in an earthy bed;

My dust would hear her and beat,
　Had I lain for a century dead;
Would start and tremble under her feet,
　And blossom in purple and red.

ALFRED, LORD TENNYSON (1809-1892)
Maud

HATING NATURE

CYRIL: (*coming in through the open window from the terrace*)

My dear Vivian, don't coop yourself up all day in the library. It is a perfectly lovely afternoon. The air is exquisite. There is a mist upon the woods, like the purple bloom upon a plum. Let us go and lie on the grass and smoke cigarettes and enjoy Nature.

VIVIAN: Enjoy Nature! I am glad to say that I have entirely lost that faculty. People tell us that Art makes us love Nature more than we loved her before; that it reveals her secrets to us; and that after a careful study of Corot and Constable we see things in her that had escaped our observation. My own experience is that the more we study Art, the less we care for Nature. What Art really reveals to us is Nature's lack of design, her curious crudities, her extraordinary monotony, her absolutely unfinished condition. Nature has good intentions, of course, but, as Aristotle once said, she cannot carry them out. When I look at a landscape I cannot help seeing all its defects. It is fortunate for us, however, that Nature is so imperfect, as otherwise we should have no art at all. Art is our spirited protest, our

gallant attempt to teach Nature her proper
place. As for the infinite variety of Nature,
that is pure myth. It is not to be found in
Nature herself. It resides in the imagination,
or fancy, or cultivated blindness of the man
who looks at her.

CYRIL: Well, you need not look at the landscape. You
can lie on the grass and smoke and talk.

VIVIAN: But Nature is so uncomfortable. Grass is hard
and lumpy and damp, and full of dreadful
black insects. Why, even Morris's poorest
workman could make you a more comfortable
seat than the whole of Nature can. Nature
pales before the furniture of "the street which
from Oxford has borrowed its name", as the
poet you love so much once vilely phrased it.
I don't complain. If Nature had been comfortable, mankind would never have invented
architecture, and I prefer houses to the open
air. In a house we all feel of the proper proportions. Everything is subordinated to us,
fashioned for our use and our pleasure. Egotism
itself, which is so necessary to a proper sense of
human dignity, is entirely the result of indoor
life. Out of doors one becomes abstract and
impersonal. One's individuality absolutely
leaves one. And then Nature is so indifferent,
so unappreciative. Whenever I am walking
in the park here, I always feel that I am no more
to her than the cattle that browse on the slope,
or the burdock that blooms in the ditch. Nothing is more evident than that Nature hates
Mind. Thinking is the most unhealthy thing
in the world, and people die of it just as they
die of any other disease. Fortunately, in

England at any rate, thought is not catching. Our splendid physique as a people is entirely due to our national stupidity. I only hope we shall be able to keep this great historic bulwark of our happiness for many years to come; but I am afraid that we are beginning to be over-educated; at least everybody who is incapable of learning has taken to teaching— that is really what our enthusiasm for education has come to. In the meantime, you had better go back to your wearisome uncomfortable Nature, and leave me to correct my proofs.

OSCAR WILDE (1856-1900)
The Decay of Lying

Going to the Play

TUDOR THEATRE: THREE VIEWS

(1) HAUNT OF VICE

In our assemblies at plays in London you shall see such heaving and shoving, such itching and shouldering to sit by women; such care for their garments that they be not trod on; such eyes to their laps, that no chips light in them; such pillows to their backs, that they take no hurt; such masking in their ears, I know not what; such giving them pippins to pass the time; such playing at foot-saunt without cards; such tickling, such toying, such smiling, such winking and such manning them home when the sports are ended, that it is a right comedy to mark their behaviour, to watch their conceits, as the cat for the mouse, and as good as a course at the game itself, to dog them a little, or follow aloof by the print of their feet and so discover by slot where the deer taketh soil.

If these were as well noted as ill seen, or as openly punished as secretly practised, I have no doubt but the cause would be feared to dry up the effect and these pretty rabbits very cunningly ferreted from their burrows. For they that lack customers all the week, either because their haunt is unknown or the constables and officers of their parish watch them so narrowly that they dare not queach,[1] to celebrate the Sabbath, flock to the theatres and there keep a general market of bawdry. Not that any filthiness indeed is committed

[1] Stir

within the compass of that ground, as was done in Rome, but that every wanton and his paramour, every man and his mistress, every John and his Joan, every knave and his quean, are there first acquainted.

STEPHEN GOSSON (1554-1624)
The School of Abuse, 1579

(2) BEYOND BELIEF

Sidney wrote in 1580, before the Tudor dramatists were in full flow of excellence. His pedantic objections to theatrical conventions seem unworthy of so rich a mind and fine a spirit. But they represented the academic frown upon the new and boisterous art of the strolling players and young University Wits. Had he lived to see and hear more he might have written otherwise.

Now ye shall have three ladies walk to gather flowers, and then we must believe the stage to be a garden. By and by we hear news of shipwreck in the same place, and then we are to blame if we accept it not for a rock. Upon the back of that comes out a hideous monster, with fire and smoke, and then the miserable beholders are bound to take it for a cave; while in the meantime, two armies fly in, represented with four swords and bucklers, and then what hard heart will not receive it for a pitched field?

Now, of time they are much more liberal, for ordinary it is that two young princes fall in love. After many traverses, she is got with child, delivered of a fair boy; he is lost, groweth a man, falls in love, and is ready to get another child; and all this in two hours space, which how absurd it is in sense, even sense may imagine, and Art hath taught, and all the ancient examples justified, and, at this day, the ordinary players in Italy will not err in.

. . . And besides these gross absurdities, how all their

plays be neither right tragedies, nor right comedies, mingling kings and clowns, not because the matter so carrieth it, but thrust in clowns by head and shoulders, to play a part in majestical matters, with neither decency nor discretion, so as neither the admiration and commiseration, nor the right sportfulness, is by their mongrel tragi-comedy obtained.

. . . So falleth it out, that having indeed no right comedy in that comical part of our tragedy, we have nothing but scurrility, unworthy of any chaste ears, or some extreme show of doltishness, indeed fit to lift up a loud laughter, and nothing else, where the whole tract of a comedy should be full of delight, as the tragedy should be still maintained in a well-raised admiration.

SIR PHILIP SIDNEY (1554-1586)
Apology for Poetry

(3) LIGHT TOYS, BUT USEFUL

If the affairs of the State be such as cannot exhale all these corrupt excrements, it is very expedient they have some light toys to busy their heads withal cast before them as bones to gnaw upon, which may keep them from having leisure to intermeddle with higher matters. To this effect, the policy of plays is very necessary, howsoever some shallow-brained censurers (not the deepest searchers into the secrets of government) mightily oppugn them. For, whereas the afternoon being the idlest time of the day, wherein men that are their own masters (as gentlemen of the Court, the Inns of the Court, and the number of captains and soldiers about London) do wholly bestow themselves upon pleasure, and that pleasure they divide (how virtuously it skills now) either into gaming, following of harlots, drinking,

WESTMORLAND: LAKE WINDERMERE

Windermere, photographed here from Bowness, is the largest lake in
England, 10½ miles long but never more than a mile wide. The shores
are beautifully wooded and there are many pleasant little bays.

WESTMORLAND: WORDSWORTH'S HOUSE AT RYDAL

The village of Rydal lies about 2 miles to the north-west of Ambleside,
in the Lake District, and it was here at Rydal Mount that Wordsworth
lived for some years before his death in 1850. He is buried in the nearby
churchyard of Grasmere.

WESTMORLAND: RED BANK, ABOVE GRASMERE

Grand scenery such as this is to be found everywhere in "the Lakes",
and is easily reached by the tourist as well as by the thousands of hill-
walkers and mountaineers who flock there each year. Beyond these hills
lies the famous Kirkstone Pass, leading north towards Penrith.

or seeing a play. Is it not then better (since of four extremes all the world cannot keep them, but they will choose one) that they should betake them to the least, which is plays? Nay, what if I prove plays to be no extreme, but a rare exercise of virtue?

First, for the subject of them (for the most part) it is borrowed out of our English Chronicles, wherein our forefathers' valiant acts (that have lain long buried in rusty brass and worm-eaten books) are revived, and they themselves raised from the grave of oblivion, and brought to plead their aged honours in open presence: than which, what can be a sharper reproof to these degenerate days of ours? How would it have joyed brave Talbot (the terror of the French) to think that after he had lain two hundred years in his tomb, he should triumph again on the stage, and have his bones new embalmed with the tears of ten thousand spectators at least (at several times) who, in the tragedian that represents his person, imagine they behold him fresh bleeding. I will defend it against any cullion,[1] or club-fisted usurer of them all, there is no immortality can be given a man on earth like unto plays.

THOMAS NASHE (1567-1601)
Piers Penniless

[1] Scoundrel

BOY PLAYER

Weep with me, all you that read
   This little story;
And know, for whom a tear you shed
   Death's self is sorry.
'Twas a child that so did thrive
   In grace and feature,
As Heaven and Nature seem'd to strive
   Which own'd the creature.

10

Years he number'd scarce thirteen
    When Fates turn'd cruel,
Yet three fill'd Zodiacs had he been
    The stage's jewel;
And did act (what now we moan)
    Old men so duly,
As sooth the Parcae[1] thought him one,
    He play'd so truly.
So, by error, to his fate
    They all consented;
But, viewing him since, alas, too late!
    They have repented;
And have sought, to give new birth,
    In baths to steep him;
But, being so much too good for earth,
    Heaven vows to keep him.

BEN JONSON (1573-1637)
Epitaph for Salathiel Pavy
A Child of Queen Elizabeth's Chapel

[1] The Fates

JULIUS CÆSAR

A Swiss traveller, Thomas Platter of Basel, visited England in 1599. On 21st September, in the afternoon, he saw a performance of a play on Julius Cæsar, which is very likely to have been Shakespeare's, since his *Julius Cæsar* is generally ascribed to that year. It is noticeable that the acting company, "some fifteen," was not large, and so a number of parts must have been "doubled". In Shakespeare's play there are thirty-five parts, apart from the "Senators, citizens, Guards and Attendants". The tragedy was followed by the "jig" in which the Fools and dancers had their chance, a chance denied them in this particular play. Shakespeare had to admit these "jigs", sketches with music and antics, to keep his comedians satisfied and in order, no doubt, to please the public too. They do not appear to have pleased him, since his references to jigs are contemptuous. In *Julius Cæsar* there is the line:

"What should the wars do with these jigging fools?"

which sounds like a dig at a player of Fools' parts importunate for

ore to do. Polonius is jeered at by Hamlet because of his addiction
o these trifles—"He's for a jig or a tale of bawdry, or he sleeps."
latter seems to have enjoyed at least the dancing of the jig which
e saw.

. . There in the house with the thatched roof witnessed
n excellent performance of the tragedy of the first
Emperor Julius Cæsar with a cast of some fifteen people;
vhen the play was over, they danced very marvellously
nd gracefully together as is their wont, two dressed
s men and two as women. . . . The actors are most
xpensively and elaborately costumed; for it is the
English usage for eminent lords or Knights at their
ecease to bequeath and leave almost the best of their
lothes to their serving men, which it is unseemly for the
atter to wear, so that they offer them then for sale for
small sum to the actors.

THOMAS PLATTER
Travels in England, 1599
Translated and Edited by Clare Williams

FAVOURITES

o have I seene, when Cesar would appeare,
And on the Stage at halfe-sword parley were,
Brutus and *Cassius*: oh how the Audience,
Were ravish'd, with what wonder they went thence,
When some new day they would not brooke a line,
Of tedious (though well laboured) *Catilines*;
ejanus too was irkesome, they priz'de more
Honest Iago, or the jealous Moore,
And though the Fox and subtill Alchimist,
Long intermitted could not quite be mist,
Though these have sham'd all the Ancients, and might
 raise,
Their Authour's merit with a crowne of Bayes.
Yet these sometimes, even at a friend's desire
Acted, have scarce defraied the Seacoale fire

And doore-keepers: when let but *Falstaffe* come,
Hall, *Poines*, the rest you scarce shall have a roome
All is so pester'd: let but *Beatrice*
And *Benedicke* be seene, loe in a trice
The Cockpit Galleries, Boxes, all are full
To heare *Maluoglio* that crosse garter'd Gull.

LEONARD DIGGES (1588-1635)
Verses contributed to the Second Folio o,
Shakespeare's Plays, published in 164

AN EXCELLENT ACTOR

Whatsoever is commendable to the grave orator, is
most exquisitely perfect in him; for by a full and
significant action of body, he charmes our attention:
sit in a full theater, and you will thinke you see so many
lines drawn from the circumference of so many eares,
whiles the *actor* is the *center*. He doth not strive to make
nature monstrous, she is often seene in the same scene
with him, but neither on stilts nor crutches; and for
his voice, 'tis not lower than the prompter; not lowder
then the foile and target. By his action hee fortifies
morall precepts with examples; for what we see him
personate, we thinke truly done before us: a man of a
deepe thought might apprehend, the ghost of our
ancient *heroes* walk't againe, and take him (at several
times) for many of them. He is much affected to paint-
ing, and 'tis a question whether that make him an
excellent player, or his playing an exquisite painter.
He addes grace to the poets labours: for what in the poet
is but ditty in him is both ditty and musick. He enter-
taines us in the best leasure of our life, that is betweene
meales, the most unfit time either for study or bodily
exercise. The flight of hawkes and chase of wilde beasts,
either of them are delights noble; but some thinke this
sport of men the worthier, despight all *calumny*. All men

have beene of his occupation: and indeed, what he doth fainedly, that doe others essentially: this day one playes a monarch, the next a private person. Here one acts a tyrant, on the morrow an exile: a parasite this man to night, to morrow a precisian, and so of divers others. I observe, of all men living, a worthy actor in one kinde is the strongest motive of affection that can be: for when he dyes, we cannot be perswaded any man can doe his parts like him.

SIR THOMAS OVERBURY (1581-1613)
Characters

MASQUES, PLAYS, AND MUSIC

Towered cities please us then,
And the busy hum of men,
Where throngs of knights and barons bold,
In weeds of peace high triumphs hold,
With store of ladies, whose bright eyes
Rain influence, and judge the prize
Of wit, or arms, while both contend
To win her grace, whom all commend.
There let Hymen oft appear
In saffron robe, with taper clear,
And pomp, and feast, and revelry,
With mask, and antique pageantry,
Such sights as youthful poets dream
On summer eves by haunted stream.
Then to the well-trod stage anon,
If Jonson's learned sock be on,
Or sweetest Shakespeare, fancy's child,
Warble his native wood-notes wild.
And ever against eating cares,
Lap me in soft Lydian airs,
Married to immortal verse,
Such as the meeting soul may pierce

In notes, with many a winding bout
Of linkèd sweetness long drawn out,
With wanton head, and giddy cunning,
The melting voice through mazes running;
Untwisting all the chains that tie
The hidden soul of harmony:
That Orpheus' self may heave his head
From golden slumber on a bed
Of heaped Elysian flowers, and hear
Such strains as would have won the ear
Of Pluto, to have quite set free
His half-regained Eurydice.
These delights if thou canst give,
Mirth, with thee I mean to live.

JOHN MILTON (1608-1674)
L'Allegro

MR. PEPYS AS CRITIC

Extracts from Samuel Pepys's Diaries

March 1, 1662.   To the Opera and there saw "Romeo and Juliet", the first time it was ever acted, but it is a play of itself the worst that ever I heard and the worst acted that ever I saw these people do.

Betterton played Romeo but apparently did not know his lines in this first revival after the closing of the theatres under the discipline of the Puritan rulers. It can be claimed on behalf of Pepys that he may have heard a garbled text.

Sept. 29, 1662.   To the King's Theatre, where we saw "Midsummer Night's Dream", which I had never seen before nor shall ever again, for it is the most insipid ridiculous play that ever I saw in my life.

Nov. 2, 1669.   To the King's Playhouse and there saw "Henry IV" and, contrary to expectation, was pleased in nothing more than in Cartwright's speaking of the speech about "What is Honour?" The house full of Parliament, it being holyday with them, and it was observable how a gentleman of good habit sitting just before us, eating of some fruit in the midst of the play, did drop down as dead, being choked: but with much ado Orange Moll did thrust her finger down his throat and brought him to life again.

Cartwright was a leading player in Killigrew's Company and by his will (1686) left his books, pictures and furnishings to Dulwich College, where his portrait was hung.

Pepys rarely enjoyed any comedy by Shakespeare. He saw *The Merry Wives of Windsor* three times, "which did not please me at all in no part of it." *The Taming of the Shrew* he found "a mean play with same very good pieces in it". In this he came nearest to contemporary opinion. He was furthest from our views in his estimation of *Twelfth Night*. This he saw three times: he dismissed it as "a burthen to me"; "a silly play and not relating at all to the name and day", and "one of the weakest plays that ever I saw on the stage". *The Tempest* he found "most innocent" and "of not great wit", but "good above ordinary plays".

He was kinder to the tragedies, greatly approving Betterton's *Hamlet*. *Macbeth* he saw seven times, evidently in highly spectacular productions. He approved "the deep tragedy" but also found it "a most excellent play for variety" and one of the best plays for "variety of dancing and musick". Evidently *Macbeth* was by then viewed chiefly as a vehicle for vaudeville.

Henry VIII he liked for "its shows". Of *Othello*, once seen, he

commented only that "a very pretty lady that sat by me called out, to
see Desdemona smothered". Of the text he wrote, (Aug. 20, 1666)
"To Deptford by water reading Othello, Moor of Venice, which I
ever heretofore esteemed a mighty good play, but having so lately
read *The Adventures of Five Houres*, it seems a mean thing."

It is plain that Mr. Pepys, like many of his period, found Shakespeare, on the whole, weak and tiresome in comedy and, except for
Betterton's *Hamlet*, only endurable in tragedy when there were
"shows" and "variety" added.

SO MUCH FOR "OTHELLO"

In the *Neighing* of an Horse, or in the *growling* of a
Mastiff, there is a meaning, there is as lively expression,
and, may I say, more humanity, than many times in
the Tragical flights of *Shakespear*.

Step then amongst the Scenes to observe the Conduct
in this Tragedy. . . .

Whence comes it then, that this is the top scene
(III, 3), the Scene that raises *Othello* above all other
Tragedies on our Theatres? It is purely from the
Action; from the Mops and the Mows, the Grimace, the
Grins and Gesticulation. Such scenes as this have made
all the World run after *Harlequin* and *Scaramuccio*. . . .

So much ado, so much stress, so much passion and
repetition about an Handkerchief? Why was not this
call'd the *Tragedy of the Handkerchief*? Had it been
Desdemona's Garter the Sagacious Moor might have
smelt a Rat: but the Handkerchief is so remote a trifle,
no Booby, on this side *Mauritania*, cou'd make any consequence from it. . . .

What can remain with the Audience to carry home
with them from this sort of Poetry, for their use and
edification? how can it work, unless (instead of settling
the mind, and purging our passions) to delude our
senses, disorder our thoughts, addle our brain, pervert
our affections, hair our imaginations, corrupt our

DURHAM: THE CASTLE AND CATHEDRAL

Both buildings stand on high ground above the River Wear. The Norman cathedral, one of the most magnificent in England, contains the tomb of the Venerable Bede. The castle, the earliest parts of which were built in 1072, was restored in 1928, and is now used by Durham University.

YORKSHIRE: FOUNTAINS ABBEY

Yorkshire is extremely rich in ecclesiastical architecture, but Fountains Abbey, about 3 miles south-west of Ripon, is outstanding in that it is the finest and most complete of the ruined English abbeys. It was a Cistercian house, founded about 1130.

YORKSHIRE: HIGH FORCE WATERFALL
A spectacular waterfall created by a solid wall of rock in the path of the River Tees as it makes it way through the Pennine moors a few miles west of Middleton in Teesdale. The Tees forms the northern boundary of Yorkshire.

YORKSHIRE: THE MOORS
Black-face sheep crossing Mossdale Moor, near Hawes, while being "gathered" for the annual dipping. The North and West Ridings of Yorkshire are among the principal sheep-farming districts in England.

appetite, and fill our head with vanity, confusion, *Tintamarre*, and Jingle-jangle, beyond what all the Parish Clarks of *London*, with their *old Testament farces*, and interludes, in *Richard* the seconds time cou'd ever pretend to? Our only hopes, for the good of their Souls, can be, that these people go to the Play-house, as they do to Church, to sit still, look on one another, make no reflection, not mind the play, more than they would a Sermon.

There is in this Play, some burlesk, some humour, and ramble of Comical Wit, some shew, and some Mimickry to divert the spectators: but the tragical part is, plainly none other, than a Bloody Farce, without salt or savour.

THOMAS RYMER (1641-1713)
A Short View of Tragedy, 1692

LITTLE MR. GARRICK

In the first row then of the first gallery did Mr. Jones, Mrs. Miller, her youngest daughter, and Partridge, take their places. Partridge immediately declared it was the finest place he had ever been in. When the first music was played, he said, "It was a wonder how so many fiddlers could play at one time, without putting one another out." While the fellow was lighting the upper candles, he cried out to Mrs. Miller, "Look, look, madam, the very picture of the man in the end of the common-prayer book before the gunpowder-treason service." Nor could he help observing, with a sigh, when all the candles were lighted, "That here were candles enough burnt in one night, to keep an honest poor family for a whole twelvemonth."

As soon as the play, which was Hamlet, Prince of Denmark, began, Partridge was all attention, nor did he break silence till the entrance of the ghost; upon which he asked Jones, "What man that was in the strange dress; something," said he, "like what I have seen in a picture. Sure it is not armour, is it?" Jones answered, "That is the ghost." To which Partridge replied with a smile, "Persuade me to that, sir, if you can. Though I can't say I ever actually saw a ghost in my life, yet I am certain I should know one, if I saw him, better than that comes to. No, no, sir, ghosts don't appear in such dresses as that, neither." In this mistake, which caused much laughter in the neighbourhood of Partridge, he was suffered to continue, till the scene between the ghost and Hamlet, when Partridge gave that credit to Mr. Garrick, which he had denied to Jones, and fell into so violent a trembling, that his knees knocked against each other. Jones asked him what was the matter, and whether he was afraid of the warrior upon the stage? "O la! sir," said he, "I perceive now it is what you told me. I am not afraid of anything; for I know it is but a play, and if it was really a ghost, it could do one no harm at such a distance, and in so much company; and yet if I was frightened, I am not the only person." "Why who," cried Jones, "dost thou take to be such a coward here besides thyself?" "Nay, you may call me coward if you will; but if that little man there upon the stage is not frightened, I never saw any man frightened in my life."

. . . The grave-digging scene next engaged the attention of Partridge, who expressed much surprize at the number of skulls thrown upon the stage. To which Jones answered, "That it was one of the most famous burial-places about town." "No wonder then," cried Partridge, "that the place is haunted. But I never saw in my life a worse grave-digger. I had a sexton, when I was clerk, that should have dug three graves while he is digging one. The fellow handles a spade as if it was the first time he had ever had one in his hand. Ay, ay, you may sing. You had rather sing than work, I believe."—Upon Hamlet's taking up the skull, he cried out, "Well! it is strange to see how fearless some men are: I never could bring myself to touch anything belonging to a dead man, on any account.—He seemed frightened enough too at the ghost, I thought."

Little more worth remembering occurred during the play, at the end of which Jones asked him, "Which of the players he had liked best?" To this he answered, with some appearance of indignation at the question, "The king, without doubt." "Indeed, Mr. Partridge," says Mrs. Miller, "you are not of the same opinion with the town; for they are all agreed, that Hamlet is acted by the best player who ever was on the stage." "He the best player!" cried Partridge, with a contemptuous sneer, "why, I could act as well as he myself. I am sure, if I had seen a ghost, I should have looked in the very same manner, and done just as he did. And then, to be sure, in that scene, as you called it, between him and his mother, where you told me he acted so fine, why, Lord help me, any man, that is, any good man, that had such a mother, would have done exactly the same. I know you are only joking with me; but indeed, madam, though I was never at a play in London, yet I have seen acting before in the country; and the king for my money; he speaks all his words distinctly, half as loud again as the other.—Anybody may see he is an actor."

HENRY FIELDING (1707-1754)
Tom Jones

ALWAYS THE ACTOR

At David Garrick's death, Dr. Johnson made the immortal epitaphic comment that this loss (in 1779) "has eclipsed the gaiety of nations and impoverished the public stock of harmless pleasure." Oliver Goldsmith, writing before Garrick's death, had criticised his posturing and vanity, but paid full tribute to his goodness of heart as well as to his unrivalled excellence in his craft of acting.

Here lies David Garrick, describe me who can,
An abridgement of all that was pleasant in man;
As an actor, confest without rival to shine,
As a wit, if not first, in the very first line,
Yet with talents like these, and an excellent heart,
The man had his failings, a dupe to his art;
Like an ill-judging beauty, his colours he spread,
And beplaistered with rouge his own natural red.
On the stage he was natural, simple, affecting,
'Twas only that, when he was off, he was acting:
With no reason on earth to go out of his way,
He turn'd and he varied full ten times a-day;
Tho' secure of our hearts, yet confoundedly sick
If they were not his own by finessing and trick,
He cast off his friends, as a huntsman his pack,
For he knew when he pleas'd he could whistle them back.
Of praise a mere glutton, he swallow'd what came,
And the puff of a dunce, he mistook it for fame;
'Till his relish grown callous, almost to disease,
Who pepper'd the highest, was surest to please.

But peace to his spirit, wherever it flies,
To act as an angel, and mix with the skies:
Those poets, who owe their best fame to his skill,
Shall still be his flatterers, go where he will.

Old Shakespeare, receive him, with praise and with love,
And Beaumonts and Bens be his Kellys[1] above.

OLIVER GOLDSMITH (1730-1774)
Retaliation

[1] Hugh Kelly was a popular eighteenth century dramatist. Garrick
played in his comedy, "False Delicacy" in 1768.

RACHEL'S MUSE OF FIRE

The theatre was full—crammed to its roof: royal and
noble were there: palace and hotel had emptied their
inmates into those tiers so thronged and so hushed.
Deeply did I feel myself privileged in having a place
before that stage; I longed to see a being of whose powers
I had heard reports which made me conceive peculiar
anticipations. I wondered if she would justify her
renown: with strange curiosity, with feelings severe
and austere, yet of riveted interest, I waited. She was a
study of such nature as had not encountered my eyes
yet: a great and new planet she was: but in what shape?
I waited her rising.

She rose at nine that December night; above the
horizon I saw her come. She could shine yet with pale
grandeur and steady might: but that star verged already
on its judgment-day. Seen near, it was a chaos—hollow,
half-consumed: an orb perished or perishing—half
lava, half glow.

I had heard this woman termed "plain", and I expected
bony harshness and grimness—something large, angular,
sallow. What I saw was the shadow of a royal Vashti:
a queen, fair as the day once, turned pale now like twilight, and wasted like wax in flame.

For a while—a long while—I thought it was only a
woman, though an unique woman, who moved in
might and grace before this multitude. By-and-by I
recognised my mistake. Behold! I found upon her

something neither of woman nor of man: in each of
her eyes sat a devil. These evil forces bore her through
the tragedy, kept up her feeble strength—for she was
but a frail creature; and as the action rose and the stir
deepened, how wildly they shook her with their passions
of the pit! They wrote HELL on her straight, haughty
brow. They tuned her voice to the note of torment.
They writhed her regal face to a demoniac mask. Hate
and Murder and Madness incarnate she stood.

It was a marvellous sight: a mighty revelation.

It was a spectacle low, horrible, immoral.

Swordsmen thrust through, and dying in their blood
on the arena sand; bulls goring horses disembowelled,
made a meeker vision for the public—a milder condi-
ment for a people's palate—than Vashti torn by seven
devils: devils which cried sore and rent the tenement
they haunted, but still refused to be exorcised.

Suffering had struck that stage empress: and she stood
before her audience neither yielding to, nor enduring,
nor, in finite measure, resenting it: she stood locked
in struggle, rigid in resistance. She stood, not dressed,
but draped in pale antique folds, long and regular like
sculpture. A background and entourage and flooring
of deepest crimson threw her out, white like alabaster—
like silver: rather, be it said, like Death.

. . . Scarcely a substance herself, she grapples to conflict with abstractions. Before calamity she is a tigress:
she rends her woes, shivers them in compulsed abhor-
ence. Pain, for her, has no result in good; tears water no
harvest of wisdom: on sickness, on death itself, she
looks with the eye of a rebel. Wicked, perhaps, she is,
but also she is strong: and her strength has conquered
Beauty, has overcome Grace, and bound both at her side,
captives peerlessly fair, and docile as fair. Even in the
uttermost frenzy of energy is each mænad movement
royally, imperially, incedingly upborne. Her hair,

flying loose in revel or war, is still an angel's hair, and glorious under a halo. Fallen, insurgent, banished, she remembers the heaven where she rebelled. Heaven's light, following her exile, pierces its confines, and discloses their forlorn remoteness.

. . . The strong magnetism of genius drew my heart out of its wonted orbit: the sunflower turned from the south to a fierce light, not solar—a rushing, red, cometary light—hot on vision and to sensation. I had seen acting before, but never anything like this: never anything which astonished Hope and hushed Desire: which outstripped Impulse and paled Conception; which, instead of merely irritating imagination with the thought of what *might* be done, at the same time fevering the nerves because it was *not* done, disclosed power like a deep, swollen winter river, thundering in cataract, and bearing the soul, like a leaf, on the steep and steely sweep of its descent.

CHARLOTTE BRONTË (1816-1855)
Villette

MUNDEN'S MANY FACES

Not many nights ago I had come home from seeing this extraordinary performer in Cockletop; and when I retired to my pillow, his whimsical image still stuck by me, in a manner as to threaten sleep. In vain I tried to divest myself of it, by conjuring up the most opposite associations. I resolved to be serious, I raised up the gravest topics of life; private misery, public calamity. All would not do:

——There the antic sate
Mocking our state——

his queer visnomy—his bewildering costume—all the strange things which he had raked together—his serpentine rod, swagging about in his pocket—Cleopatra's tear, and the rest of his relics—O'Keefe's wild farce, and *his* wilder commentary—till the passion of laughter, like grief in excess, relieved itself by its own weight, inviting the sleep which in the first instance it had driven away.

But I was not to escape so easily. No sooner did I fall into slumbers, than the same image, only more perplexing, assailed me in the shape of dreams. Not one Munden, but five hundred, were dancing before me, like the faces which, whether you will or no, come when you have been taking opium—all the strange combinations, which this strangest of all strange mortals ever shot his proper countenance into, from the day he came commissioned to dry up the tears of the town for the loss of the now almost forgotten Edwin. O for the power of the pencil to have fixed them when I awoke! A season or two since, there was exhibited a Hogarth gallery. I do not see why there should not be a Munden gallery. In richness and variety, the latter would not fall far short of the former.

There is one face of Farley,[1] one face of Knight,[2] one (but what a one it is!) of Liston[3]; but Munden has none that you can properly pin down, and call *his*. When you think he has exhausted his battery of looks, in unaccountable warfare with your gravity, suddenly he sprouts out an entirely new set of features, like Hydra. He is not one, but legion; nor so much a comedian, as a company. If his name could be multiplied like his countenance, it might fill a play-bill. He, and he alone, literally *makes faces*: applied to any other person, the phrase is a mere figure, denoting certain modifications

---

[1] Charley Farley (1771-1859)
[2] Thomas Knight (d. 1804)
[3] John Liston (1776-1846)

of the human countenance. Out of some invisible wardrobe he dips for faces, as his friend Suett used for wigs, and fetches them out as easily. I should not be surprised to see him some day put out the head of a river-horse; or come forth a pewitt, or lap-wing, some feathered metamorphosis.

I have seen this gifted actor in Sir Christopher Curry—in old Dornton—diffuse a glow of sentiment which has made the pulse of a crowded theatre beat like that of one man; when he has come in aid of the pulpit, doing good to the moral heart of a people. I have seen some faint approaches to this sort of excellence in other players. But in the grand grotesque of farce, Munden stands out as single and unaccompanied as Hogarth. Hogarth, strange to tell, had no followers. The school of Munden began, and must end, with himself.

Can any man *wonder*, like him? can any man *see ghosts*, like him? or *fight with his own shadow* "SESSA"—as he does in that strangely neglected thing, the *Cobbler of Preston*—where his alternations from the Cobbler to the Magnifico, and from the Magnifico to the Cobbler, keep the brain of the spectator in as wild a ferment, as if some Arabian Night were being acted before him. Who like him can throw, or ever attempted to throw, a preternatural interest over the commonest daily-life objects? A table or a joint-stool, in his conception, rises into a dignity equivalent to Cassiopeia's chair. It is invested with constellatory importance. You could not speak of it with more deference, if it were mounted into the firmament.

A beggar in the hands of Michael Angelo, says Fuseli, rose the Patriarch of Poverty. So the gusto of Munden antiquates and ennobles what it touches. His pots and his ladles are as grand and primal as the seething-pots and hooks seen in old prophetic vision. A tub of butter, contemplated by him, amounts to a Platonic idea. He understands a leg of mutton in its quiddity. He stands

wondering, amid the common-place materials of life,
like primeval man with the sun and stars about him.

CHARLES LAMB (1775-1834)
From *Essays of Elia*

PRIME MINISTER OF MIRTH

Mr. George Robey is at the head of that one art of the
theatre which really lives, with the full vehemence of
life, in England; its shows are crowded because people like
them, and not because somebody else does, nor because
they think they ought to like them, or that if they
can stand them for some time they may yet come to like
them. While Mr. Robey is on the stage nearly the whole
audience laughs, and part of it deliriously, as you would
see people laugh at Toole and other low comedians of
genius—not at any one speech or grimace, but at the
whole idea of a being so grotesque as the one before
them.

Mr. Robey's range of characterization, like that of
most of his peers at the halls, is very small, but the study
is diabolically intimate, and the execution edged and
finished like a cut jewel. He will come on the stage
first as that veteran theme, the middle-aged toper in
black, frock-coated, tieless and collarless, leering with
imbecile knowingness, Stiggins and Bardolph and Ally
Sloper in one, his face all bubukles and whelks and
knobs and flames o' fire. He will end as the equally
trite old woman, also of bibulous aspect, also half
cunning, half crazy, a scold, farcical with relics of
vanity, ugly as a gargoyle. Nothing could be staler than
the matter, nothing more keen with fresh gusto than the
craftsman's manner. In a sense Mr. Robey attempts
nothing hard; he does not even sketch a character;
he only isolates and caricatures a few odd traits. But
the relatively easy task is done amazingly well. He will

stand in mid-stage and suggest a dialogue with an invisible second person, he himself uttering no complete speeches, but only the trimmings of speech, the humming and hawing, grinning, bowing, odds and ends of suspensive or stimulatory "Yes," and "Oh, I see!" and "Oh, then," and yet the affluent expressiveness of each inflection and each twitch of a muscle makes everything radiantly clear. What he sings is naught; he might leave it out without taking much from the fun; as he has grown great his music has withered and his patter has grown more and more; the patter is everything now, and yet he says, altogether, wonderfully little; first a word, and then he seems to detect some misplaced laugh in the audience, checks, bridles up, passes in pantomime from tantrum to tantrum, the gusts and squalls of temper coming and going in him visibly. You may call the topics outworn and trivial, the mere words insignificant, the humour metallic, rasping, or worse, but the art, within its limits, is not to be surpassed in its gleaming, elliptical terseness, the volumes it speaks in some instants, its suddenness, fire and zest.

At the theatre everything has a long pedigree; current fashions have sometimes the longest. Perhaps music-hall performances like Dan Leno's and Mr. Robey's keep nearer than anything else on the West European stage of to-day to the origin of modern professional acting in the Italian "Comedy of Art" of the Renaissance. The old practitioners exploited a few stock butts, as the music-hall men do now; like them, they owed nothing directly to eminent authors; like them, they depended mainly on patter, improvised or crammed up; like them, they started with some little rag of a written part and embroidered upon it as genius might prompt; like them, they were tied pretty fast by convention to certain accepted standard lines of comic observation; they did not go into the streets to note and reproduce some more of their interminable humours—all they might do was to add a gesture here and a phrase there to the traditional business or gag of a roguish valet, or swaggering soldier, or didactic doctor, or cursing father, just as Mr. Robey will leave his little store of shrews and boozers much as he found them. Indeed, some of the sallies that detonate on every week-night in a thousand English music-halls, the old stuff about frumps and termagants and comic tipsiness, may have been going off in Western Europe without a break, except at some festivals of the Church, since some wag first tried them on the Medici at Florence.

C. E. MONTAGUE (1867-1928)
Dramatic Values, 1911

Colleges and Schools

PEERLESS PAIR

There are also in this Island two famous Universities, the one *Oxford*, the other *Cambridge*, both for the profession of all sciences, for Divinity, Physick, Law, and all kinds of learning, excelling all the Universities in Christendom.

I was myself in either of them, and like them both so well that I mean not in the way of controversy to refer any for the better in *England*, but both for the best in the world, saving this, that Colleges in *Oxenford* are much more stately for the building, and *Cambridge* much more sumptuous for the houses in the town; but the learning neither lieth in the free stones of the one, nor the fine streets of the other, for out of them both do daily proceed men of great wisdom to rule in the commonwealth, of learning to instruct the common people, of all singular kind of professions to do good to all. And let this suffice, not to inquire which of them is the superior, but that neither of them have their equal; neither to ask which of them is the most ancient, but whether any other be so famous.

JOHN LYLY (1554-1606)
Euphues and his England

The King, observing with judicious eyes,
The state of both his universities,
To Oxford sent a troop of horse, and why?
That learned body wanted loyalty;

To Cambridge books, as very well discerning,
How much that loyal body wanted learning.

JOSEPH TRAPP (1679-1747)
Literary Anecdotes

REDBRICK

They call them Redbrick, those dozen or so of English Universities and University Colleges that have not the ancientry and authority of Oxford and Cambridge. Redbrick they often are not: yet, if they were, what harm? For brick can be a rich, rewarding material of the builder, as the Tudor architects well knew. There is, however, a deal of grey stone in these other Academies. What nobler than Durham's rock above the curling river, the rock where College and Cathedral now share the stronghold of the Prince Bishops of the North?

The new Universities work under handicap. Lacking the status and allure of Oxford and Cambridge, they find that the leaders in learning of the arts and sciences prefer, on leaving school, to avail themselves of the scholarships and bursaries inviting them to three or four years beside the Thames or Cam. So the exceptional talents of our industrial towns do frequently pass by the Universities which during the last century have been planted beside the Grammar Schools of their own places. The cream, as they say, is drawn off and goes to nourish the two Senior foundations. But much of merit remains.

The Redbricks were once mainly frequented by students living at home or scattered in lodgings. They lacked the fellowship of living in and living together, but now there are more and more hostels where the pleasures of association and of constant company can be enjoyed and so the frustration of youth isolated, youth merely attending lectures and then catching train or bus for a suburb, is increasingly defeated. There can be more of those activities of clubs and societies, more

midnight sessions of happily heretical discussion in
which much of the best education is discovered. The
Redbricks are overcoming their housing problem and
gaining a new and vigorous collegiate life.

The new Universities are, after all, much more
numerous in their members. In England there are as a
rule some 80,000 undergraduates at work (and play) each
year and of these Oxford and Cambridge claim but
15,000. And in those populous juniors the technicians
and scientists of to-morrow are especially prominent
and most capably trained. They may not have prompted
poets to sing of them in exquisite nostalgia. Nor have
they drawn the foreign traveller to muse upon their
spires or penetrate their quadrangles. But, without the
pomp or panache of their seniors, they are known to their
own and serve the cities and the nation in their distinct
and valuable ways. They may lack the spectacular
glory and the storied heritage of Oxford and Cambridge,
but to be short of such magnetism is not to lack authentic
merit.

ANONYMOUS

TWO OXFORD MEN

There was an *Oxford Cleric* too, a student,
Long given to Logic, longer than was prudent;
The horse he had was leaner than a rake,
And he was not too fat, I undertake,
But had a hollow look, a sober stare;
The thread upon his overcoat was bare.
He had found no preferment in the church
And he was too unworldly to make search.
He thought far more of having by his bed
His twenty books all bound in black and red,
Of Aristotle and philosophy
Than of gay music, fiddles or finery.

Though a philosopher, as I have told,
He had not found the stone for making gold.
Whatever money from his friends he took
He spent on learning or another book
And prayed for them most earnestly, returning
Thanks to them thus for paying for his learning.
His only care was study, and indeed
He never spoke a word more than was need,
Formal at that, respectful in the extreme,
Short, to the point, and lofty in his theme.
The thought of moral virtue filled his speech
And he would gladly learn, and gladly teach.

*   *   *

Some time ago there was a rich old codger
Who lived in Oxford and who took a lodger.
The fellow was a carpenter by trade,
His lodger a poor student who had made
Some studies in the arts, but all his fancy
Turned to astrology and geomancy,
And he could deal with certain propositions
And make a forecast under some conditions
About the likelihood of drought or showers
For those who asked at favourable hours,
Or put a question how their luck would fall
In this or that, I can't describe them all.
This lad was known as Nicholas the Spark.
He was a dab at love, but kept it dark,
For he was sly and secret and he took
Advantage of his meek and girlish look.
He rented a small chamber in the kip
All by himself without companionship.
He decked it charmingly with herbs and fruit
And he himself was sweeter than the root
Of liquorice or any fragrant herb.
His astronomic text-books were superb,

YORKSHIRE: YORK MINSTER

As Eboracum, York was the military capital of Roman Britain. In the 10th century it was known as Iorvik. The Minster, mainly of 12th and 13th century construction, is one of the finest Gothic churches in England. The walls and gateways of the medieval city remain.

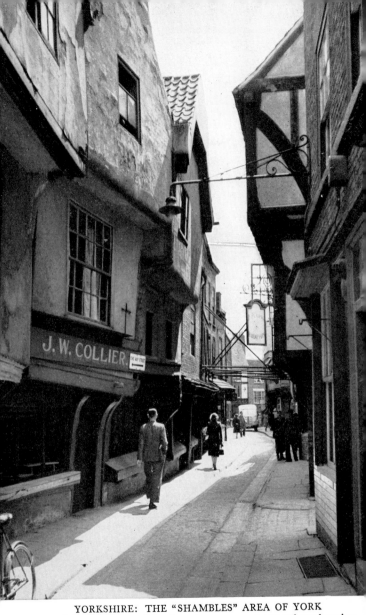

YORKSHIRE: THE "SHAMBLES" AREA OF YORK

One of the oldest parts of the city, where narrow streets and overhanging, half-timbered buildings of the Middle Ages are constant reminders of York's great antiquity. The 15th century Guildhall was destroyed by bombing in World War II.

He had an astrolabe to match his art
And calculating counters laid apart
On handy shelves that stood·above his bed.
His press was curtained coarsely and in red;
Above there lay a gallant harp in sight
On which he played melodiously at night
With such a touch that all the chamber rang;
It was *The Virgin's Angelus* he sang,
And after that he sang *King William's Note*,
And people often blessed his merry throat.
And that was how this charming scholar spent
His time and money, which his friends had sent.

GEOFFREY CHAUCER (1340-1400)
*The Canterbury Tales—Prologue
and The Miller's Tale
Translated by Nevill Coghill*

PUBLIC SCHOOLS

A youth should not be made to hate study before he
know the causes to love it: or taste the bitterness before
the sweet; but called on, and allured, entreated, and
praised: Yea, when he deserves it not. For which cause
I wish them sent to the best school, and a publike, which
I think the best. Your Lordship I fear hardly hears of
that, as willing to breed them in your eye, and at home;
and doubting their manners may be corrupted abroad.
They are in more danger in your own Family, among ill
servants (allowing, they be safe in their School-Master),
than amongst a thousand boys, however immodest:
would we did not spoil our own children and overthrow
their manners ourselves by too much Indulgence.
To breed them at home is to breed them in a shade;
where in a school they have the light and heat of the
Sun. They are used and accustomed to things and men.
When they come forth into the Commonwealth they

find nothing new or to seek. They have made their friendships and aids; some to last till their Age. They hear what is commanded to others as well as themselves. Much approved, much corrected; all which they bring to their own store and use, and learn as much as they hear. *Eloquence* would be but a poor thing if we should only converse with singulars; speak but man and man together. Therefore I like no private breeding. I would send them where their industry should be daily increased by praise; and that kindled by emulation. It is a good thing to inflame the mind. . . . And from the rod, or ferule, I would have them free, as from the menace of them: for it is both deformed and servile.

BEN JONSON (1573-1637)
Discoveries

DISCIPLINE FOR DAUGHTERS

I would have their breeding like to the Dutch woman's clothing, tending to profit only and comeliness.

Though she never have a dancing-schoolmaster, a French tutor, nor a Scotch tailor to make her shoulders of the breadth of Bristow Cowsway, it makes no matter; for working in curious Italian purls or French borders, it is not worth the while. Let them learn plain works of all kind, so they take heed of too open seaming. Instead of song and music, let them learn cookery and laundry. And instead of reading Sir Philip Sidney's *Arcadia*, let them read the *Grounds of Good Housewifery*. I like not a female poetess at any hand. Let greater personages glory their skill in music, the posture of their bodies, their knowledge in languages, the greatness and freedom of their spirits, and their arts in arraigning of men's affections at their flattering faces. This is not the way to breed a private gentleman's daughter.

If the mother of them be a good housewife and religiously disposed, let her have the bringing up of one of them. Place the other two forth betimes, and before they can judge of a good manly leg. The one in the house of some good merchant, or citizen of civil and religious government; the other in the house of some lawyer, some judge, or well reported justice or gentleman of the country, where the serving man is not too predominant. In any of these she may learn what belongs to her improvement: for sempstry, for confectionery, and all requisites of housewifery. She shall be sure to be restrained of all rank company and unfitting liberty, which are the overthrow of too many of their sex. . . .

WILLIAM POWELL (1631)
Tom of All Trades

HEAD OF A HOUSE

John Aubrey, the gifted gossip, whose *Brief Lives* I regard as one of the most enchanting feats of English biographical writing, went to Trinity College, Oxford. Its president was, during his first year of residence, Ralph Kettle, D.D., of whom Aubrey wrote:

. . He was then a good deale above eighty, and he had then a fresh ruddy complexion. He was a very tall well growne man. His gowne and surplice and hood being on, he had a terrible gigantique aspect, with his sharp gray eies. The ordinary gowne he wore was a russet cloath gowne. He was, they say, white very soon; he had a very venerable presence, and was an excellent governour. One of his maximes of governing was to keepe-downe the *juvenilis impetus* ('Tis Seneca's expression).

. . He observed that the howses that had the smallest

beer had most drunkards, for it forced them to goe into the town to comfort their stomachs; wherfore Dr. Kettle alwayes had in his College excellent beer, not better to be had in Oxon; so that we could not goe to any other place but for the worse, and we had the fewest drunkards of any howse in Oxford.

He was constantly at lectures and exercises in the hall to observe them, and brought along with him his hower-glasse; and one time, being offended at the boyes, he threatened them, that if they would not doe their exercise better he "would bring an hower-glass two howers long".

He was irreconcileable to long haire; called them hairy scalpes, and as for periwigges (which were then very rarely worne) he beleeved them to be the scalpes of men cutt off after they were hang'd, and so tanned and dressed for use. When he observed the scholars' haire longer then ordinary (especially if they were scholars of the howse), he would bring a paire of cizers in his muffe (which he commonly wore), and woe be to them that sate on the outside of the table. I remember he cutt Mr. Radford's haire with the knife that chipps the bread on the buttery-hatch. . . .

. . . Dr. Kettle, when he scolded at the idle young boies of his colledge, he used these names, *viz.*, *Tarrarages* (these were the worst sort, Rude Rakells), *Rascal-Jacks*, *Blindcinques, Scabberlotchers* (these did no hurt, were sober, but went idleing about the grove with their hands in their pocketts, and telling the number of the trees there, or so).

JOHN AUBREY (1626-97)
Brief Lives

PRAISE TO THE BUILDER

Tax not the royal Saint with vain expense,
With ill-match'd aims the Architect who plann'd
(Albeit labouring for a scanty band
Of white-robed Scholars only) this immense

And glorious work of fine intelligence!
—Give all thou canst; high Heaven rejects the lore
Of nicely-calculated less or more:—
So deem'd the man who fashion'd for the sense

These lofty pillars, spread that branching roof
Self-poised, and scoop'd into ten thousand cells
Where light and shade repose, where music dwells

Lingering—and wandering on as loth to die:
Like thoughts whose very sweetness yieldeth proof
That they were born for immortality.

WILLIAM WORDSWORTH (1770-1850)
Within King's College Chapel, Cambridge

WORDSWORTH AT CAMBRIDGE

It was a dreary morning when the wheels
Rolled over a wide plain o'erhung with clouds,
And nothing cheered our way till first we saw
The long-roofed chapel of King's College lift
Turrets and pinnacles in answering files,
Extended high above a dusky grove.

   Advancing, we espied upon the road
A student clothed in gown and tasselled cap,
Striding along as if o'ertasked by Time,
Or covetous of exercise and air;

He passed—nor was I master of my eyes
Till he was left an arrow's flight behind.
As near and nearer to the spot we drew,
It seemed to suck us in with an eddy's force.
Onward we drove beneath the Castle; caught,
While crossing Magdalene Bridge, a glimpse of Cam;
And at the *Hoop* alighted, famous Inn.

My spirit was up, my thoughts were full of hope;
Some friends I had, acquaintances who there
Seemed friends, poor simple schoolboys, now hung round
With honour and importance; in a world
Of welcome faces up and down I roved;
Questions, directions, warnings and advice,
Flowed in upon me, from all sides; fresh day
Of pride and pleasure! to myself I seemed
A man of business and expense, and went
From shop to shop about my own affairs,
To Tutor or to Tailor, as befell,
From street to street with loose and careless mind. . . .

. . . The Evangelist St. John my patron was;
Three Gothic courts are his, and in the first
Was my abiding-place, a nook obscure;
Right underneath, the College kitchens made
A humming sound, less tuneable than bees,
But hardly less industrious; with shrill notes
Of sharp command and scolding intermixed.
Near me hung Trinity's loquacious clock,
Who never let the quarters, night or day,
Slip by him unproclaimed, and told the hours
Twice over with a male and female voice.
Her pealing organ was my neighbour too;
And from my pillow, looking forth by light
Of moon or favouring stars, I could behold
The antechapel where the statue stood
Of Newton with his prism and silent face,

The marble index of a mind for ever
Voyaging through strange seas of Thought, alone. . . .

. . . Beside the pleasant Mill of Trompington
I laughed with Chaucer in the hawthorn shade;
Heard him, while birds were warbling, tell his tales
Of amorous passion. And that gentle Bard,
Chosen by the Muses for their Page of State—
Sweet Spenser, moving through his clouded heaven
With the moon's beauty and the moon's soft pace,
I called him Brother, Englishman, and Friend!
Yes, our blind Poet, who, in his later day,
Stood almost single; uttering odious truth—
Darkness before, and danger's voice behind,
Soul awful—if the earth has ever lodged
An awful soul—I seemed to see him here
Familiarly and in his scholar's dress
Bounding before me, yet a stripling youth—
A boy, no better, with his rosy cheeks
Angelical, keen eye, courageous look,
And conscious step of purity and pride.
Among the band of my compeers was one
Whom chance had stationed in the very room
Honoured by Milton's name.

WILLIAM WORDSWORTH (1770-1850)
The Prelude, Book III

TRIBUTE DENIED

To the University of Oxford *I* acknowledge no obliga-
tion; and she will as cheerfully renounce me for a son,
as I am willing to disclaim her for a mother. I spent
fourteen months at Magdalen College; they proved
the fourteen months the most idle and unprofitable of
my whole life: the reader will pronounce between the
school and the scholar; but I cannot affect to believe

that Nature had disqualified me for all literary pursuits.

The schools of Oxford and Cambridge were founded in a dark age of false and barbarous science; and they are still tainted with the vices of their origin. Their primitive discipline was adapted to the education of priests and monks; and the government still remains in the hands of the clergy, an order of men whose manners are remote from the present world, and whose eyes are dazzled by the light of philosophy. The legal incorporation of these societies by the charters of popes and kings had given them a monopoly of the public instruction; and the spirit of monopolists is narrow, lazy, and oppressive; their work is more costly and less productive than that of independent artists; and the new improvements, so eagerly grasped by the competition of freedom, are admitted with slow and sullen reluctance in those proud corporations. We may scarcely hope that any reformation will be a voluntary act; and so deeply are they rooted in law and prejudice, that even the omnipotence of parliament would shrink from an inquiry into the state and abuses of the two universities. . . .

As a gentleman commoner, I was admitted to the society of the fellows, and fondly expected that some questions of literature would be the amusing and instructive topic of their discourse. Their conversation stagnated in a round of college business, Tory politics, personal anecdotes, and private scandal: their dull and deep potations excused the brisk intemperance of youth; and their constitutional toasts were not expressive of the most lively loyalty for the house of Hanover. . . .

EDWARD GIBBON (1737-1794)
Memoirs

CUMBERLAND: ISEL BRIDGE

A quiet stretch of the River Derwent, at Isel Bridge. The Derwent rises in the tarns around Great Gable (2,949 ft.) and Scafell Pike (3,210 ft., the highest mountain in England). It then flows north through wooded Borrowdale to form Derwentwater and Bassenthwaite.

CUMBERLAND: KESWICK

One of the main centres for visitors to the Lake District, Keswick is also a busy market town and manufactures lead pencils from locally mined plumbago. Southey and Samuel Taylor Coleridge are among the famous poets and writers who lived at Keswick.

CUMBERLAND: WETHERAL WOODS, CARLISLE

A pleasant stretch of the river Eden, near Carlisle. Even in Roman and
Saxon times Carlisle was a thriving city and later, in the centuries of
border strife, its castle formed the main bulwark against the Scots in
the west. It is now one of the chief railway centres in Britain.

NORTHUMBERLAND: NEWCASTLE-UPON-TYNE

A view of the famous Tyneside shipyards. The prosperity of Newcastle
is based on its situation on a great tidal river and the rich coalfields
nearby. Its exports include coal, chemicals, iron, steel and machinery,
and it is one of the chief ports for Norwegian tourist traffic.

BLISS AT ETON

Ye distant spires, ye antique towers
   That crown the watery glade,
Where grateful Science still adores
   Her Henry's holy shade;
And ye, that from the stately brow
Of Windsor's heights th'expanse below
Of grove, of lawn, or mead survey,
Whose turf, whose shade, whose towers among
Wanders the hoary Thames along
   His silver-winding way:

Ah happy hills! ah pleasing shade!
   Ah fields beloved in vain!
Where once my careless childhood stray'd,
   A stranger yet to pain!
I feel the gales that from ye blow
A momentary bliss bestow,
As waving fresh their gladsome wing
My weary soul they seem to soothe,
And, redolent of joy and youth,
   To breathe a second spring.

Say, Father Thames, for thou hast seen
   Full many a sprightly race
Disporting on thy margent green
   The paths of pleasure trace;
Who foremost now delight to cleave
With pliant arm, thy glassy wave?
The captive linnet which enthral?
What idle progeny succeed
To chase the rolling circle's speed
   Or urge the flying ball?

While some on earnest business bent
    Their murmuring labours ply
'Gainst graver hours, that bring constraint
    To sweeten liberty:
Some bold adventurers disdain
The limits of their little reign
And unknown regions dare descry;
Still as they run they look behind,
They hear a voice in every wind,
    And snatch a fearful joy.

Gay hope is theirs by fancy fed,
    Less pleasing when possest;
The tear forgot as soon as shed,
    The sunshine of the breast:
Theirs buxom health, of rosy hue,
Wild wit, invention ever new,
And lively cheer, of vigour born;
The thoughtless day, the easy night,
The spirits pure, the slumbers light
    That fly th'approach of morn.

Alas! regardless of their doom
    The little victims play;
No sense have they of ills to come
    Nor care beyond to-day;
Yet see how all around 'em wait
The ministers of human fate
And black Misfortune's baleful train!
Ah show them where in ambush stand
To seize their prey, the murderous band!
    Ah, tell them they are men!

       *   *   *

To each his sufferings: all are men,
    Condemn'd alike to groan;
The tender for another's pain,
    Th'unfeeling for his own.

Yet, ah! why should they know their fate,
Since sorrow never comes too late,
And happiness too swiftly flies?
Thought would destroy their paradise.
No more;—where ignorance is bliss,
　'Tis folly to be wise.

THOMAS GRAY (1716-1771)
Ode on a Distant Prospect of Eton College

BLISS AT HARROW

Byron, although he played cricket for Harrow, had warmer recollection of his play-acting than of his batting and bowling. He thus gave early evidence of a theatrical disposition and affection for display, 'with spectators surrounded". Mossop was an Irish actor who considered himself the equal of Garrick but was not accepted as such and remained an embittered rival. Zanga was the role in which he had made the most impression upon London.

Ye scenes of my childhood, whose loved recollection
　Embitters the present, compared with the past;
Where science first dawn'd on the powers of reflection,
　And friendships were form'd, too romantic to last!

＊　　　　＊　　　　＊

Again I behold where for hours I have ponder'd,
　As reclining, at eve, on yon tombstone I lay;
Or round the steep brow of the churchyard I wander'd,
　To catch the last gleam of the sun's setting ray.

I once more view the room, with spectators surrounded,
　Where, as Zanga, I trod on Alonzo o'er thrown;
While, to swell my young pride, such applauses resounded,
　I fancied that Mossop himself was out-shone;

Or, as Lear, I pour'd forth the deep imprecation,
  By my daughters of kingdom and reason depriv'd;
Till, fired by loud plaudits and self-adulation,
  I regarded myself as a Garrick revived.

Ye dreams of my boyhood, how much I regret you!
  Unfaded your memory dwells in my breast;
Though sad and deserted, I ne'er can forget you;
  Your pleasure may still be in fancy possest.

LORD BYRON (1788-1824)
Hours of Idleness

PRIZE-WINNERS PUT DOWN

A lad with a sickly constitution and no very active
mind, who can just retain what is pointed out to him
and has neither sagacity to distinguish nor spirit to
enjoy for himself, will generally be at the head of his
form. An idler at school, on the other hand, is one who
has high health and spirits, who has the free use of his
limbs, with all his wits about him, who feels the circulation of his blood and the motion of his heart, who is
ready to laugh and cry in a breath, and who had rather
chase a ball or a butterfly, feel the open air in his face,
look at the fields or the sky, follow a winding path, or
enter with eagerness into all the little conflicts and
interests of his acquaintances and friends, than doze
over a musty spelling-book, repeat barbarous distichs
after his master, sit so many hours pinioned to a writing-
desk, and receive his reward for the loss of time and
pleasure in paltry prize-medals at Christmas and Midsummer. There is indeed a degree of stupidity which
prevents children from learning the usual lessons, or even
arriving at these puny academic honours. But what
passes for stupidity is much oftener a want of interest,
of a sufficient motive to fix the attention and force a

reluctant application to the dry and unmeaning pursuits of school-learning. The best capacities are as much above this drudgery as the dullest are beneath it. Our men of the greatest genius have not been most distinguished for their acquirements at school or at the university.

"Th' enthusiast Fancy was a truant ever."

Gray and Collins were among the instances of this wayward disposition. Such persons do not think so highly of the advantages, nor can they submit their imaginations so servilely to the trammels of strict scholastic discipline. There is a certain kind and degree of intellect in which words take root, but into which things have not power to penetrate. A mediocrity of talent, with a certain slenderness of moral constitution, is the soil that produces the most brilliant specimens of successful prize-essayists and Greek epigrammatists. It should not be forgotten that the least respectable character among modern politicians was the cleverest boy at Eton.

WILLIAM HAZLITT (1778-1830)
On the Ignorance of the Learned

AT SALEM HOUSE

When David Copperfield was sent by his steely step-father, Mr. Murdstone, to a boarding school, Salem House, kept by Mr. Creakle, it was during the school-holidays and he was looked after by the gentle Mr. Mell. Since Dickens has left such repulsive pictures of the brutal Creakle, as well as of the more famous and infamous Squeers of Dotheboys Hall, it is pleasant to find that not all his schoolmasters are sadistic scoundrels, and that he could feel compassion as much for a distressed usher as for ill-treated boys.

Mr. Mell was a gaunt, sallow young man, with hollow

cheeks, and a chin almost as black as Mr. Murdstone's; but there the likeness ended, for his whiskers were shaved off, and his hair instead of being glossy, was rusty and dry. He was dressed in a suit of black clothes which were rather rusty and dry too, and rather short in the sleeves and legs; and he had a white neckerchief on, that was not over-clean. I did not, and do not, suppose that this neckerchief was all the linen he wore, but it was all he showed or gave any hint of.

"You're the new boy," he said.

"Yes, sir," I said.

I supposed I was. I didn't know.

"I'm one of the masters at Salem House," he said.

Later, Mr. Mell, the Master, arranges for the hungry boy to have a good breakfast outside the school.

I sat down to my brown loaf, my egg, and my rasher of bacon, with a basin of milk besides, and made a most delicious meal. While I was yet in the full enjoyment of it, the old woman of the house said to the Master:

"Have you got your flute with you?"

"Yes," he returned.

"Have a blow at it," said the old woman, coaxingly. "Do!"

The Master, upon this, put his hand underneath the skirts of his coat, and brought out his flute in three pieces, which he screwed together, and began immediately to play. My impression is, after many years of consideration, that there never can have been anybody in the world who played worse. He made the most dismal sounds I have ever heard produced by any means, natural or artificial. I don't know what the tunes were —if there were such things in the performance at all, which I doubt—but the influence of the strain upon me was, first to make me think of all my sorrows until I could hardly keep my tears back; then to take away my appetite; and lastly, to make me so sleepy that I couldn't keep my eyes open.

. . . When I seemed to have been dozing a long while, the Master at Salem House unscrewed his flute into the three pieces, put them up as before, and took me away. We found the coach very near at hand, and got upon the roof; but I was so dead sleepy, that when we stopped on the road to take up somebody else, they put me inside where there were no passengers, and where I slept profoundly, until I found the coach going at a footpace up a steep hill among green leaves. Presently, it stopped, and had come to its destination.

. . . Salem House was a square brick building with wings, of a bare and unfurnished appearance. All about it was so very quiet, that I said to Mr. Mell I supposed the boys were out; but he seemed surprised at my not knowing that it was holiday-time. That all the boys were at their several homes. That Mr. Creakle, the proprietor, was down by the sea-side with Mrs. and Miss Creakle. And that I was sent in holiday-time as a punishment for my misdoing. All of which he explained as we went along.

I gazed upon the schoolroom into which he took me, as the most forlorn and desolate place I had ever seen. I see it now. A long room, with three long rows of desks, and six of forms, and bristling all round with pegs for hats and slates. Scraps of old copy-books and exercises litter the dirty floor. Some silkworms' houses, made of the same materials, are scattered over the desks. Two miserable little white mice, left behind by their owner, are running up and down in a fusty castle made of pasteboard and wire, looking in all the corners with their red eyes for anything to eat. A bird, in a cage very little bigger than himself, makes a mournful rattle now and then in hopping on his perch, two inches high, or dropping from it; but neither sings nor chirps. There is a strange unwholesome smell upon the room, like mildewed corduroys, sweet apples wanting air, and rotten books. There could not well be more ink splashed about it, if it had been roofless from its first construction, and the skies had rained, snowed, hailed, and blown ink through the varying seasons of the year.

. . . I had long tasks every day to do with Mr. Mell; but I did them, there being no Mr. and Miss Murdstone here, and got through them without disgrace. Before, and after them, I walked about—supervised, as I have mentioned, by the man with the wooden leg. How vividly I call to mind the damp about the house, the green cracked flagstones in the court, an old leaky water-butt, and the discoloured trunks of some of the grim trees, which seemed to have dripped more in the rain than other trees, and to have blown less in the sun! At one we dined, Mr. Mell and I, at the upper end of a long bare dining-room, full of deal tables, and smelling of fat. Then, we had more tasks until tea, which Mr. Mell drank out of a blue tea-cup, and I out of a tin pot. All day long, and until seven or eight in the evening, Mr. Mell, at his own detached desk in the school-room, worked hard with pen, ink, ruler, books, and writing-paper, making out the bills (as I found) for last half-year. When he had put up his things for the night, he took out his flute, and blew at it, until I almost thought he would gradually blow his whole being into the large hole at the top, and ooze away at the keys.

. . . Mr. Mell never said much to me, but he was never harsh to me. I suppose we were company to each other, without talking. I forgot to mention that he would talk to himself sometimes, and grin, and clench his fist, and grind his teeth, and pull his hair in an unaccountable

YORKSHIRE: SELBY ON MARKET DAY

An old market town on the Ouse, 14 miles south of York, and about 16 miles east of Leeds. Its splendid Abbey Church was once a Benedictine house, founded in 1069, and is one of the most perfect monastic survivals in the north.

YORKSHIRE: STEEL MILLS AT SHEFFIELD

Iron was smelted at Sheffield in early times, and the city is now the centre of the special steel and cutlery trade. This picture shows the cold rolling of steel strip at the Shepcote Lane Mills of Firth-Vickers Stainless Steels, Ltd.

LINCOLNSHIRE: LINCOLN CATHEDRAL

As early as Roman times Lincoln was an important city, a route centre
at the junction of Fosse Way and Ermine Street. The cathedral, standing
on a hill, is a landmark for miles around, and is one of the most magnificent Gothic buildings in the world.

manner. But he had these peculiarities. At first they frightened me, though I soon got used to them.

CHARLES DICKENS (1812-1870)
David Copperfield

DO-THE-GIRLS-HALL

The severity and even down-right cruelty of English schooling during the nineteenth century are emphasized by Charlotte Brontë in *Jane Eyre*, whose heroine is sent to the Charity School of Lowood and finds herself half-frozen and half-starved. But just as Smike found a protector in Nicholas Nickleby at Dotheboys Hall, and David Copperfield met one kindly usher at Mr. Creakle's Salem House, so did Jane encounter not only the tyrannical and flagellant Miss Scatcherd but the wisdom and benignity of Miss Temple and the precious friendship of the long-suffering Helen Burns.

Miss Scatcherd nagged, scolded and even flayed the girls, especially Helen, without cease.

"You dirty, disagreeable girl! you have never cleaned your nails this morning!"

Burns made no answer: I wondered at her silence.

"Why," thought I, "does she not explain that she could neither clean her nails nor wash her face, as the water was frozen?"

My attention was now called off by Miss Smith desiring me to hold a skein of thread: while she was winding it, she talked to me from time to time, asking whether I had ever been at school before, whether I could mark, stitch, knit, &c.; till she dismissed me. I could not pursue my observations on Miss Scatcherd's movements. When I returned to my seat, that lady was just delivering an order of which I did not catch the import; but Burns immediately left the class, and going into the small inner room where the books were kept, returned in half a minute, carrying in her hand a bundle of twigs tied together at one end. This ominous tool she presented to Miss Scatcherd with a respectful courtesy;

then she quietly, and without being told, unloosed her pinafore, and the teacher instantly and sharply afflicted on her neck a dozen strokes with the bunch of twigs. Not a tear rose to Burns' eye: and, while I paused from my sewing, because my fingers quivered at this spectacle with a sentiment of unavailing and impotent anger, not a feature of her pensive face altered its ordinary expression.

"Hardened girl!" exclaimed Miss Scatcherd; "nothing can correct you of your slatternly habits: carry the rod away."

Burns obeyed: I looked at her narrowly as she emerged from the book-closet; she was just putting her handkerchief into her pocket and the trace of a tear glistened on her thin cheek.

* * *

But there were compensations, when the vicious Scatcherd's kindly colleague entertained girls in her own way.

We feasted that evening as on nectar and ambrosia; and not the least delight of the entertainment was the smile of gratification with which our hostess regarded us, as we satisfied our famished appetites on the delicate fare she liberally supplied. Tea over and the tray removed, she again summoned us to the fire; we sat one on each side of her, and now a conversation followed between her and Helen, which it was indeed a privilege to be admitted to hear.

Miss Temple had always something of serenity in her air, of state in her mien, of refined propriety in her language, which precluded deviation into the ardent, the excited, the eager: something which chastened the pleasure of those who looked on her and listened to her, by a controlling sense of awe; and such was my feeling now: but as to Helen Burns, I was struck with wonder.

The refreshing meal, the brilliant fire, the presence and kindness of her beloved instructress, or, perhaps, more than all these, something in her own unique mind, had roused her powers within her. They woke, they kindled: first, they glowed in the bright tint of her cheek, which till this hour I had never seen but pale and bloodless; then they shone in the liquid lustre of her eyes, which had suddenly acquired a beauty more singular than that of Miss Temple's—a beauty neither of fine colour nor long eyelash, nor pencilled brow, but of meaning, of movement, of radiance. Then her soul sat on her lips, and language flowed, from what source I cannot tell: has a girl of fourteen a heart large enough, vigorous enough to hold the swelling spring of pure, full, fervid eloquence? Such was the characteristic of Helen's discourse on that, to me, memorable evening; her spirit seemed hastening to live within a very brief span as much as many live during a protracted existence.

They conversed of things I had never heard of; of nations and times past; of countries far away: of secrets of nature discovered or guessed at: they spoke of books: how many they had read! What stores of knowledge they possessed! Then they seemed so familiar with French names and French authors; but my amazement reached its climax when Miss Temple asked Helen if she sometimes snatched a moment to recall the Latin her father had taught her, and taking a book from a shelf, bade her read and construe a page of Virgil; and Helen obeyed, my organ of Veneration expanding at every sounding line. She had scarcely finished ere the bell announced bedtime: no delay could be admitted; Miss Temple embraced us both, saying, as she drew us to her heart—

"God bless you, my children!"

Helen she held a little longer than me: she let her go more reluctantly; it was Helen her eye followed

to the door; it was for her she a second time breathed
a sad sigh; for her she wiped a tear from her cheek.

On reaching the bed-room, we heard the voice of Miss
Scatcherd: she was examining drawers; she had just
pulled out Helen Burns's, and when we entered Helen
was greeted with a sharp reprimand, and told that
to-morrow she should have half-a-dozen of untidily
folded articles pinned to her shoulder.

"My things were indeed in shameful disorder," murmured Helen to me, in a low voice: "I intended to have
arranged them, but I forgot."

Next morning, Miss Scatcherd wrote in conspicuous
characters on a piece of pasteboard the word "Slattern",
and bound it like a phylactery round Helen's large,
mild, intelligent, and benign looking forehead. She
wore it till evening, patient, unresentful, regarding it as
a deserved punishment.

CHARLOTTE BRONTË (1816-1855)
Jane Eyre

ARNOLD OF RUGBY

We looked upon every trumpery little custom and habit
which had obtained in the school as though it had been
a law of the Medes and Persians, and regarded the in-
fringement or variation of it as a sort of sacrilege. And
the Doctor, than whom no man or boy had a stronger
liking for old school customs which were good and
sensible, had, as has already been hinted, come into
most decided collision with several which were neither
the one nor the other. And as old Brooke had said, when
he came into collision with boys or customs, there was
nothing for them but to give in or take themselves off;
because what he said had to be done, and no mistake
about it. And this was beginning to be pretty clearly
understood; the boys felt that there was a strong man

over them, who would have things his own way; and hadn't yet learned that he was a wise and loving man also. His personal character and influence had not had time to make itself felt, except by a very few of the bigger boys with whom he came more directly in contact; and he was looked upon with great fear and dislike by the great majority even of his own house. For he had found school, and school-house, in a state of monstrous licence and misrule, and was still employed in the necessary but unpopular work of setting up order with a strong hand.

THOMAS HUGHES (1822-1896)
Tom Brown's Schooldays

OXFORD BY MOONLIGHT

Beautiful city! so venerable, so lovely, so unravaged by the fierce intellectual life of our century, so serene!

There are our young barbarians, all at play!

And yet, steeped in sentiment as she lies, spreading her gardens to the moonlight, and whispering from her towers the last enchantments of the Middle Ages, who will deny that Oxford, by her ineffable charm, keeps ever calling us near to the true goal of all of us, to the ideal, to perfection—to beauty, in a word, which is only truth seen from another side?—nearer, perhaps, than all the science of Tübingen. Adorable dreamer, whose heart has been so romantic! who has given thyself, so prodigally given thyself, to sides and to heroes not mine, only never to the Philistines! home of lost causes and forsaken beliefs, and unpopular names, and impossible loyalties. . . .

MATTHEW ARNOLD (1822-1888)
Essays in Criticism

THE ABSENT FRIEND[1]

How changed is here each spot man makes or fills!
  In the two Hinkseys nothing keeps the same;
    The village street its haunted mansion lacks,
  And from the sign is gone Sibylla's name,
    And from the roofs the twisted chimney-stacks—
      Are ye too changed, ye hills?
See, 'tis no foot of unfamiliar men
  To-night from Oxford up your pathway strays;
    Here came I often, often, in old days—
Thyrsis and I; we still had Thyrsis then.

Runs it not here, the track by Childsworth Farm,
  Past the high wood, to where the elm-tree crowns
    The hill behind whose ridge the sunset flames?
The signal-elm, that looks on Ilsley Downs,
    The Vale, the three lone weirs, the youthful
        Thames?—
    This winter-eve is warm,
Humid the air! leafless, yet soft as spring,
  The tender purple spray on copse and briers!
  And that sweet city with her dreaming spires,
She needs not June for beauty's heightening.

Lovely all times she lies, lovely to-night!—
  Only, methinks, some loss of habit's power
    Befalls me wandering through this upland dim.
Once pass'd I blindfold here, at any hour;
    Now seldom come I, since I came with him.
    That single elm-tree bright
Against the west—I miss it! is it gone?
  We prized it dearly; while it stood, we said,
  Our friend, the Gipsy-Scholar, was not dead;
While the tree lived, he in these fields lived on. . . .

[1] The absent friend, spoken of as Thyrsis, was the poet, A. H. Clough,
who died in 1861.

. . . It irk'd him to be here, he could not rest.
He loved each simple joy the country yields,
  He loved his mates; but yet he could not keep,
For that a shadow lour'd on the fields,
  Here with the shepherds and the silly sheep.
    Some life of men unblest
  He knew, which made him droop, and fill'd his head.
    He went; his piping took a troubled sound
    Of storms that rage outside our happy ground;
  He could not wait their passing, he is dead.

MATTHEW ARNOLD (1822-1888)
Thyrsis

GOING BACK TO SCHOOL

It was always the most bitter thing, in my own drive to the station, to see other people, quite happy, as it seemed, with no upheaval of their lives; people in cabs, who were going out to dinner and would sleep in London; grown-up people! Than the impotent despair of those drives—I had exactly fifteen of them—I hope that I shall never experience a more awful emotion. Those drives have something, surely, akin with drowning. In their course the whole of a boy's home-life passes before his eyes, every phase of it standing out against the black curtain of his future. The author of *Vice-Versa* has well analysed the feeling, and he is right, I think, in saying that all boys, of whatsoever temperament, are preys to it. Well do I remember how, on the last day of the holidays, I used to rise early, and think that I had got twelve more whole hours of happiness, and how those hours used to pass me with mercifully slow feet. . . . Three more hours! . . . Sixty more minutes! . . . Five! . . . I used to draw upon my tips for a first-class ticket, that I might not be plunged suddenly among my companions,

with their hectic and hollow mirth, their dreary dis-
interment of last term's jokes. I used to revel in the
thought that there were many stations before G—— . . ;
The dreary walk, with my small bag, up the hill! I
was not one of those who made a rush for the few cabs.
. . . The awful geniality of the House Master! The jugs
in the dormitory! . . . Next morning, the bell that woke
me! The awakening!

Not that I had any special reason for hating school!
Strange as it may seem to my readers, I was not unpopular
there. I was a modest, good-humoured boy. It is Oxford
that has made me insufferable. At school, my character
remained in a state of undevelopment. I had a few
misgivings, perhaps. In some respects, I was always
too young, in others, too old, for a perfect relish of the
convention. As I hovered, in grey knickerbockers, on
a cold and muddy field, round the outskirts of a crowd
that was tearing itself limb from limb for the sake of a
leathern bladder, I would often wish for a nice, warm
room and a good game of hunt-the-slipper. And when
we sallied forth, after dark, in the frost, to the swimming-
bath, my heart would steal back to the fireside in Writing
School and the plot of Miss Braddon's latest novel.
Often, since, have I wondered whether a Spartan system
be really well for youths who are bound mostly for
Capuan Universities. It is true, certainly that this
system makes Oxford or Cambridge doubly delectable.
Undergraduates owe their happiness chiefly to the
consciousness that they are no longer at school. The
nonsense which was knocked out of them at school is
all put gently back at Oxford or Cambridge. And the
discipline to which they are subject is so slight that it
does but serve to accentuate their real freedom.

SIR MAX BEERBOHM (1872-1955)
More

ENGLISH SCHOOLMASTER

My father was a schoolmaster, and a very good one, with an almost ludicrous passion for acquiring and imparting knowledge. He was not a born scholar, but he was a born teacher. Outside his school, he did a great deal of useful public service—speaking, helping to organize, working on committees, and so on—not because he was a busybody or was socially ambitious, but because he was essentially public-spirited, the type of citizen that democratic theorists have in mind but rarely in actual view. But there was nothing of the smooth committee humbug about him. He was very brisk, humorous, stout-hearted, not to be patronized or bullied. I am commonly supposed to be pugnacious, but he was at heart ten times more pugnacious than I am, and if you went one step too far with him, his ruddy face turned scarlet, his eyes were electric blue, and he came roaring at you like a little lion. He had the only sensible way of dealing with money, and I am glad to say that he bequeathed it to me. This is to realize as soon as possible what kind of life you can lead with the money at your disposal (and he had never much, yet was never dissatisfied) then within that circle to live at your ease, never worrying about money. He deliberately shut out one sort of life—the more expensive life of hotels, restaurants, cabs, theatre stalls, Havana cigars, liqueur brandies—and then lived like a king in the dominions left to him.

To think hard and realistically about money, then to forget it, that is what neither spendthrifts nor misers can do, and it is the only way to be merry and wise. He was not a romantic figure, did not pretend to be. His world lacked glitter and glamour. I never remember seeing him either in ecstasies nor yet defeated by despair. But he never failed a duty, left the world better than he found it, was loved by his friends and respected by his army of acquaintances, and had a lot of fun. Beneath the rather droll surface peculiarities—his love of making acquaintances, of asking questions, of imparting information; his fear of minor social criticism; his distrust of the picturesque, romantic, grandiose things of this life; his odd mixture of patience and explosive hot temper— he was a living rock of good solid human nature. If I was picking a team to go and colonize another planet, I would choose his kind first. Years ago, when my first scribblings were achieving print, he was proud of me; and now, too long after we exchanged our last words, I think I am prouder still of him.

J. B. PRIESTLEY (Born 1894)
Midnight on the Desert

WEALTH AND DR. WORTLE

Dr. Wortle's School, a pleasant contrast to Salem House, was established as "preparatory to Eton". His fees of £200 a year, with extras, were, when his tale was told in 1881, equivalent to £700 or £800 a year to-day. Yet the equivalents of Dr. Wortle are probably charging half or less than half that at the present time.

There had, too, been some fighting between Dr. Wortle and the world about his school. He was, as I have said, a thoroughly generous man, but he required, himself, to be treated with generosity. Any question as to the charges made by him as schoolmaster was unendurable. He explained to all parents that he charged for each boy at the rate of two hundred a-year for board, lodging, and tuition, and that anything required for a boy's benefit or comfort beyond that ordinarily supplied

would be charged for as an extra at such price as Dr.
Wortle himself thought to be an equivalent. Now the
popularity of his establishment no doubt depended in a
great degree on the sufficiency and comfort of the good
things of the world which he provided. The beer was
of the best; the boys were not made to eat fat; their
taste in the selection of joints was consulted. The
morning coffee was excellent. The cook was a great
adept at cakes and puddings.

The Doctor would not himself have been satisfied
unless everything had been plentiful, and everything of
the best. He would have hated a butcher who had
attempted to seduce him with meat beneath the usual
price. But when he had supplied that which was sufficient
according to his own liberal ideas, he did not give more
without charging for it. Among his customers there
had been a certain Honourable Mr. Stantiloup, and,—
which had been more important—an Honourable Mrs.
Stantiloup. Mrs. Stantiloup was a lady who liked all the
best things which the world could supply, but hardly
liked paying the best price. Dr. Wortle's school was the
best thing the world could supply of that kind, but then
the price was certainly the very best.

Young Stantiloup was only eleven, and as there were
boys at Bowick as old as seventeen,—for the school had
not altogether maintained its old character as being
merely preparatory,—Mrs. Stantiloup had thought that
her boy should be admitted at a lower fee. The correspondence which had ensued had been unpleasant.
Then young Stantiloup had had the influenza, and
Mrs. Stantiloup had sent her own doctor. Champagne
had been ordered, and carriage exercise. Mr. Stantiloup
had been forced by his wife to refuse to pay sums
demanded for these undoubted extras. Ten shillings a-
day for a drive for a little boy seemed to her a great deal,
—seemed so to Mrs. Stantiloup. Ought not the Doctor's
wife to have been proud to take out her little boy in her

own carriage? And then £2 10s. for champagne for the little boy! It was monstrous.

Mr. Stantiloup remonstrated. Dr. Wortle said that the little boy had better be taken away and the bill paid at once. The little boy was taken away and the money was offered, short of £5. The matter was instantly put into the hands of the Doctor's lawyer, and a suit commenced. The Doctor, of course, got his money, and then there followed an acrimonious correspondence in the "Times" and other newspapers. Mrs. Stantiloup did her best to ruin the school, and many very eloquent passages were written not only by her or by her own special scribe, but by others who took the matter up, to prove that two hundred a-year was a great deal more than ought to be paid for the charge of a little boy during three quarters of the year. But in the course of the next twelve months Dr. Wortle was obliged to refuse admittance to a dozen eligible pupils because he had not room for them.

ANTHONY TROLLOPE (1815-1882)
Dr. Wortle's School

BELLOC'S OXFORD

We kept the Rabelaisian plan:
    We dignified the dainty cloisters
With Natural Law, the Rights of Man,
    Song, Stoicism, Wine and Oysters.

The library was most inviting:
    The books upon the crowded shelves
Were mainly of our private writing:
    We kept a school and taught ourselves.

We taught the art of writing things
   On men we still should like to throttle:
And where to get the Blood of Kings
   At only half a crown a bottle.

     *   *   *

They say that in the unchanging place,
   Where all we loved is always dear,
We meet our morning face to face
   And find at last our twentieth year. . . .

They say (and I am glad they say)
   It is so; and it may be so:
It may be just the other way,
   I cannot tell. But this I know:

From quiet homes and first beginning,
   Out to the undiscovered ends,
There's nothing worth the wear of winning,
   But laughter and the love of friends.

     *   *   *

And oh! the days, the days, the days,
   When all the four were off together:
The infinite deep of summer haze,
   The roaring charge of autumn weather.

     *   *   *

I will not try the reach again,
   I will not set my sail alone,
To moor a boat bereft of men
   At Yarnton's tiny docks of stone.

But I will sit beside the fire,
   And put my hand before my eyes,
And trace, to fill my heart's desire,
   The last of all our Odysseys.

The quiet evening kept her tryst:
   Beneath an open sky we rode,
And passed into a wandering mist
   Along the perfect Evenlode.

The tender Evenlode that makes
   Her meadows hush to hear the sound
Of waters mingling in the brakes,
   And binds my heart to English ground.

A lovely river, all alone,
   She lingers in the hills and holds
A hundred little towns of stones,
   Forgotten in the western wolds.

HILAIRE BELLOC (1870-1953)
Dedicatory Ode

BROOKE'S CAMBRIDGE

I only know that you may lie
Day long and watch the Cambridge sky,
And, flower-lulled in sleepy grass,
Hear the cool lapse of hours pass,
Until the centuries blend and blur
In Grantchester, in Grantchester. . . .
Still in the dawnlit waters cool
His ghostly Lordship swims his pool,
And tries the strokes, essays the tricks,
Long learnt on Hellespont, or Styx.
Dan Chaucer hears his river still
Chatter beneath a phantom mill.

Tennyson notes, with studious eye,
How Cambridge waters hurry by . . .
And in that garden, black and white,
Creep whispers through the grass all night;
And spectral dance, before the dawn,
A hundred Vicars down the lawn;
Curates, long dust, will come and go
On lissom, clerical, printless toe;
And oft between the boughs is seen
The sly shade of a Rural Dean . . .
Till, at a shiver in the skies,
Vanishing with Satanic cries,
The prim ecclesiastical rout
Leaves but a startled sleeper-out,
Grey heavens, the first bird's drowsy calls,
The falling house that never falls. . . .

. . . Ah, God! to see the branches stir
Across the moon at Grantchester!
To smell the thrilling-sweet and rotten
Unforgettable, unforgotten
River-smell, and hear the breeze
Sobbing in the little trees.
Say, do the elm-clumps greatly stand
Still guardians of that holy land?
The chestnuts shade, in reverend dream,
The yet unacademic stream?
Is dawn a secret shy and cold
Anadyomene, silver-gold?
And sunset still a golden sea
From Haslingfield to Madingley?
And after, ere the night is born,
Do hares come out about the corn?
Oh, is the water sweet and cool,
Gentle and brown, above the pool?
And laughing the immortal river still
Under the mill, under the mill?

Say, is there Beauty yet to find?
And Certainty? and Quiet kind?
Deep meadows yet, for to forget
The lies, and truths, and pain? . . . Oh! yet
Stands the Church clock at ten to three?
And is there honey still for tea?

RUPERT BROOKE (1887-1915)
The Old Vicarage, Grantchester

LINCOLNSHIRE: TENNYSON'S BIRTHPLACE, SOMERSBY
Somersby Rectory, where Alfred, Lord Tennyson, was born in 1809, in the room with the balcony. The chapel-like portion on the right is a dining-room built while Tennyson was living there. The rich pastoral scenery of this part of Lincolnshire influenced his early poetry.

NOTTINGHAMSHIRE: MAKING CRICKET BATS, NOTTINGHAM
Although Nottingham is an industrial city, producing lace, hosiery, clothing, bicycles, machinery and chemicals, most of us first hear of it in connection with Robin Hood and nearby Sherwood Forest. It is also one of the homes of cricket, with a fine ground at Trent Bridge and craftsmen skilled in the making of bats.

DERBYSHIRE: CHATSWORTH HOUSE

The seat of the Duke of Devonshire, Chatsworth House stands on the River Derwent, about 3 miles east of Bakewell. Ionic in style, it is built foursquare, with famous gardens decorated with sculptures and fountains said to be surpassed only by those at Versailles.

LEICESTERSHIRE: LITTLE DALBY

A typical stretch of countryside in Leicestershire, which is primarily a dairy-farming county, although there is some coal-mining. This village was once the home of Mrs. Orton, said to be the first maker of Stilton cheese, which is now mainly produced in Leicestershire.

Seas and Sailors

THE MOAT DEFENSIVE

I will make no other Introduction to the following Discourse, than that as the Importance of our being strong at Sea was ever very great, so in our present Circumstances it is grown to be much greater; because, as formerly our Force in Shipping contributed greatly to our Trade and Safety, so now it is become indispensably necessary to our very being.

It may be said now to *England*, Martha, Martha, *thou art busy about many things, but one thing* is necessary. To the question, What shall we do to be saved in this World? there is no other answer but this, Look to your *Moat*.

The first Article of an Englishman's Political Creed must be, That he believeth in the Sea, &c., without that there needeth no General Council to pronounce him incapable of Salvation here.

We are in an Island, confined to it by God Almighty, not as a Penalty but a Grace, and one of the greatest that can be given to Mankind. Happy confinement, that hath made us Free, Rich, and Quiet; a fair Portion in this World, and very well worth the preserving; a Figure that ever hath been envied, and could never be imitated by our Neighbours.

THE MARQUESS OF HALIFAX (1635-1695)
A Draft of a New Model at Sea

AU REVOIR—MAID TO MAN

The sea-faring life has always involved sad partings and farewells:
England has been rich in ballads and lyrics crying "Au revoir".

Shall I thus ever long, and be no whit the neare?
   And shall I still complain to thee, the which me will
      not hear?
   Alas! say nay! say nay! and be no more so dumb,
But open thou thy manly mouth and say that thou
     wilt come:
   Whereby my heart may think, although I see not thee,
That thou wilt come—thy word so sware—if thou a live
     man be.
   The roaring hugy waves they threaten my poor ghost,
And toss thee up and down the seas in danger to be lost.
   Shall they not make me fear that they have swallowed
     thee?
—But as thou art most sure alive, so wilt thou come to
     me?
   Whereby I shall go see thy ship ride on the strand,
And think and say *Lo where he comes* and *Sure here will he
    land*:
   And then I shall lift up to thee my little hand,
And thou shalt think thine heart in ease, in health to see
     me stand.
   And if thou come indeed (as Christ thee send to do!)
Those arms which miss thee now shall then embrace thee
     too:
   Each vein to every joint the lively blood shall spread
Which now for want of thy glad sight doth show full
     pale and dead.
   But if thou slip thy troth, and do not come at all,
As minutes in the clock do strike so call for death I
     shall:

To please both thy false heart and rid myself from
    woe,
That rather had to die in troth than live forsaken so!

ANONYMOUS (1557)

AU REVOIR—MAN TO MAID

All in the Downs the fleet was moor'd,
    The streamers waving in the wind,
When black-eyed Susan came aboard;
    "O! where shall I my true-love find?
Tell me, ye jovial sailors, tell me true
If my sweet William sails among the crew."

William, who high upon the yard
    Rock'd with the billow to and fro,
Soon as her well-known voice he heard
    He sigh'd and cast his eyes below:
The cord slides swiftly through his glowing hands,
And quick as lightning on the deck he stands.

So the sweet lark, high poised in air,
    Shuts close his pinions to his breast
If chance his mate's shrill call he hear,
    And drops at once into her nest:—
The noblest captain in the British fleet
Might envy William's lip those kisses sweet.

"O Susan, Susan, lovely dear,
    My vows shall ever true remain;
Let me kiss off that falling tear;
    We only part to meet again.
Change as ye list, ye winds; my heart shall be
The faithful compass that still points to thee.

"Believe not what the landmen say
    Who tempt with doubts thy constant mind:
They'll tell thee, sailors, when away,
    In every port a mistress find:

Yes, yes, believe them when they tell thee so,
For Thou art present whereso'er I go.

" If to fair India's coast we sail,
　　Thy eyes are seen in diamonds bright,
Thy breath in Afric's spicy gale,
　　Thy skin is ivory so white.
Thus every beauteous object that I view
Wakes in my soul some charm of lovely Sue.

" Though battle call me from thy arms
　　Let not my pretty Susan mourn;
Though cannons roar, yet safe from harms
　　William shall to his Dear return.
Love turns aside the balls that round me fly,
Lest precious tears should drop from Susan's eye."

The boatswain gave the dreadful word,
　　The sails their swelling bosom spread,
No longer must she stay aboard;
　　They kiss'd, she sigh'd, he hung his head.
Her lessening boat unwilling rows to land;
" Adieu!" she cried; and waved her lily hand.

　　　　　　　　　　JOHN GAY (1685-1732)
　　　　　Sweet William's Farewell to Black-Eyed Susan

THE ELIZABETHAN SAILORS

To harp no longer upon this string and to speak a word
of that just commendation which our nation do indeed
deserve; it cannot be denied, but as in all former ages
they have been men full of activity, stirrers abroad and
searchers of the remote parts of the world, so in this
most famous and fearless government of her Most
Excellent Majesty, through the special assistance and
blessing of God, in search of the most opposite corners
and quarters of the world, and to speak plainly in com-

passing the vast globe of the earth more than once they have excelled all the nations and people of the earth. For which of the kings of this land before her Majesty had their banners ever seen in the Caspian Sea? Which of them hath ever dealt with the Emperor of Persia, as her Majesty hath done, and obtained for her merchant large and loving privileges? Whoever saw before this regiment an English ligier in the stately porch of the Grand Signior at Constantinople? Whoever found English consuls and agents at Tripolis in Syria at Aleppo, at Babylon, at Balsara, and, which is more, whoever heard of Englishmen at Goa before now? What English ships did heretofore ever anchor in the mighty river of Plate? Pass and repass the unpassable (in former opinion) Strait of Magellan, range along the coast of Chile, Peru, and all the backside of Nova Hispania, further than any Christian ever passed, traverse the mighty breadth of the South Sea, land upon the Luzones in despite of the enemy, enter into alliance, amity, and traffic with the Princes of the Moluccaes and the Isle of Java, double the famous Cape of Bona Speranza, arrive at the Isle of Santa Helena, and, last of all, return most richly laden with the commodities of China, as the subjects of this now flourishing monarchy have done?

RICHARD HAKLUYT (*c.* 1552-1616)
Principal Voyages of the English Nation, 1589

ADVICE TO CAPTAINS

Young gentlemen that desires command ought well to consider the condition of his ship, victual and company; for if there be more learners than sailors, how slightly soever many esteem sailors, all the work to save ship, goods and lives must lie upon them, especially in foul weather; the labour, hazard, wet and cold is so incredible I cannot express it. It is not then the number of them that here will say at home, what I cannot do I can quickly learn, and what a great matter it is to sail a ship or go to sea. Surely those for a good time will do most trouble than good. I confess it is more necessary such should go, but not too many in one ship; for if the labour of sixty should lie upon thirty, as many times it doth, they are so overcharged with labour, bruises and overstraining themselves (for there is no dallying nor excuses with storms, gusts, over-grown seas and lee shores), they fall sick of one disease or other, and then if their victuals be putrefied, it endangers all.

Men of all other professions, in lightning, thunder, storms and tempests, with rain and snow, may shelter themselves in dry houses, by good fires and good cheer; but those are the chief times that seamen must stand to their tacklings, and attend with all diligence their greatest labour upon the decks. Many supposeth anything is good enough to serve men at sea and yet nothing sufficient for them ashore, either for their healths, for their ease, or estates, or state. A commander at sea should do well to think the contrary, and provide for himself and company in like manner: also seriously to consider what will be his charge to furnish himself at sea with bedding, linen, arms and apparel; how to keep his table aboard, his expenses on shore, and his petty tally, which is a competent proportion according to your number, of these particulars following.

Fine wheat-flour, close and well packed, rice, currants, sugar, prunes, cinnamon, ginger, pepper, cloves, green-ginger, oil, butter, old cheese, or holland, wine vinegar, canary sack, aqua-vitæ, the best wines, the best waters, the juice of lemons for the scurvy, white biscuit, oatmeal, gammons of bacon, dried neats' tongues, roasted beef packed up in vinegar, legs of mutton minced and stewed, and close packed up with butter in earthen pots. To entertain strangers, marmalet, suckets, almonds, comfits and such-like.

Some it may be will say I would have men rather to
feast than fight. But I say the want of those necessaries
occasions the loss of more men than in any English
fleet hath been slain in any fight since 1588: for when a
man is ill, sick, or at the point of death, I would know
whether a dish of buttered rice, with a little cinnamon
and sugar, a little minced meat, or roast beef, a few
stewed prunes, a race of green-ginger, a flap-jack,[1] a can
of fresh brewed water with a little cinnamon, ginger and
sugar, be not better than a little poor John,[2] or salt fish
with oil and mustard, or biscuit, butter, cheese or
oatmeal pottage on fish days, salt beef, pork and pease,
and six shillings' beer. This is your ordinary ship's
allowance and good for them are well, if well con-
ditioned, which is not always, as seamen can too well witness; and after a storm, when poor men are all wet and
some not so much a cloth to shift him, shaking with
cold, few of those but will tell you a little sack or aqua-
vitæ is much better to keep them in health than a little
small beer or cold water, although it be sweet.

JOHN SMITH
An Accidence for Young Seamen, 1626

[1] Pancake [2] Salt cod

THE CLIFFS OF DOVER

Come on, sir; here's the place. Stand still. How fearful
And dizzy 'tis to cast one's eyes so low!
The crows and choughs that wing the midway air
Show scarce so gross as beetles: half way down
Hangs one that gathers samphire,—dreadful trade!
Methinks he seems no bigger than his head:
The fishermen, that walk upon the beach,
Appear like mice; and yond tall anchoring bark,
Diminisht to her cock,—her cock, a buoy

Almost too small for sight: the murmuring surge,
That on the unnumber'd idle pebbles chafes,
Cannot be heard so high.

WILLIAM SHAKESPEARE (1564-1616)
King Lear

SHAKESPEARE AT SEA

From the journal of Captain William Keeling, of the *Dragon*, bound for the East Indies with the *Hector*, whose captain was William Hawkins, and the *Consent*. In September, 1607, the ships were in the neighbourhood of Sierra Leone. The reason for this exercise in amateur theatricals is of interest considering the current suspicion that play-acting was likely to lead to immorality. Captain Keeling evidently looked on drama as a prop of discipline. Remembering the size of vessels at that time we may surmise that the productions were, as we say, "intimate". Perhaps some failed actor, who had taken to a seaman's life with the East India Company's fleet, was there, with copies of the plays, to stimulate and organise. Or Keeling himself may have been one of the early devotees of the Bard, finding Shakespeare an abiding comfort on the High Seas.

1607. *Sept. 5.*   I sent the interpreter, according to his desire, aboard the Hector where he broke fast and afterward came aboard me where we gave the tragedy of Hamlet.

Sept. 30.   Captain Hawkins dined with me, where my companions acted King Richard the Second.

1608. *March 31.*   I invited Captain Hawkins to a fish dinner and had Hamlet acted aboard me; which I permit to keep my people from idleness and unlawful games, or sleep.

CAPTAIN WILLIAM KEELING
Journal

CHESHIRE: LOCOMOTIVE WORKS AT CREWE

Crewe is a great railway junction, with lines converging from London, Manchester and Wales. It has one of the busiest railway stations in the world, and one of the biggest locomotive and rolling stock works.

STAFFORDSHIRE: THE POTTERIES

The Potteries is a name given to a district of North Staffordshire, the centre of the earthenware and china industry. It comprises Hanley, Stoke-on-Trent, Burslem, Longton, Tunstall and Fenton, and is the scene of many of Arnold Bennett's novels, such as *Clayhanger*. Coal for these kilns at Stoke is brought by canal.

STAFFORDSHIRE: LICHFIELD

The city of Lichfield has a long history, being first mentioned in Bede's
Ecclesiastical History in 731. This picture of the 13th-14th century cathedral
shows the Garden of Remembrance in the foreground. The many
interesting old houses include the birthplace of Dr. Johnson.

SLEEP AND THE SHIP-BOY

The King is speaking. Shakespeare's interest in, and possibly experience of, storms at sea is remarkable. Had he seen a ship-boy thus unperturbed?

How many thousand of my poorest subjects
Are at this hour asleep!—O sleep, O gentle sleep,
Nature's soft nurse, how have I frighted thee,
That thou no more wilt weigh my eyelids down,
And steep my senses in forgetfulness?
Why rather, sleep, liest thou in smoky cribs,
Upon uneasy pallets stretching thee,
And husht with buzzing night-flies to thy slumber,
Than in the perfumed chambers of the great,
Under the canopies of costly state,
And lull'd with sound of sweetest melody?
O thou dull god, why liest thou with the vile
In loathsome beds, and leavest the kingly couch
A watch-case or a common 'larum-bell?
Wilt thou upon the high and giddy mast
Seal up the ship-boy's eyes, and rock his brains
In cradle of the rude imperious surge,
And in the visitation of the winds,
Who take the ruffian billows by the top,
Curling their monstrous heads, and hanging them
With deafening clamour in the slippery shrouds,
That, with the hurly, death itself awakes?—
Canst thou, O partial sleep, give thy repose
To the wet sea-boy in an hour so rude;
And in the calmest and most stillest night,
With all appliances and means to boot,
Deny it to a king? Then, happy low, lie down!
Uneasy lies the head that wears a crown.

WILLIAM SHAKESPEARE (1564-1616)
Henry IV, Part 2

12

PRESS GANG

June 30th, 1666. Mightily troubled all this morning with going to my Lord Mayor, (Sir Thomas Bludworth, a silly man I think), and other places, about getting shipped some men that they have these two last nights pressed in the City out of houses: the persons wholly unfit for sea, and many of them people of very good fashion, which is a shame to think of, and carried to Bridewell they are, yet without being impressed with money legally as they ought to be. But to see how the King's business is done; my Lord Mayor himself did scruple at this time of extremity to do this thing, because he had not money to pay the pressed-money to the men. I did out of my own purse disburse 15£. to pay for their pressing and diet last night and this morning; which is a thing worth record of my Lord Mayor. Busy about this all the morning, and about the getting off men pressed by our officers of the fleet into the service; even our own men that are at the office, and the boats that carry us. So that it is now become impossible to have so much as a letter carried from place to place, or any message done for us: nay, out of Victualling ships, full loaden to go down to the fleet, and out of the vessels of the officers of the Ordnance they press men, so that for want of discipline in this respect I do fear all will be undone.

July 1st. . . . To the Tower several times, about the business of the pressed men, and late at it till twelve at night shipping of them. But, Lord! how some poor women did cry; and in my life I never did see such natural expression of passion as I did here in some women's bewailing themselves, and running to every parcel of men that were brought, one after another, to

look for their husbands, and wept over every vessel
that went off, thinking they might be there, and looking
after the ship as far as ever they could by moone-light,
that it grieved me to the heart to hear them. Besides, to
see poor patient labouring men and house-keepers
leaving poor wives and families, taken up on a sudden
by strangers, was very hard, and that without press-
money, but forced against all law to be gone. It is a great
tyranny.

SAMUEL PEPYS (1633-1703)
Diary

SAILOR SUITOR

In Congreve's comedy <i>Love for Love</i>, Sir Sampson Legend would have
his son Ben, a bluff, rough sailor, get married. Ben is a reluctant
suitor, but he dutifully does propose to Miss Prue Foresight, herself
described as "a silly, awkward country girl". This meeting of land
and water makes a stormy wooing.

BEN   Come, mistress, will you please to sit down?
       For an you stand astern o' that'n, we shall never
       grapple together. Come, I'll haul a chair. There,
       an you please to sit, I'll sit by you.

MISS   You need not sit so near one. If you have anything
       to say, I can hear you farther off. I ain't deaf.

BEN   Why, that's true, as you say, nor I ain't dumb.
       I can be heard as far as another. I'll heave off,
       to please you. [<i>sits farther off</i>] An we were a
       league asunder, I'd undertake to hold discourse
       with you, an 'twere not a main high wind
       indeed, and full in my teeth. Look you, forsooth,
       I am, as it were, bound for the land of
       matrimony. 'Tis a voyage, d'ye, that was none of
       my seeking. I was commanded by father, and if

you like of it, mayhap I may steer into your harbour. How say you, mistress? The short of the thing is that if you like me, and I like you, we may chance to swing in a hammock together.

MISS I don't know what to say to you, nor I don't care to speak with you at all.

BEN No, I'm sorry for that. But pray, why are you so scornful?

MISS As long as one must not speak one's mind, one had better not speak at all, I think, and truly I won't tell a lie for the matter.

BEN Nay, you say true in that. It's but a folly to lie. For to speak one thing, and to think just the contrary way is, as it were, to look one way and to row another. Now, for my part, d'ye see, I'm for carrying things above board. I'm not for keeping anything under hatches. So that if you ben't as willing as I, say so i' God's name, there's no harm done. Mayhap you may be shamefaced. Some maidens though they love a man well enough yet they don't care to tell 'n so to's face. If that's the case, why silence gives consent.

MISS But I'm sure it is not so, for I'll speak sooner than you should believe that. And I'll speak truth, though one should always tell a lie to a man, and I don't care, let my father do what he will. I'm too big to be whipped, so I'll tell you plainly I don't like you, nor love you at all, nor never will, that's more. So, there's your answer for you, and don't trouble me no more, you ugly thing.

BEN   Look you, young woman, you may learn to give good words, however. I spoke you fair, d'ye see, and civil. As for your love or your liking, I don't value it of a rope's end. And mayhap I like you as little as you do me. What I said was in obedience to father. Gad, I fear a whipping no more than you do. But I tell you one thing, if you should give such language at sea, you'd have a cat-o'-ninetails laid across your shoulders. Flesh! who are you? You heard t'other handsome young woman speak civilly to me of her own accord. Whatever you think of yourself, gad, I don't think you are any more to compare to her than a can of small-beer to a bowl of punch.

MISS   Well, and there's a handsome gentleman, and a fine gentleman, and a sweet gentleman, that was here that loves me, and I love him. And if he sees you speak to me any more, he'll thrash your jacket for you, he will, you great sea-calf.

BEN   What, do you mean that fair-weather spark that was here just now? Will he thrash my jacket? Let'n, let'n. But if an comes near me, mayhap I may give'n a salt eel for his supper, for all that. What does father mean to leave me alone as soon as I come home with such a dirty dowdy? Sea-calf! I ain't calf enough to lick your chalked face, you cheese-curd, you. Marry thee! 'Oons, I'll marry a Lapland witch as soon, and live upon selling contrary winds, and wrecked vessels.

MISS   I won't be called names, nor I won't be abused thus, so I won't. If I were a man—(cries)—you durst not talk at this rate. No, you durst not, you stinking tar-barrel.

WILLIAM CONGREVE (1670-1728)
Love for Love

THE HAPPY EMIGRANT

Where the remote Bermudas ride
In the ocean's bosom unespied,
From a small boat that row'd along
The listening winds received this song.
" What should we do but sing His praise
That led us through the watery maze
Where He the huge sea-monsters wracks,
That lift the deep upon their backs,
Unto an isle so long unknown,
And yet far kinder than our own?
He lands us on a grassy stage,
Safe from the storms, and prelate's rage:
He gave us this eternal Spring
Which here enamels everything,
And sends the fowls to us in care
On daily visits through the air.
He hangs in shades the orange bright
Like golden lamps in a green night,
And does in the pomegranates close
Jewels more rich than Ormus shows:
He makes the figs our mouths to meet
And throws the melons at our feet;
But apples plants of such a price,
No tree could ever bear them twice.
With cedars chosen by His hand
From Lebanon He stores the land;
And makes the hollow seas that roar
Proclaim the ambergris on shore.
He cast (of which we rather boast)
The Gospel's pearl upon our coast;
And in these rocks for us did frame
A temple where to sound His name.
Oh! let our voice His praise exalt
Till it arrive at Heaven's vault,

Which thence (perhaps) rebounding may
Echo beyond the Mexique bay!"
—Thus sung they in the English boat
A holy and a cheerful note:
And all the way, to guide their chime,
With falling oars they kept the time.

ANDREW MARVELL (1620-1678)
The English Emigrants in Bermuda

T. STUMP AND THE SAVAGES

Captain Thomas Stump, of Malmesbury. 'Tis pity the
strange adventures of him should be forgotten. He was
the eldest sonn of Mr. William Stump, rector of Yatton
Keynell; was a boy of most daring spirit; he would
climb towers and trees most dangerously; nay, he would
walke on the battlements of the tower there.

He had too much spirit to be a scholar, and about
sixteen went in a voyage with his uncle, since Sir Thomas
Ivy, to Guyana, in *anno* 1633, or 1632. When the ship
put in somewhere there, four or five of them straggled
into the countrey too far, and in the interim the wind
served, and the sails were hoist, and the stragglers left
behind. It was not long before the wild people seized
on them and strip't them, and those that had beards
they knocked their braines out, and (as I remember) did
eat them; but the Queen saved T. Stump, and the other
boy. Stump threw himself into the river Oronoque
to have drowned himself, but could not sinke; he is
very full chested. The other youth shortly died. He
lived with them till 1636 or 1637.

His narrations are very strange and pleasant; but so
many yeares have made me almost forgett all. He sayes
there is incomparable fruite there, and that it may be
termed the Paradise of the World. He says that the
spondyles of the backbones of the huge serpents there

are used to sit on, as our women sitt upon butts. He taught them to build hovills, and to thatch and wattle. I wish I had a good account of his abode there; he is *fide dignus*.[1] I never heard of any man that lived so long among those savages. A ship then sayling by, a Portughese, he swam to it; and they took him up and made use of him for a seaboy. As he was sayling near Cornwall he stole out of a port-hole and swam to shore; and so begged to his father's in Wiltshire. When he came home nobody knew him, and they would not own him; only Jo. Harris the carpenter knew him. At last he recounted so many circumstances that he was owned, and in 1642 had a commission for a Captain of Foot in King Charles the First's army.

JOHN AUBREY (1626-1697)
Brief Lives

[1] Worthy to be believed

SEA-DOG ON LAND

This loquacious publican soon gave him sketches of all the characters in the county; and, among others, described that of his next neighbour, Commodore Trunnion, which was altogether singular and odd. "The commodore and your worship," said he, "will in a short time be hand and glove; he has a power of money, and spends it like a prince—that is, in his own way—for to be sure he is a little humorsome, as the saying is, and swears woundily; though I'll be sworn he means no more harm than a sucking babe. Lord help us! it will do your honour's heart good to hear him tell a story, as how he lay along-side of the French, yard-arm and yard-arm, board and board, and of heaving grapplings, and stink-pots, and grapes, and round and double-headed partridges, crows and carters.[1] Lord have mercy upon us! he has

[1] Various names for missiles fired at sea

been a great warrior in his time, and lost an eye and a heel in the service. Then he does not live like any other Christian land-man; but keeps garrison in his house, as if he were in the midst of his enemies, and makes his servants turn out in the night, watch and watch as he calls it, all the year round. His habitation is defended by a ditch, over which he had laid a draw-bridge, and planted his court-yard with patereroes continually loaded with shot, under the direction of one Mr. Hatchway, who had one of his legs shot away while he acted as lieutenant on board the commodore's ship; and now, being on half-pay, lives with him as his companion.

"The lieutenant is a very brave man, a great joker, and, as the saying is, hath got the length of his commander's foot—though he has another favourite in the house called Tom Pipes, that was his boatswain's mate, and now keeps the servants in order. Tom is a man of few words, but an excellent hand at a song concerning the boatswain's whistle, hustle-cap, and chuck-farthing—there is not such another pipe in the county—so that the commodore lives very happy in his own manner; tho' he be sometimes thrown into perilous passions and quandaries, by the application of his poor kinsmen, whom he can't abide, because as how some of them were the first occasion of his going to sea. Then he sweats with agony at the sight of an attorney, just, for all the world, as some people have an antipathy to a cat; for it seems he was once at law, for striking one of his officers, and cast in a swinging sum.

"He is, moreover, exceedingly afflicted with goblins that disturb his rest, and keep such a racket in his house, that you would think (God bless us!) all the devils in hell had broke loose upon him. It was no longer ago than last year about this time, that he was tormented the livelong night by the mischievous spirits that got into his chamber, and played a thousand pranks about his hammock, for there is not one bed within his walls.

Well, sir, he rang his bell, called up all his servants, got lights, and made a thorough search; but the devil a goblin was to be found. He had no sooner turned in again, and the rest of the family gone to sleep, than the foul fiends began their game anew.

"True it is, Mr. Hatchway makes a mock of the whole affair; and told his commander, in this very blessed spot, that the two goblins were no other than a couple of jackdaws which had fallen down the chimney, and made a flapping with their wings up and down the apartment. But the commodore, who is very choleric, and does not like to be jeered, fell into a main high passion, and stormed like a perfect hurricane, swearing that he knew a devil from a jackdaw as well as e'er a man in the three kingdoms. He owned, indeed, that the birds were found, but denied that they were the occasion of the uproar. For my own part, master, I believe much may be said on both sides of the question; though to be sure, the devil is always going about, as the saying is."

TOBIAS SMOLLETT (1721-1771)
Peregrine Pickle

THE SEA-DOG'S WEDDING

Another day was fixed for the nuptials; and in order to balk the curiosity of idle people, which had given great offence, the parson was prevailed upon to perform the ceremony in the garrison, which all that day was adorned with flags and pendants displayed; and at night illuminated, by the direction of Hatchway, who also ordered the patereroes to be fired, as soon as the marriage-knot was tied. Neither were the other parts of the entertainment neglected by this ingenious contriver, who produced undeniable proofs of his elegance and art in the wedding-supper, which had been committed to his management and direction. This genial banquet was entirely composed of sea-dishes; a huge pillaw, consisting of a large piece of beef sliced, a couple of fowls, and half a peck of rice, smoked in the middle of the board; a dish of hard fish, swimming in oil, appeared at each end; the sides being furnished with a mess of that savoury composition known by the name of lob's-course,[1] and a plate of salmagundy.[2] The second course displayed a goose of a monstrous magnitude, flanked with two Guinea-hens, a pig barbacued, a hock of salt pork in the midst of a pease-pudding, a leg of mutton roasted, with potatoes, and another boiled with yams. The third service was made up of a loin of fresh pork, with apple-sauce, a kid smothered with onions, and a terrapin baked in the shell; and, last of all, a prodigious sea-pie was presented, with an infinite volume of pancakes and fritters. That everything might be answerable to the magnificence of this delicate feast, he had provided vast quantities of strong beer, flip,[3] rumbo, and burnt brandy, with plenty of Barbadoes water for the ladies; and hired all the fiddles within six miles, which, with the addition of a drum, bagpipe, and Welsh harp, regaled the guests with a most melodious concert.

The company, who were not at all exceptious, seemed extremely well pleased with every particular of the entertainment; and the evening being spent in the most social manner, the bride was by her sister conducted to her apartment, where, however, a trifling circumstance had like to have destroyed the harmony which had been hitherto maintained.

I have already observed, that there was not one standing bed within the walls; therefore the reader will not wonder that Mrs. Trunnion was out of humour, when she found herself under the necessity of being confined with her spouse in a hammock, which, though enlarged

---

[1] Meat stewed with vegetables
[2] A rich dish of chopped meat
[3] A hot mixture of beer and spirits

with a double portion of canvass, and dilated with a
yoke for the occasion, was at best but a disagreeable, not
to say dangerous, situation. She accordingly complained with some warmth of this inconvenience, which
she imputed to disrespect; and, at first, absolutely refused
to put up with the expedient: but Mrs. Pickle soon
brought her to reason and compliance, by observing
that one night would soon be elapsed, and next day she
might regulate her own economy.

Thus persuaded, she ventured into the vehicle, and was
visited by her husband in less than an hour, the company being departed to their own homes, and the
garrison left to the command of his lieutenant and mate.
But it seems the hooks that supported this swinging
couch were not calculated for the addition of weight
which they were now destined to bear; and therefore
gave way in the middle of the night, to the no small
terror of Mrs. Trunnion, who perceiving herself falling,
screamed aloud, and by that exclamation brought
Hatchway, with a light into the chamber. Though she
had received no injury by the fall, she was extremely
discomposed and incensed at the accident, which she
even openly ascribed to the obstinacy and whimsical
oddity of the commodore, in such petulant terms as
evidently declared that she thought her great aim
accomplished, and her authority secured against all the
shocks of fortune. Indeed her bedfellow seemed to be
of the same opinion, by his tacit resignation; for he
made no reply to her insinuations, but with a most
vinegar aspect crawled out of his nest, and betook
himself to rest in another apartment: while his irritated
spouse dismissed the lieutenant, and from the wreck of
the hammock made an occasional bed for herself on the
floor, fully determined to provide better accommodation
for the next night's lodging.

TOBIAS SMOLLETT (1721-1771)
Peregrine Pickle

BECALMED: A PUNISHMENT

And a good south wind sprung up behind;
The albatross did follow,
And every day, for food or play,
Came to the mariners' hollo!

In mist or cloud, on mast or shroud,
It perch'd for vespers nine;
Whiles all the night, through fog-smoke white,
Glimmer'd the white moonshine.

"God save thee, ancient Mariner,
From the fiends, that plague thee thus!—
Why look'st thou so?"—"With my crossbow
I shot the Albatross."

"The Sun now rose upon the right:
Out of the sea came he,
Still hid in mist, and on the left
Went down into the sea.

And the good south wind still blew behind,
But no sweet bird did follow,
Nor any day for food or play
Came to the mariners' hollo!

And I had done a hellish thing,
And it would work 'em woe:
For all averr'd I had kill'd the bird
That made the breeze to blow.
Ah wretch! said they, the bird to slay,
That made the breeze to blow!

Nor dim nor red, like God's own head,
The glorious Sun uprist:
Then all averr'd I had kill'd the bird
That brought the fog and mist.
'Twas right, said they, such birds to slay,
That bring the fog and mist.

The fair breeze blew, the white foam flew,
The furrow follow'd free;
We were the first that ever burst
Into that silent sea.

Down dropt the breeze, the sails dropt down,
'Twas sad as sad could be;
And we did speak only to break
The silence of the sea!

All in a hot and copper sky,
The bloody Sun, at noon,
Right up above the mast did stand,
No bigger than the Moon.

Day after day, day after day,
We stuck, nor breath nor motion;
As idle as a painted ship
Upon a painted ocean.

Water, water, everywhere,
And all the boards did shrink;
Water, water, everywhere,
Nor any drop to drink.

The very deep did rot: O Christ!
That ever this should be!
Yea, slimy things did crawl with legs
Upon the slimy sea.

About, about, in reel and rout
The death-fires danced at night;
The water, like a witch's oils,
Burnt green, and blue, and white.

And some in dreams assurèd were
Of the Spirit that plagued us so;
Nine fathom deep he had follow'd us
From the land of the mist and snow.

And every tongue, through utter drought,
Was wither'd at the root;
We could not speak, no more than if
We had been choked with soot.

Ah! well a-day! what evil looks
Had I from old and young!
Instead of the cross, the Albatross
About my neck was hung.

S. T. COLERIDGE (1772-1834)
The Rime of the Ancient Mariner

NEPTUNE'S OWN

The more aggressively patriotic sea-poetry of England, though plentiful, has been sparingly used. It becomes monotonous. But Dibdin's rollicking songs have a humorous gusto and there is no taint of "British Imperialism" (long defunct anyway) in defending one's own island. The events of 1939-1945 have kept his ditty topical.

Daddy Neptune, one day, to Freedom did say,
    "If ever I lived upon dry land,
The spot I should hit on would be little Britain!"
    Says Freedom, "Why that's my own Island!"
        O, it's a snug little Island!
            A right little, tight little Island!
        Search the globe round, none can be found
            So happy as this little Island.

Julius Cæsar the Roman, who yielded to no man,
   Came by water—he couldn't come by land;
And Dane, Pict, and Saxon, their homes turn'd their
                                   backs on
    And all for the sake of our island.
      O, what a snug little Island!
        They'd all have a touch at the Island!
    Some were shot dead, some of them fled,
      And some stayed to live on the Island.

Then a very great war-man, called Billy the Norman,
   Cried, "Damn it, I never liked my land.
It would be much more handy to leave this Normandy,
   And live on your beautiful Island."
      Says he, "'Tis a snug little Island;
        Shan't we go visit the Island?"
      Hop, skip, and jump, there he was plump,
        And he kick'd up a dust in the Island.

But party deceit help'd the Normans to beat;
   Of traitors they managed to buy land;
By Dane, Saxon or Pict, Britons ne'er had been lick'd,
   Had they stuck to the King of their Island.
      Poor Harold the King of the Island!
        He lost both his life and the Island.
        That's all very true: what more could he do?
        Like a Briton he died for his Island.

The Spanish Armada set out to invade-a,
   'Twill sure if they ever come nigh land.
They couldn't do less than tuck up Queen Bess,
   And take their full swing on the Island.
      O, the poor Queen of the Island!
        The Dons came to plunder the Island;
      But snug in her hive, the Queen was alive,
        And "buzz" was the word in the Island.

Those proud puff'd-up cakes thought to make ducks and
                                          drakes
   Of our wealth; but they hardly could spy land
When our Drake had the luck to make their pride duck
   And stoop to the lads of the Island!
      Huzza for the lads of the Island!
        The good wooden walls of the Island;
      Devil or Don, let them come on,
        But see how they'd come off at the Island.

Since Freedom and Neptune have hitherto kept tune,
   In each saying, "This shall be my land";
Should the "Army of England," or all it could bring,
                                         land.
   We'd show 'em some play for the Island.
     We'd fight for our right to the Island;
       We'd give them enough of the Island;
     Invaders should just—bite at the dust,
      But not a bit more of the Island.

THOMAS DIBDIN (1771-1841)
The Snug Little Island

OMNIPOTENT OCEAN

Roll on, thou deep and dark blue Ocean—roll!
Ten thousand fleets sweep over thee in vain;
Man marks the earth with ruin—his control
Stops with the shore; upon the watery plain
The wrecks are all thy deed, nor doth remain
A shadow of man's ravage, save his own,
When, for a moment, like a drop of rain,
He sinks into thy depths with bubbling groan,
Without a grave, unknell'd, uncoffin'd, and unknown.

His steps are not upon thy paths,—thy fields
Are not a spoil for him,—thou dost arise
And shake him from thee; the vile strength he wields
For earth's destruction thou dost all despise,
Spurning him from thy bosom to the skies,
And sends't him, shivering in thy playful spray
And howling, to his Gods, where haply lies
His petty hope in some near port or bay,
And dashest him again to earth;—there let him lay.

The armaments which thunderstrike the walls
Of rock-built cities, bidding nations quake,
And monarchs tremble in their capitals,
The oak leviathans, whose huge ribs make
Their clay creator the vain title take
Of lord of thee, and arbiter of war—
These are thy toys, and, as the snowy flake,
They melt into thy yeast of waves, which mar
Alike the Armada's pride or spoils of Trafalgar.

Thy shores are empires, changed in all save thee—
Assyria, Greece, Rome, Carthage, what are they?
Thy waters wash'd them power while they were free,
And many a tyrant since: their shores obey
The stranger, slave, or savage; their decay
Has dried up realms to deserts:—not so thou;—
Unchangeable, save to thy wild waves' play
Time writes no wrinkle on thine azure brow;
Such as creation's dawn beheld, thou rollest now.

Thou glorious mirror, where the Almighty's form
Glasses itself in tempests; in all time,—
Calm or convulsed, in breeze, or gale, or storm,
Icing the pole, or in the torrid clime
Dark-heaving—boundless, endless, and sublime,
The image of eternity, the throne
Of the Invisible; even from out thy slime

The monsters of the deep are made; each zone
Obeys thee; thou goest forth, dread, fathomless, alone.

And I have loved thee, Ocean! and my joy
Of youthful sports was on thy breast to be
Borne, like thy bubbles, onward: from a boy
I wanton'd with thy breakers—they to me
Were a delight; and if the freshening sea
Made them a terror—'twas a pleasing fear,
For I was as it were a child of thee,
And trusted to thy billows far and near,
And laid my hand upon thy mane—as I do here.

LORD BYRON (1778-1824)
Childe Harold

BY SAIL TO MARGATE

A Hoy was a small vessel travelling small distances along the sea-coast. Here is Lamb's most flowery style of writing, characteristic, but not to be copied by intending essayists.

Can I forget thee, thou old Margate Hoy, with thy weather-beaten, sunburnt captain, and his rough accommodations—ill exchanged for the foppery and fresh-water niceness of the modern steam-packet? To the winds and waves thou committedst thy goodly freightage, and didst ask no aid of magic fumes, and spells, and boiling cauldrons. With the gales of heaven thou wentest swimmingly; or, when it was their pleasure, stoodest still with sailor-like patience. Thy course was natural, not forced, as in a hot-bed; nor didst thou go poisoning the breath of ocean with sulphureous smoke—a great sea chimera, chimneying and furnacing the deep; or liker to that fire-god parching up Scamander.

Can I forget thy honest, yet slender crew, with their coy reluctant responses (yet to the suppression of anything like contempt) to the raw questions, which we of the great city would be ever and anon putting to them, as to the uses of this or that strange naval implement? 'Specially can I forget thee, thou happy medium, thou shade of refuge between us and them, conciliating interpreter of their skill to our simplicity, comfortable ambassador between sea and land!—whose sailor-trousers did not more convincingly assure thee to be an adopted denizen of the former, than thy white cap, and whiter apron over them, with thy neat-fingered practice in thy culinary vocation, bespoke thee to have been of inland nurture heretofore—a master cook of Eastcheap?

How busily didst thou ply thy multifarious occupation, cook, mariner, attendant, chamberlain: here, there, like another Ariel, flaming at once about all parts of the deck, yet with kindlier ministrations— not to assist the tempest, but, as if touched with a kindred sense of our infirmities, to soothe the qualms which that untried motion might haply raise in our crude land-fancies. And when the o'erwashing billows drove us below deck (for it was far gone in October, and we had stiff and blowing weather) how did thy officious minister-ings, still catering for our comfort, with cards, and cordials, and thy more cordial conversation, alleviate the closeness and the confinement of thy else (truth to say) not very savoury, nor very inviting, little cabin!

CHARLES LAMB (1775-1834)
The Old Margate Hoy

MAN OVERBOARD

On the morning of the tenth of November, 1835, I found myself off the coast of Galicia, whose lofty mountains, gilded by the rising sun, presented a magnificent appearance. I was bound for Lisbon; we passed

Cape Finisterre, and standing farther out to sea, speedily lost sight of land. On the morning of the eleventh the sea was very rough, and a remarkable circumstance occurred. I was on the forecastle, discoursing with two of the sailors: one of them, who had but just left his hammock, said, "I have had a strange dream, which I do not much like, for," continued he, pointing up to the mast, "I dreamt that I fell into the sea from the cross-trees." He was heard to say this by several of the crew besides myself.

A moment after, the captain of the vessel perceiving that the squall was increasing, ordered the topsails to be taken in, whereupon this man with several others instantly ran aloft; the yard was in the act of being hauled down, when a sudden gust of wind whirled it round with violence, and a man was struck down from the cross-trees into the sea, which was working like yeast below. In a short time he emerged; I saw his head on the crest of a billow, and instantly recognised in the unfortunate man the sailor who a few moments before had related his dream.

I shall never forget the look of agony he cast whilst the steamer hurried past him. The alarm was given, and everything was in confusion; it was two minutes at least before the vessel was stopped, by which time the man was a considerable way astern; I still, however, kept my eye upon him, and could see that he was struggling gallantly with the waves. A boat was at length lowered, but the rudder was unfortunately not at hand, and only two oars could be procured, with which the men could make but little progress in so rough a sea. They did their best, however, and had arrived within ten yards of the man, who still struggled for his life, when I lost sight of him, and the men on their return said that they saw him below the water, at glimpses, sinking deeper and deeper, his arms stretched out and his body apparently stiff, but that they

found it impossible to save him; presently after, the
sea, as if satisfied with the prey which it had acquired,
became comparatively calm. The poor fellow who
perished in this singular manner was a fine young man
of twenty-seven, the only son of a widowed mother;
he was the best sailor on board, and was beloved by all
who were acquainted with him. This event occurred
on the eleventh of November, 1835; the vessel was the
London Merchant steamship. Truly wonderful are the
ways of Providence![1]

GEORGE BORROW (1803-1881)
The Bible in Spain

[1] Borrow's adjective for the "ways of Providence" in this case may
itself be thought wonder-making.

SEA SUMMONS

To sea, to sea! The calm is o'er;
   The wanton water leaps in sport,
And rattles down the pebbly shore;
   The dolphin wheels, the sea-cows snort,
And unseen mermaids' pearly song
Comes bubbling up, the weeds among.
   Fling broad the sail, dip deep the oar;
   To sea, to sea! The calm is o'er.

To sea, to sea! our wide-winged bark
   Shall billowy cleave its sunny way,
And with its shadow, fleet and dark,
   Break the caved Tritons' azure day,
Like mighty eagle soaring light
O'er antelopes on Alpine height.
   The anchor heaves, the ship swings free,
   The sails swell full. To sea, to sea!

T. L. BEDDOES (1798-1851)
Death's Jest-Book

CHEERFUL PASSENGER

It is due to Mark Tapley to state that he suffered at least
as much from sea-sickness as any man, woman or
child, on board; and that he had a peculiar faculty of
knocking himself about on the smallest provocation,
and losing his legs at every lurch of the ship. But
resolved, in his usual phrase, to "come out strong"
under disadvantageous circumstances, he was the life
and soul of the steerage, and made no more of stopping
in the middle of a facetious conversation to go away and
be excessively ill by himself, and afterwards come back
in the very best and gayest of tempers to resume it,
than if such a course of proceeding had been the
commonest in the world.

It cannot be said that as his illness wore off, his cheerfulness and good nature increased, because they would
hardly admit of augmentation; but his usefulness
among the weaker members of the party was much
enlarged; and at all times and seasons there he was
exerting it. If a gleam of sun shone out of the dark sky,
down Mark tumbled into the cabin, and presently up
he came again with a woman in his arms, or half-a-
dozen children, or a man, or a bed, or a saucepan, or a
basket, or something animate or inanimate, that he
thought would be the better for the air. If an hour or
two of fine weather in the middle of the day tempted
those who seldom or never came on deck at other times
to crawl into the long-boat, or lie down upon the spare
spars, and try to eat, there, in the centre of the group,
was Mr. Tapley, handing about salt beef and biscuit,
or dispensing tastes of grog, or cutting up the children's
provisions with his pocket-knife, for their greater ease
and comfort, or reading aloud from a venerable news-

paper, or singing some roaring old song to a select party, or writing the beginnings of letters to their friends at home for people who couldn't write, or cracking jokes with the crew, or nearly getting blown over the side, or emerging, half-drowned, from a shower of spray, or lending a hand somewhere or other: but always doing something for the general entertainment.

At night, when the cooking-fire was lighted on the deck, and the driving sparks that flew among the rigging, and the cloud of sails, seemed to menace the ship with certain annihilation by fire, in case the elements of air and water failed to compass her destruction; there, again, was Mr. Tapley, with his coat off and his shirt-sleeves turned up to his elbows, doing all kinds of culinary offices; compounding the strangest dishes; recognised by everyone as an established authority; and helping all parties to achieve something which, left to themselves, they never could have done, and never would have dreamed of. In short, there never was a more popular character than Mark Tapley became, on board that noble and fast-sailing line-of-packet ship, the Screw; and he attained at last to such a pitch of universal admiration, that he began to have grave doubts within himself whether a man might reasonably claim any credit for being jolly under such exciting circumstances.

CHARLES DICKENS (1812-70)
Martin Chuzzlewit

COLD, GRAY STONES

Break, break, break,
   On thy cold gray stones, O Sea!
And I would that my tongue could utter
   The thoughts that arise in me.

O well for the fisherman's boy,
  That he shouts with his sister at play!
O well for the sailor lad,
  That he sings in his boat on the bay!

And the stately ships go on
  To their haven under the hill;
But O for the touch of a vanish'd hand,
  And the sound of a voice that is still!

Break, break, break,
  At the foot of thy crags, O Sea!
But the tender grace of a day that is dead
  Will never come back to me.

ALFRED, LORD TENNYSON (1809-1892)
Poems

TIME AND TIDE

The sea is calm to-night.
The tide is full, the moon lies fair
Upon the Straits;—on the French coast the light
Gleams and is gone; the cliffs of England stand,
Glimmering and vast, out in the tranquil bay.
Come to the window, sweet is the night-air!
Only, from the long line of spray
Where the sea meets the moon-blanch'd land,
Listen! you hear the grating roar
Of pebbles which the waves draw back, and fling,
At their return, up the high strand,
Begin, and cease, and then again begin,
With tremulous cadence slow, and bring
The eternal note of sadness in.

Sophocles long ago
Heard it on the Aegean, and it brought
Into his mind the turbid ebb and flow
Of human misery; we
Find also in the sound a thought,
Hearing it by this distant northern sea.

The Sea of Faith
Was once, too, at the full, and round earth's shore
Lay like the folds of a bright girdle furl'd.
But now I only hear
Its melancholy, long, withdrawing roar,
Retreating, to the breath
Of the night-wind, down the vast edges drear
And naked shingles of the world.

Ah, love let us be true,
To one another! for the world, which seems
To lie before us like a land of dreams,
So various, so beautiful, so new,
Hath really neither joy, nor love, nor light,
Nor certitude, nor peace, nor help for pain:
And we are here as on a darkling plain
Swept with confused alarms of struggle and flight,
Where ignorant armies clash by night.

MATTHEW ARNOLD (1828-1888)
Dover Beach

THE WAVES: A HAPPIER VIEW

Say not the struggle nought availeth,
    The labour and the wounds are vain,
The enemy faints not, nor faileth,
    And as things have been they remain.

If hopes were dupes, fears may be liars;
    It may be, in yon smoke concealed,
Your comrades chase e'en now the fliers,
    And, but for you, possess the field.

For while the tired waves, vainly breaking,
    Seem here no painful inch to gain,
Far back, through creeks and inlets making,
    Comes silent, flooding in, the main,

And not by eastern windows only,
    When daylight comes, comes in the light,
In front, the sun climbs slow, how slowly,
    But westward, look, the land is bright.

A. H. CLOUGH (1819-1861)
Poems

CAPTAIN CUTTLE

But an addition to the little party now made its appearance, in the shape of a gentleman in a wide suit of blue, with a hook instead of a hand attached to his right wrist; very bushy black eyebrows; and a thick stick in his left hand, covered all over (like his nose) with knobs. He wore a loose black silk handkerchief round his neck, and such a very large coarse shirt-collar, that it looked like a small sail. He was evidently the person for whom the spare wine-glass was intended, and evidently knew it; for having taken off his rough outer coat, and hung up, on a particular peg behind the door, such a hard glazed hat as a sympathetic person's head might ache at the sight of, and which left a red rim round his own forehead as if he had been wearing a tight basin, he brought a chair to where the clean glass was, and sat himself down behind it. He was usually addressed as Captain, this visitor; and had been a pilot, or a skipper, or a privateersman, or all three perhaps; and was a very salt-looking man indeed.

His face, remarkable for a brown solidity, brightened as he shook hands with uncle and nephew; but he seemed to be of a laconic disposition, and merely said:

"How goes it?"

"All well," said Mr. Gills, pushing the bottle towards him.

He took it up, and having surveyed and smelt it, said with extraordinary expression:

"*The?*"

"*The,*" returned the Instrument-maker.

Upon that he whistled as he filled his glass, and seemed to think they were making holiday indeed.

THE CAPTAIN AT HOME

Captain Cuttle lived on the brink of a little canal near the India Docks, where there was a swivel bridge which opened now and then to let some wandering monster of a ship come roaming up the street like a stranded leviathan. The gradual change from land to water, on the approach to Captain Cuttle's lodgings, was curious. It began with the erection of flag-staffs, as appurtenances to public-houses; then came slopsellers' shops, with Guernsey shirts, sou'wester hats, and canvas pantaloons, at once the tightest and the loosest of their order, hanging up outside. These were succeeded by anchor and chain-cable forges, where sledge-hammers were dinging upon iron all day long. Then came rows of houses, with little vane-surmounted masts up-rearing themselves from among the scarlet beans. Then, ditches. Then pollard willows. Then more ditches. Then unaccountable patches of dirty water, hardly to be described, for the ships that covered them. Then, the air was perfumed with chips; and all other trades were swallowed up in mast, oar, and block-making, and boat-building. Then, the ground grew marshy and un-settled. Then, there was nothing to be smelt but rum and sugar. Then, Captain Cuttle's lodgings—at once a first floor and a top story, in Brig Place—were close before you.

The Captain was one of those timber-looking men, suits of oak as well as hearts, whom it is almost im-possible for the liveliest imagination to separate from any part of their dress, however insignificant. Accord-ingly, when Walter knocked at the door, and the Captain instantly poked his head out of one of his little front windows, and hailed him, with the hard glazed hat already on it, and the shirt-collar like a sail, and the wide suit of blue, all standing as usual, Walter was as fully persuaded that he was always in that state, as if the Captain had been a bird and those had been his feathers.

"Wal'r, my lad!" said Captain Cuttle. "Stand by and knock again. Hard! It's washing day."

Walter, in his impatience, gave a prodigious thump with the knocker.

"Hard it is!" said Captain Cuttle, and immediately drew in his head, as if he expected a squall.

Nor was he mistaken; for a widow-lady, with her sleeves rolled up to her shoulders, and her arms frothy with soapsuds and smoking with hot water, replied to the summons with startling rapidity. Before she looked at Walter she looked at the knocker, and then, measuring him with her eyes from head to foot, said she wondered he had left any of it.

"Captain Cuttle's at home, I know," said Walter with a conciliatory smile.

"Is he?" replied the widow lady. "In-deed!"

"He has just been speaking to me," said Walter, in breathless explanation.

"Has he," replied the widow lady. "Then p'raps you'll give him Mrs. MacStinger's respects, and say that the next time he lowers himself and his lodgings by talking out of winder she'll thank him to come down and open the door too." Mrs. MacStinger spoke loud, and listened for any observations that might be offered from the first floor.

"I'll mention it," said Walter, "if you'll have the goodness to let me in, ma'am."

For he was repelled by a wooden fortification extending across the doorway, and put there to prevent the little MacStingers in their moments of recreation from tumbling down the steps.

"A boy that can knock my door down," said Mrs MacStinger, contemptuously, "can get over that, I should hope!" But Walter, taking this as a permission to enter, and getting over it, Mrs. MacStinger immediately demanded whether an Englishwoman's house was her castle or not; and whether she was to be broke in upon by "raff". On these subjects her thirst for information was still very importunate, when Walter, having made his way up the little staircase through an artificial fog occasioned by the washing, which covered the banisters with a clammy perspiration, entered Captain Cuttle's room, and found that gentleman in ambush behind the door.

"Never owed her a penny, Wal'r," said Captain Cuttle, in a low voice, and with visible marks of trepidation on his countenance. "Done her a world of good turns, and the children too. Vixen at times, though. Whew!"

"*I* should go away, Captain Cuttle," said Walter.

"Dursn't do it, Wal'r," returned the Captain. "She'd find me out, wherever I went."

CHARLES DICKENS (1812-1876)
Dombey and Son

HOME-THOUGHTS

Nobly, nobly Cape Saint Vincent to the North-west died
 away;
Sunset ran, one glorious blood-red, reeking into Cadiz
 Bay;
Bluish 'mid the burning water, full in face Trafalgar lay;
In the dimmest North-east distance dawn'd Gibraltar
 grand and gray;
Here and here did England help me: how can I help
 England?—say,
Whoso turns as I, this evening, turn to God to praise and
 pray,
While Jove's planet rises yonder, silent over Africa.

ROBERT BROWNING (1812-1889)
Home-Thoughts from the Sea

GETTING ABOARD

Lucy Snowe, the heroine of *Villette*, emigrates alone to seek a career
(certainly no fortune) as a governess or teacher in Villette, another
name for Brussels. For an early Victorian young woman to set out
in this way for a foreign country completely unknown to her showed
her boldness and resolution. Her first experience of embarkation
was discouraging—and costly.

That same evening I obtained from my friend the
waiter information respecting the sailing of vessels
for a certain Continental port, Boue-Marine. No time,
I found, was to be lost; that very night I must take my
berth. I might, indeed, have waited till the morning
before going on board, but would not run the risk of
being too late.

"Better take your berth at once, ma'am," counselled
the waiter. I agreed with him, and, having discharged

my bill, and acknowledged my friend's services at a rate which I now know was princely, and which in his eyes must have seemed absurd—and indeed, while pocketing the cash, he smiled a faint smile which intimated his opinion of the donor's *savoir faire*—he proceeded to call a coach. To the driver he also recommended me, giving at the same time an injunction about taking me, I think, to the wharf, and not leaving me to the watermen; which that functionary promised to observe, but failed in keeping his promise. On the contrary, he offered me up as an oblation, served me as a dripping roast, making me alight in the midst of a throng of watermen.

This was an uncomfortable crisis. It was a dark night. The coachman instantly drove off as soon as he had got his fare. The watermen commenced a struggle for me and my trunk. Their oaths I hear at this moment. They shook my philosophy more than did the night, or the isolation, or the strangeness of the scene. One laid hands on my trunk. I looked on and waited quietly; but when another laid hands on me, I spoke up, shook off his touch, stepped at once into a boat, desired austerely that the trunk should be placed beside me—"just there" —which was instantly done; for the owner of the boat I had chosen became now an ally. I was rowed off.

Black was the river as a torrent of ink. Lights glanced on it from the piles of building round, ships rocked on its bosom. They rowed me up to several vessels. I read by lantern-light their names painted in great, white letters on a dark ground. The *Ocean*, the *Phoenix*, the *Consort*, the *Dolphin* were passed in turn; but the *Vivid* was my ship, and it seemed she lay farther down.

Down the sable flood we glided; I thought of the Styx, and of Charon rowing some solitary soul to the Land of Shades. Amidst the strange scene, with a chilly wind blowing in my face, and midnight clouds dropping rain above my head, with two rude rowers for com-

WARWICKSHIRE: NEW STREET, BIRMINGHAM
Although mainly in Warwickshire, Birmingham has suburbs extending
into Staffordshire and Worcestershire, and is the second largest city in
England. It is the greatest manufacturing centre in the world, the products being mainly associated with metals and including motor vehicles,
jewellery, guns, tools and hardware.

WARWICKSHIRE: HAMS HALL POWER STATION
Water cooling towers and tall chimneys such as these at this important
power station near Birmingham are typical features of the "Black
Country" landscape. There is, however, much unspoiled and lovely
scenery within easy reach of the big industrial cities.

WARWICKSHIRE: BROADGATE, COVENTRY
The rebuilding of Coventry after the severe bombing in World War II,
a programme which includes the reconstruction of the cathedral to a
new and striking design. Motor cars, cycles, sewing machines, watches
and textiles are among the products of Coventry's numerous industries.

WARWICKSHIRE: RUGBY SCHOOL
One of England's great public schools, founded in 1567. It is the scene
of *Tom Brown's Schooldays* which keeps alive the fame of Dr. Arnold, one
of the school's many outstanding Headmasters, and the birthplace of
Rugby football, "invented" by an enterprising pupil in 1823.

panions, whose insane oaths still tortured my ear, I asked myself if I was wretched or terrified. I was neither. Often in my life have I been far more so under comparatively safe circumstances. "How is this?" said I. "Methinks I am animated and alert instead of being depressed and apprehensive!" I could not tell how it was.

The *Vivid* started out, white and glaring, from the black night at last. "Here you are!" said the waterman, and instantly demanded six shillings.

"You ask too much," I said. He drew off from the vessel, and swore he would not embark me till I paid it. A young man, the steward as I found afterwards, was looking over the ship's side; he grinned a smile in anticipation of the coming contest. To disappoint him I paid the money. Three times that afternoon I had given crowns where I should have given shillings; but I consoled myself with the reflection, "It is the price of experience."

"They've cheated you!" said the steward exultingly when I got on board. I answered phlegmatically that "I knew it," and went below.

CHARLOTTE BRONTË (1816-1855)
Villette

THE SHELL

I thought of life, the outer and the inner,
    As I was walking by the sea:
How vague, unshapen this, and that, though thinner,
    Yet hard and clear in its rigidity.
Then I took up the fragment of a shell,
    And saw its accurate loveliness,
And searched its filmy lines, its pearly cell,
    And all that keen contention to express

A finite thought. And then I recognised
  God's working in the shell from root to rim,
And said: "He works till He has realized—
  O Heaven! if I could only work like Him!"
                                    T. E. BROWN (1830-1897)
                                                    Poem

MARINE PARADE: NEW LOOK

The small English seaside town has been a social
chronicle as well as a decoration of our shores. It wears
its history on its sleeve—in stripes. First came the
Georgian stucco, a midget replica of Brighton's
splendours. George III had favoured Weymouth and
now dipping in the sea, with due precautions, was
medically recommended. Sea-baths demanded the
elegance of Bath itself. So there came to the bay the
classic Terrace and its suave Crescent, while bow-
windowed cottages jostled, more snug than sanitary
around the river-mouth and harbour.

The following Victorians laid out a Marine Parade
in front of the Terrace and created behind it a lodging-
house belt, stark, severe, grimly basemented. Then
came a chapel or two. One sensed in this region a powerful odour of chill piety and boiled cabbage. The narrow
little High Street grew out of its sombre clothes and in
summer became almost pagan with a new prosperity
of garish shopping; beside the old-established merchants
there sprouted those bulging holiday emporia which
spill spades and buckets into the street and flaunt those
picture-postcards whose maritime fun is broad-based
upon the tremendous buttocks of bathing Mums.
Then commerce ordained a pier, absurdly Oriental, all
bulbs and minarets, as though the pier-master were
Sinbad the Sailor.

Further back, where the slopes began rising to down

or heather, were the houses of the retired Colonels and Indian Civilians, built when pensions were solid props of comfort; they were ample homes with tennis-lawn and kitchen garden, demanding the service of two "domestics" and a half-time gardener. The Anglo-Indians retired at fifty and matured tranquilly, like the peaches on their walls.

Fourth layer from the sea was the villadom of the nineteen twenties, with cosy names like Land o' Nod and Bide-a-wee. Shopkeepers in a small way came from the big towns to find repose here. Behind this arrived a few exhibits of the functional architecture of the nineteen-thirties, blatantly cubic, the "veritable sun-traps" of the house-agents, serving the new sun-cult with huge square windows and the new transport with built-in garages.

All was peaceable enough. Society, like the architecture, was cut in steps. The Golf Club and the Tennis Club belonged to the Colonels and the Indian Civilians and their young on holiday. The Bowling Green was shop-keepers' territory and there was no general urge to trespass either way. But there were some bitter actions fought over Tennis Club Status. Bank-managers, even bank-clerks, made the grade. But could a Vet or a Dentist? No, said the doctors.

The economic revolution of our time has blown the strip-system away. The Anglo-Indians, with their pensions shrivelled, have gone: their houses are carved up or taken over as schools and hostels. The old owners have dwindled, departed, and found labour-saving bungalows in quieter spots. Where the Tennis Club kept its privacy, a score of caravans are resting.

Welfare State, holidays for all, holidays on pay, "inflation money" from the big wages in the big inland towns, general motoring, coach parties and mass "outings" have swept over the small seaside town. To the departing Colonels this is gate-crashing: to the shopkeepers it is good money. A trippers' paradise? The up-to-date incomers evidently find it paradisal. For in they swarm—and stay while the money lasts.

The cash is spent as well as taken by the town. Marine Parade, which was getting shabby, has had its face lifted. Flaking and dingy stucco gleams again. The Guest Houses—there are no more Boarders now—have painted their cheeks in a lively fashion. They adopt Riviera names and have awnings and sun-shades outside. The Town Council, free of the Sahibs who once snubbed the shopkeeper members and regarded "development" as Satanic, has rolled up its sleeves to serve the new patrons.

At sundown the seafront is a ribbon of fairy-lights. At the pier-head Hot Dogs and Choc Ice are devoured according to climatic variations. On the pier itself there is a fun-fair, stridently alluring. From the pier-head Pierrot has gone, but you will not see bare, ruined choirs where once the soubrette sang: a packed dance-hall mingles the solemnities of Old Time Dancing with the pulsations of Rock and Roll.

Close packing is general and popular. The August beach-huts, tents and deck-chairs leave the sand invisible round the pierhead. People like bathing and paddling limb to limb. This crowding makes things easier for the few who like a bit of space: half-a-mile away along the sands and "it's all yours". So each to his own. Money flows, for the Channel trip and the moorland drive, and especially for gew-gaws and mementoes; these would shock a panel of artists, but they are essential to the holiday. When South Wales pours into South Devon, it must go to Widecombe and bring Widecombe home, not a tin of cream only but an Uncle Tom Cobley mug, playing Widecombe Fair when you lift it. The old folk at home must know all that Dartmoor offers and there is no stinting at the gew-gaw counter.

There are nuisances: the day-trippers bring their own victuals, do not spend enough, and make a beastly mess for the rate-payers to clean up. The villa-folk who offer "bed and breakfast" cannot, as a rule, provide the other meals. Over-full employment means no domestic labour for hire. You can hardly blame the lonely landlady. One pair of hands cannot lay on three meals a day. So the visitors must hunt round the cafés for their dinners and suppers, crowding and queueing for the "cuppa", the baked beans, and the fish and chips. The British have been queue-broken since 1940. Their patience is a miracle. But "chips" and "cuppas" are unfailing consolation.

The town toils at its job for three months and makes enough to provide a basking winter; enough also to go on with "development". This is not all raucous and unsightly. Prosperity opens its paint box and gives radiance to once glum façades. The town evidently satisfies its customers and the customers swarm in with "the lolly" and go home with their skins brown or scarlet and sufficient gew-gaws to load grandma's mantelpiece. The children say "Are we coming next year?" and the old residents, no longer residing, growl about trippers. But they cannot be heard. The buzz of happiness can.

IVOR BROWN (Born 1891)
The Observer

Sport

CRICKET

A game played with a crooked stick, later called a bat. According to
Mr. Samuel Looker, one of the game's many enthusiasts, anthologists,
and historians, it was first mentioned in the poetic writings of Joseph
of Exeter, A.D. 1180.

> The youths at cricks did play
> Throughout the merry day.

In Joseph's time the knights batted and bowled at two sticks or
wickets, with a third across the top: the wicket-keeper was a serf
and presumably other fielders were also less than gentlemen. During
the Middle Ages cricket was popular but frowned upon by those
engaged in raising military forces: it interfered with the practice of
archery. (A similar objection to golf was raised in Scotland.) The
creation of modern cricket owed much to the sturdy fathers of the
game who played on Broad Halfpenny Down at Hambledon in Hampshire and added powerful refreshment to vigorous recreation.

In the middle of the eighteenth century cricket had its laureate
in John Love, who composed, in the manner of his period, a Heroic
Poem to the game.

> Hail Cricket! glorious, manly, British Game!
> First of all sports! be first alike in fame!
> To my fir'd Soul thy busy transports bring,
> That I may feel thy Raptures, while I sing!
> O thou, sublime Inspirer of my Song!
> What matchless trophies to thy worth belong!
> Look round the earth, inclin'd to mirth, and see
> What daring sport can claim the prize from *thee*!

> Not puny Billiards, where, with sluggish pace,
> The dull ball trails before the foolish face,
> Where nothing can your languid spirits move,
> Save when the Marker bellows out, Six love!

Nor yet that happier Game, where the smooth Bowl,
In circling mazes, wanders to the goal;
Not Tennis self, thy sister sport, can charm,
Or with thy fierce delights our bosoms warm.
For, to small space confined, ev'n she must yield
To nobler Cricket, the disputed field.

O parent Britain! minion of renown!
Whose far-extended fame all nations own;
Nurs'd on thy plains, first Cricket learnt to please,
And taught thy sons to slight inglorious ease;
And see where busy Counties strive for fame,
Each greatly potent at this mighty game.
Fierce Kent, ambitious of the first applause,
Against the world combin'd, asserts her cause;
Gay Sussex sometimes triumphs o'er the field,
And fruitful Surrey cannot brook to yield.
While London, Queen of Cities! proudly vies,
And often grasps the well-disputed prize.

JOHN LOVE
Cricket
(published in 1744)

BAT, BEEF, AND BEER

The Hambledon Men and their inspiriting forms of nourishment
were celebrated by John Nyren.

There was high feasting held on Broad Halfpenny during
the solemnity of one of our grand matches. Oh! it was
a heart-stirring sight to witness the multitude forming
a complete and dense circle round that noble green.
Half the county would be present, and all their hearts
with us—Little Hambledon, pitted against All England
was a proud thought for the Hampshire men. Defeat
was glory in such a struggle—victory, indeed, made us
only "a little lower than angels." How those fine

brawn-faced fellows of farmers would drink to our success! And then, what stuff they had to drink! Punch—not your new Ponche à la Romaine, or Ponche à la Groseille, or your modern cat-lap milk-punch— punch be-devilled; but good, unsophisticated, John Bull stuff—stark!—that would stand on end—punch that would make a cat speak! Sixpence a bottle!

The ale too!—not the modern horror under that name, that drives as many men melancholy-mad as the hypocrites do—not the beastliness of these days, that will make a fellow's inside like a shaking bog, and as rotten; but barley-corn, such as would put the souls of three butchers into one weaver. Ale that would flare like turpentine—genuine Boniface!—This immortal viand (for it was more than liquor) was vended at two-pence per pint. The immeasurable villainy of our vintners would, with their march of intellect (if ever they could get such a brewing), drive a pint of it out into a gallon. Then the quantity the fellows would eat! Two or three of them would strike dismay into a round of beef. They could no more have pecked in that style than they could have flown, had the infernal black stream (that type of Acheron!) which soddens the carcass of a Londoner, been the fertilizer of their clay. There would this company, consisting most likely of some thousands, remain patiently and anxiously watching every turn of fate in the game, as if the event had been the meeting of two armies to decide their liberty. And whenever a Hambledon man made a good hit, worth four or five runs, you would hear the deep mouths of the whole multitude baying away in pure Hampshire— " Go hard!—go hard!—Tich and turn!—tich and turn!" To the honour of my countrymen, let me bear testimony upon this occasion also, as I have already done upon others. Although their provinciality in general, and personal partialities individually, were naturally inter-ested in behalf of the Hambledon men, I cannot call to

WARWICKSHIRE: WARWICK CASTLE

The castle of the earls of Warwick, built in Norman times, stands on a rock overlooking the River Avon. It houses a famous collection of pictures. Among the many interesting buildings in Warwick is the Leicester hospital, founded by Robert Dudley, Earl of Leicester.

WARWICKSHIRE: KENILWORTH CASTLE

At various times the residence of Henry III, John of Gaunt, Henry VIII and the Earl of Leicester, this great castle remains famous through the pages of Scott's *Kenilworth* and the tragic story of Amy Robsart. It was destroyed by Cromwell's troops during the Civil War.

WARWICKSHIRE: MEMORIAL THEATRE, STRATFORD-ON-AVON

As Shakespeare's birthplace and a pleasant riverside town standing in a beautiful countryside, Stratford is one of the busiest tourist centres in England. The Shakespeare Memorial Theatre was opened in 1932 to replace an earlier theatre destroyed by fire.

OXFORDSHIRE: THE GRAND UNION CANAL

There are about 2000 miles of inland waterways in England. Railway competition caused a decline in canal traffic in the 19th century, although motor traction later helped them to recover some lost trade. Many people would like to see the old waterways kept in use, and even extended.

recollection an instance of their wilfully stopping a ball that had been hit out among them by one of our opponents. Like true Englishmen, they would give an enemy fair play. How strongly are all those scenes of fifty years by-gone, painted in my memory!—and the smell of that ale comes upon me as freshly as the new May flowers.

JOHN NYREN (1764-1837)
The Young Cricketer's Tutor
and <i>Cricketers of My Time</i></div>

MR. JINGLE—COMMENTATOR

The Georgian and Regency aristocrats took up the game as a form of exercise and means of gambling. They backed their teams with heavy stakes. In his youth George IV is said to have played cricket with "great condescension and ability."

Dickens gave cricket some prominence in his *Pickwick Papers*. The Pickwickians encountered a village match (and the famous Mr. Jingle of staccato speech) early in their travels. All-Muggleton were playing Dingley Dell.

"Capital game—smart sport—fine exercise—very," were the words which fell upon Mr. Pickwick's ear as he entered the tent: and the first object that met his eyes was his green-coated friend of the Rochester coach, holding forth, to the no small delight and edification of a select circle of the chosen of All-Muggleton. His dress was slightly improved, and he wore boots; but there was no mistaking him.

The stranger recognised his friends immediately: and, darting forward and seizing Mr. Pickwick by the hand, dragged him to a seat with his usual impetuosity, talking all the while as if the whole of the arrangements were under his especial patronage and direction.

"This way—this way—capital fun—lots of beer—hogs-heads; rounds of beef—bullocks; mustard—cart loads; glorious day—down with you—make yourself at home—glad to see you—very."

*　　　*　　　*

"Well; and how came you here?" said Mr. Pickwick, with a smile in which benevolence struggled with surprise.

"Come," replied the stranger—"stopping at Crown—Crown at Muggleton—met a party—flannel jackets—white trousers—anchovy sandwiches—devilled kidneys—splendid fellows—glorious."

*　　　*　　　*

All-Muggleton had the first innings; and the interest became intense when Mr. Dumkins and Mr. Podder, two of the most renowned members of that most distinguished club, walked, hat in hand to their respective wickets. Mr. Luffey, the highest ornament of Dingley Dell, was pitched to bowl against the redoubtable Dumkins, and Mr. Struggles was selected to do the same kind office for the hitherto unconquered Podder. Several players were stationed, to "look out", in different parts of the field, and each fixed himself into the proper attitude by placing one hand on each knee, and stooping very much as if he were "making a back" for some beginner at leap-frog. All the regular players do this sort of thing;—indeed it's generally supposed that it is quite impossible to look out properly in any other position.

The umpires were stationed behind the wickets; the scorers were prepared to notch the runs; a breathless silence ensued. Mr. Luffey retired a few paces behind the wicket of the passive Podder, and applied the ball to his right eye for several seconds. Dumkins confidently awaited its coming with his eyes fixed on the motions of Luffey.

"Play!" suddenly cried the bowler. The ball flew from his hand straight and swift towards the centre stump of the wicket. The wary Dumkins was on the alert; it fell upon the tip of the bat, and bounded far away over the heads of the scouts, who had just stooped low enough to let it fly over them.

"Run—run—another.—Now, then, throw her up—up with her—stop there—another—no—yes—no—throw her up, throw her up!"—Such were the shouts which followed the stroke; and at the conclusion of which All-Muggleton had scored two. Nor was Podder behind-hand in earning laurels wherewith to garnish himself and Muggleton. He blocked the doubtful balls, missed the bad ones, took the good ones, and sent them flying to all parts of the field. The scouts were hot and tired; the bowlers were changed and bowled till their arms ached; but Dumkins and Podder remained unconquered. Did an elderly gentleman essay to stop the progress of the ball, it rolled between his legs or slipped between his fingers. Did a slim gentleman try to catch it, it struck him on the nose, and bounded pleasantly off with redoubled violence, while the slim gentleman's eye filled with water, and his form writhed with anguish. Was it thrown straight up to the wicket, Dumkins had reached it before the ball. In short, when Dumkins was caught out and Podder stumped out, All-Muggleton had notched some fifty-four, while the score of the Dingley Dellers was as blank as their faces. The advantage was too great to be recovered. In vain did the eager Luffey, and the enthusiastic Struggles, do all that skill and experience could suggest, to regain the ground Dingley Dell had lost in the contest; it was of no avail; and in an early period of the winning game Dingley Dell gave in, and allowed the superior prowess of All-Muggleton.

*   *   *

"Capital game—well played—some strokes admirable," said the stranger, as both sides crowded into the tent, at the conclusion of the game.

"You have played it, sir?" inquired Mr. Wardle, who had been much amused by his loquacity.

"Played it! Think I have—thousands of times—not here—West Indies—exciting thing—hot work—very."

"It must be rather a warm pursuit in such a climate," observed Mr. Pickwick.

"Warm!—red hot—scorching—glowing. Played a match once—single wicket—friend the Colonel—Sir Thomas Blazo—who should get the greatest number of runs.—Won the toss—first innings—seven o'clock A.M. —six natives to look out—went in; kept in—heat intense—natives all fainted—taken away—fresh half-dozen ordered—fainted also—Blazo bowling—supported by two natives—couldn't bowl me out—fainted too—cleared away the Colonel—wouldn't give in—faithful attendant—Quanko Samba—last man left—sun so hot, bat in blisters, ball scorched brown—five hundred and seventy runs—rather exhausted—Quanko mustered up last remaining strength—bowled me out—had a bath, and went out to dinner."

"And what became of what's-his-name, sir?" inquired an old gentleman.

"Blazo?"

"No—the other gentleman."

"Quanko Samba?"

"Yes, sir."

"Poor Quanko—never recovered it—bowled on, on my account—bowled off, on his own—died, sir." Here the stranger buried his countenance in a brown jug, but whether to hide his emotion or imbibe its contents, we cannot distinctly affirm. We only know that he paused suddenly, drew a long and deep breath, and looked anxiously on, as two of the principal members of the Dingley Dell club approached Mr. Pickwick, and said—

"We are about to partake of a plain dinner at the Blue Lion, sir; we hope you and your friends will join us."

"Of course," said Mr. Wardle, "among our friends we include Mr.——;" and he looked towards the stranger.

"Jingle," said that versatile gentleman, taking the hint at once. "Jingle—Alfred Jingle, Esq., of No Hall, No-where."

CHARLES DICKENS (1812-1870)
The Pickwick Papers

THE PRODIGY

"W.G.", William Gilbert Grace (1848-1915), was not only the Grand Old Man of Victorian and Edwardian English cricket: he was also the Boy Marvel. One of a family of addicts and experts (ten Gloucestershire Graces are mentioned in the Births and Deaths section of *Wisden's Cricketers' Almanack*), he reached man's prowess in boyhood's years. Here is Bernard Darwin's imagining of the child being reared in the way in which he should so triumphantly go.

Everybody must have played, strictly by himself, that game of the imagination in which, by means of some enchantment, he can turn back the clock and call up scenes long past. I have a whole theatre full of them in the domain of sport alone, the centuries sadly mixed up. There is George Osbaldeston after his great ride on Newmarket Heath and John Gully to force a way for him through the cheering crowd; Allan Robertson playing at St. Andrews; M. J. Brooks jumping six feet for the first time, when it was deemed impossible, and, for cricket, of course Hambledon against All England, and my own Kent with Alfred Mynn and Fuller Pilch in their pride. But perhaps best of all I should like to see that family game in the orchard, with a cousin or two, a Rees or a Gilbert, thrown in, and to hear what they all said with their pleasant touch of Gloucestershire accent. "These Graces chatter so," was said years afterwards by a fiery and much tried batsman. I don't imagine W. G.

saying much then, but no doubt there is plenty of cheerful noise from the elders. The small W.G. shall be batting, with Mrs. Grace holding the still smaller Fred by the hand, and Uncle Pocock looking on with mingled pride and anxiety, and the daughters, the poor unconsidered daughters whose names are almost lost, throwing up the ball if it comes their way. And then the boy's five minutes are up and my picture melts away and dissolves.

I have been told by one who played against Gloucestershire in Mr. Jessop's first match how some of the other side, seeing only the rough-hewn and almost rustic hitting and not discerning the greatness that lay beneath, dared gently to chaff W.G. and to ask him, "What have you got here, Old Man?" Thereupon W.G. turned on them truculently and told them, "Ah, you'll soon see what I've got here." Uncle Pocock might have used those very words, and he had not long to wait for his prophecies to come true. Let anyone look at this briefest record—I must have a few figures here—and then talk of any other youthful prodigy if he dare. In 1858 when he was ten young Gilbert played his first march for the West Gloucestershire Club. Two years later, at twelve, he made fifty-one for the club against Clifton. In 1863, just before his fifteenth birthday, he faced the All England eleven, with the two famous fast bowlers of the day, Tarrant and Jackson, and the bowling had to be changed and Tinley put on, with his cunning lobs, before the boy was out, for thirty-two. He was still only fifteen when in 1864, he played for the All England eleven himself, and then, a month or two after his sixteenth birthday, he made 170 and fifty-six not out against Sussex. By 1865 he had played twice for the Gentlemen against the Players, and for England against Surrey. As far as such representative honours were concerned he had no more worlds left to conquer, and he was but a little over seventeen.

And yet to-day the world is greatly impressed if a boy
after his last summer at a public school is given a trial
for his county. Was there ever such a "riband in the
cap of youth?"

BERNARD DARWIN (Born 1876)
Every Idle Dream

VILLAGE GREEN

International Test Matches and County Games are the high level of
English Cricket. But the village game, weaving its pattern as Gerald
Bullett has described it, is one of the wide-spread and unchanging
pleasures of the countryside. Few can pass by a village green while
play is in progress: they must stop their walk (or their horse or their
car) and watch a while.

Flowing together by devious channels
From farm and brickyard, forest and dene,
Thirteen men in glittering flannels
Move to their stations out on the green.

Long-limbed Waggoner, stern, unbudging,
Stands like a rock behind the bails.
Dairyman umpire, gravely judging,
Spares no thought for his milking-pails.

Bricklayer bowls, a perfect length,
Grocery snicks and sneaks a run.
Law, swiping with all his strength,
Is caught by Chemist at mid-on.

Two to the boundary, a four and a six,
Put the spectators in fear of their lives:
Shepherd the slogger is up to his tricks,
Blithely unwary of weans and wives.

Lord of the manor makes thirty-four.
Parson contributes, smooth and trim,
A cautious twelve to the mounting score:
Leg-before-wicket disposes of him.

Patient, dramatic, serious, genial,
From over to over the game goes on,
Weaving a pattern of hardy perennial
Civilization under the sun.

GERALD BULLETT (1893-1958)
News from the Village

LANCASHIRE CRICKET

Soon I reached the inn where we were all staying. In
the bar the Lancashire cricketers had already come back
from the match. There was Harry Dean, a hero of my
boyhood, now entering on his last years in the field.
I had seen him through many summers bowling for
Lancashire in the pomp of Maclaren's day, a willing
horse and a Lancashire lad from the richest soil. He
wore blue serge and a watch-chain across his waistcoat,
and strong boots. The old professional cricketers did not
go to the cinema theatres in the evenings after a long
day's play; they sat in bar-parlours and talked cricket.
Or you would see them walking slowly and gravely
along the streets, two by two, hands in pockets, and
smoking their pipes. There was also "Lol" Cook, bosom
friend of Dean, and he was a portly little man whose
head hung on one side in a sort of patient acquiescence
to a world that was always expecting him to bowl
against the wind and would so seldom see eye to eye
with him in appeals for leg before wicket. Harry Dean
spoke with a deliberate accent, the purest Lancashire,
and by his use of certain words and cadences revealed
that he had once on a time attended Sunday School and
had escaped the advancing blight of industrialism and
half-education. He would utter audible capital letters
when he extolled the great cricketers of the time of his
apprenticeship. "The reason why we young 'uns learned
t' Principles was that we pla-ayed with Wise Men. It

were an Education to bat wi' Maister Spooner"—(Harry by the way, was usually number ten in the order of the innings, and his one and only stroke was an elegant but unproductive forward push, usually straight back to the bowler)—"aye, it were an Education. And Maister Maclaren were a Great Captain, and once at Kennington Oval he coom in dressing-room before start of match and said, ' Harry, I've lost toss, so put on three pairs of socks. You'll open at Pavilion end and you'll be bowlin' at half-past six, if I'm not mistaken, because that bloody villain, Sam Apted, has made one of his Shirt Front Wickets.' And, by gum, Maister Maclaren were reight; Ah were. Ah bowled mi left toe-nail raw that day and Tom Hayward made two 'undred fit for Buckingham Palace. Hey, bah gum, and that was day when Jimmy 'Eap come back in team after 'e'd been dropped . . ."

James Heap was a slow left-hand spinner with a charming action, a little jump, right hand pointing to heaven, side to the batsman, then a "swing-through" of easeful rhythm. On a "sticky" wicket he could bowl as dangerously as Rhodes himself; but his misfortune was lumbago. For weeks in dry weather, and on cruel hard wickets, he would slave away spinless and harmless. Then the weather would break; he would hear the rain in the night and chuckle. But alas! to quote his own account of the tragedy—"in t' mornin', Maister Maclaren coom into t' dressin'-room, and says, ' At last, Jimmy, you've got your "sticky" wicket! I'll put you on right away—and it's a real "glue-pot" already, and made for you, my lad! '" But, continued Heap, "Ah 'as to tell 'im ' Ah'm sorry, Maister Maclaren, but Ah can 'ardly stand oop this mornin'—lumbago's coom back.'"

NEVILLE CARDUS (Born 1889)
Second Innings

RUGBY FOOTBALL — OLD STYLE

And now that the two sides have fairly sundered, and
each occupies its own ground, and we get a good look
at them, what absurdity is this? You don't mean to say
that those fifty or sixty boys in white trousers, many
of them quite small, are going to play that huge mass
opposite? Indeed I do, gentlemen; they're going to
try at any rate, and won't make such a bad fight of it
either, mark my word: for hasn't old Brooke won the
toss, with his lucky halfpenny, and got choice of goals
and kick-off? The new ball you may see lie there quite
by itself, in the middle, pointing towards the School
or island goal; in another minute it will be well on its
way there. Use that minute in remarking how the
School-house side is drilled.

You will see in the first place, that the sixth-form boy,
who has the charge of goal, has spread his force (the goal-
keepers) so as to occupy the whole space behind the goal-
posts, at distances of about five yards apart; a safe and
well-kept goal is the foundation of all good play. Old
Brooke is talking to the captain of quarters; and now
he moves away. See how that youngster spreads his men
(the light brigade) carefully over the ground, half-way
between their own goal and the body of their own
players-up (the heavy brigade). These again play in
several bodies; there is young Brooke and the bull-
dogs—mark them well—they are the "fighting brigade",
the "die-hards", larking about at leap-frog to keep themselves warm, and playing tricks on one another. And
on each side of old Brooke, who is now standing in the
middle of the ground and just going to kick-off, you
see a separate wing of players-up, each with a boy of
acknowledged prowess to look to—here Warner, and
there Hedge; but over all is old Brooke, absolute as he of

Russia, but wisely and bravely ruling over willing and worshipping subjects, a true football king. His face is earnest and careful as he glances a last time over his array, but full of pluck and hope, the sort of look I hope to see in my general when I go out to fight.

    *   *   *

And now the last minutes are come, and the School gather for their last rush, every boy of the hundred and twenty who has a run left in him. Reckless of the defence of their own goal, on they come across the level big-side ground, the ball well down amongst them, straight for our goal, like the column of the Old Guard up the slope at Waterloo. All former charges have been child's play to this. Warner and Hedge have met them, but still on they come. The bull-dogs rush in for the last time; they are hurled over or carried back, striving hand, foot, and eyelids. Old Brooke comes sweeping round the skirts of the play, and turning short round picks out the very heart of the scrummage, and plunges in. It wavers for a moment—he has the ball! No, it has passed him, and his voice rings out clear over the advancing tide, "Look out in goal." Crab Jones catches it for a moment; but before he can kick, the rush is upon him and passes over him; and he picks himself up behind them with his straw in his mouth, a little dirtier, but as cool as ever.

The ball rolls slowly in behind the School-house goal not three yeards in front of a dozen of the biggest School players-up.

There stand the School-house præpostor, safest of goal-keepers, and Tom Brown by his side, who has learned his trade by this time. Now is your time, Tom. The blood of all the Browns is up, and the two rush in together, and throw themselves on the ball, under the very feet of the advancing column; the præpostor on his hands and knees arching his back, and Tom all along on his face. Over them topple the leaders of the rush, shooting over the back of the præpostor, but falling flat on Tom, and knocking all the wind out of his small carcase. "Our ball," says the præpostor, rising with his prize; "but get up there, there's a little fellow under you." They are hauled and roll off him, and Tom is discovered a motionless body.

Old Brooke picks him up. "Stand back, give him air," he says; and then feeling his limbs, adds, "No bones broken. How do you feel, young un?"

"Hah-hah," gasps Tom as his wind comes back, "pretty well, thank you—all right."

"Who is he?" says Brooke. "Oh, it's Brown, he's a new boy; I know him," says East, coming up.

"Well, he is a plucky youngster, and will make a player," says Brooke.

And five o'clock strikes. "No side," is called, and the first day of the School-house match is over.

THOMAS HUGHES (1822-1896)
Tom Brown's School Days

FISHING: MUCH VIRTUE NEEDED

A skilful angler ought to be a general scholar, and seen in all the liberal sciences, as a grammarian, to know how either to write or discourse of his art in true and fitting terms, without affection or rudeness. He should have sweetness of speech, to persuade and entice others to delight in an exercise so much laudable. He should have strength of arguments, to defend and maintain his profession against envy or slander. He should have knowledge in the sun, moon and stars, that by their aspects he may guess the seasonableness or unseasonableness of the weather, the breeding of storms, and from what coasts the winds are ever delivered. He should be a good knower of countries, and well used to highways, that by taking the readiest paths to every lake, brook or river, his journeys may be more certain and less wearisome. He should have knowledge in proportions of all sorts, whether circular, square or diametrical, that when he shall be questioned of his diurnal progresses, he may give a geographical description of the angles and channels of rivers, how they fall from their heads, and what compasses they fetch in their several windings. He must also have the perfect art of numbering, that in the sounding of lakes and rivers, he may know how many foot or inches each severally containeth; and by adding, subtracting, or multiplying the same, he may yield the reason of every river's swift or slow current. He should not be unskilful in music, that whensoever either melancholy, heaviness of his thoughts, or the perturbations of his own fancies stirreth up sadness in him, he may remove the same with some godly hymn or anthem, of which David gives him ample examples.

He must be of a well settled and constant belief, to enjoy the benefit of his expectation; for then to despair, it were better never to be put in practice: and he must ever think where the waters are pleasant, and anything likely, that there the Creator of all good things hath stored up much of plenty; and though your satisfaction be not as ready as your wishes, yet you must hope still, that with perseverance, you shall reap the fullness of your harvest with contentment. Then he must be full of love, both to his pleasure and to his neighbour. To his pleasure, which otherwise will be irksome and tedious, and to his neighbour, that he neither give offence in any particular, nor be guilty of any general destruction. Then he must be exceeding patient, and neither vex nor excruciate himself with losses or mischances, as in losing the prey when it is almost in the hand, or by breaking his tools by ignorance or negligence, but with pleased sufferance amend errors, and think mischances instructions to better carefulness.

He must then be full of humble thoughts, not disdaining when occasion commands to kneel, lie down, or wet his feet or fingers as oft as there is any advantage given thereby, unto the gaining the end of his labour. Then must he be strong and valiant, neither to be amazed with storms, nor affrighted with thunder, but hold them according to their natural causes, and the pleasure of the Highest. Neither must he, like the fox which preyeth upon lambs, employ all his labour against the smaller fry; but like the lion that seizeth elephants, think the greatest fish which swimmeth a reward little enough for the pains which he endureth. Then must he be liberal, and not working only for his own belly, as if it could never be satisfied, but he must with much cheerfulness bestow the fruits of his skill amongst his honest neighbours, who, being partners of his gain, will doubly renown his triumph; and that is ever a pleasing reward to virtue.

GERVASE MARKHAM (1568-1637)
Country Contentments

THE FINE ART

O, Sir, doubt not but that Angling is an art; is it not an art to deceive a Trout with an artificial fly? a Trout! that is more sharp-sighted than any Hawk you have named, and more watchful and timorous than your high mettled Merlin is bold? and yet, I doubt not to catch a brace or two to-morrow, for a friend's breakfast: doubt not therefore, Sir, but that angling is an art, and an art worth your learning: the question is rather, whether you be capable of learning it? for Angling is somewhat like poetry, men are to be born so: I mean with inclinations to it, though both may be heightened by discourse and practice; but he that hopes to be a good Angler, must not only bring an inquiring, searching, observing wit; but he must bring a large measure of hope and patience, and a love and propensity to the art itself; but having once got and practised it, then doubt not that Angling will prove to be so pleasant, that it will prove to be like virtue, a reward to itself.

IZAAK WALTON (1593-1683)
The Compleat Angler

THE VARIOUS JOYS

Look, under that broad *Beech-tree*, I sat down, when I was last this way a-fishing, and the birds in the adjoining grove seemed to have a friendly contention with an Echo, whose dead voice seemed to live in a hollow cave, near to the brow of that Primrose-hill; there I sat viewing the silver streams glide silently towards their centre, the tempestuous sea; yet, sometimes opposed by rugged roots, and pebble stones, which broke their waves, and turned them into foam: and sometimes I beguiled time by viewing the harmless Lambs, some leaping securely in the cool shade, whilst others sported themselves in the cheerful Sun: and saw others were craving comfort from the swollen udders of their bleating Dams. As I thus sat, these and other sights had so fully possessed my soul with content, that I thought as the Poet has happily expressed it:

> I was for that time lifted above earth;
> And possessed joys not promised in my birth.

As I left this place, and entered into the next field, a second pleasure entertained me, 'twas a handsome Milkmaid that had not yet attained so much age and wisdome as to load her mind with any fears of many things that will never be (as too many men too often do), but she cast away all care, and sung like a *Nightin-gale*: her voice was good, and the Ditty fitted for it; 'twas that smooth song, which was made by *Kit Marlow*, now at least fifty years ago: and the Milkmaid's Mother sung an answer to it, which was made by *Sir Walter Rawleigh* in his younger days.

They were old-fashioned Poetry, but choicely good, I think much better than the strong lines that are now in fashion in this critical age. Look yonder! on my word, yonder they both be a-milking again. I will give her the *Chub*, and persuade them to sing those two songs to us.

God speed you good woman, I have been a-fishing, and am going to *Bleak-Hall* to my bed, and having caught more fish than will sup myself and my friend, I will bestow this upon you and your daughter, for I use to sell none.

Milkwoman. Marry, God requite you Sir, and we'll eat it cheerfully, and if you come this way a-fishing two months hence, a grace of God I'll give you a silly-bub of new verjuice, in a new made haycock for it, and my *Maudlin* shall sing you one of her best *Ballads*; for she and I both love all *Anglers*, they be such honest, civil, quiet men.

IZAAK WALTON (1593-1683)
The Compleat Angler

THE WORMING WAY

There is nowadays, among our august fly-fishers, a disdain of worm-fishers, but some of the old devotees were more concerned with the substance of the catch than with the dignity of the bait. Such a one was John Gay, who combined the composition of *The Beggar's Opera* with a sportsman's guide to success in the field or on the river.

When floating clouds their spongy fleeces drain,
Troubling the streams with swift-descending rain,

OXFORDSHIRE: OXFORD FROM THE AIR

Several University buildings can be identified in this photograph. Christchurch is in the centre foreground, with Christchurch Cathedral at the lower right corner of the quadrangle and the tower of Great Tom, the old curfew bell, to the left of it. Directly above this quadrangle is the circular Radcliffe Camera, reading room of the Bodleian Library.

OXFORDSHIRE: MAGDALEN COLLEGE, OXFORD

Oxford University is the oldest residential university in Britain, University College being founded in 1249. Magdalen College was founded in 1458 by William of Waynflete, Bishop of Winchester. Its alumni have included William Camden, John Hampden and Edward Gibbon

BEDFORDSHIRE: WOBURN ABBEY

The sculpture gallery of Woburn Abbey, country seat of the Duke of Bedford. This famous mansion lies about 12 miles south of Bedford within easy reach of London, and is now open to the public.

And waters tumbling down the mountain's side,
Bear the loose soil into the swelling tide,
Then, soon as vernal gales begin to rise,
And drive the liquid burden through the skies,
The fisher to the neighbouring current speeds,
Whose rapid surface purls, unknown to weeds;
Upon a rising border of the brook
He sits him down, and ties the treacherous hook;
Now expectation cheers his eager thought,
His bosom glows with treasures yet uncaught;
Before his eyes a banquet seems to stand,
Where every guest applauds his skilful hand.

Far up the stream the twisted hair he throws,
Which down the murmuring current gently flows;
When if or chance or hunger's powerful sway
Directs the roving trout this fatal way,
He greedily sucks in the twining bait,
And tugs and nibbles the fallacious meat;
Now, happy fisherman, now twitch the line!
How thy rod bends! behold, the prize is thine!
Cast on the bank, he dies, with gasping pains,
And trickling blood his silver mail distains.

You must not every worm promiscuous use;
Judgment will tell thee proper bait to choose;
The worm that draws a long immoderate size
The trout abhors, and the rank morsel flies;
And if too small, the naked fraud's in sight,
And fear forbids, while hunger does invite.
Those baits will best reward the fisher's pains,
Whose polish'd tails a shining yellow stains;
Cleanse them from filth, to give a tempting gloss,
Cherish the sullied reptile race with moss;
Amid the verdant bed they twine, they toil,
And from their bodies wipe their native soil.

JOHN GAY (1685-1732)
Rural Sports

RIDERS' JOY

John Masefield's poem, *Right Royal*, describes the race for the English
"Chasers" Cup on Compton Course, and this passage catches the
ecstasy of the grand rider on a grand horse.

In front was the curving street of Course,
Barred black by the leaps unsmashed by horse.
A cloud blew by and the sun shone bright,
Showing the guard-rails gleaming white.
Little red flags, that gusts blew tense,
Streamed to the wind at each black fence.

And smiting the turf to clods that scattered
Was the rush of the race, the thing that mattered,
A tide of horses in fury flowing,
Beauty of speed in glory going,
Kubbadar pulling, romping first,
Like a big black fox that had made his burst,

And away and away and away they went,
A visible song of what life meant.

Living in houses, sleeping in bed,
Going to business, all seemed dead,
Dead as death to that rush in strife,
Pulse for pulse with the heart of life.

"For to all," Charles thought, "when the blood beats
      high
Comes the glimpse of that which may not die;
When the world is stilled, when the wanting dwindles,
When the mind takes light and spirit kindles,
One stands on a peak of this old earth."

Charles eyed his horses and sang with mirth.
What of this world that spins through space?
With red blood running he rode a race,
The beast's red spirit was one with his,
Emulous and in ecstasies;
Joy that from heart to wild heart passes
In the wild things going through the grasses;
In the hares in the corn, in shy gazelles
Running the sand where no man dwells;
In horses scared at the prairie spring;
In the dun deer noiseless, hurrying;
In fish in the dimness scarcely seen,
Save as shadows shooting in a shaking green;
In birds in the air, neck-straining, swift,
Wing touching wing while no wings shift,
Seen by none, but when stars appear
A reaper wandering home may hear
A sigh aloft where the stars are dim,
Then a great rush going over him:
This was his; it had linked him close
To the force by which the comet goes,
With the rein none sees, with the lash none feels,
But with fire-mane tossing and flashing heels.

JOHN MASEFIELD (Born 1878)
Right Royal

SHOOTING

Pope has included several ways of killing beast and bird: as a boyhood
resident of Binfield near Windsor Park, he wrote of what he knew
but not of what he liked. His sympathies are with the target, not the
marksman, and his sympathies, by evoking the last line of the passage,
here showed him a true poet as well as a master of the rhyming couplet
and the formal style.

The reference to Albion's warring sons shows an attitude to "acts
of oppression" which now would be deemed regrettable. This passage
probably refers to the capture of Gibraltar in 1704. No less regrettable

seems the slaughter of larks. Pope's "doves" are presumably wood-
pigeons which often swarm in our woods and fields and are a farmer's
pest.

Ye vig'rous swains! while youth ferments your blood,
And purer spirits swell the sprightly flood,
Now range the hills, the gameful woods beset,
Wind the shrill horn, or spread the waving net.
When milder autumn summer's heat succeeds,
And in the new-shorn field the partridge feeds,
Before his lord the ready spaniel bounds,
Panting with hope, he tries the furrow'd grounds;
But when the tainted gales the game betray,
Couch'd close he lies, and meditates the prey:
Secure they trust th' unfaithful field beset,
Till hov'ring o'er 'em sweeps the swelling net.
Thus (if small things we may with great compare)
When Albion sends her eager sons to war,
Some thoughtless Town, with ease and plenty blest,
Near, and more near, the closing lines invest;
Sudden they seize th' amaz'd, defenceless prize,
And high in air Britannia's standard flies.
See! from the brake the whirring pheasant springs,
And mounts exulting on triumphant wings:
Short is his joy; he feels the fiery wound,
Flutters in blood, and panting beats the ground.
Ah! what avail his glossy, varying dyes,
His purple crest, and scarlet-circled eyes,
The vivid green his shining plumes unfold,
His painted wings, and breast that flames with gold?
Nor yet, when moist Arcturus clouds the sky,
The woods and fields their pleasing toils deny.
To plains with well-breath'd beagles we repair,
And trace the mazes of the circling hare:
(Beasts, urg'd by us, their fellow-beasts pursue,
And learn of man each other to undo).
With slaught'ring guns th' unwearied fowler roves,
When frosts have whiten'd all the naked groves;

Where doves in flocks the leafless trees o'ershade,
And lonely woodcocks haunt the wat'ry glade,
He lifts the tube, and levels with his eye;
Straight a short thunder breaks the frozen sky:
Oft, as in airy rings they skim the heath,
The clam'rous lapwings feel the leaden death:
Oft, as the mounting larks their notes prepare,
They fall, and leave their little lives in air.

ALEXANDER POPE (1688-1744)
Windsor Forest

RIDERS TO HOUNDS

Mr. Jorrocks was a great city grocer of the old school, one who was neither ashamed of his trade, nor of carrying it on in a dingy warehouse that would shock the managers of the fine mahogany-countered, gilt-canistered, puffing, poet-keeping establishments of modern times. He had been in business long enough to remember each succeeding Lord Mayor before he was anybody—"reg'lar little tuppences in fact", as he used to say. Not that Mr. Jorrocks decried the dignity of civic honour, but his ambition took a different turn. He was for the field, not the forum.

As a merchant he stood high—country traders took his teas without tasting, and his bills were as good as bank-notes. Though an unlettered man, he had great powers of thought and expression in his peculiar way. He was "highly respectable", as they say on 'Change—that is to say, he was very rich, the result of prudence and economy—not that he was stingy, but his income outstripped his expenses, and money, like snow, rolls up amazingly fast.

A natural-born sportsman, his lot being cast behind a counter instead of in the country, is one of those frolics of fortune that there is no accounting for. To remedy

the error of the blind goddess, Mr. Jorrocks had taken
to hunting as soon as he could keep a horse, and although
his exploits were long confined to the suburban county
of Surrey, he should rather be "credited", for keenness
in following the sport in so unpropitious a region,
than "debited" as a Cockney and laughed at for his
pains. But here the old adage of "where ignorance is
bliss", etc., came to his aid, for before he had seen any
better country than Surrey, he was impressed with the
conviction that it was the "werry best", and their hounds
the finest in England.

"Doesn't the best of everything come to London?"
he would ask, "and doesn't it follow as nattaral consequence, that the best 'unting is to be had from it?"

*   *   *

When the gates of the world were opened by railways,
our friend's active mind saw that business might be
combined with pleasure, and as first one line opened
and then another, he shot down into the different
countries—bags and all—Beckford in one pocket—
order book in the other—hunting one day and selling
teas another. Nay, he sometimes did both together,
and they tell a story of him in Wiltshire, holloaing out
to a man who had taken a fence to get rid of him,
"Did you say *two* chests o' black and *one* o' green?"

Then when the Great Northern opened he took a turn
down to Peterborough, and emboldened by what he
saw with Lord Fitzwilliam, he at length ventured right
into the heaven of heavens—the grass—or what he calls
the "cut 'em down" countries.[1] What a commotion
he caused! Which is Jorrocks? Show me Jorrocks! Is
that old Jorrocks? And men would ride to and fro
eyeing him as if he were a wild beast. Gradually the
bolder ventured a word at him—observed it was a fine

[1] "Cut 'em down and hang 'em up to dry!"—Leicestershire phrase

day—asked him how he liked their country, or their hounds. Next, perhaps, the M.F.H. would give him a friendly lift—say "Good morning, Mr. Jorrocks"— then some of what Jorrocks calls the "hupper crusts" of the hunt would begin talking to him, until he got fairly launched among them—when he would out with his order-book and do no end of business in tea. None but Jorrocks & Co.'s tea goes down in the Midland counties. Great, however, as he is in the country, he is equally famous in London, where his "Readings in Beckford" and sporting lectures in Oxenden Street procured him the attentions of the police.

Mr. Jorrocks had now passed the grand climacteric, and balancing his age with less accuracy than he balanced his books, called himself somewhere between fifty and sixty. He wouldn't own to three pund, as he called sixty, at any price. Neither could he ever be persuaded to get into the scales to see whether he was nearer eighteen "stun" or twenty. He was always "'ticlarly engaged" just at the time, either goin' to wet samples of tea with his traveller, or with someone to look at "an 'oss", or, if hard pressed, to take Mrs. J. out in the chay. "He didn't ride stipple chases", he would say, "and wot matter did it make 'ow much he weighed? It was altogether 'twixt him and his 'oss, and weighin' wouldn't make him any lighter". In person he was a stiff, square-built, middle-sized man, with a thick neck and a large round head. A woolly, broad-brimmed, lowish-crowned hat sat with a jaunty sidelong sort of air upon a bushy, nut-brown wig, worn for comfort and not deception. Indeed his grey whiskers would have acted as a contradiction if he had, but deception formed no part of Mr. Jorrocks's character. He had a fine open countenance, and though his turn-up nose, little grey eyes, and rather twisted mouth were not handsome, still there was a combination of fun and good humour in his looks that pleased at first sight,

and made one forget all the rest. His dress was generally
the same—a puddingy white neckcloth tied in a knot,
capacious shirt frill (shirt made without collars), a
single-breasted, high-collared, buff waistcoat with
covered buttons, a blue coat with metal ones, dark
blue stocking-net pantaloons, and hessian boots with
large tassels, displaying the liberal dimensions of his
full, well-turned limbs. The coat pockets were outside,
and the back buttons far apart.

His business place was in St. Botolph's Lane, in the
City, but his residence was in Great Coram Street. This
is rather a curious locality—city people considering it
west, while those in the west consider it east. The fact
is, that Great Coram Street is somewhere about the
centre of London, near the London University, and not
a great way from the Euston station of the Birmingham
railway. Jorrocks says it is close to the two best cover
hacks in the world, the Great Northern and Euston
stations. Approaching it from the east, which seems the
proper way of advancing to a city man's residence,
you pass the Foundling Hospital in Guildford Street,
cross Brunswick Square, and turning short to the left
you find yourself in "Great Coram Street". Neat
unassuming houses form the sides, and the west end is
graced with a building that acts the double part of a
reading-room and swimming-bath; "literature and
lavement" is over the door.

MR. SPONGE

. . . It was a murky October day that the hero of our
tale, Mr. Sponge, or Soapey Sponge, as his good-natured
friends called him, was seen mizzling along Oxford
Street, wending his way to the West. Not that there
was anything unusual in Sponge being seen in Oxford
Street, for when in town his daily perambulations

CAMBRIDGESHIRE: ST. JOHN'S COLLEGE CHAPEL, CAMBRIDGE

A view from The Backs, the stretch of the River Cam which passes the back of some of the colleges. Schools existed in Cambridge in the 12th century and the first college, Peterhouse, was founded in 1284. Famous men educated at Cambridge include Bacon, Milton, Cromwell, Wordsworth and Darwin.

HUNTINGDONSHIRE: THE GEORGE HOTEL, HUNTINGDON

A splendid old coaching inn, with a fine courtyard and an interesting outside gallery, a reminder that Huntingdon for long owed its prosperity to its situation on the Roman road, Ermine Street. The famous grammar school had Oliver Cromwell and Samuel Pepys among its pupils.

NORTHAMPTONSHIRE: PETERBOROUGH CATHEDRAL

The Cathedral of St. Peter, seen here by moonlight, was consecrated in 1238 and is the third church to occupy the site. The styles range through Norman to Early English and Perpendicular. Peterborough has large railway works and is a focal point for road and rail communications.

consist of a circuit, commencing from the Bantam
Hotel in Bond Street into Piccadilly, through Leicester
Square, and so on to Aldridge's, in St. Martin's Lane,
thence by Moore's sporting-print-shop, and on through
some of those ambiguous and tortuous streets that,
appearing to lead all ways at once and none in particular,
land the explorer, sooner or later, on the south side of
Oxford Street.

Mr. Sponge had pursued this enterprising life for
some "seasons"—ten at least—and, supposing him to
have begun at twenty or one-and-twenty, he would be
about thirty at the time we have the pleasure of introducing him to our readers—a period of life at which
men begin to suspect they were not quite so wise at
twenty as they thought. Not that Mr. Sponge had any
particular indiscretions to reflect upon, for he was
tolerably sharp, but he felt that he might have made
better use of his time, which may be shortly described
as having been spent in hunting all the winter, and in
talking about it all the summer. With this popular
sport he combined the diversion of fortune-hunting,
though we are concerned to say that his success, up to the
period of our introduction had not been commensurate
with his deserts. Let us, however, hope that brighter
days are about to dawn upon him.

Having now introduced our hero to our male and
female friends, under his interesting pursuits of fox and
fortune-hunter, it becomes us to say a few words as to his
qualifications for carrying them on.

Mr. Sponge was a good-looking, rather vulgar-looking
man. At a distance—say ten yards—his height, figure,
and carriage gave him somewhat of a commanding
appearance, but this was rather marred by a jerky,
twitchy, uneasy sort of air, that too plainly showed he
was not the natural, or what the lower orders call the
real gentleman. Not that Sponge was shy. Far from it.
He never hesitated about offering to a lady, after a three

14

days' acquaintance, or in asking a gentleman to take
him a horse in over-night, with whom he might chance
to come in contact in the hunting-field. And he did it
all in such a cool, off-hand, matter-of-course sort of
way, that people who would have stared with astonishment if anybody else had hinted at such a proposal,
really seemed to come into the humour and spirit of the
thing, and to look upon it rather as a matter of course
than otherwise. Then his dexterity in getting into
people's houses was only equalled by the difficulty of
getting him out again.

R. S. SURTEES (1805-1864)
Handley Cross
and *Mr. Sponge's Sporting Tour*

AFTER THE HUNT

The fox lay still in the rabbit-meuse,
On the dry brown dust of the plumes of yews.
In the bottom below a brook went by,
Blue, in a patch, like a streak of sky.
There one by one, with a clink of stone,
Came a red or dark coat on a horse half-blown.
And man to man with a gasp for breath
Said: "Lord, what a run! I'm fagged to death."

*   *   *

After an hour no riders came,
The day drew by like an ending game;
A robin sang from a pufft red breast,
The fox lay quiet and took his rest.
A wren on a tree-stump carolled clear,
Then the starlings wheeled in a sudden sheer,
The rooks came home to the twiggy hive
In the elm-tree tops which the winds do drive.

Then the noise of the rooks fell slowly still,
And the lights came out in the Clench Brook Mill;
Then a pheasant cocked, then an owl began,
With the cry that curdles the blood of man.

*   *   *

The stars grew bright as the yews grew black,
The fox rose stiffly and stretched his back.
He flaired the air, then he padded out
To the valley below him, dark as doubt,
Winter-thin with the young green crops,
For old Cold Crendon and Hilcote Copse.

*   *   *

The stars grew bright in the winter sky,
The wind came keen with a tang of frost,
The brook was troubled for new things lost,
The copse was happy for old things found,
The fox came home and he went to ground.

*   *   *

And the hunt came home and the hounds were fed,
They climbed to their bench and went to bed;
The horses in stable loved their straw.
"Good-night, my beauties," said Robin Dawe.

*   *   *

Then the moon came quiet and flooded full
Light and beauty on clouds like wool,
On a feasted fox at rest from hunting,
In the beech-wood grey where the brocks were grunting.

*   *   *

The beech-wood grey rose dim in the night
With moonlight fallen in pools of light,
The long dead leaves on the ground were rimed;
A clock struck twelve and the church-bells chimed.

JOHN MASEFIELD (Born 1878)
Reynard the Fox

HUNTING: BYRON'S VIEW

A fox-hunt to a foreigner is strange;
  'Tis also subject to the double danger
Of tumbling first, and having in exchange
  Some pleasant jesting at the awkward stranger;
But Juan had been early taught to range
  The wilds, as doth an Arab turn'd avenger,
So that his horse, or charger, hunter, hack,
Knew that he had a hunter on his back.

And now in this new field with some applause,
  He clear'd hedge, ditch, and double post, and rail,
And never craned, and made but few *faux pas*,
  And only fretted when the scent 'gan fail.
He broke, 'tis true, some statutes of the laws
  Of hunting—for the sagest youth is frail;
Rode o'er the hounds, it may be, now and then,
And once o'er several country gentlemen.

But, on the whole, to general admiration
  He acquitted both himself and horse: the squires
Marvell'd at merit of another nation;
  The boors cried, "Dang it! who'd have thought it?"
    Sires,
The Nestors of the sporting generation,
  Swore praises and recall'd their former fires;
The huntsman's self relented to a grin,
And rated him almost a whipper-in.

Such were his trophies,—not of spear and shield,
    But leaps, and bursts, and sometimes foxes' brushes;
Yet I must own,—although in this I yield
    To patriot sympathy a Briton's blushes,—
He thought at heart like courtly Chesterfield,
    Who, after a long chase o'er hills, dales, bushes,
And what not, though he rode beyond all price,
Ask'd next day, "if men ever hunted *twice*?"

He also had a quality uncommon
    To early risers after a long chase,
Who wake in winter ere the cock can summon
    December's drowsy day to his dull race,—
A quality agreeable to a woman,
    When her soft, liquid words run on apace,
Who likes a listener, whether saint or sinner,—
He did not fall asleep just after dinner.

LORD BYRON (1788-1824)
Don Juan

SKATING

And in the frosty season, when the sun
Was set, and visible for many a mile
The cottage windows blazed through twilight gloom,
I heeded not their summons: happy time
It was indeed for all of us—for me
It was a time of rapture! Clear and loud
The village clock tolled six,—I wheeled about,
Proud and exulting like an untired horse
That cares not for his home. All shod with steel,
We hissed along the polished ice in games
Confederate, imitative of the chase
And woodland pleasures,—the resounding horn,
The pack loud chiming, and the hunted hare.
So through the darkness and the cold we flew,

And not a voice was idle; with the din
Smitten, the precipices rang aloud;
The leafless trees and every icy crag
Tinkled like iron; while far distant hills
Into the tumult sent an alien sound
Of melancholy not unnoticed, while the stars
Eastward were sparkling clear, and in the west
The orange sky of evening died away.
Not seldom from the uproar I retired
Into a silent bay, or sportively
Glanced sideway, leaving the tumultuous throng,
To cut across the reflex of a star
That fled, and, flying still before me, gleamed
Upon the glassy plain; and oftentimes,
When we had given our bodies to the wind,
And all the shadowy banks on either side
Came sweeping through the darkness, spinning still
The rapid line of motion, then at once
Have I, reclining back upon my heels,
Stopped short; yet still the solitary cliffs
Wheeled by me—even as if the earth had rolled
With visible motion her diurnal round!
Behind me did they stretch in solemn train,
Feebler and feebler, and I stood and watched
Till all was tranquil as a dreamless sleep.

WILLIAM WORDSWORTH (1770-1850)
The Prelude

SKATING—PICKWICKIAN

"Now," said Wardle, after a substantial lunch, with the agreeable items of strong beer and cherry-brandy, had been done ample justice to; "what say you to an hour on the ice? We shall have plenty of time."

"Capital!" said Mr. Benjamin Allen.

"Prime!" ejaculated Mr. Bob Sawyer.

"You skate, of course, Winkle?" said Wardle.

"Ye-yes; oh, yes," replied Mr. Winkle. "I-I-am *rather* out of practice."

"Oh, *do* skate, Mr. Winkle," said Arabella. "I like to see it so much."

"Oh, it is so graceful," said another young lady.

A third young lady said it was elegant, and a fourth expressed her opinion that it was "swan-like."

"I should be very happy, I'm sure," said Mr. Winkle, reddening; "but I have no skates."

This objection was at once overruled. Trundle had a couple of pair, and the fat boy announced that there were half-a-dozen more downstairs: whereat Mr. Winkle expressed exquisite delight, and looked exquisitely uncomfortable.

Old Wardle led the way to a pretty large sheet of ice, and the fat boy and Mr. Weller, having shovelled and swept away the snow which had fallen on it during the night, Mr. Bob Sawyer adjusted his skates with a dexterity which to Mr. Winkle was perfectly marvellous, and described circles with his left leg, and cut figures of eight, and inscribed upon the ice, without once stopping for breath, a great many other pleasant and astonishing devices, to the excessive satisfaction of Mr. Pickwick, Mr. Tupman, and the ladies: which reached a pitch of positive enthusiasm, when old Wardle and Benjamin Allen, assisted by the aforesaid Bob Sawyer, performed some mystic evolutions, which they called a reel.

All this time, Mr. Winkle, with his face and hands blue with the cold, had been forcing a gimlet into the soles of his feet, and putting his skates on, with the points behind, and getting the straps into a very complicated and entangled state, with the assistance of Mr. Snodgrass, who knew rather less about skates than a Hindoo. At length, however, with the assistance of Mr. Weller, the unfortunate skates were firmly screwed and buckled on, and Mr. Winkle was raised to his feet.

"Now then, sir," said Sam, in an encouraging tone; "off vith you, and show 'em how to do it."

"Stop, Sam, stop!" said Mr. Winkle, trembling violently, and clutching hold of Sam's arms with the grasp of a drowning man. "How slippery it is, Sam!"

"Not an uncommon thing upon ice, sir," replied Mr. Weller. "Hold up, sir!"

"These—these—are very awkward skates; ain't they, Sam?" inquired Mr. Winkle, staggering.

"I'm afeerd there's a orkard gen'l'm'n in 'em, sir," replied Sam.

"Now, Winkle," cried Mr. Pickwick, quite unconscious that there was anything the matter. "Come; the ladies are all anxiety."

"Yes, yes," replied Mr. Winkle, with a ghastly smile. "I'm coming."

"Just a goin' to begin," said Sam, endeavouring to disengage himself. "Now, sir, start off! . . ."

"Just hold me at first, Sam; will you?" said Mr. Winkle. "There—that's right. I shall soon get in the way of it, Sam. Not too fast, Sam; not too fast."

Mr. Winkle stooping forward, with his body half doubled up, was being assisted over the ice by Mr. Weller, in a very singular and un-swan-like manner, when Mr. Pickwick most innocently shouted from the opposite bank:

"Sam!"

"Sir?"

"Here. I want you."

"Let go, sir," said Sam. "Don't you hear the governor a callin'? Let go, sir."

With a violent effort, Mr. Weller disengaged himself from the grasp of the agonised Pickwickian, and, in so doing, administered a considerable impetus to the unhappy Mr. Winkle. With an accuracy which no degree of dexterity or practice could have insured, that unfortunate gentleman bore swiftly down into the centre of the reel, at the very moment when Mr. Bob Sawyer was performing a flourish of unparalleled beauty. Mr. Winkle struck wildly against him, and with a loud crash they both fell heavily down. Mr. Pickwick ran to the spot. Bob Sawyer had risen to his feet, but Mr. Winkle was far too wise to do anything of the kind, in skates. He was seated on the ice, making spasmodic efforts to smile; but anguish was depicted on every lineament of his countenance.

"Are you hurt?" inquired Mr. Benjamin Allen, with great anxiety.

"Not much," said Mr. Winkle, rubbing his back very hard.

"I wish you'd let me bleed you," said Mr. Benjamin, with great eagerness.

"No, thank you," replied Mr. Winkle hurriedly.

"I really think you had better," said Allen.

"Thank you," replied Mr. Winkle; "I'd rather not."

"What do *you* think, Mr. Pickwick?" inquired Bob Sawyer.

Mr. Pickwick was excited and indignant. He beckoned to Mr. Weller, and said in a stern voice, "Take his skates off."

"No; but really I had scarcely begun," remonstrated Mr. Winkle.

"Take his skates off," repeated Mr. Pickwick firmly.

The command was not to be resisted. Mr. Winkle allowed Sam to obey it in silence.

"Lift him up," said Mr. Pickwick. Sam assisted him to rise.

Mr. Pickwick retired a few paces apart from the bystanders; and, beckoning his friend to approach, fixed a searching look upon him, and uttered in a low, but distinct and emphatic tone, these remarkable words:

"You're a humbug, sir."

" A what ? " said Mr. Winkle, starting.

" A humbug, sir. I will speak plainer, if you wish it.
An impostor, sir."

CHARLES DICKENS (1812-1870)
Pickwick Papers

THE TRIUMVIRATE

In the years before the 1914 war, British golf was dominated by three
men, J. H. Taylor, Harry Vardon, and James Braid. The American
invasion had not arrived, and for some time these three, known as
the Triumvirate after the world-dividing Triumvirs of the Roman
Empire, shared the major honours—there were small rewards then—
in rotation.

I managed to see each of the three win two champion-
ships, Braid at Prestwick and St. Andrews in 1908 and
1910, Taylor at Deal and Hoylake, 1909 and 1913, Vardon
at Sandwich and Prestwick, 1911 and 1914. I suppose
the most exciting was in 1914 when Vardon and Taylor,
leading the field, were drawn together on the last day,
and the whole of the West of Scotland was apparently
moved with a desire to watch them. Braid, too, played
his part on that occasion, for had he not designed the
bunker almost in the middle of the fairway at the
fourth hole? And was it not fear of that bunker that
drove Taylor too much to the right into the other one
by the Pow Burn, so that he took a seven? No wonder
J.H. said that the man who made that bunker should
be buried in it with a niblick through his heart. Yes,
that was a tremendous occasion, and Braid's golf in
1908—291 with an eight in it at the Cardinal—was
incredibly brilliant; and Vardon's driving when he
beat Massy in playing off the tie at Sandwich was, I
think, the most beautiful display of wooden club hitting
I ever saw; but for sheer thrilling quality give me
Taylor at Hoylake in 1913. There was no great excite-

ment since, after qualifying by the skin of his teeth, he won by strokes and strokes; but I have seen nothing else in golf which so stirred me and made me want to cry. The wind and the rain were terrific, but not so terrific as Taylor, with his cap pulled down, buffeting his way through them. There are always one or two strokes which stick faster in the memory than any others, and I noticed the other day that my friend Mr. Macfarlane recalled just the one that I should choose. It was the second shot played with a cleek to the Briars hole in the very teeth of the storm. I can still see Taylor standing on rocklike feet, glued flat on the turf, watching that ball as it whizzes over the two cross bunkers straight for the green. There never was such a cleek shot; there never will be such another as long as the world stands.

It is surely a curious fact that, though these three players dominated golf for so long, and the golfer is essentially an imitative animal, no one of them has been the founder of a school. They made people play better by having to live up to their standard, but they did not make people play like them. Here are three strongly-marked and characteristic styles to choose from, and yet where are their imitators? Vardon had one, to be sure, in Mr. A. C. Lincoln, an excellent player who belonged to Totteridge; he had at any rate many of the Vardonian mannerisms and a strong superficial likeness. There is George Duncan, too, with a natural talent for mimicry; he remodelled the swing he had learnt in Scotland after he first saw the master. Imagine Duncan slowed down and there is much of Vardon. Beyond those two, I can think of no one in the least like him. It is much the same with Taylor. His two sons, J. H. Junior and Leslie, have something of the tricks of the back swing, but nobody has got the flat-footed hit and the little grunt that goes with it. Braid, with that strange combination of a portentous gravity and a sudden, furious lash, seems the most impossible model of all. I know no one who has even copied his waggle, with that little menacing shake of the club head in the middle of it. Each of the three was so unlike the other two that the world hesitated which model to take and ended by taking none.

American players look as if they had all been cast in one admirable mould. Ours look as if they came out of innumerable different ones, and as if in nearly every mould there had been some flaw. It was part of the fascination of the triumvirate that each was so extraordinarily individual, but now it seems almost a pity for British golf. If only just one of them could have been easier to imitate! In other respects, of course, they did all three of them leave a model which could be imitated. By all the good golfing qualities of courage and sticking power and chivalry, by their modesty and dignity and self-respect, they helped to make the professional golfer a very different person from what he was when they first came on the scene. Their influence as human beings has been as remarkable as their achievements as golfers.

BERNARD DARWIN (Born 1876)
Out of the Rough

SOCCER THEN AND NOW

Football started as a game without rules, often played in the street. Not until the 19th century did it become an organised sport.

The ball consisted of a large bullock's bladder well filled with air, and secured in a stout leathern case ... The moment for starting being announced by the tolling of the town bell ... the task developed upon Mr. Redford, of the Castle Hotel, to give the starting kick, which he executed in a lofty and effective manner. By this time, an immense concourse of persons, of all denominations, had assembled in the grand market street . . . The competitors at the ball were divided into two classes—namely, the inhabitants at Thames-street end of the Castle, and those of the Town's end . . . To surmount the roofs of houses, scale the walls, and to plunge into the creek or river, were comparatively trifles. Had a mad bull been let loose it could not have afforded greater satisfaction to the Kingston people than this leathern ball.

The Sporting Magazine

———————

The Beswick Prize Band rose nobly to the occasion and gave a rendering of the Brabançonne more or less in line with the intentions of the composer. As soon as the teams got to grips the first Belgian attack revealed the presence of treacherous pools of water on the surface. Dewael, beautifully fed by Mermans, had the track to goal miraculously split open for him, but as he darted along on his scoring mission he left the ball far behind him. It stopped dead as though held by glue. Nine minutes only of sparkling football had gone by when United produced one of the great goals of all time. Byrne cleared his lines with a superb volley and at the same time gave Pegg the sort of pass a winger dreams about. Pegg needed no second bidding. He ran off down the track, rounded his man like an eel, and dropped his centre just where Taylor wanted it. A leap, a downward header, a shower of raindrops from the goalnet, and United were one up on the night, three up on the aggregate.

H. D. DAVIES
The Manchester Guardian

Character and Comedy

CONSCRIPTS

Sir John Falstaff has gone into Gloucestershire to raise recruits for
Henry IV in his putting down of rebellion. He interviews some
local types, gallant and the reverse, who have been summoned for
"pricking," *i.e.*, marking on the call-up roll, by that twittering fribble,
Mr. Justice Shallow and his colleague, Silence. The two latter are
talking of memories and country matters before Sir John arrives.

SHALLOW: Jesu, Jesu, the mad days that I have spent!
and to see how many of my old acquaintances are dead!

SILENCE: We shall all follow, cousin.

SHALLOW: Certain, 'tis certain; very sure, very sure;
death, as the Psalmist saith, is certain to all, all shall
die.—How a good yoke of bullocks at Stamford fair?

SILENCE: Truly, cousin, I was not there.

SHALLOW: Death is certain.—Is old Double of your
town living yet?

SILENCE: Dead, sir.

SHALLOW: Jesu, Jesu, dead!—a' drew a good bow.—
and dead?—a' shot a fine shoot:—John o' Gaunt loved
him well, and betted much money on his head. Dead!—
a' would have clapt i' th' clout at twelve score; and
carried you a forehand shaft a fourteen and fourteen
and a half, that it would have done a man's heart good
to see.—How a score of ewes now?

SILENCE: Thereafter as they be: a score of good ewes
may be worth ten pounds.

SHALLOW: And is old Double dead?

❋   ❋   ❋

Enter: FALSTAFF *with his man* BARDOLPH.

SHALLOW: Here comes good Sir John. Give me your good hand, give me your worship's good hand: by my troth, you like well, and bear your years very well: welcome, good Sir John.

FALSTAFF: I am glad to see you well, good Master Robert Shallow:—Master Surecard, as I think?

SHALLOW: No, Sir John, it is my cousin Silence, in commission with me.

FALSTAFF: Good Master Silence, it well befits you should be of the peace.

SILENCE: Your good worship is welcome.

FALSTAFF: Fie! this is hot weather, gentlemen. Have you provided me here half a dozen sufficient men?

SHALLOW: Marry, have we, sir. Will you sit?

FALSTAFF: Let me see them, I beseech you.

SHALLOW: Where's the roll? where's the roll? where's the roll?—Let me see, let me see, let me see. So, so, so, so, so, so, so: yea, marry, sir;—Ralph Mouldy!—let them appear as I call; let them do so, let them do so.— Let me see, where is Mouldy?

MOULDY: Here, an't please you.

SHALLOW: What think you, Sir John? a good-limbed fellow; young, strong, and of good friends.

FALSTAFF: Is thy name Mouldy?

MOULDY: Yea, an't please you.

FALSTAFF: 'Tis the more time thou wert used.

SHALLOW: Ha, ha, ha! most excellent, i' faith! things that are mouldy lack use: very singular good!—in faith, well said, Sir John; very well said.

FALSTAFF: (*to* SHALLOW) Prick him.

MOULDY: I was prickt well enough before, an you could have let me alone: my old dame will be undone now, for one to do her husbandry and her drudgery: you need not to have prickt me; there are other men fitter to go out than I.

FALSTAFF: Go to! peace, Mouldy; you shall go. Mouldy, it is time you were spent.

MOULDY: Spent!

SHALLOW: Peace, fellow, peace; stand aside: know you where you are?—For th'other, Sir John:—let me see;—Simon Shadow!

FALSTAFF: Yea, marry, let me have him to sit under: he's like to be a cold soldier.

SHALLOW: Where's Shadow?

SHADOW: Here, sir.

FALSTAFF: Shadow, whose son art thou?

SHADOW: My mother's son, sir.

FALSTAFF: Thy mother's son! like enough; and thy father's shadow: so the son of the female is the shadow of the male: it is often so, indeed; but much of the father's substance!

SHALLOW: Do you like him, Sir John?

FALSTAFF: Shadow will serve for summer,—prick him; for we have a number of shadows to fill up the muster-book.

SHALLOW: Thomas Wart!

FALSTAFF: Where's he?

WART: Here, sir.

FALSTAFF: Is thy name Wart?

WART: Yea, sir.

FALSTAFF: Thou art a very ragged wart.

SHALLOW: Shall I prick him, Sir John?

FALSTAFF: It were superfluous; for his apparel is built upon his back, and the whole frame stands upon pins: prick him no more.

SHALLOW: Ha, ha, ha!—you can do it, sir; you can do it: I commend you well—Francis Feeble!

FEEBLE: Here, sir.

FALSTAFF: What trade art thou, Feeble?

FEEBLE: A woman's tailor, sir.

SHALLOW: Shall I prick him, sir?

FALSTAFF: You may: but if he had been a man's

tailor, he'd ha' prickt you.—Wilt thou make as many holes in an enemy's battle as thou hast done in a woman's petticoat?

FEEBLE: I will do my good will, sir; you can have no more.

FALSTAFF: Well said, good woman's tailor! well said, courageous Feeble! thou wilt be as valiant as the wrathful dove or most magnanimous mouse.—Prick the woman's tailor well, Master Shallow; deep, Master Shallow.

FEEBLE: I would Wart might have gone, sir.

FALSTAFF: I would thou wert a man's tailor, that thou mightst mend him, and make him fit to go. I cannot put him to a private soldier, that is the leader of so many thousands: let that suffice, most forcible Feeble.

FEEBLE: It shall suffice, sir.

FALSTAFF: I am bound to thee, reverend Feeble.— Who is next?

SHALLOW: Peter Bullcalf o' th' green!

FALSTAFF: Yea, marry, let's see Bullcalf.

BULLCALF: Here, sir.

FALSTAFF: 'Fore God, a likely fellow!—Come, prick me Bullcalf till he roar again.

BULLCALF: O Lord! good my lord captain,—

FALSTAFF: What, dost thou roar before thou art prickt?

BULLCALF: O Lord, sir! I am a diseased man.

FALSTAFF: What disease hast thou?

BULLCALF: A whoreson cold, sir,—a cough, sir,— which I caught with ringing in the king's affairs upon his coronation-day, sir.

FALSTAFF: Come, thou shalt go to the wars in a gown; we will have away thy cold; and I will take such order, that thy friends shall ring for thee.—Is here all?

SHALLOW: Here is two more call'd than your number; you must have but four here, sir:—and so, I pray you, go in with me to dinner.

FALSTAFF: Come, I will go drink with you, but I cannot tarry dinner. I am glad to see you, by my troth, Master Shallow.

SHALLOW: O, Sir John, do you remember since we lay all night in the windmill in Saint George's field?

FALSTAFF: No more of that, good Master Shallow, no more of that.

SHALLOW: Ha, 'twas a merry night. And is Jane Nightwork alive?

FALSTAFF: She lives, Master Shallow.

SHALLOW: She never could away with me.

FALSTAFF: Never, never; she would always say she could not abide Master Shallow.

SHALLOW: By the mass, I could anger her to the heart. She was then a bona-roba. Doth she hold her own well?

FALSTAFF: Old, old, Master Shallow.

SHALLOW: Nay, she must be old; she cannot choose but be old; certain she's old; and had Robin Nightwork by old Nightwork before I came to Clement's-Inn.

SILENCE: That's fifty-five year ago.

SHALLOW: Ha, cousin Silence, that thou hadst seen that that this knight and I have seen!—Ha, Sir John, said I well?

FALSTAFF: We have heard the chimes at midnight, Master Shallow.

SHALLOW: That we have, that we have, that we have; in faith, Sir John, we have: our watch-word was, "Hem, boys!"—Come, let's to dinner, come, let's to dinner.—Jesus, the days that we have seen!—come, come.

Exeunt FALSTAFF, SHALLOW *and* SILENCE.

BULLCALF: Good master corporate Bardolph, stand my friend; and here's four Harry ten shillings in French crowns for you. In very truth, sir, I has as lief be hang'd, sir, as go: and yet, for mine own part, sir, I do not care;

but rather, because I am unwilling, and, for mine own part, have a desire to stay with my friends, else, sir, I did not care, for mine own part, so much.

BARDOLPH: Go to; stand aside.

MOULDY: And, good master corporal captain, for my old dame's sake, stand my friend: she has nobody to do any thing about her when I am gone; and she is old, and cannot help herself; you shall have forty, sir.

BARDOLPH: Go to; stand aside.

FEEBLE: By my troth, I care not; a man can die but once,—we owe God a death: I'll ne'er bear a base mind: an't be my destiny, so; an't be not, so: no man's too good to serve's Prince; and let it go which way it will, he that dies this year is quit for the next.

BARDOLPH: Well said; thou'rt a good fellow.

FEEBLE: Faith, I'll bear no base mind.

WILLIAM SHAKESPEARE (1564-1616)
Henry IV, Part II

ENGLISH MAID

There is a garden in her face
    Where roses and white lilies grow;
A heavenly paradise is that place,
    Wherein all pleasant fruits do flow;
There cherries grow which none may buy,
Till "Cherry-Ripe" themselves do cry.

Those cherries fairly do enclose
    Of orient pearl a double row,
Which when her lovely laughter shows,
    They look like rose-buds fill'd with snow;
Yet them nor peer nor prince can buy,
Till "Cherry-Ripe" themselves do cry.

Her eyes like angels watch them still;
    Her brows like bended bows do stand,
Threat'ning with piercing frowns to kill
    All that attempt with eye or hand
Those sacred cherries to come nigh,
—Till "Cherry-Ripe" themselves do cry!

THOMAS CAMPION (1567-1619)
There is a Garden in Her Face

MRS. MALAPROP'S WAY

The humour of words misused is common and popular in English comedy. Shakespeare had set a notable example with his watchman, Dogberry, in *Much Ado About Nothing*. H. G. Wells, to be quoted later, added to this kind of fun with the wildly inventive vocabulary of his Mr. Polly.

SIR ANTHONY: In my way hither, Mrs. Malaprop, I observed your niece's maid coming forth from a circulating library!—She had a book in each hand—they were half-bound volumes, with marble covers!—From that moment I guessed how full of duty I should see her mistress!

MRS. MALAPROP: Those are vile places, indeed!

SIR ANTHONY: Madam, a circulating library in a town is as an evergreen tree of diabolical knowledge! It blossoms through the year!—And depend on it, Mrs. Malaprop, that they who are so fond of handling the leaves will long for the fruit at last.

MRS. MALAPROP: Fie, fie, Sir Anthony, you surely speak laconically.

SIR ANTHONY: Why, Mrs. Malaprop, in moderation, now, what would you have a woman know?

MRS. MALAPROP: Observe me, Sir Anthony.—I would by no means wish a daughter of mine to be a progeny of learning; I don't think so much learning becomes a young woman; for instance, I would never let her meddle with Greek, or Hebrew, or Algebra, or Simony, or Fluxions, or Paradoxes, or such inflammatory branches of learning—neither would it be necessary for her to handle any of your mathematical, astronomical diabolical instruments:—But, Sir Anthony, I would send her, at nine years old, to a boarding-school, in order to learn a little ingenuity and artifice. Then, sir, she should have a supercilious knowledge in accounts;— and as she grew up, I would have her instructed in geometry, that she might know something of the contagious countries;—but above all, Sir Anthony, she should be mistress of orthodoxy, that she might not mis-spell, and mis-pronounce words so shamefully as girls usually do; and likewise that she might reprehend the true meaning of what she is saying. This, Sir Anthony, is what I would have a woman know;—and I don't think there is a superstitious article in it.

SIR ANTHONY: Well, well, Mrs. Malaprop, I will dispute the point no further with you; though I must confess that you are a truly moderate and polite arguer, for almost every third word you say is on my side of the question. But, Mrs. Malaprop, to the more important point in debate,—you say you have no objection to my proposal.

MRS. MALAPROP: None, I assure you. I am under no positive engagement with Mr. Acres, and as Lydia is so obstinate against him, perhaps your son may have better success.

SIR ANTHONY: Well, madam, I will write for the boy directly. He knows not a syllable of this yet, though I have for some time had the proposal in my head. He is at present with his regiment.

MRS. MALAPROP: We have never seen your son, Sir Anthony; but I hope no objection on his side.

SIR ANTHONY: Objection!—let him object if he dare! —No, no, Mrs. Malaprop, Jack knows that the least demur puts me in a phrensy directly. My process was always very simple—in their younger days, 'twas "Jack, do this";—if he demurred, I knocked him down—and if he grumbled at that, I always sent him out of the room.

MRS. MALAPROP: Ay, and the properest way, o' my conscience!—nothing is so conciliating to young people as severity.

R. B. SHERIDAN (1751-1816)
The Rivals

OLD-FASHIONED

SCENE: *A Chamber in an old-fashioned House.*

Enter MRS. HARDCASTLE *and* MR. HARDCASTLE.

MRS. HARDCASTLE: I vow, Mr. Hardcastle, you're very particular. Is there a creature in the whole country, but ourselves, that does not take a trip to town now and then, to rub off the rust a little? There's the two Miss Hoggs, and our neighbour, Mrs. Grigsby, go to take a month's polishing every winter.

HARDCASTLE: Ay, and bring back vanity and affectation to last them the whole year. I wonder why London cannot keep its own fools at home. In my time, the follies of the town crept slowly among us, but now they travel faster than a stage-coach. Its fopperies come down, not only as inside passengers, but in the very basket.

MRS. HARDCASTLE: Ay, *your* times were fine times, indeed; you have been telling us of *them* for many a long year. Here we live in an old rumbling mansion, that looks for all the world like an inn, but that we never see company. Our best visitors are old Mrs. Oddfish, the curate's wife, and little Cripplegate, the lame dancing-master: And all our entertainment your old stories of Prince Eugene and the Duke of Marlborough. I hate such old-fashioned trumpery.

HARDCASTLE: And I love it. I love every thing that's old: old friends, old times, old manners, old books, old wine; and, I believe, Dorothy (*taking her hand*) you'll own I have been pretty fond of an old wife.

MRS. HARDCASTLE: Lord, Mr. Hardcastle, you're for ever at your Dorothy's and your old wife's. You may be a Darby, but I'll be no Joan, I promise you. I'm not so old as you'd make me, by more than one good year. Add twenty to twenty, and make money of that.

HARDCASTLE: Let me see; twenty added to twenty, makes just fifty and seven.

MRS. HARDCASTLE: It's false, Mr. Hardcastle: I was but twenty when I was brought to bed of Tony, that I had by Mr. Lumpkin, my first husband; and he's not come to years of discretion yet.

HARDCASTLE: Nor ever will, I dare answer for him. Ay, you have taught *him* finely.

MRS. HARDCASTLE: No matter, Tony Lumpkin has a good fortune. My son is not to live by his learning. I don't think a boy wants much learning to spend fifteen hundred a year.

HARDCASTLE: Learning, quotha! A mere composition of tricks and mischief.

MRS. HARDCASTLE: Humour, my dear; nothing but humour. Come, Mr. Hardcastle, you must allow the boy a little humour.

HARDCASTLE: I'd sooner allow him an horse-pond. If burning the footmen's shoes, frighting the maids, and worrying the kittens, be humour, he has it. It was but yesterday he fastened my wig to the back of my chair, and when I went to make a bow, I popt my bald head in Mrs. Frizzle's face.

MRS. HARDCASTLE: And am I to blame? The poor boy was always too sickly to do any good. A school would be his death. When he comes to be a little stronger, who know what a year or two's Latin may do for him?

HARDCASTLE: Latin for him! A cat and fiddle. No,

no, the ale-house and the stable are the only schools he'll ever go to.

MRS. HARDCASTLE: Well, we must not snub the poor boy now, for I believe we shan't have him long among us. Any body that looks in his face may see he's consumptive.

HARDCASTLE: Ay, if growing too fat be one of the symptoms.

MRS. HARDCASTLE: He coughs sometimes.

HARDCASTLE: Yes, when his liquor goes the wrong way.

MRS. HARDCASTLE: I'm actually afraid of his lungs. .

HARDCASTLE: And truly so am I; for he sometimes whoops like a speaking trumpet.

OLIVER GOLDSMITH (1730-1774)
She Stoops to Conquer

HOSTESS—AND HOST

Emma was so busy in admiring those soft blue eyes, in talking and listening, and forming all these schemes in the in-betweens, that the evening flew away at a very unusual rate; and the supper-table, which always closed such parties, and for which she had been used to sit and watch the due time, was all set out and ready, and moved forwards to the fire, before she was aware. With an alacrity beyond the common impulse of a spirit which yet was never indifferent to the credit of doing everything well and attentively, with the real good-will of a mind delighted with its own ideas, did she then do all the honours of the meal, and help and recommend the minced chicken and scalloped oysters, with an urgency which she knew would be acceptable to the early hours and civil scruples of their guests.

Upon such occasions poor Mr. Woodhouse's feelings were in sad warfare. He loved to have the cloth laid, because it had been the fashion of his youth, but his conviction of suppers being very unwholesome made him rather sorry to see anything put on it; and while his hospitality would have welcomed his visitors to everything, his care for their health made him grieve that they would eat.

Such another small basin of thin gruel as his own was all that he could, with thorough self-approbation, recommend; though he might constrain himself, while the ladies were comfortably clearing the nicer things, to say——

"Mrs. Bates, let me propose your venturing on one of these eggs. An egg boiled very soft is not unwholesome. Serle understands boiling an egg better than anybody. I would not recommend an egg boiled by anybody else—but you need not be afraid, they are very small, you see—one of our small eggs will not hurt you. Miss Bates, let Emma help you to a *little* bit of tart—a *very* little bit. Ours are all apple-tarts. You need not be afraid of unwholesome preserves here. I do not advise the custard. Mrs. Goddard, what say you to *half* a glass of wine? A *small* half-glass, put into a tumbler of water? I do not think it could disagree with you."

Emma allowed her father to talk—but supplied her visitors in a much more satisfactory style.

JANE AUSTEN (1775-1817)
Emma

ENGLISH GENTLEMAN

Since the word "gentleman" has been misused and therefore misprised and even ridiculed, it is refreshing to meet this beautifully phrased and finely considered definition.

He has his eyes on all his company; he is tender towards the bashful, gentle towards the distant, and merciful towards the absurd; he is seldom prominent in conversation, and never wearisome. He makes light of favours while he does them, and seems to be receiving when he is conferring. He never speaks of himself except when compelled, never defends himself by a mere retort, he has no ears for slander or gossip, is scrupulous in imputing motives to those who interfere with him, and interprets everything for the best. He is never mean or little in his disputes, never takes unfair advantage, never mistakes personalities or sharp saying for arguments, or insinuates evil which he dare not say out. From a long-sighted prudence, he observes the maxim of the ancient sage, that we should ever conduct ourselves towards our enemy as if he were one day to be our friend.

He has too much good sense to be affronted at insults, he is too well employed to remember injuries, and too indolent to bear malice. He is patient, forbearing, and resigned, on philosophical principles; he submits to pain, because it is inevitable, to bereavement, because it is irreparable, and to death, because it is his destiny. If he engages in controversy of any kind, his disciplined intellect preserves him from the blundering discourtesy of better, though less educated, minds; who, like blunt weapons, tear and hack instead of cutting clean, who mistake the point in argument, waste their strength on trifles, misconceive their adversary, and leave the question more involved than they find it. He may be right or wrong in his opinion, but he is too clear-headed to be unjust; he is as simple as he is forcible, and as brief as he is decisive.

JOHN HENRY, CARDINAL NEWMAN (1801-1890)
Idea of a University

THE CHATTER-BOX

Supper was announced. The move began; and Miss Bates might be heard from that moment without interruption, till her being seated at table and taking up her spoon.

"Jane, Jane, my dear Jane, where are you? Here is your tippet. Mrs. Weston begs you to put on your tippet. She says she is afraid there will be draughts in the passage, though everything has been done—one door nailed up—quantities of matting—my dear Jane, indeed you must. Mr. Churchill, oh! you are too obliging. How well you put it on—so gratified! Excellent dancing indeed. Yes, my dear, I ran home, as I said I should, to help grandmamma to bed, and got back again, and nobody missed me. I set off without saying a word, just as I told you. Grandmamma was quite well, had a charming evening with Mr. Woodhouse, a vast deal of chat, and backgammon. Tea was made downstairs, biscuits and baked apples, and wine before she came away: amazing luck in some of her throws: and she inquired a great deal about you, how you were amused, and who were your partners. "Oh!" said I, "I shall not forestall Jane; I left her dancing with Mr. George Otway; she will love to tell you all about it herself to-morrow: her first partner was Mr. Elton; I do not know who will ask her next, perhaps Mr. William Cox." My dear sir, you are too obliging. Is there nobody you would not rather? I am not helpless. Sir, you are most kind. Upon my word, Jane on one arm, and me on the other. Stop, stop, let us stand a little back, Mrs. Elton is going; dear Mrs. Elton, how elegant she looks—beautiful lace. Now we all follow in her train. Quite the queen of the evening!

Well, here we are at the passage. Two steps, Jane, take

care of the two steps. Oh, no, there is but one. Well,
I was persuaded there were two. How very odd! I
was convinced there were two, and there is but one.
I never saw anything equal to the comfort and style—
candles everywhere. I was telling you of your grandmamma. Jane—there was a little disappointment.
The baked apples and biscuits, excellent in their way,
you know; but there was a delicate fricassée of sweetbread and some asparagus brought in at first, and good
Mr. Woodhouse, not thinking the asparagus quite
boiled enough, sent it all out again. Now there is
nothing grandmamma loves better than sweetbread and
asparagus—so she was rather disappointed; but we
agreed we would not speak of it to anybody, for fear of
its getting round to dear Miss Woodhouse, who would
be so very much concerned. Well, this is brilliant!
I am all amazement!—could not have supposed anything
—such elegance and profusion! I have seen nothing like
it since—Well, where shall we sit? Where shall we sit?
Anywhere, so that Jane is not in a draught. Where *I*
sit is of no consequence. Oh! do you recommend this
side? Well, I am sure, Mr. Churchill—only it seems
too good—but just as you please. What you direct in
this house cannot be wrong. Dear Jane, how shall we
ever recollect half the dishes for grandmamma? Soup
too! Bless me! I should not be helped so soon, but it
smells most excellent, and I cannot help beginning."

Emma had no opportunity of speaking to Mr.
Knightley till after supper.

JANE AUSTEN (1775-1817)
Emma

NEW RICH

Mr. and Mrs. Veneering were bran-new people in a bran-new house in a bran-new quarter of London. Everything about the Veneerings was spick and span new. All their furniture was new, all their friends were new, all their servants were new, their plate was new, their carriage was new, their harness was new, their horses were new, their pictures were new, they themselves were new, they were as newly married as was lawfully compatible with their having a bran-new baby, and if they had set up a great grandfather, he would have come home in matting from the Pantechnicon, without a scratch upon him, French-polished to the crown of his head.

For, in the Veneering establishment, from the hall-chairs with the new coat of arms, to the grand piano-forte with the new action, and upstairs again to the new fire-escape, all things were in a state of high varnish and polish. And what was observable in the furniture was observable in the Veneerings—the surface smelt a little too much of the workshop and was a trifle sticky.

CHARLES DICKENS (1812-1870)
Our Mutual Friend

PODSNAPPERY

Mr. Podsnap was well to do, and stood very high in Mr. Podsnap's opinion. Beginning with a good inheritance, he had married a good inheritance, and had thriven exceedingly in the Marine Insurance way, and was quite satisfied. He never could make out why everybody was not quite satisfied, and he felt conscious that he set a brilliant social example in being particularly well satisfied with most things, and, above all other things, with himself.

Thus happily acquainted with his own merit and importance, Mr. Podsnap settled that whatever he put behind him he put out of existence. There was a dignified conclusiveness—not to add a grand convenience—in this way of getting rid of disagreeables, which had done much towards establishing Mr. Podsnap in his lofty place in Mr. Podsnap's satisfaction. "I don't want to know about it; I don't choose to discuss it; I don't admit it!" Mr. Podsnap had even acquired a peculiar flourish of his right arm in often clearing the world of its most difficult problems, by sweeping them behind him (and consequently sheer away) with those words and a flushed face. For they affronted him.

Mr. Podsnap's world was not a very large world, morally; no, nor even geographically: seeing that although his business was sustained upon commerce with other countries, he considered other countries, with that important reservation, a mistake, and of their manners and customs would conclusively observe, "Not English!" when, PRESTO! with a flourish of the arm, and flush of the face, they were swept away.

*   *   *

As a so eminently respectable man, Mr. Podsnap was sensible of its being required of him to take Providence under his protection. Consequently he always knew exactly what Providence meant. Inferior and less respectable men might fall short of that mark, but Mr. Podsnap was always up to it. And it was very remarkable (and must have been very comfortable) that what Providence meant, was invariably what Mr. Podsnap meant.

CHARLES DICKENS (1812-1870)
Our Mutual Friend

BOXING DAY AT MR. ACKWORTH'S

"Good lad! Glad to see you," roared Mr. Ackworth in the hall, helping me off with my heavy overcoat. "Got a bit o' good stuff i' this overcoat an' all. Ah'll bet your Uncle Miles chose that for you, didn't he? Well, you know one or two of 'em 'ere, but not so many. Mostly neighbours. Introduce yourself, lad. Ah can't be bothered. 'Ere's the wife, though. Better be introduced to 'er or there'll be ructions. Annie, this is young Gregory Dawson who 'elps me in t'sample-room."

"How do you do?" said Mrs. Ackworth in a very deep voice. She was a stately, rather handsome woman, who seemed to think that it was her duty to have dignity enough for both of them, with the result that she was not unlike a duchess in a George Edwardes musical comedy. "Seasonable weather, isn't it?"

"Ay, an' what this lad needs is a drop o' summat to warm 'im up an' get 'im started," said Mr. Ackworth, winking at me.

He took me into a little room full of books, told me to look around it, and then after a minute or two came back with a steaming glass of a very generous size. "Mulled old ale. Warm you up in a jiffy, lad. Now get it down."

It was the strongest stuff I had ever tasted up to that time, and it was hot and I drank it quickly. Then I found I had a great desire to giggle. Mr. Ackworth, Mrs. Ackworth, and their party that I had not yet seen, they all seemed to me exquisitely droll. Mr. Ackworth led me across the hall into a drawing-room packed with people, most of them very hot and many of them very fat. The Bruddersfield agent of the Canal Company, whom I recognised although at that moment he was blindfolded, was trying to pin a paper tail on to an outline of a donkey. And then I saw that the three Allington girls were there, Joan and Eva and Bridget. They smiled, and I made my way, through a solid but almost steaming ton or so of wool merchants and wives, to join them in their corner. I was one of the magic circle. And this, I realized at once, was a wonderful party.

. . . Some game that involved the billiards-table was now proposed, and most of the guests went to play this game, but our little group stayed on in the drawing-room. After a few minutes Mr. Ackworth himself, carrying more food and drink, joined us. "If that lot stays out," he said, "Ah'll get 'Erbert Leaton to play a bit for us."

"Can that man really play?" asked Bridget, rather loftily.

But you couldn't take that line with Mr. Ackworth. "Nah then, young Bridget," he said, grinning at her, "that'll do from you. Ah suppose you think 'cos 'Erbert's a slammocky lookin' sort o' chap an' earns 'is livin' in t'insurance, he amounts to nowt. Well, that's where you're wrong. 'Erbert could 'ave easy earned 'is livin' by music, but bein' an independent sort of chap he'd rather keep it as a 'obby. An' tak' that grin off your face, young woman," he added sternly.

"All right, Mr. Ackworth," Bridget was demure now. "I'd love to hear him play."

"An' what 'ave you brought with you? Summat good, Ah 'ope. None o' this caffy music. We like solid stuff up 'ere on t'Glen. Go an' fetch it, lass."

*　　　*　　　*

"Ah'll tell you what it is," said Mr. Ackworth to the two girls, "Gregory 'ere's a bit of a Clever Dick. An' either 'e'll 'ave to make summat special out of 'imself

NORFOLK: PULLS FERRY, NORWICH

The ferry boat, which in pre-war days used to ply on the River Wensum, now lies sunk at its moorings. Beyond can be seen the Cathedral spire. The importance of Norwich in the wool trade dates from the reign of Edward III, and it has long been famous for its boots and shoes.

NORFOLK: THE BROADS

Yachting on Barton Broad, up the River Ant, at Easter. The "Broads" are lakes formed by the rivers meandering through the low-lying country between Norwich and the coast, and there are nearly 200 miles of navigable waterway in this part of East Anglia.

SUFFOLK: LOWESTOFT HARBOUR

Drifters, after landing the herring catch, prepare for the next trip to the North Sea fishing grounds. Lowestoft, besides being one of the chief fishing ports in England, has important ship- and boat-building yards and is a popular seaside resort.

or he'll be one o' them that nobody wants to talk to or listen to."

I stared at him, for this matched exactly my secret thoughts about myself. He gave me a knowing wink. I glanced at the girls. Eva was looking faintly puzzled, but Joan was nodding wisely. It was a queer moment, and I never forgot it.

Herbert Leaton came up again, still rubbing his huge hands and pulling his long bony fingers and making them crack. He was followed by Bridget, carrying her violin and music case.

"Nah, sitha, 'Erbert lad," said Mr. Ackworth, in an even broader accent than his usual one, "Ah'm goin' to give thee a glass o' right good whisky—special stuff, lad—an' then tha's goin' to play t'piano for us. An' Ah want thee to show these clever bairns just 'ow to do it, 'cos they think they knaw summat an' they knaw nowt yet. Nah, 'ere's thi whisky— an' Ah'll fix t'piano up for thee."

Leaton guffawed, and looked like a lanky North Country comedian in a pantomime. "Thanks, Joe. An' 'ere's to me an' my wife's 'usband." And down went the whisky.

Bridget made a face at us. By this time Mr. Ackworth had cleared some plates and ash-trays off the top of the grand piano and had opened it. Leaton went shambling across, cracking his fingers harder than ever. "What's to be, Joe?" he asked as he sat down.

"Please thysen, lad," replied Mr. Ackworth, lighting a cigar. "But a bit o' Bach 'ud do me."

"Me an' all," said Leaton, hunching himself up over the keyboard and spreading those long bony fingers.

Bridget looked surprised. Then she stopped fidgeting with her own music and settled down to listen.

With one clean stroke, as clean as his opening phrases, Leaton cut straight through the insurance business, the wool trade, Bruddersfield, and the twentieth century, straight through to the eighteenth century and Johann Sebastian Bach. These huge hands of his brought out every note, unfaltering and crystal clear. He had too, what many Bach pianists never quite achieve, a singing tone, a warmth and flush, as of sunlight on the marble. Preludes and fugues sang and climbed, and went thundering by. Joe Ackworth's piano became a whole world of changing tone and colour.

"No, no, no, please!" cried Bridget, running over to him when he stopped, and almost embracing him. "You can't stop now, you can't—you mustn't. Go on. Go on—*please*, Mr. Leaton." There was a break in her voice, and her eyes were very bright.

"Ah told you—didn't Ah—that you knew nowt," observed Mr. Ackworth complacently. "'Ave another drop o' whisky, 'Erbert?"

"Never mind whisky," cried Bridget. "And I admit we know *nowt*. But tell him he must keep on playing. He's wonderful. And I couldn't possibly play now."

Leaton wheeled round on his stool. "'Ow d'yer mean?"

"Not after you I couldn't——"

"Nah stop that." And Leaton held out one hand for the whisky, and held out the other for Bridget's music. "What you got there? Let's 'ave a look. Nah 'ere's a bit o' Bach——"

"I couldn't, I couldn't—not after you." Bridget danced about in her apprehension. "It would sound frightful. Joan—Gregory—back me up—wouldn't it sound frightful?"

"What about the César Franck?" asked Joan.

"Well—I might try——" said Bridget, hesitating.

"Me an' 'Erbert thinks that's thinnish stuff," said Mr. Ackworth, once again surprising me.

"It'll do, Joe, it'll do," said Leaton.

"Do you know it?" asked Bridget.

"Ay, Ah've played it——"

"Didn't you play it that time at Gladstone 'All when Thingumbob's accompanist didn't turn up?" began Mr. Ackworth.

"Never mind about that, Joe."

"Yes, all right, Mr. Leaton," said Bridget. "But who was Thingumbob?"

Herbert Leaton grinned and winked, looking more grotesque than ever. "Ysaye."

. . . So they played the César Franck sonata, and I could see and hear them still, two World Wars away as I closed my eyes to the Cornish sunlight and shut out of my mind the whole fretting and half-ruined planet of this later year. I could still hear Bridget's brave if rather uncertain tone, with its growing tenderness and grave passion, and Leaton's easy and fluid piano tone; and with an effort I could still catch a glimpse of his ungainly hunched figure and Bridget's frowning little face and her tumbling hair. We had, I remembered, more Bach after that, then food and drink with the rest of the party, and more games and nonsense, with Bridget now in tearing high spirits. I could recall too walking down to the Allingtons' with the three girls, through the thickening snow and the blanket of the night, and after that the trudging and slipping, slipping and trudging, from the Allingtons' to Brigg Terrace, alone but aglow with the immense vague dreams of youth. For wasn't my world, in the snow and darkness, opening like a flower?

J. B. PRIESTLEY (Born 1894)
Bright Day

MR. POLLY

H. G. Wells's Mr. Polly was a shop-assistant who inherited enough money to buy his own little shop and fail therein. He had always been a romantic, a lover of words. In his youth with his friends, Parsons and Platt, he roamed the country on Sundays and read Rabelais. Both beer and books gave him a pleasant intoxication.

Mr. Polly was not so picturesque a youth as Parsons. He lacked richness in his voice, and went about in those days with his hands in his pockets looking quietly speculative.

He specialised in slang and the misuse of English, and he played the rôle of an appreciative stimulant to Parsons. Words attracted him curiously, words rich in suggestion, and he loved a novel and striking phrase. His school training had given him little or no mastery of the mysterious pronunciation of English, and no confidence in himself. His schoolmaster indeed had been both unsound and variable. New words had terror and fascination for him; he did not acquire them, he could not avoid them, and so he plunged into them. His only rule was not to be misled by the spelling. That was no guide anyhow. He avoided every recognised phrase in the language, and mispronounced everything in order that he should be suspected of whim rather than of ignorance.

"Sesquippledan," he would say. "Sesquippledan verboojuice."

"Eh?" said Platt.

"Eloquent Rapsodooce."

"Where?" asked Platt.

"In the warehouse, O' Man. All among the table-cloths and blankets. Carlyle. He's reading aloud. Doing the High Froth. Spuming! Windmilling! Waw, waw! It's a sight worth seeing. He'll bark his blessed knuckles one of these days on the fixtures, O' Man."

He held an imaginary book in one hand and waved an eloquent gesture. "So too shall every Hero inasmuch as notwithstanding for evermore come back to Reality," he parodied the enthusiastic Parsons, "so that in fashion and thereby, upon things and not *under* things articulariously He stands."

"I should laugh if the Governor dropped on him," said Platt. "He'd never hear him coming."

"The O' Man's drunk with it—fair drunk," said Polly. "*I* never did. It's worse than when he got on to Raboloose."

When Mr. Polly set up as a shop-keeper on his own, he had a bookish neighbour of a very different kind.

One of his last friendships was with Rusper, the ironmonger. Rusper took over Worthington's shop about three years after Mr. Polly opened. He was a tall, lean, nervous, convulsive man, with an upturned, back-thrown, oval head, who read newspapers and the *Review of Reviews* assiduously, had belonged to a Literary Society somewhere once, and had some defect of the palate that at first gave his lightest word a charm and interest for Mr. Polly. It caused a peculiar clinking sound, as though he had something between a giggle and a gas-meter at work in his neck.

His literary admirations were not precisely Mr. Polly's literary admirations; he thought books were written to enshrine Great Thoughts, and that art was pedagogy in fancy dress; he had no sense of phrase or epithet or richness of texture, but still he knew there were books. He did know there were books, and he was full of large, windy ideas of the sort he called "Modern (kik) Thought," and seemed needlessly and helplessly concerned about "(kik) the Welfare of the Race."

Mr. Polly would dream about that (kik) at nights.

It seemed to that undesirable mind of his that Rusper's head was the most egg-shaped head he had ever seen; the similarity weighed upon him, and when he found an argument growing warm with Rusper he would say, "Boil it some more, O' Man; boil it harder!" or "Six minutes at least," allusions Rusper could never make head or tail of, and got at last to disregard as a part of Mr. Polly's general eccentricity. For a long time that little tendency threw no shadow over their intercourse, but it contained within it the seeds of an ultimate disruption.

Often during the days of this friendship Mr. Polly would leave his shop and walk over to Mr. Rusper's establishment and stand in his doorway and inquire, "Well, O' Man, how's the Mind of the Age working?" and get quite an hour of it; and sometimes Mr. Rusper would come into the outfitter's shop with "Heard the (kik) latest?" and spend the rest of the morning.

H. G. WELLS (1866-1946)
The History of Mr. Polly

First and Last Things

SACRED AND PROFANE LOVE

Let me not to the marriage of true minds
Admit impediments. Love is not love
Which alters when it alteration finds,
Or bends with the remover to remove:
O, no! it is an ever-fixed mark,
That looks on tempests, and is never shaken:
It is the star to every wandering bark,
Whose worth's unknown, although his height be taken.
Love's not Time's fool, though rosy lips and cheeks
Within his bending sickle's compass come;
Love alters not with his brief hours and weeks,
But bears it out even to the edge of doom.
   If this be error, and upon me proved,
   I never writ, nor no man ever loved.

Th' expense of spirit in a waste of shame
Is lust in action; and till action, lust
Is perjur'd, murd'rous, bloody, full of blame,
Savage, extreme, rude, cruel, not to trust;
Enjoy'd no sooner but despised straight;
Past reason hunted; and no sooner had,
Past reason hated, as a swallow'd bait,
On purpose laid to make the taker mad:
Mad in pursuit, and in possession so;
Had, having, and in quest to have, extreme;
A bliss in proof, and prov'd, a very woe;
Before, a joy propos'd; behind, a dream.
   All this the world well knows; yet none knows well
   To shun the heaven that leads men to this hell.

WILLIAM SHAKESPEARE (1564-1616)
Sonnets, 116 and 129

455

UTOPIA

Dreaming of a perfect human society and of one that could be quickly achieved has been a constant habit of the sanguine English people. Sir Thomas More (1478-1535) compiled his *Utopia*. (The word, of Greek derivation, means Nowhere, but to all Utopians it is somewhere.) H. G. Wells, in the early part of this century, was particularly fertile in Utopian planning. Nowadays we are so apprehensive of the future that we are more concerned to read the grim forebodings of George Orwell's "1984" than to indulge in visions of any earthly paradise. Shakespeare, though dealing more often with the crimes, follies, and humours of mankind, drew one Utopian, Gonzalo in *The Tempest*. His dream was of universal idleness. At the end of the eighteenth century, with Revolution in the air, Shelley, Godwin and their circle had ideas of a Utopian Pantisocracy, a community wherein general equality of wealth and power prevailed. For a while Coleridge was one of these visionary optimists, and gave an actual location to his paradise, anticipating the advice, "Go West, young man, go West."

SHAKESPEARE'S UTOPIA

(*Gonzalo speaks*)

I' the commonwealth I would by contraries
Execute all things; for no kind of traffic
Would I admit; no name of magistrate;
Letters should not be known; riches, poverty,
And use of service, none; contract, succession,
Bourn, bound of land, tilth, vineyard, none;
No use of metal, corn, or wine, or oil;
No occupation; all men idle, all;
And women too,—but innocent and pure;
No sovereignty . . .
All things in common nature should produce
Without sweat or endeavour: treason, felony,
Sword, pike, knife, gun, or need of any engine,
Would I not have; but nature should bring forth,

SUFFOLK: THE TOWER MILL AT PAKENHAM
Many windmills in England have fallen into disrepair, but this old mill near Bury St. Edmunds was completely restored to its original state. Suffolk is one of the principal grain-growing counties of England, and is also famous for its punch horses, cows and sheep.

SUFFOLK: THE ANCIENT HOUSE, IPSWICH

This beautiful old building, formerly known as Sparrowe's House, stands in the Butter Market. Its date is 1557 and practically no alterations have been made to it since. In the Middle Ages, Ipswich was an important wool town, and its industries still include clothing and sacking.

SUFFOLK: CAVENDISH VILLAGE

The flint-and-stone church tower and thatched cottages of Cavendish stand near the River Stour and on the road from Clare to Sudbury, a locality beloved by Constable and Gainsborough.

Of its own kind, all foison, all abundance,
To feed my innocent people . . .
I would with such perfection govern, sir,
T'excel the golden age.

WILLIAM SHAKESPEARE (1564-1616)
The Tempest

COLERIDGE'S YOUNG IDEA

Truth I pursued, as fancy sketch'd the way,
And wiser men than I went worse astray.

I was never myself, at any period of my life, a convert
to the Jacobinical system. From my earliest manhood,
it was an axiom in politics with me, that in every
country where property prevailed, property must be the
grand basis of the government; and that that government was the best, in which the power or political
influence of the individual was in proportion to his
property, provided that the free circulation of property
was not impeded by any positive laws or customs, nor
the tendency of wealth to accumulate in abiding masses
unduly encouraged. I perceived, that if the people
at large were neither ignorant nor immoral, there
could be no motive for a sudden and violent change of
government; and if they were, there could be no hope
but of a change for the worse. The temple of despotism,
like that of the Mexican God, would be rebuilt with
human skulls, and more firmly, though in a different
style of architecture.

Thanks to the excellent education which I had received,
my reason was too clear not to draw this circle of power
round me, and my spirit too honest to attempt to break
through it. My feelings, however, and imagination
did not remain unkindled in this general conflagration;
and I confess I should be more inclined to be ashamed

than proud of myself, if they had. I was a sharer in the general vortex, though my little world described the path of its revolution in an orbit of its own. What I dared not expect from constitutions of government and whole nations, I hoped from religion and a small company of chosen individuals.

I formed a plan, as harmless as it was extravagant, of trying the experiment of human perfectibility on the banks of the Susquehanna; where our little society, in its second generation, was to have combined the innocence of the patriarchal age with the knowledge and genuine refinements of European culture; and where I dreamed that in the sober evening of my life, I should behold the cottages of independence in the undivided dale of industry,—

> And oft, soothed sadly by some dirgeful wind,
> Muse on the sore ills I had left behind!

Strange fancies, and as vain as strange! yet to the intense interest and impassioned zeal, which called forth and strained every faculty of my intellect for the organization and defence of this scheme, I owe much of whatever I at present possess, my clearest insight into the nature of individual man, and my most comprehensive views of his social relations, of the true uses of trade and commerce, and how far the wealth and relative power of nations promote or impede their welfare and inherent strength. Nor were they less serviceable in securing myself, and perhaps some others, from the pitfalls of sedition: and when we at length alighted on the firm ground of common sense from the gradually exhausted balloon of youthful enthusiasm, though the air-built castles, which we had been pursuing, had vanished with all their pageantry of shifting forms and glowing colours, we were yet free from the stains and impurities which might have remained upon us, had we been travel-

ling with the crowd of less imaginative malcontents,
through the dark lanes and foul by-roads of ordinary
fanaticism.

S. T. COLERIDGE (1772-1834)
The Friend

DEATH'S DISCIPLINE

It is therefore Death alone that can suddenly make man
to know himselfe. He tells the proud and insolent that
they are but Abjects, and humbles them at the instant,
makes them crie, complaine and repent, yea, even to hate
their forepassed happinesse. He takes the account of the
rich and proves him a beggar, a naked beggar, which
hath interest in nothing, but in the gravell that fills his
mouth. He holds a Glasse before the eyes of the most
beautifull, and makes them see therein their deformitie
and rottennesse; and they acknowledge it.

O eloquent, just and mighty Death! Whom none could
advise, thou hast persuaded; what none hath dared,
thou hast done; and whom all the world hath flattered,
thou only hast cast out of the world and despised;
thou hast drawne together all the farre stretched greatnesse, all the pride, crueltie and ambition of man, and
covered it over with these two narrow words, *hic jacet.*

SIR WALTER RALEIGH (1552-1618)
A History of the World

DEATH THE LEVELLER

The glories of our blood and state
    Are shadows, not substantial things;
There is no armour against fate;
    Death lays his icy hand on kings:

Sceptre and Crown
Must tumble down
And in the dust be equal made
With the poor crooked scythe and spade.

Some men with swords may reap the field,
    And plant fresh laurels where they kill:
But their strong nerves at last must yield;
    They tame but one another still:
        Early or late
        They stoop to fate,
And must give up their murmuring breath
When they, pale captives, creep to death.

The garlands wither on your brow;
    Then boast no more your mighty deeds;
Upon Death's purple altar now
    See where the victor-victim bleeds:
        Your heads must come
        To the cold tomb;
Only the actions of the just
Smell sweet, and blossom in their dust.

JAMES SHIRLEY (1596-1666)
from *The Contention of Ajax and Ulysses*

IN PRAISE OF POVERTY

At last they upbraided my poverty; I confess she is my
Domestick; sober of diet, simple of habit; frugal,
painful; a good Counsellor to me; that keeps me from
Cruelty, Pride, or other more delicate impertinences;
which are the Nurse-children of Riches. But let them
look over all the great and monstrous wickednesses,
they shall never find those in poor families. They are
the issue of the wealthy *Giants*, and the mighty Hunters:
whereas no great work, or worthy of praise, or memory,

but came out of poor cradles. It was the ancient poverty that founded Commonweals, built Cities, invented Arts, made wholesome Laws; armed men against vices; rewarded them with their own virtues; and preserved the honour, and state of Nations, till they betrayed themselves to Riches.

BEN JONSON (1573-1637)
Discoveries

VIRTUE ON TRIAL

It was from out the rind of one apple tasted that the knowledge of good and evil as two twins cleaving together leapt forth into the World. And perhaps this is that doom which *Adam* fell into of knowing good and evil, that is to say of knowing good by evil. As therefore the state of man now is, what wisdom can there be to choose, what continence to forbeare, without the knowledge of evil? He that can apprehend and consider vice with all her baits and seeming pleasures, and yet abstain, and yet distinguish, and yet prefer that which is truly better, he is the true warfaring Christian. I cannot praise a fugitive and cloistered virtue, un-exercised and unbreathed, that never sallies out and sees her adversary, but slinks out of the race, where that immortal garland is to be run for not without dust and heat. Assuredly we bring not innocence into the world, we bring impurity much rather: that which purifies us is trial, and trial is by what is contrary.

JOHN MILTON (1608-1674)
Areopagitica

OLD AGE

When we for age could neither read nor write,
The subject made us able to indite;
The soul, with nobler resolutions decked,
The body stooping, does herself erect.
No mortal parts are requisite to raise
Her that, unbodied, can her Maker praise.

The seas are quiet when the winds give o'er;
So, calm are we when passions are no more!
For then we know how vain it was to boast
Of fleeting things, so certain to be lost.
Clouds of affection from our younger eyes
Conceal that emptiness which age descries.

The soul's dark cottage, battered and decayed,
Lets in new light through chinks that time has made;
Stronger by weakness, wiser men become,
As they draw near to their eternal home.
Leaving the old, both worlds at once they view,
That stand upon the threshold of the new.

EDMUND WALLER (1606-1687)
Poems

THE ASPIRATION

How long, great God, how long must I
Immur'd in this dark prison lie;
Where at the gates and avenues of sense,
My soul must watch to have intelligence;
Where but faint gleams of Thee salute my sight,
Like doubtful moonshine in a cloudy night:
When shall I leave this magic sphere,
And be all mind, all eye, all ear?

How cold this clime! And yet my sense
Perceives e'en here Thy influence.
E'en here Thy strong magnetic charms I feel,
And pant and tremble like the amorous steel.
To lower good, and beauties less divine,
Sometimes my erroneous needle does decline,
    But yet, so strong the sympathy,
    It turns, and points again to Thee.

I long to see this excellence
Which at such distance strikes my sense.
My impatient soul struggles to disengage
Her wings from the confinement of her cage.
Wouldst thou, great Love, this prisoner once set free,
How would she hasten to be link'd to Thee!
    She'd for no angels' conduct stay,
    But fly, and love-on, all the way.

JOHN NORRIS (1657-1711)
Poems

THE FIRST CHRISTMAS

It was the winter wild
While the heaven-born Child
All meanly wrapt in the rude manger lies;
Nature in awe to Him
Had doff'd her gaudy trim,
With her great Master so to sympathise:
It was no season then for her
To wanton with the sun, her lusty paramour.

Only with speeches fair
She woos the gentle air
To hide her guilty front with innocent snow;
And on her naked shame,
Pollute with sinful blame,
The saintly veil of maiden white to throw;

Confounded, that her Maker's eyes
Should look so near upon her foul deformities.

But He, her fears to cease,
Sent down the meek-eyed Peace;
She, crown'd with olive green, came softly sliding
Down through the turning sphere,
His ready harbinger,
With turtle wing the amorous clouds dividing;
And waving wide her myrtle wand,
She strikes a universal peace through sea and land.

No war, or battle's sound
Was heard the world around:
The idle spear and shield were high uphung;
The hookéd chariot stood
Unstain'd with hostile blood;
The trumpet spake not to the arméd throng;
And kings sat still with awful eye,
As if they surely knew their sovran Lord was by.

But peaceful was the night
Wherein the Prince of Light
His reign of peace upon the earth began:
The winds, with wonder whist,
Smoothly the waters kist
Whispering new joys to the mild océan—
Who now hath quite forgot to rave,
While birds of calm sit brooding on the charméd wave.

The stars, with deep amaze,
Stand fix'd in the steadfast gaze,
Bending one way their precious influence;
And will not take their flight
For all the morning light,
Or Lucifer that often warn'd them thence;
But in their glimmering orbs did glow
Until their Lord Himself bespake, and bid them go.

And though the shady gloom
Had given day her room,
The sun himself withheld his wonted speed,
And hid his head for shame,
As his inferior flame
The new-enlighten'd world no more should need;
He saw a greater Sun appear
Than his bright throne, or burning axletree could bear.

The Shepherds on the lawn
Or ere the point of dawn
Sate simply chatting in a rustic row;
Full little thought they than
That the mighty Pan
Was kindly come to live with them below;
Perhaps their loves, or else, their sheep
Was all that did their silly[1] thoughts so busy keep:—

When such music sweet
Their hearts and ears did greet
As never was by mortal finger strook—
Divinely-warbled voice
Answering the stringéd noise,
As all their souls in blissful rapture took:
The air, such pleasure loth to lose,
With thousand echoes still prolongs each heavenly close.

JOHN MILTON (1608-1674)
Ode on the Morning of Christ's Nativity
[1] Simple

MAN, SPIRIT AND FLESH

These (i.e. Spirits) are certainly the Magisteriall &
master pieces of the Creator, the Flower or (as we may
say) the best part of nothing, actually existing, what
we are but in hopes, and probabilitie; we are only that

amphibious piece betweene a corporall and spirituall essence, that middle forme that linkes those two together, and makes good the method of God and nature, that jumps not from extreames, but unites the incompatible distances by some middle and participating natures; that wee are the breath and similitude of God, it is indisputable, and upon record of holy Scripture, but to call our selves a Microcosme, or little world, I thought it onely a pleasant trope of Rhetorick, till my nearer judgement and second thoughts told me there was a reall truth therein: for first wee are a rude masse, and in the ranke of creatures, which only are, and have a dull kinde of being not yet privileged with life, or preferred to sense or reason; next we live the life of plants, the life of animals, the life of men, and at last the life of spirits, running on in one mysterious nature those five kinds of existences, which comprehend the creatures not onely of the world, but of the Universe; thus is man that great and true *Amphibium*, whose nature is disposed to live not onely like other creatures in divers elements, but in divided and distinguished worlds; for though there bee but one world to sense, there are two to reason; the one, visible, the other invisible, whereof *Moses* seemes to have left description, and of the other so obscurely, that some parts thereof are yet in controversie; and truely for the first chapters of *Genesis*, I must confesse a great deale of obscurity, though Divines have to the power of humane reason endeavoured to make all goe in a literall meaning, yet those allegoricall interpretations are also probable, and perhaps the mysticall method of *Moses* bred up in the Hieroglyphicall Schooles of the *Egyptians*.

. . . The whole Creation is a mystery, and particularly that of man; at the blast of his mouth were the rest of the creatures made, and at his bare word they started out of nothing: but in the frame of man (as the text describes it) he played the sensible operator, and seemed not so much to create, as make him; when hee had separated the materials of other creatures, there consequently resulted a forme and soule, but having raised the walls of man, he was driven to a second and harder creation of a substance like himselfe, an incorruptible and immortall soule.

SIR THOMAS BROWNE (1605-1682)
Religio Medici

A BISHOP'S VIEW

The motion and situation of the planets, are they not admirable for use and order? Were those (miscalled *erratique*) globes once known to stray, in their repeated journies through the pathless void? Do they not measure areas round the sun, ever proportioned to the times? So fixed, so immutable are the laws by which the unseen Author of Nature actuates the universe. How vivid and radiant is the lustre of the fixed stars! How magnificent and rich that negligent profusion with which they appear to be scattered through the whole azure vault! Yet, if you take the telescope, it brings into your view a new host of stars that escape the naked eye. Here they seem contiguous and minute, but, to a nearer view, immense orbs of light at various distances far sunk in the abyss of space.

Now you must call imagination to your aid. The feeble narrow sense cannot descry innumerable worlds revolving round the central fires, and, in those worlds, the energy of an all-perfect mind displayed in endless forms. But neither sense nor imagination are big enough to comprehend the boundless extent, with all its dazzling furniture. Though the labouring mind exert and strain each power to its utmost reach, there still stands out ungrasped a surplusage immeasurable. Yet all the vast bodies that compose this mighty frame, how distant and remote soever, are, by some secret mechanism, some divine art and force, linked in a mutual dependence and intercourse with each other, even with this earth, which almost slipt from my thoughts, and was lost in the crowd of worlds. Is not the whole system immense, beautiful, glorious beyond expression and beyond thought? What treatment then do those Philosophers deserve, who would deprive these noble and delightful scenes of all reality? How should those principles be entertained, that lead us to think all the visible beauty of the creation a false imaginary glare?

BISHOP BERKELEY (1684-1753)
Dialogues

A DEAN'S OPINIONS

1

I am in all opinions to believe according to my own impartial reason; which I am bound to inform and improve, as far as my capacity and opportunities will permit.

2

It may be prudent in me to act sometimes by other men's reason, but I can think only by my own.

3

If another man's reason fully convinceth me, it becomes my own reason.

4

To say a man is bound to believe, is neither true nor sense.

5

You may force men, by interest or punishment, to say or swear they believe, and to act as if they believed: You can go no further.

6

Every man, as a member of the common wealth, ought to be content with the possession of his own opinion in private, without perplexing his neighbour or disturbing the public.

7

Violent zeal for truth hath an hundred to one odds to be either petulancy, ambition, or pride.

8

The want of belief is a defect that ought to be concealed when it cannot be overcome.

9

God's mercy is over all his works, but divines of all sorts lessen that mercy too much.

10

I look upon myself, in the capacity of a clergyman, to be one appointed by Providence for defending a post assigned me, and for gaining over as many enemies as I can. Although I think my cause is just, yet one great motion is my submitting to the pleasure of Providence, and to the laws of my country.

11

I am not answerable to God for the doubts that arise in my own breast, since they are the consequence of that reason which he hath planted in me, if I take care to conceal those doubts from others, if I use my best endeavours to subdue them, and if they have no influence on the conduct of my life.

12

I never saw, heard, nor read, that the clergy were beloved
in any nation where Christianity was the religion of the
country. Nothing can render them popular but some
degree of persecution.

13

Those fine gentlemen who affect the humour of railing
at the clergy, are, I think, bound in honour to turn
parsons themselves and shew us better examples.

14

It is impossible that anything so natural, so necessary,
and so universal as death, should ever have been designed
by providence as an evil to mankind.

15

Although reason were intended by providence to govern
our passions, yet it seems that, in two points of the
greatest moment to the being and continuance of the
world, God hath intended our passions to prevail over
reason. The first is, the propagation of our species,
since no wise man ever married from the dictates of
reason. The other is, the love of life, which, from the
dictates of reason, every man would despise, and wish it
at an end, or that it never had a beginning.

DEAN SWIFT (1667-1745)
Thoughts on Religion

TOLERATION

Some people talk as if they were quite teazed and worried
by the eternal clamours of the Catholics; but if you are
eternally unjust, can you expect any thing more than
to be eternally vexed by the victims of your injustice?

You want all the luxury of oppression, without any of its inconvenience. I should think the Catholics very much to blame, if they ever ceased to importune the legislature for justice, so long as they could find one single member of Parliament who would advocate their cause.

The putting the matter to rest by an effort of the county of York, or by any decision of Parliament against them, is utterly hopeless. Every year increases the Catholic population, and the Catholic wealth, and the Catholic claims, till you are caught in one of those political attitudes to which all countries are occasionally exposed, in which you are utterly helpless, and must give way to their claims: and if you do it then, you will do it badly; you may call it an arrangement, but arrangements made at such times are much like the bargains between an highwayman and a traveller, a pistol on one side, and a purse on the other: the rapid scramble of armed vigilance, and the unqualified surrender of helpless timidity. *If you think the thing must be done at some time or another, do it when you are calm and powerful, and when you need not do it.*

There are a set of high-spirited men who are very much afraid of being afraid; who cannot brook the idea of doing any thing from fear, and whose conversation is full of fire and sword, when any apprehension of resistance is alluded to; I have a perfect confidence in the high and unyielding spirit, and in the military courage of the English: and I have no doubt, but that many of the country gentlemen, who now call out No Popery, would fearlessly put themselves at the head of their embattled yeomanry, to control the Irish Catholics. My objection to such courage is, that it would certainly be exercised unjustly, and probably exercised in vain. I should deprecate any rising of the Catholics as the most grievous misfortune which could happen to the Empire and to themselves. They had far better endure all they do endure, and a great deal worse, than try the experiment. *But if they do try it, you may depend upon it, they will do it at their own time, and not at yours.* They will not select a fortnight in the summer, during a profound peace, when corn and money abound, and when the Catholics of Europe are unconcerned spectators. If you make a resolution to be unjust, you must make another resolution to be always strong, always vigilant, and always rich; you must commit no blunders, exhibit no deficiencies, and meet with no misfortunes; you must present a square phalanx of impenetrable strength, for keen-eyed revenge is riding round your ranks; and if one heart falter, or one hand tremble, you are lost.

SYDNEY SMITH (1771-1845)
*A Letter to the Electors
on the Catholic Question*

THE DIVINE IMAGE

To Mercy, Pity, Peace and Love,
All pray in their distress:
And to these virtues of delight
Return their thankfulness.

For Mercy, Pity, Peace, and Love
Is God, our Father dear,
And Mercy, Pity, Peace, and Love
Is man, His child and care.

For Mercy has a human heart,
Pity a human face,
And Love, the human form divine,
And Peace, the human dress.

ESSEX: THE ABBEY GATEWAY, COLCHESTER

The gateway of St. John's Abbey, a fine flint-and-stone structure of Perpendicular style with interesting panel work. In early times the city was known as Camulodunum and was the capital of the British chief Cunobelin. It is still an important military headquarters.

CHRISTMAS IN ENGLAND

Rehearsal for the Christmas Carol Service in the chapel of Christ's Hospital, popularly known as the Bluecoat School, at Horsham, Sussex.

CHRISTMAS IN ENGLAND

In Piccadilly Circus, and neighbouring Piccadilly and Regent Street, decorations appear as stores prepare for their busiest season.

Then every man, of every clime,
That prays in his distress,
Prays to the human form divine,
Love, Mercy, Pity, Peace.

And all must love the human form,
In heathen, Turk, or Jew;
Where Mercy, Love, and Pity dwell
There God is dwelling too.

WILLIAM BLAKE (1757-1827)
Songs of Innocence

STRENGTH AND BEAUTY

Strong is the lion—like a coal
His eyeball—like a bastion's mole
   His chest against the foes:
Strong the gier-eagle on his sail,
Strong against tide the enormous whale
   Emerges as he goes.

But stronger still in earth and air,
And in the sea the man of prayer,
   And far beneath the tide:
And in the seat to faith assigned,
Where ask is have, where seek is find,
   Where knock is open wide.

Beauteous the fleet before the gale;
Beauteous the multitudes in mail,
   Ranked arms, and crested heads:
Beauteous the garden's umbrage mild,
Walk, water, meditated wild,
   And all the bloomy beds.

Beauteous the moon full on the lawn;
And beauteous when the veil's withdrawn,
    The virgin to her spouse:
Beauteous the temple, decked and filled,
When to the heaven of heavens they build
    Their heart-directed vows.

Beauteous, yea beauteous more than these,
The Shepherd King upon his knees,
    For his momentous trust;
With wish of infinite conceit,
For man, beast, mute, the small and great,
    And prostrate dust to dust.

CHRISTOPHER SMART (1722-1771)
Song to David

ART AND NATURE

Nor, whilst I recommend studying the Art from Artists, can I be supposed to mean that Nature is to be neglected; I take this study in aid, and not in exclusion of the other. Nature is and must be the fountain which alone is inexhaustible, and from which all excellencies must originally flow.

The great use of studying our predecessors is, to open the mind, to shorten our labour, and to give us the result of the selection made by those great minds of what is grand or beautiful in Nature; her rich stores are all spread out before us; but it is an art, and no easy art, to know how or what to choose, and how to attain and secure the object of our choice.

Thus the highest beauty of form must be taken from nature; but it is an art of long deduction and great experience to know how to find it.

We must not content ourselves with merely admiring and relishing; we must enter into the principles on which

the work is wrought: these do not swim on the super-
ficies, and consequently are not open to superficial
observers.

Art in its perfection is not ostentatious; it lies hid and
works its effect, itself unseen. It is the proper study and
labour of an artist to uncover and find out the latent
cause of conspicuous beauties, and from thence form
principles for his own conduct; such an examination
is a continual exertion of the mind; as great, perhaps,
as that of the Artist whose works he is thus studying.

SIR JOSHUA REYNOLDS (1723-1792)
Sixth Discourse

SIN AND SOCIETY

Some writers have so confounded society with government, as to leave little or no distinction between them;
whereas they are not only different, but have different
origins. Society is produced by our wants and government by our wickedness; the former promotes our
happiness *positively* by uniting our affections, the latter
negatively by restraining our vices. The one encourages
intercourse, the other creates distinctions. The first is
a patron, the last a punisher.

Society in every state is a blessing, but government,
even in its best state, is but a necessary evil; in its worst
state an intolerable one; for when we suffer, or are
exposed to the same miseries *by a government*, which we
might expect in a country *without government*, our calamity is heightened by reflecting that we furnish the means
by which we suffer. Government, like dress, is the badge
of lost innocence; the palaces of kings are built upon the
ruins of the bowers of paradise. For were the impulses
of conscience clear, uniform and irresistibly obeyed,
man would need no other law-giver; but that not being
the case, he finds it necessary to surrender up a part of

his property to furnish means for the protection of the
rest; and this he is induced to do by the same prudence
which in every other case advises him, out of two evils
to choose the least. Wherefore, security being the true
design and end of government, it unanswerably follows
that whatever form thereof appears most likely to ensure
it to us, with the least expence and greatest benefit,
is preferable to all others.

. . . Here then is the origin and rise of government:
namely, a mode rendered necessary by the inability of
moral virtue to govern the world; here too is the
design and end of government, viz. freedom and security.
And however our eyes may be dazzled with show, or
our ears deceived by sound; however prejudice may warp
our wills, or interest darken our understanding, the
simple voice of nature and reason will say, 'tis right.

I draw my idea of the form of government from a
principle in nature which no art can overturn, viz.
that the more simple any thing is, the less liable it is to
be disordered, and the easier repaired when disordered;
and with this maxim in view I offer a few remarks on
the so much boasted Constitution of England. That it
was noble for the dark and slavish times in which it
was erected, is granted. When the world was overrun
with tyranny the least remove therefrom was a glorious
rescue. But that it is imperfect, subject to convulsions,
and incapable of producing what it seems to promise, is
easily demonstrated.

THOMAS PAINE (1737-1809)
Common Sense

COMFORT

A thing of beauty is a joy for ever:
Its loveliness increases; it will never
Pass into nothingness; but still will keep
A bower quiet for us, and a sleep
Full of sweet dreams, and health, and quiet breathing.
Therefore, on every morrow, are we wreathing
A flowery band to bind us to the earth,
Spite of despondence, of the inhuman dearth
Of noble natures, of the gloomy days,
Of all the unhealthy and o'er-darkened ways
Made for our searching: yes, in spite of all,
Some shape of beauty moves away the pall
From our dark spirits. Such the sun, the moon,
Trees old and young, sprouting a shady boon
For simple sheep; and such are daffodils
With the green world they live in; and clear rills
That for themselves a cooling covert make
'Gainst the hot season; the mid-forest brake,
Rich with a sparkling of fair musk-rose blooms:
And such too is the grandeur of the dooms
We have imagined for the mighty dead;
All lovely tales that we have heard or read:
An endless fountain of immortal drink,
Pouring into us from the heaven's brink.

JOHN KEATS (1795-1821)
Endymion

IN PRAISE OF SOLITUDE

The first work therefore that a man must do to make
himself capable of the good of Solitude is the very
Eradication of all Lusts, for how is it possible for a Man
to enjoy himself while his Affections are tied to things

without Himself? In the second place, he must learn
the Art and get the Habit of Thinking; for this, too, no
less than well speaking, depends upon much practice,
and Cogitation is the thing which distinguishes the
Solitude of a God from a wild Beast. Now because the
soul of Man is not by its own Nature or observation
furnished with sufficient Materials to work upon, it is
necessary for it to have continual recourse to Learning
and Books for fresh supplies, so that the solitary Life
will grow indigent, and be ready to starve without
them; but if once we be thoroughly engaged in the
Love of Letters, instead of being wearied with the length
of any days, we shall only complain of the shortness of
our whole Life.

> *O vita, stulto longa, sapienti brevis!*
> O Life, long to the Fool, short to the Wise!

The first Minister of State has not so much business
in public as a wise man has in private; if the one have
little leisure to be alone, the other has less leisure to be
in company; the one has but part of the affairs of one
Nation, the other all the works of God and Nature under
his consideration. There is no saying shocks me so
much as that which I hear very often. That a man
does not know how to pass his Time. 'Twould have
been but ill-spoken by *Methusalem* in the Nine hundred
sixty-ninth year of his Life; so far it is from us, who have
not time enough to attain to the utmost perfection
of any part of any Science, to have cause to complain
that we are forced to be idle for want of work. But
this, you'll say, is work only for the Learned: others
are not capable either of the employments or divertise-
ments that arrive from Letters. I know they are not,
and therefore cannot much recommend Solitude to a
man totally illiterate.

ABRAHAM COWLEY (1618-1667)
Essays

THAT BLESSED MOOD

These beauteous forms,
Through a long absence, have not been to me
As is a landscape to a blind man's eye:
But oft, in lonely rooms, and 'mid the din
Of towns and cities, I have owed to them,
In hours of weariness, sensations sweet,
Felt in the blood, and felt along the heart;
And passing even into my purer mind,
With tranquil restoration:—feelings too
Of unremembered pleasure: such, perhaps,
As have no slight or trivial influence
On that best portion of a good man's life,
His little, nameless, unremembered, acts
Of kindness and of love. Nor less, I trust,
To them I may have owed another gift,
Of aspect more sublime; that blessed mood,
In which the burthen of the mystery,
In which the heavy and the weary weight
Of all this unintelligible world,
Is lightened:—that serene and blessed mood,
In which the affections gently lead us on,—
Until, the breath of this corporeal frame
And even the motion of our human blood
Almost suspended, we are laid asleep
In body, and become a living soul:
While with an eye made quiet by the power
Of harmony, and the deep power of joy,
We see into the life of things.

If this
Be but a vain belief, yet, oh! how oft—
In darkness and amid the many shapes
Of joyless daylight, when the fretful stir

Unprofitable, and the fever of the world,
Have hung upon the beatings of my heart—
How oft, in spirit, have I turned to thee,
O sylvan Wye! thou wanderer thro' the woods,
How often has my spirit turned to thee!

                              . . . For I have learned
To look on nature, not as in the hour
Of thoughtless youth; but hearing oftentimes
The still, sad music of humanity,
Nor harsh nor grating, though of ample power
To chasten and subdue. And I have felt
A presence that disturbs me with the joy
Of elevated thoughts: a sense sublime
Of something far more deeply interfused,
Whose dwelling is the light of setting suns,
And the round ocean and the living air,
And the blue sky, and in the mind of man:
A motion and a spirit, that impels
All thinking things, all objects of all thought,
And rolls through all things.

WILLIAM WORDSWORTH (1770-1850)
Lines Composed a Few Miles Above Tintern Abbey

REPLY TO WORDSWORTH

In the neighbourhood of latitude fifty north, and for
the last hundred years or thereabouts, it has been an
axiom that Nature is divine and morally uplifting.
For good Wordsworthians—and most serious-minded
people are now Wordsworthians, either by direct inspira-
tion or at second hand—a walk in the country is the
equivalent of going to church, a tour through Westmorland is as good as a pilgrimage to Jerusalem. To commune with the fields and waters, the woodlands and the
hills, is to commune, according to our modern and

northern ideas, with the visible manifestations of the "Wisdom and Spirit of the Universe."

The Wordsworthian who exports this pantheistic worship of Nature to the tropics is liable to have his religious convictions somewhat rudely disturbed. Nature, under a vertical sun, and nourished by the equatorial rains, is not at all like that chaste, mild deity who presides over the *Gemütlichkeit*, the prettiness, the cosy sublimities of the Lake District. The worst that Wordsworth's goddess ever did to him was to make him hear

> Low breathings coming after me, and sounds
> Of undistinguishable motion, steps
> Almost as silent as the turf they trod;

and was to make him realize, in the shape of "a huge peak, black and huge", the existence of "unknown modes of being." He seems to have imagined that this was the worst Nature *could* do. A few weeks in Malaya or Borneo would have undeceived him. Wandering in the hothouse darkness of the jungle, he would not have felt so serenely certain of those "Presences of Nature", those "Souls of Lonely Places", which he was in the habit of worshipping on the shores of Windermere and Rydal. The sparse inhabitants of the equatorial forest are all believers in devils. When one has visited, in even the most superficial manner, the places where they live, it is difficult not to share their faith. The jungle is marvellous, fantastic, beautiful; but it is also terrifying, it is also profoundly sinister. There is something in what, for lack of a better word, we must call the character of great forests—even in those temperate lands—which is foreign, appalling, fundamentally and utterly inimical to intruding man.

The life of those vast masses of swarming vegetation is alien to the human spirit and hostile to it. Meredith, in his "Woods of Westermain", has tried reassuringly

16

to persuade us that our terrors are unnecessary, that the hostility of these vegetable forces is more apparent than real, and that if we will but trust Nature we shall find our fears transformed into serenity, joy, and rapture. This may be sound philosophy in the neighbourhood of Dorking; but it begins to be dubious even in the forests of Germany—there is too much of them for a human being to feel himself at ease within their enormous glooms; and when the woods of Borneo are substituted for those of Westermaine, Meredith's comforting doctrine becomes frankly ridiculous.

ALDOUS HUXLEY (Born 1894)
Do What You Will

BLAKE'S TESTAMENT

To see a World in a grain of sand,
And a Heaven in a wild flower,
Hold Infinity in the palm of your hand,
And Eternity in an hour.

A robin redbreast in a cage
Puts all Heaven in a rage.
A dove-house fill'd with doves and pigeons
Shudders Hell thro' all its regions.
A dog starv'd at his master's gate
Predicts the ruin of the State.
A horse misus'd upon the road
Calls to Heaven for human blood.
Each outcry of the hunted hare
A fibre from the brain does tear.
A skylark wounded in the wing,
A cherubin does cease to sing.
The game-cock clipt and arm'd for fight
Does the rising sun affright.
Every wolf's and lion's howl
Raises from Hell a Human soul.

The wild deer, wandering here and there,
Keeps the Human soul from care.
The lamb misus'd breeds public strife,
And yet forgives the butcher's knife.
He who shall hurt the little wren
Shall never be belov'd by men.
He who the ox to wrath has mov'd
Shall never be by woman lov'd.
The wanton boy that kills the fly
Shall feel the spider's enmity.
He who torments the chafer's sprite
Weaves a bower in endless night.
The caterpillar on the leaf
Repeats to thee thy mother's grief.
Kill not the moth nor butterfly,
For the Last Judgement draweth nigh.
He who shall train the horse to war
Shall never pass the polar bar.
The beggar's dog and widow's cat,
Feed them, and thou wilt grow fat.

The bat that flits at close of eve
Has left the brain that won't believe.
The owl that calls upon the night
Speaks the unbeliever's fright.
The gnat that sings his summer's song
Poison gets from Slander's tongue.
The poison of the snake and newt
Is the sweat of Envy's foot.
The poison of the honey-bee
Is the artist's jealousy.
A truth that's told with bad intent
Beats all the lies you can invent.

Joy and woe are woven fine,
A clothing for the soul divine;
Under every grief and pine
Runs a joy with silken twine.

It is right it should be so;
Man was made for joy and woe;
And when this we rightly know,
Thro' the world we safely go.

* * *

The strongest poison ever known
Came from Cæsar's laurel crown.
Nought can deform the human race
Like to the armour's iron brace.
When gold and gems adorn the plough
To peaceful arts shall Envy bow.
To be in a passion you good may do,
But no good if a passion is in you.
The whore and gambler, by the state
Licensed, build that nation's fate.
The harlot's cry from street to street
Shall weave Old England's winding-sheet.
The winner's shout, the loser's curse,
Dance before dead England's hearse.

WILLIAM BLAKE (1757-1827)
Miscellaneous Poems

THE HIGHER PANTHEISM

The sun, the moon, the stars, the seas, the hills and the
  plains—
Are not these, O Soul, the Vision of Him who reigns?

Is not the Vision He? tho' He be not that which He
  seems?
Dreams are true while they last, and do we not live in
  dreams?

Earth, these solid stars, this weight of body and limb,
Are they not sign and symbol of thy division from Him?

Dark is the world to thee: thyself art the reason why;
For is He not all but that which has power to feel "I
am I"?

Glory about thee, without thee; and thou fulfillest thy
doom
Making Him broken gleams, and a stifled splendour and
gloom.

Speak to Him, thou, for He hears, and Spirit with Spirit
can meet—
Closer is He than breathing, and nearer than hands and
feet.

God is law, say the wise; O Soul, and let us rejoice,
For if He thunder by law the thunder is yet His voice.

Law is God, say some: no God at all, says the fool;
For all we have power to see is a straight staff bent in
a pool;

And the ear of man cannot hear, and the eye of man
cannot see;
But if we could see and hear, this Vision—were it not He?

ALFRED, LORD TENNYSON (1809-1892)
Poems

THE SILENT FRIENDS

Still-born Silence! thou that art
Flood-gate of the deeper heart!
Offspring of a heavenly kind!
Frost o' the mouth, and thaw o' the mind!
Secrecy's confidant, and he
Who makes religion mystery!

> Admiration's speaking'st tongue !
> Leave, thy desert shades among,
> Reverend hermit's hallow'd cells,
> Where retired devotion dwells !
> With thy enthusiasms come,
> Seize our tongues, and strike us dumb ! [1]

Reader, would'st thou know what true peace and quiet mean; would'st thou find a refuge from the noises and clamours of the multitude; would'st thou enjoy at once solitude and society; would'st thou possess the depth of thine own spirit in stillness, without being shut out from the consolatory faces of thy species; would'st thou be alone and yet accompanied; solitary, yet not desolate; singular, yet not without some to keep thee in countenance; a unit in aggregate; a simple in composite:—come with me into a Quakers' Meeting.

Dost thou love silence deep as that "before the winds were made"? Go not out into the wilderness, descend not into the profundities of the earth; shut not up thy casements; nor pour wax into the little cells of thy ears, with little-faith'd self-mistrusting Ulysses.— Retire with me into a Quakers' Meeting.

For a man to refrain even from good words, and to hold his peace, it is commendable; but for a multitude it is great mastery.

There are wounds which an imperfect solitude cannot heal. By imperfect I mean that which a man enjoyeth by himself. The perfect is that which he can sometimes attain in crowds, but nowhere so absolutely as in a Quakers' Meeting.—Those first hermits did certainly understand this principle, when they retired into Egyptian solitudes, not singly, but in shoals, to enjoy one another's want of conversation. The Carthusian is bound to his brethren by this agreeing spirit of incommunicativeness. In secular occasions, what so pleasant

[1] From *Poems of All Sorts*, by Richard Fleckno, 1653

as to be reading a book through a long winter evening,
with a friend sitting by—say, a wife—he, or she, too,
(if that be probable) reading another without interruption, or oral communication?—can there be no sympathy
without the gabble of words?—away with this inhuman,
shy, single, shade-and-cavern-haunting solitariness.

. . . How far the followers of these good men in our
days have kept to the primitive spirit, or in what proportion they have substituted formality for it, the Judge of
Spirits can alone determine. I have seen faces in their
assemblies upon which the dove sate visibly brooding.
Others, again, I have watched, when my thoughts
should have been better engaged, in which I could
possibly detect nothing but a blank inanity. But quiet
was in all, and the disposition to unanimity, and the
absence of the fierce controversial workings.—If the
spiritual pretensions of the Quakers have abated, at
least they make few pretences. Hypocrites they certainly
are not, in their preaching. It is seldom, indeed, that
you shall see one get up amongst them to hold forth.
Only now and then a trembling, female, generally
ancient, voice is heard—you cannot guess from what
part of the meeting it proceeds—with a low, buzzing,
musical sound, laying out a few words which "she
thought might suit the condition of some present,"
with a quaking diffidence, which leaves no possibility
of supposing that anything of female vanity was mixed
up, where the tones were so full of tenderness, and a
restraining modesty.—The men, for what I have observed
speak seldomer.

. . . More frequently the Meeting is broken up without
a word having been spoken. But the mind has been
fed. You go away with a sermon not made with hands.
You have been in the milder caverns of Trophonius;
or as in some den, where that fiercest and savagest of

all wild creatures, the TONGUE, that unruly member,
has strangely lain tied up and captive. You have bathed
with stillness.—O, when the spirit is sore fretted, even
tired to sickness of the janglings and nonsense-noises
of the world, what a balm and a solace it is to go and
seat yourself for a quiet half-hour upon some un-
disputed corner of a bench, among the gentle Quakers!

Their garb and stillness conjoined, present a uniform-
ity, tranquil and herd-like—as in the pasture—"forty
feeding like one."—

The very garments of a Quaker seem incapable of
receiving a soil; and cleanliness in them to be something more than the absence of its contrary. Every
Quakeress is a lily; and when they come up in bands
to their Whitsun conferences, whitening the easterly
streets of the metropolis, from all parts of the United
Kingdom, they show like troops of the Shining Ones.

CHARLES LAMB (1775-1834)
from *Essays of Elia: A Quakers' Meeting*

NO COWARD SOUL

No coward soul is mine,
No trembler in the world's storm-troubled sphere:
　　I see Heaven's glories shine,
And Faith shines equal, arming me from Fear.

　　O God within my breast,
Almighty, ever-present Deity!
　　Life, that in me hast rest
As I, undying Life, have power in Thee!

　　Vain are the thousand creeds
That move men's hearts: unutterably vain;
　　Worthless as withered weeds,
Or idlest froth amid the boundless main,

To waken doubt in one
Holding so fast by Thy infinity,
   So surely anchored on
The steadfast rock of Immortality.

   With wide-embracing love
Thy Spirit animates eternal years,
   Pervades and broods above,
Changes, sustains, dissolves, creates, and rears.

   Though earth and moon were gone,
And suns and universes ceased to be,
   And Thou wert left alone,
Every existence would exist in Thee.

   There is not room for Death,
Nor atom that his might could render void:
   Since Thou art Being and Breath
And what Thou art may never be destroyed.

EMILY BRONTË (1818-1848)
Poems

JOHN KEATS, IMMORTAL

Peace, peace! he is not dead, he doth not sleep—
He hath awakened from the dream of life—
'Tis we who, lost in stormy visions, keep
With phantoms an unprofitable strife,
And in mad trance strike with our spirit's knife
Invulnerable nothings.—*We* decay
Like corpses in a charnel; fear and grief
Convulse us and consume us day by day,
And cold hopes swarm like worms within our living clay.

He has outsoared the shadow of our night;
Envy and calumny and hate and pain,
And that unrest which men miscall delight,
Can touch him not and torture not again;
From the contagion of the world's slow stain
He is secure, and now can never mourn
A heart grown cold, a head grown gray in vain;
Nor, when the spirit's self has ceased to burn,
With sparkless ashes load an unlamented urn.

*   *   *

He is made one with Nature: there is heard
His voice in all her music, from the moan
Of thunder, to the song of night's sweet bird;
He is a presence to be felt and known
In darkness and in light, from herb and stone,
Spreading itself where'er that Power may move
Which has withdrawn his being to its own;
Which wields the world with never-wearied love,
Sustains it from beneath, and kindles it above.

He is a portion of that loveliness
Which once he made more lovely: he doth bear
His part, while the one Spirit's plastic stress
Sweeps through the dull dense world, compelling there,
All new successions to the forms they wear;
Torturing th'unwilling dross that checks its flight
To its own likeness, as each mass may bear;
And bursting in its beauty and its might
From trees and beasts and men into the Heaven's light.

PERCY BYSSHE SHELLEY (1792-1822)
Adonais

SONG

When I am dead, my dearest,
　Sing no sad songs for me;
Plant thou no roses at my head.
　Nor shady cypress tree:
Be the green grass above me
　With showers and dewdrops wet:
And if thou wilt, remember,
　And if thou wilt, forget.

I shall not see the shadows,
　I shall not feel the rain;
I shall not hear the nightingale
　Sing on as if in pain:
And dreaming through the twilight
　That doth not rise nor set,
Haply I may remember,
　And haply may forget.

CHRISTINA ROSSETTI (1830-1894)
Poems

ON REFUSAL OF AID
BETWEEN NATIONS

Not that the earth is changing, O my God!
　Nor that the seasons totter in their walk,—
　Not that the virulent ill of act and talk
Seethes ever as a winepress ever trod,—
Not therefore are we certain that the rod
　Weighs in thine hand to smite thy world; though
　　now
　Beneath thine hand so many nations bow,
So many kings:—not therefore, O my God!—

But because Man is parcelled out in men
   To-day; because, for any wrongful blow
      No man not stricken asks, "I would be told
Why thou dost thus;" but his heart whispers then,
   "He is he, I am I." By this we know
      That our earth falls asunder, being old.

                  DANTE GABRIEL ROSSETTI (1828-1882)
                  Miscellaneous Poems

FAITH AND DOUBT

And now what are we? unbelievers both,
Calm and complete, determinately fixed
To-day, to-morrow and for ever, pray?
You'll guarantee me that? Not so, I think!
In no wise! all we've gained is, that belief,
As unbelief before, shakes us by fits,
Confounds us like its predecessor. Where's
The gain? how can we guard our unbelief,
Make it bear fruit to us?—the problem here.
Just when we are safest, there's a sunset-touch,
A fancy from a flower-bell, someone's death,
A chorus-ending from Euripides,—
And that's enough for fifty hopes and fears
As old and new at once as Nature's self,
To rap and knock and enter in our soul,
Take hands and dance there, a fantastic ring,
Round the ancient idol, on his base again,—
The grand Perhaps! We look on helplessly.
There the old misgivings, crooked questions are—
This good God—what he could do, if he would,
Would, if he could—then must have done long since:
If so, when, where and how? some way must be,—
Once feel about, and soon or late you hit
Some sense, in which it might be, after all.
Why not, "The Way, the Truth, the Life"?

—That way
Over the mountain, which who stands upon
Is apt to doubt if it be meant for a road;
While, if he views it from the waste itself,
Up goes the line there, plain from base to brow,
Not vague, mistakable! what's a break or two
Seen from the unbroken desert either side?
And then (to bring in fresh philosophy)
What if the breaks themselves should prove at last
The most consummate of contrivances
To train a man's eye, teach him what is faith?
And so we stumble at truth's very test!
All we have gained then by our unbelief
Is a life of doubt diversified by faith,
For one of faith diversified by doubt:
We called the chess-board white,—we call it black.

ROBERT BROWNING (1812-1889)
Bishop Blougram's Apology

SEND MY ROOTS RAIN

Thou art indeed just, Lord, if I contend
With thee; but, sir, so what I plead is just,
Why do sinners' ways prosper? and why must
Disappointment all I endeavour end?
    Wert thou my enemy, O thou my friend,
How wouldst thou worse, I wonder, than thou dost
Defeat, thwart me? Oh, the sots and thralls of lust
Do in spare hours more thrive than I that spend,
Sir, life upon thy cause. See, banks and brakes
Now, leavèd how thick! lacèd they are again
With fretty chervil, look, and fresh wind shakes
Them; birds build—but not I build; no, but strain,
Time's eunuch, and not breed one work that wakes.
Mine, O thou lord of life, send my roots rain.

GERARD MANLEY HOPKINS (1844-1889)
Thou Art Indeed Just, Lord

KNOWLEDGE AND ART

Yes, but it must be practical knowledge. There is nothing less powerful than knowledge unattached, and incapable of application. That is why what little knowledge I have has done myself personally so much harm. I do not know much, but if I knew a good deal less than that little I should be far more powerful. The rule should be never to learn a thing till one is pretty sure one wants it, or that one will want it before long so badly as not to be able to get on without it. This is what sensible people do about money, and there is no reason why people should throw away their time and trouble more than their money. There are plenty of things that most boys would give their ears to know, these and these only are the proper things for them to sharpen their wits upon.

If a boy is idle and does not want to learn anything at all, the same principle should guide those who have the care of him—he should never be made to learn anything till it is pretty obvious that he cannot get on without it. This will save trouble both to boys and teachers, moreover it will be far more likely to increase a boy's desire to learn. I know in my own case no earthly power could make me learn till I had my head given me; and nothing has been able to stop me from incessant study from that day to this.

In art, never try to find out anything, or try to learn anything until the not knowing it has come to be a nuisance to you for some time. Then you will remember it, but not otherwise. Let knowledge importune you before you will hear it. Our schools and universities go on the precisely opposite system.

Never consciously agonise; the race is not to the swift, nor the battle to the strong. Moments of extreme issue are unconscious and must be left to take care of themselves. During conscious moments take reasonable pains but no more and, above all, work so slowly as never to get out of breath. Take it easy in fact, until forced not to do so.

There is no mystery about art. Do the things that you can see; they will show you those that you cannot see. By doing what you can you will gradually get to know what it is that you want to do and cannot do, and so be able to do it.

Do not hunt for subjects, let them choose you, not you them. Only do that which insists upon being done and runs right up against you, hitting you in the eye until you do it. This calls you and you had better attend to it, and do it as well as you can. But till called in this way do nothing.

Each man's mind is an unknown land to himself, so that we need not be at such pains to frame a mechanism of adventure for getting to undiscovered countries. We have not far to go before we reach them. They are like the Kingdom of Heaven, within us.

SAMUEL BUTLER (1835-1902)
Notebooks

SO SAD, SO STRANGE

Tears, idle tears, I know not what they mean,
Tears from the depth of some divine despair
Rise in the heart, and gather in the eyes,
In looking on the happy Autumn fields,
And thinking of the days that are no more.

Fresh as the first beam glittering on a sail,
That brings our friends up from the underworld,
Sad as the last which reddens over one
That sinks with all we love below the verge;
So sad, so fresh, the days that are no more.

Ah, sad and strange as in dark summer dawns
The earliest pipe of half-awaken'd birds
To dying ears, when unto dying eyes
The casement slowly grows a glimmering square;
So sad, so strange, the days that are no more.

Dear as remember'd kisses after death,
And sweet as those by hopeless fancy feign'd
On lips that are for others; deep as love,
Deep as first love, and wild with all regret;
O Death in Life, the days that are no more.

ALFRED, LORD TENNYSON (1809-1892)
The Princess

FOR MY FUNERAL

O thou that from thy mansion
    Through time and place to roam,
Dost send abroad thy children,
    And then dost call them home,

That men and tribes and nations
    And all thy hand hath made
May shelter them from sunshine
    In thine eternal shade:

We now to peace and darkness
    And earth and thee restore
Thy creature that thou madest
    And will cast forth no more.

A. E. HOUSMAN (1859-1936)
More Poems

THE SOLDIER

If I should die, think only this of me:
    That there's some corner of a foreign field
That is for ever England. There shall be
    In that rich earth a richer dust concealed;
A dust whom England bore, shaped, made aware,
    Gave, once, her flowers to love, her ways to roam,
A body of England's, breathing English air,
    Washed by the rivers, blest by suns of home.

And think, this heart, all evil shed away,
    A pulse in the eternal mind, no less
        Gives somewhere back the thoughts by England
            given,
Her sights and sounds; dreams happy as her day;
    And laughter, learnt of friends; and gentleness,
        In hearts at peace, under an English heaven.

RUPERT BROOKE (1887-1915)
Collected Poems

FARE WELL

When I lie where shades of darkness
Shall no more assail mine eyes,
Nor the rain make lamentation
    When the wind sighs;
How will fare the world whose wonder
Was the very proof of me?
Memory fades, must the remembered
    Perishing be?

Oh, when this my dust surrenders
Hand, foot, lip, to dust again,
May these loved and loving faces
    Please other men!
May the rusting harvest hedgerow
Still the Traveller's Joy entwine,
And as happy children gather
    Posies once mine.

Look thy last on all things lovely,
Every hour. Let no night
Seal thy sense in deathly slumber
    Till to delight
Thou hast paid thy utmost blessing;
Since that all things thou wouldst praise
Beauty took from those who loved them
    In other days.

WALTER DE LA MARE (1873-1956)
Collected Poems

EPILOGUE

So it works round to this—the delights of one place or another reside rather more in ourselves than they do in the place. The Alps at after-glow may be made trite and dull by some failure of ours to master a mean little fear or desire; the finest fairy-tale that Nature ever told may come to nothing more than a lifeless humming in your ears if you see a lot of her other children not minding it and have not learnt to do your own listening for yourself. All the details of our own state affect, in some little measure at least, the quality of things that we see and even of things that we saw long ago. To many English exiles long in the tropics, well branded and drenched with years of the extravagant unfriendliness of soddening rains and skies of hard, hot tin, there comes a boundless increase in the beauty of the common English country town that they see in their thoughts. Its friendly glow, its air of reasonable contentment, of order temperately kept, and of unflustered diligence, the slowly-printed record of many generations of cheerful and good-natured people, easy to understand and to live with—these things come by their rights; they establish more fully than ever before the claims of their beauty. A long-familiar country house or farm that you remember flushing to heart-warming reds in the horizontal light of the endless English summer evening, the longest and kindest in the world, or standing up out of low meadow mists in the primeval-seeming stillness of late afternoon in the grave October weather when fires in deep hearths begin to grow wonderful—this is not just one good-looking thing, but a long scale of things ascending from dreary plainness to the loveliness that makes your small heart ache with over-filling; and some state of oneself, not of any-thing else, is registered by the place where it seems to stand on the scale. It may be to you the occasion of some vision as trivial and poor as a bilious man's vision of food, or a vision all on fire with heart-rending beauty and truth, like the one a man gets of the life of his mother when she has just died.

Away, then, with the critical pertness that classes one place as sufficiently fair to be loved and sets another place aside as unsightly. It has been airily said, in our time, that Sheffield and even London are ugly. London! London on an early autumn afternoon of quiet sunshine, when all the air is mysterious with a vaporous gold-dust of illuminated motes and the hum of the traffic seems to fall pensive and muted round the big, benign London policeman

with uplifted hand
Conducting the orchestral Strand.

London ugly! Or Leeds not an Athens! Or Birmingham not the right place! Just look at them all, with your own mind and body decently fit, and your feelers well out and your retina burnished. For all places, when properly looked at, illuminate or set off one another: they do not fight for crowns of beauty in your esteem; members one of another, while ministering also to your sense of effective contrast, they join to lead you on towards conscious possessorship of your whole visible world as a single estate, wholly yours now and the whole of it always implied in any one of its parts that you may happen to see. Attain to that and you carry the centre of things about in your mind, and the right place is wherever you are.

C. E. MONTAGUE (1867-1928)
The Right Place

LEADING EVENTS AND DATES
IN ENGLISH HISTORY
55 B.C.—1945

55 B.C.	Roman expedition to Britain under Julius Cæsar.
43 A.D.	Annexation of Britain by Roman Empire begins.
c. 449 A.D.	Invasion by Angles, Jutes and Saxons begins.
596	Mission of St. Augustine to Kent.
617	Christianity adopted in Northumbria.
664	Synod of Whitby. Roman form of Christianity adopted.
829	Egbert, king of Wessex first king of English.
870	Defeat of Alfred the Great by Danes at Ashdown.
878	Alfred defeats Danes at Ethandune (Eddington).
980	Viking attacks on English coast.
1016	Canute king of England and Denmark.
1066	Battle of Hastings. William of Normandy crowned William I.
1086	Completion of Domesday Book.
1170	Murder of Thomas à Becket at Canterbury.
1190	Departure of Richard I on First Crusade.
1215	Magna Carta.
1295	Edward I's Model Parliament.
1337	Beginning of 100 Years' War.
1346	Battle of Crécy.
1348	Beginning of Black Death (ends 1349).
1356	Battle of Poitiers.
1381	Peasants' Revolt under Wat Tyler.
1399	Deposition of Richard II. Henry IV king.
1415	Battle of Agincourt.
1420	Treaty of Troyes. Henry V Regent of France.
1455	Beginning of Wars of the Roses with Battle of St. Albans.
1476	Caxton sets up his printing press at Westminster.
1485	Battle of Bosworth ends Wars of the Roses. Henry VII king.
1515	Cardinal Wolsey becomes Chancellor.
1536	Dissolution of the Monasteries (1536-9).
1553	Accession of Mary Tudor.
1558	Accession of Elizabeth I.
1577	Sir Francis Drake's circumnavigation of the globe begins.
1584	Virginia discovered and colonised.
1588	Defeat of Spanish Armada.
1603	Union of the Crowns of Scotland and England.
1605	Gunpowder Plot.
1611	Authorised Version of the Bible.
1620	Pilgrim Fathers sail for America.
1628	Petition of Right.

1642   Civil War. Battle of Edgehill.
1644   Battle of Marston Moor.
1649   Execution of Charles I.
1653-1660   Protectorate.
1660   Restoration of the Monarchy. Charles II.
1665   Great Plague of London.
1666   Great Fire of London.
1679   Habeas Corpus Act passed.
1685   Monmouth's rebellion crushed at Battle of Sedgemoor.
1688   William of Orange lands in England.
1689   Bill of Rights.
1694   The Bank of England founded.
1704   Battle of Blenheim.
1707   Union of Parliaments of England and Scotland.
1713   Treaty of Utrecht.
1715   Jacobite Rebellion.
1720   Financial disaster of the South Sea Bubble.
1745   Jacobite rebellion.
1756   Outbreak of Seven Years' War.
1757   Battle of Plassey.
1759   Capture of Quebec from French.
1763   Treaty of Paris.
1775   Outbreak of American War of Independence.
1793   Britain enters War of the French Revolution.
1805   Battle of Trafalgar.
1815   Battle of Waterloo.
1825   Trade Unions made legal.
1832   First Reform Act.
1833   Abolition of Slavery.
1837   Accession of Queen Victoria.
1840   Penny Postage introduced by Rowland Hill.
1854-6   Crimean War.
1857   Indian Mutiny.
1870   Education Act.
1885   Fall of Khartoum and the death of General Gordon.
1899   Beginning of the Boer War (ends 1902).
1901   Death of Queen Victoria.
1909   Old Age Pensions introduced for first time.
1914   Outbreak of Great War.
1915-16   Gallipoli Campaign.
1916   Battle of Jutland.
1918   Armistice signed November 11th.
1926   General Strike.
1936   Abdication of Edward VIII.
1939   Outbreak of World War II.
1940   Evacuation of Dunkirk. Battle of Britain.
1942   Battle of El Alamein.
1944   D-day landings in Normandy. Airborne landings at Arnhem.
1945   Surrender of Germany and Japan.

INDEX OF AUTHORS, SOURCES, FIRST LINES